LET'S LIBERATE THE TEMPLE
A
DR. BEN-JOCHANNAN ADMONITION

FREDERICK MONDERSON

SUMON PUBLISHERS

ISBN - 9781610230544
LCCN – 2016900723

In the Tribute to Professor George Simmonds, "Unsung Hero," Dr. Fred Monderson "sat at the feet of his heroes," Brother X, Michael Carter, Dr. Leonard Jeffries, Elombe Brathe, Dr. Lewis, Prof. George Simmonds, Dr. ben-Jochannan, Sister Camille Yarbrough, among others.

ABOUT THE AUTHOR

Dr. Frederick Monderson is a retired college professor and public-school teacher who taught **African History** in the City University of New York and **American History and Government** in the New York public schools. He has written some 1000 articles in the "New York Black Press," *Daily Challenge*, *Afro Times* and *New American* newspapers. In this venture, Monderson lends his expertise as a historian, Egyptologist, journalist and author of several books including *Ladies in the House*; *Michael Jackson: The Last Dance*; *50 on Point*; *Barack Obama: Ready, Fit to Lead*; *Barack Obama: Master of Washington D.C.*; *Obama: Master and Commander* and *Obama: The Journey Completed*; *Sonny Carson: The Final Triumph (5 Volumes)*; *Black Nationalism: Alive and Well*; *Black Nationalism: Still Alive and Well*; *African Nationalist: Poetry* *and Prose*; *Guyana: Land of Beauty and Many Waters*; and on **Ancient Egypt** *Seven Letters to Mike Tyson on Egyptian Temples*; *10 Poems Praising Great Blacks for Mike Tyson*; *Research Essays on Ancient Egypt*; *Temple of Karnak: The Majestic Architecture of Ancient Kemet*; *Where are the Kamite Kings?*; *Abydos and Osiris*; *Temple of Luxor*; *Medinet Habu: Mortuary Temple of Rameses III*; *The Quintessential Book on Ancient Egypt: "Holy Land"* (A Tour Guide Novel on Egypt); *Hatshepsut's Temple at Deir el Bahari*; *Intrigue Through Time*; *An Egyptian Resurrection*, (a Novel on Ancient Egypt); *The Majesty of Egyptian Gods and Temples* (a book of Egyptian Poems); *Egypt Essays on Ancient Kemet*; *The Ramesseum: Mortuary Temple of Rameses II*; *The Colonnade: Then and Now*; *Reflections on Ancient Kemet*; *The Hypostyle Hall*; *Grassroots View of Ancient Egypt*; *Glory of the Ancestors: 19 Letters to O.J. Simpson on Ancient African History*; *Celebrating Dr. Ben-Jochannan*; *Black History Extravaganza: Honoring Dr. Ben Jochannan*; *Into the Egyptian Mind*; *More Woman, More Power*; *Reflections on Ancient Egypt - Book One*; *Reflections on Ancient Egypt - Book Two*; *Black History Everyday - Part One*; *Black History Everyday - Part Two*; and more. A student of the esteemed Dr. Yosef ben-Jochannan, Dr. Monderson conducts tours to Egypt.

For Tour information, Contact Orleane Brooks-Williams at Nostrand Travel, 730 Nostrand Avenue, Brooklyn, New York 11216. Phone Number 718-756-5300. Next Tour of Egypt is July 27-August 10, 2018.

fredsegypt.com@fredsegypt.com
sumonpublishers.com@sumonpublishers.com
blackegyptbooks.com@blackegyptbooks.com
blackfolksbooks.com@blackfolksbooks.com

I. LIBERATING THE TEMPLE
BY
DR. FRED MONDERSON

While there is a "Ben Trilogy" comprising his *Africa: Mother of Western Civilization*; *African Origins of the "Major" Western Religions*; and *Black Man of the Nile and His Family*; this volume, *Let's Liberate the Temple* is the third volume of "**A Trilogy to Ben**." That is, together with *Celebrating Dr. Ben Jochannan, Black History Extravaganza: Honoring Dr. Ben-Jochannan* and *Let's Liberate the Temple*, these works represent the "**Trilogy to Ben**." The insistence on these three volumes is not simply to demonstrate respect and admiration for the life and work of Dr. Yosef A.A. Ben-Jochannan, but to underscore the influence his teachings have had on "One of the young cubs." That is to demonstrate, while the "Old Lion" today basks in the glory of the sacred Black ancestral pantheon, the inspiration, fortitude and tenacity he helped generate recognizes and continues the great work he instituted in terms of educating and enlightening the great masses of the African people whom Dr. Ben considered his constituency. This work is simply a tribute to a Great African scholar, researcher, nationalist, humanitarian, courageous intellectual freedom fighter who uplifted African people, man, woman, and child and helped generate the light of knowledge in preaching to and encouraging all forms of African empowerment.

As such then, the question as to what is meant by "Liberating the Temple" is a valid one. In this, the idea of liberating the temple is of a two-fold nature. First, it is to recognize the constituent parts, the materials of its composition and construction and the role each constituent part has played in the structure described as *The Temple in Man* as in each of these, the pharaoh embodies its metaphysical and esoteric nature and the cosmological and spiritual substance and significance it represents. Second and equally important, the individual who visits the temple, to gain the maximum benefit, must himself be liberated to truly envision the object he encounters as a manifestation of himself as a human being which is a form of cosmological consciousness, given that man is made in the image of god, and that god manifests inexorably in the temple in heaven as here on earth. In that phenomenal experience, man must free himself, function purely, to see both himself and the temple as divine manifestations experienced here on earth. Thus, once the visitor becomes aware and seeks to understand the meaning and significance of the temple's totality in its artistic and architectural beauty, the quintessence of its potent purity, then he or she can achieve the essence of cosmic consciousness embodied in the religious, spiritual and philosophic path to liberation this divine work represents and seeks to encourage. This cerebral, human and psychic elevation thus enables the observer to recognize the potency of constituent parts of the wonderful experiment called the Egyptian temple. This cosmic consciousness is what divinity ordained when it invested and imbued Pharaoh to be a shepherd of his people, manifested through the practice of Ma'at and its constituent elements maintained in the practice of truth, justice and righteousness.

Now, while each temple is essentially a replica of each other, there are still peculiarities of some temples that distinguish them from others. Notwithstanding, the temple of Karnak and Luxor, New Kingdom cosmic creations as abodes of God Amon-ra, are unique; but Luxor is more particularly so; given, Karnak is a "vegetation construction" while Luxor a numerical expression. As such then, among other factors, their uniqueness rests in time duration of the structure's construction. To this we may add, the potency of the multitude of spiritual powers who as divine essence manifest in the holy place. To this we may add the particularities and care taken to achieve the specific objective of the temple which is to "Give the house to its master" and thereby undertake the liturgy and ritual necessary to safeguard and ritualize the god force inhabiting the sacred space. As such, again in comparison, Luxor temple can be viewed as the quintessential temple, "built for eternity" but despite the assaults in its preserved state it is still able to exhibit the principal features of a holy site. Karnak, on the other hand, because of its massive structure and the principal source of invading enmity, the spiritual quintessence is wanting. Still, for these in-tuned metaphysically, spiritually and intellectually, applying a tincture of imagination, the visitor can conceive and consider all that the temple represents is simply a library of cosmic consciousness.

Naturally, and despite the showcase the visitor comes to admire, it is nevertheless a challenge if such persons lack the wherewithal to recognize the essential features of the temple as a manifestation of "sacred science." This conundrum may very well be heightened since the original creators have left unrecognizable esoteric elements that only the highest sages can truly comprehend in totality the cosmic phenomenon the holy site represents.

Nonetheless, as such, visitors must consider, first and foremost, the object one views in approach to the temple is not all there is to it. In fact, there is, metaphysically speaking, a spiritual "invisible shield," a sort of umbrella that surrounds and protects this abode of the god, which in itself is difficult to comprehend. In this, one has to possess a certain degree of esoteric knowledge to comprehend the higher sciences so involved. Notwithstanding, we know the king commissioned the temple and he "stretched the cord" to create the "House of eternity" for his heavenly father, but it was the "architectural manifestation," the actions of the architects who built the temple, viz., the dimensions, orientation, materials, decoration, layout, functions of its constituent parts, etc.; that is of the greatest significance. As such then, and in order to so complete his assigned task, his architectural skills notwithstanding, the builder or architect himself had to be psychically, spiritually, even metaphysically in-tuned with the Neter or God (the symbolist says principles) for whom the temple was being built. That is, he must know his god! To achieve such an objective there has to be no option but architectural perfection in the construction otherwise the gods would not be properly invoked or come to reside in such a structure unless every spiritual and cosmic iota was correct. Only then will the cosmic aura or shield of invisibility finally be overlaid on the temple.

Liberate the Temple. Karnak Temple of God Amon.
Temple entrance showing the "Avenue of Sphinxes," the First or Great Pylon and into the deep recesses past the "Processional Colonnade."

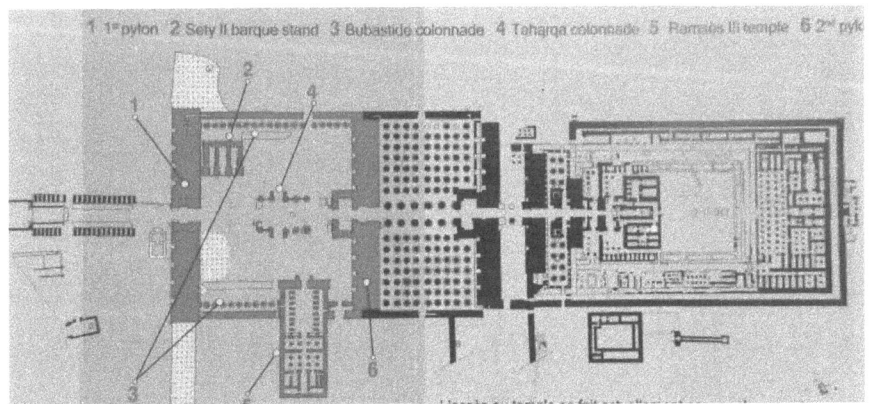

Liberate the Temple. Karnak Temple of God Amon.
Plan of the Temple with the First or Great Court highlighted.

Liberate the Temple. Karnak Temple of God Amon.
In the Great Court, two visitors plan their approach before the Taharka Kiosk and the "Processional Colonnade" beyond.

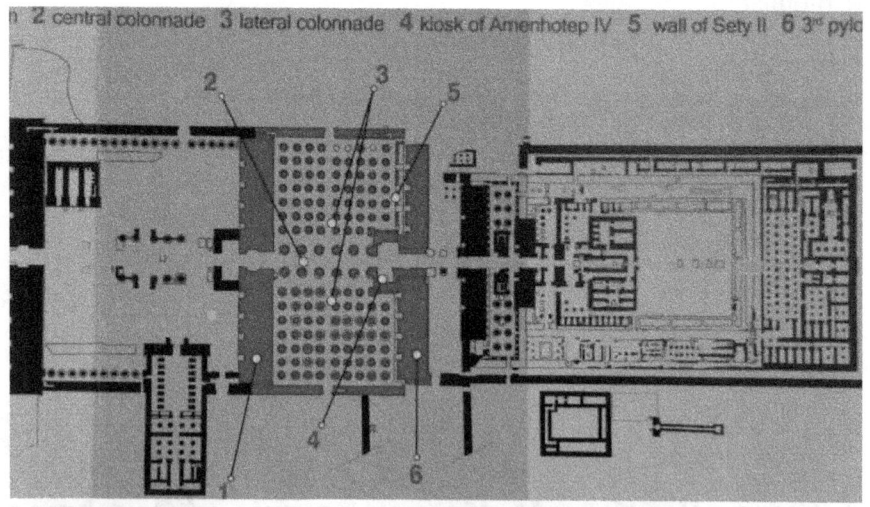

Liberate the Temple. Karnak Temple of God Amon.
Plan of the temple with the Hypostyle Hall highlighted.

Liberate the Temple. Karnak Temple of God Amon.
Contrast in column, how they were set up (left) and what they looked like when finished (right).

Given the above, as part of its protection, the frame of mind of the architect also had to fit the bill of perfection, physically and mentally, otherwise he would suffer anguish, even as he tried to complete the assigned task. This was a sort of "Don't play with fire," unless you know what you are doing" admonition or syndrome. Thereafter, every part of the temple, every gate, column, architrave, stone joint, sealing, hall, wall with appropriate decoration had to be aligned in the configuration of perfection as laid down in the envisioned foundation ceremony conducted by the king as he, the king had to give the temple to its master, the God who would reside there. Therefore, he instructed the builder as to the structural dynamics to be expected and to be achieved.

Liberate the Temple. Karnak Temple of God Amon. Colossal seated statues behind the Eighth Pylon on the North/South Axis.

One of the better explanations given of the phenomenal exercise of "stretching the cord" and achieving the principal objectives of the task before giving the house to its master is presented by Schwaller de

Lubicz in *Sacred Science: The King of Pharaonic Theocracy* (Rochester, Vermont: Inner Traditions International, (1961) 1982: 104-05) wherein, the author emphasizes the connection between the god and the monarch. As such, he writes: "The King, the inspired one, consecrated and crowned, having abstracted himself from 'private thoughts,' transmits the divine will to men through the phases of the Empire's genesis. Therefore, the King, assisted by the Neters, is represented at all the ceremonies of a temple's founding, the essential scenes of which are as follows:

"The King and Seshat, mistress of divine books, each tap a mallet upon a stake which they are driving into the ground. This scene, known as 'stretching the cord,' consists in determining the orientation of the temple according to the circumpolar stars at a specific date of the year. It is also said that Thoth is there with his books, that Ptah-Tatenen measured the ground, that Neith utters the protective formulas, and that Selket lays her hand upon those works destined for eternity….

Then the King ploughs a furrow with the hoe four times; he scatters the contents of a bushel-basket, shapes the first brick uniting earth and water four times, for the four corners of the temple, and after having circled the temple with incense, the King gives the house to its Master." It therefore seems, this is a metaphysical expression since only after completion of all the mystical, spiritual and philosophical acts associated with creating cosmic space on earth can the temple properly become an abode of the god.

Now, having done as such, the work of building the temple could commence. However, while much of this is cosmological and theological speculation, Sir Gaston Maspero, while Director the of Antiquities Department in the 1880s, discovered evidence of a foundation ceremony customary at the founding commencement of a new temple at both Deir el Bahari and also at Luxor Temple. "There" he notes, "in a bed of clean white sand, an animal was slain and its blood allowed to flow as part of the consecration foundation ceremony. Grain, milk, honey, and other liquid and solid substances were deposited along with miniature replicas of all tools to be used in the construction. In addition, the builder's cartouche [*Shennu*]; in this case Hatshepsut at Deir el Bahari and Amenhotep III at Luxor; were deposited, all as part of consecrating, blessing and protecting the work to be undertaken and the structure that will come alive" with cosmic consciousness and spiritual potency as well as the "mystical shield" that would protect the holy site.

Now in explaining some aspects of the associated religious experience that follows in actions of the principals, viz., the King and Priests, we look to Adolf Erman in *A Handbook of Egyptian Religion* (London: Archibald Constable, 1907: 52) who wrote: "For the official religion as it was accepted in the temples, there existed only the god and the king; he served them, he built their temples, and made offerings to them, and they rewarded *their beloved son* for his pious devotion with *life for millions of years*, with victory over his enemies and everlasting fame. The gods were no longer the gods of the Egyptian people, they are the gods of Pharaoh *their son.* And this relation of the sovereign to the deities is carried yet farther. It the king built a temple he did it not so much from devotion to the god, as for his own glorification. *He has made this as his monument*, thus begins every dedicatory inscription from the earliest times, and then follows the name of the temple which the king has built to the god *his father*."

Given this relationship and despite the king not being able to perform the ceremonies in the various temples scattered across the land in which the High Priest takes his place, all such ceremonies are still done in his name. In contradiction, it is as if the sacerdotal official is not a part of developments. This is again reinforced by Erman (1907: 52-53) who writes: "It is a natural result of this idea that the temple scenes give the impression that the priests are not present, but that the king takes his place. On all the walls the offerings and ceremonies are represented as they were performed before the gods, but it is always the king who is officiating. Although we can understand the king on some special occasion may have occasionally exercised priestly functions, yet that he should have taken part in the ceremonies of the countless temples of his domination can only have been a theoretical possibility. The actual performers at the Egyptian ceremonies must have been the priest, even though they represented themselves in the rituals as merely the delegates of the king."

Therefore, in the execution of that function of ritual in the liturgy the temple bureaucracy not simply adhered to a family success regimen, the priests were either practitioners of a mundane profession, medicine, astronomy, architecture, teaching, etc., or they were strictly functionaries in the temple experience, in which, "certain priestly orders are connected with certain professions. Thus, the high judicial functionaries of the Old Kingdom are at the same time priests of the goddess of truth, the physicians are priests of Sekhmet, the great artists are priests of Ptah." In this respect, Erman (1907: 53) explained: "At the head of every temple was a high-priest who acted as overseer of all the sacred offices, he is initiated into divine books and divine things and gives directions to the priests as regulating the festivals. He has a loud voice when he praises the god and a pure hand when he brings flowers and offers water and food upon the altar. The administration of the temple property is incumbent on him, and in war he had to command the contingent provided by his temple."

All this, notwithstanding, an interesting dynamic, question, presents itself in the case of the two temples, Deir el Bahari and Luxor, built by Hatshepsut and Amenhotep respectively.

In his years of conducting trips to Egypt, Dr. Yosef A.A. Ben-Jochannan has most importantly emphasized the significance of temple architecture; that is, whether worship or God and mortuary or King Temples. Suffice to say, the god's "mansion of millions of years." Thus, in his admonition to study and appreciate the temple, the good doctor instructed his students to not simply observe features of the enclosure wall, columns and colonnades, kiosks, chapels, the decorated walls, column bases, shaft, capital, abacus, architrave, altars, statues, the hieroglyphic decoration and most important to press their Guides to explain everything material, philosophic, even spiritual to the extent they could communicate some knowledge of this. Such a challenge equally relates to the temple's meaning, its art and architecture, even building materials and efforts and methods of construction. All this notwithstanding, this latter line of inquiry is still significant despite the fact, Dr. Ben-Jochannan believed, "sixty percent of what the Guides tell is false." So, do your own research in preparation for the intellectual, moral, historical, even religious and photographic adventure a trip to Egypt presents.

No less significant, for his many years of visiting and involvement in Egypt, a number of temples became his favorite including Deir el Bahari, Abydos, Luxor, Abu Simbel and particularly Karnak. In this special and significant temple; Karnak, besides the sanctuary which the Master Teacher and his associates George Simmonds and Brother Abdul, treated with great reverence, his favorite was the Hypostyle Hall built by Seti I and Rameses II. Naturally there was some disagreements as to who actually gets ownership for construction of the Hall and what was its purpose.

Nevertheless, it now seems settled, Haremhab conceived the idea, Rameses I began construction; some say Rameses I erased Horemhab's cartouche; Seti I completed the work and began the decoration that was finished by his son Rameses II. Therefore, and technically, this Hypostyle Hall with its 134 columns of the Processional Colonnade and the northern and southern segments consumed more than 100 years in construction. No less significant, inscriptions indicate the Hypostyle Hall was actually Seti's "Mortuary Temple in a Worship Temple." Nevertheless, and despite all of that, Master Teacher Dr. Ben-Jochannan insisted on two things regarding the temple.

First, however, and remindful in Pharaonic times only the king and designated priests were permitted in the "Holy of Holies," he instructed his students to avoid entering the Sanctuary as well as do dress properly and act appropriately when in the holy place. Second, Dr. Ben-Jochannan admonished his students to become familiar with the history of the temple under study, its builder and peculiarities. That is why, among many ideas he imparted, he insisted his students, "Visit the Hypostyle Hall five or six times to fully comprehend its meaning and significance." We must also and importantly seek to understand, Dr. Ben represented more than a bulwark against Western intellectual, moral, cultural, spiritual, even religious oppression and bigotry against African people on a global scale; but significantly the Master Teacher was about research and critical examination of the evidence, learning and enlightenment through reading and writing embodied in education to be on par with all other cultures. All this, therefore, as a prelude to understand the wider significance of the culture and what is at stake in the struggle to reclaim and retain Egypt as African and Black!

He was an educator beyond question and sought to have his students comprehend the temple in its multi-faceted dynamics to better understand religious architecture housing the divinity as a prelude to understand the gods and the ritual practiced daily within the temple.

Liberate the Temple. Luxor Temple of Amenhotep III and Rameses II. The Great Pylon as viewed from the North-East towards and between the Mosque of Abu Haggag (left) and the new entrance (right).

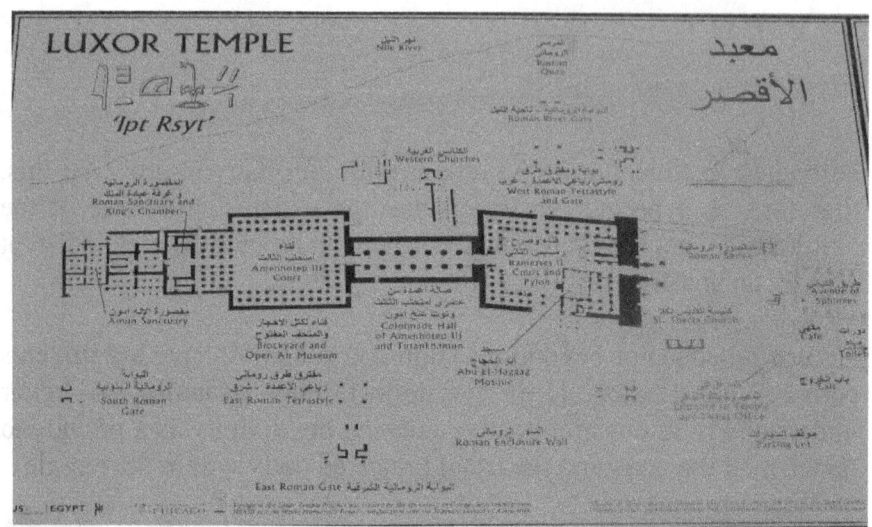

Liberate the Temple. Luxor Temple. Plan highlighting the principal parts of the home of Amon where the Opet Festival was celebrated.

Liberate the Temple. Luxor Temple of Amenhotep III and Rameses II. The Entrance to the temple with seated and standing statues and an obelisk.

Liberate the Temple. Luxor Temple of Amenhotep III and Rameses II. Close-up of the entrance showing the two seated statues before the Great Pylon, and beyond, the first column of the "Processional Colonnade" and another of two seated statues at the end of the "Peristyle Court," dubbed "The Ramessean Front."

This is interesting for, not only the stages of construction of the temple would become apparent but also the realization modern conception and propagation of the notion of the temple is founded on a misnomer or falsity. In this it is generally agreed, the king and worshippers look in to ritualize and worship while the god looks out to admire and bless his creations. That is to say, the temple is built out from the Sanctuary area towards the pylon and enclosure wall with decoration and intermediate structures between. However, as propagated and realized, modern projection of the temple is from the entrance to the sanctuary or in reverse order of how it was actually built. Now, while the projected arrangement of the pylons at Karnak is a good example of this 'reversal,' the arrangement of the Hypostyle Hall at Abydos, or any temple with succeeding Hypostyle Halls, become the perfect example of this conundrum. As such, the "First" and "Second Hypostyle Halls" at Abydos are represented in reverse. That is, in pointing to one such conundrum and to be correct; since Seti I commenced the Abydos temple to Osiris, the temple would have been built out with the "Second Hypostyle Hall" being in the first position. Given, Rameses II, in this case, found the temple unfinished, today's "the First Hypostyle Hall" as we know it should be credited to him and as such should be in the position of the "Second Hypostyle Hall." Naturally, we need to recognize this and admit, for convenience sake, the present arrangement is acceptable.

Liberate the Temple. Luxor Temple of Amenhotep III and Rameses II. From beginning of the "Processional Colonnade," towards the rising elevation of the "Court of Amenhotep," two columns of the Hypostyle Hall and the curved Transept of the inner chambers.

We see this same naming in the hypostyles of the Ramesseum and Medinet Habu, both with their multiple hypostyle halls.

One thing is certain, from the beginning of dynastic rule, the dual nature of the king has been established and perpetuated as the king of Upper and Lower Egypt. This duality is further underscored in the division of the temple but particularly the sanctuary that was divided into two parts, representing the north and the south, as similarly the earth. With its northern and southern regions, as the god looks out, the left side is considered the north and the right side the south, though each gets the same treatment in the ritual. While this may be so, however, the south, right side always enjoyed prominence over the north, whether this is in the **Suten Bat** title of King of Upper and Lower Egypt; the white crown over the red crown or the south over the north; and strange enough, even as early as on Narmer's palette, the 4 or 5 gods or "souls" accompanying the king are all southern and none from the north. This state of affairs remained unchanged throughout dynastic rule. We can, thus draw attention to two things here and they both relate to commentary by Dr. Cheikh Anta Diop. The first has to do with Alexander Moret who asked, 'By whom was the south influenced if not by the north?' to which Dr. Diop responded simply, "If so, why are all the historic monuments in the south and not in the north?" Second, Dr. Diop explained, "Naville was wrong" in placing the west over the east in some issue of contention. Dr. Diop simply meant regarding the particular orientation and following the flow of the Nile given the dichotomy discussed above with the East to the right and the West to the left; then Dr. Naville's mistake (the right side) is because he was ascending rather than descending the Nile. Let us not forget, the numbering of the nomes is from the south to north and this is ancient, while conversely today's numbering of the cataracts contradictorily is from the north to the south and this is modern. Again, we must recognize, in the flow of the Nile's cultural effluence from the south to the north, this places the right side to the east and everything should be so oriented.

Nevertheless, the temple, like so many issues in respect to recording the history and culture of ancient Egypt and the Nile Valley, particularly, and even more, regarding, as Dr. Leonard James has pointed out, "The existential data contradicts the symbolic representation;" scholars have also wondered whether the Egyptian architects constructed a temple from conception to completion based on an end-view in mind. That is, whether they worked from a stated plan. Now, in the *Religious Ritual at Abydos*, A. Rosalie David (Warminster, England, Aris and Philips, 1973) affirmatively points out, "Records were kept in temple archives explaining the stages in which a temple was built." Equally too, and reinforcing this reality, in the rear of the Temple of Edfu in the "Corridor of Victory," a plan of the temple is depicted on the middle of this outer wall. However, while this is a late period construction, it does provide an analytic basis to argue, such plans existed in the earliest times; even though none have been discovered, in this respect. In a similar yet unrelated manner, one scholar insisted and in support of the idea of created plans of Egyptian temples, "an argument from the absence of monuments is not sound."

Nevertheless, and as such, David (1973: 2) sought to explain the role of the temple in the life of the society by stating: "To understand the ancient Egyptians concept of a temple, one must first attempt to understand their concept of the universe which was so very different from our own. We accept the idea of a constantly changing society, where values are different from one generation to the next, and where fresh advances are made in most branches of learning, and where new problems bring forth new solutions. Our belief, however, would have been quite alien to the ancient Egyptian mind." These ancient Africans believed, "in the far distant past, chaos had prevailed. There was no light and water covered everything: then the world was created. Together with the physical creation of a place where mankind could live, abstract concepts such as religion, law, ethics and kingship were established, to benefit the Egyptian people for all time. In these primeval times, all the elements were established to provide for a stable society. To solve their problems or answers to questions of human existence in general, they crafted and practiced principles as established harmony, order, balance, truth, justice, righteousness, all embodied in Ma'at. In this regard, later generation had simply to emulate the conditions which had been present at the very beginning, "the First Occasion." Thus, "the Egyptians believed the universe worked according to a fixed pattern, which was unchanging, and they constantly looked back to that time when they believed all the elements of their world and society had been given to them. They did not desire change and tried to reproduce the setting which they believed to have existed on that 'First Occasion.'" Significantly, tis applied to architecture, temple construction, and the peculiar characteristics that developed in the experimental and trial mechanics that developed as the society matured.

As such and attempting to elaborate on varied yet particular characteristics of the temple, David (1973: 2) continued: "In many of the surviving temples of Egypt, the existing floor level is apparently not the original one, and in such temples as Karnak and Luxor, it is impossible to be certain or precise about the floor itself, or changes to its level. Nevertheless, it is now abundantly clear that in many temples there was a deliberate distinction made between the construction of those parts lying between the front of the Hypostyle Hall and the extreme rear of the temple (i.e. the roofed area), and the outer courts. This distinction is one which has not hitherto received adequate attention, but it is important. Two methods seem to have been employed. In one, the whole temple, from and including the Hypostyle Hall to the rear of the temple, is built on a low platform which is clearly distinguished on the outside by a cornice and roll as though it were the top of a wall. This feature can clearly be seen in the Temples of Luxor and Karnak. In other temples, there is a small but definite raising of the floor level as one passes from hall to hall, from the Hypostyle to the sanctuary. The sanctuary itself in such temples is always higher than those rooms and halls in front of it, and the floor level drops again behind it. This feature is particularly noticeable in the Temple of Medinet Habu, where the site chosen for the temple – a knoll which slopes gently away from the cultivation – conforms naturally to these requirements. At Abydos, these slopes are provided by rising pavement levels in the successive courts and halls. This is also a regular feature in Ptolemaic temples in Egypt. In all temples, the ceiling becomes lower the further one penetrates from the Hypostyle Hall into the sanctuary. It is commonly stated that the effect of this was to increase the sense of awe and oppressiveness the nearer one approached the god, and undoubtedly the effect was produced. But perhaps the basic reason for both the pedestal-type of construction and the changing floor level was a deliberate attempt to reproduce architecturally the original 'Island of creation.'"

Adding more to expand the concept of the structure in total, David writes further: "The heavy brick wall which enclosed each temple complex was sectionally built, probably in alternate units. Sections of these walls show that the courses are either concave or convex. These sections are linked with the variable level of the temple floor. According to the Edfu texts, when chaos reigned, and there was no light and the water covered the earth, there were as yet no gods. From these primeval waters there emerged a low mud-island, and the flotsam and jetsam at the edge of the waters, a piece of reed that drifted ashore was picked up by some demi-gods and stuck into the ground, near the water's edge. Out of the surrounding gloom came a falcon, which settled on the reed, and sanctified the island. As a sacred place, it needed protection, and so a simple reed wall seems to have been built around the reed and the god who perched thereon. As the waters receded, and the island grew bigger, it was possible to add rooms on either side of the first humble chamber and other rooms or halls in front of it, so that ultimately, a complete temple of reed came to be built. Always the original room in which the reed was first planted and on which the god first alighted was at a slightly higher level than the rest of the temple, and as the first room, it was always at the back; in developed temples, this became the sanctuary at the rear. The pedestal or rising floor level in Pharaonic temples is an attempt to reproduce in stone this original site of the creation of the first temple."

First and foremost, a rather cogent observation is that most Western writers, writing for a Western audience, only use the West or South-West Asia as reference points in explaining ancient Egypt. They never use, see or make any connection with Africa proper, where reasonably intelligent people see the light! However, among early Egyptologists, E.A. Wallis budge alone did researches among various peoples, culture and regions of Africa Surprisingly, he found great similarities among early Egyptians and ancient Africa. Naturally, this changed his perception on the origin of the Egyptian culture. Alas, and sadly, most of his contemporaries held to the today's fast crumbling false notion of a "Caucasian Egypt."

Liberate the Temple. Qurna (Kurneh) Mortuary Temple of Seti I. Entrance colonnade of eight-sided papyrus bundle columns with two bands and entranceway.

Liberate the Temple. Qurna (Kurneh) Mortuary Temple of Seti I. The Bases of Eight-sided Papyrus Bundle Columns.

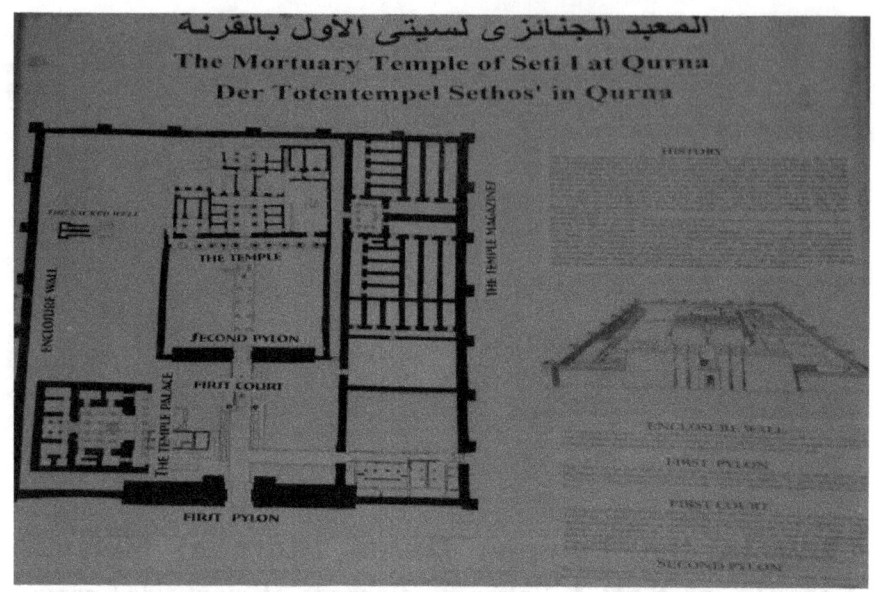

Liberate the Temple. Qurna (Kurneh) Mortuary Temple of Seti I. Plan of the temple in which the First and Second Pylons are now destroyed and entrance generally begins in the Second Court.

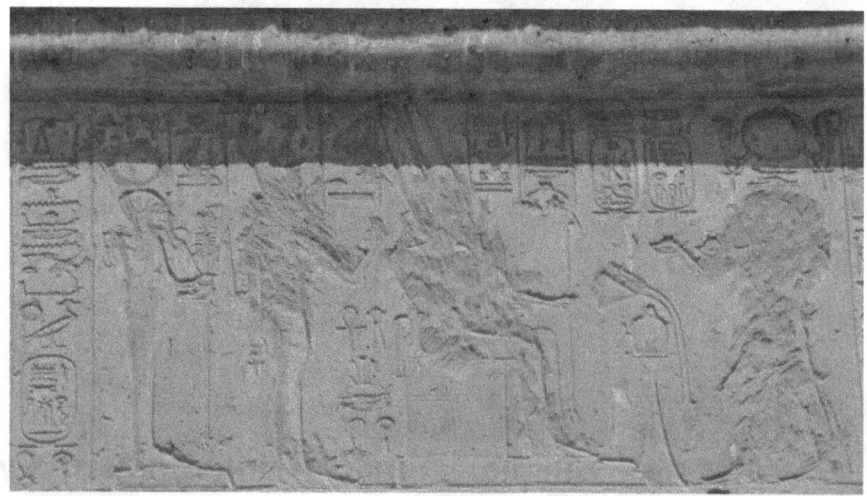

Liberate the Temple. Qurna (Kurneh) Mortuary Temple of Seti I. Defaced image of the Theban Triad of Amon, Mut and Khonsu as well as Pharaoh Seti I.

Liberate the Temple. Qurna (Kurneh) Mortuary Temple of Seti I. Trees with Dates stand before the colonnade and afford a look deep into the opening.

Liberate the Temple. Qurna (Kurneh) Mortuary Temple of Seti I. View from the rear, the pillared Hypostyle Hall housing the Sanctuary looking toward the date palm trees.

Liberate the Temple. Qurna (Kurneh) Mortuary Temple of Seti I. A surviving stela shows Seti kneeling with empty hands raised in adoration before enthroned Ra-Horakhty.

In the **Geography of Egypt**, we hear of "standing with one foot in the desert and one foot on cultivated land." Well, it seems when Western writers reference Egypt they stand with one leg in the Delta and one leg in the Mediterranean Sea or Western Asia. On the other hand, Cheikh Anta Diop in his *Cultural Unity of Black Africa*, saw the entire continent as interrelated and interestingly enough, currently it seems his Associate Theophile Obenga is one of few writers who recognizes and points to Egyptian ideas and cultural practices using the same lens showing Egyptian similarities with other African people and cultures continent-wide. On the other hand, as stated, of the "old Egyptologists," Dr. Wallis Budge was able to relate, much of Egypt could be observed particularly in the Upper Nile and in Central Africa. In this particular regard, and tremendously significant, Theophile Obenga in *African Philosophy: The Pharaonic Period - 2780 to 330 B.C.* in a point-counter-point analysis relates much of that relevance in Egypt as extant cultural practices in many contemporary African societies. Thus, it can be argued, and given the Egyptians had no recollection of their "ancestors from South-West Asia," neither in pyramid building, types of tomb structure, even religious practices that is extant in modern Africa, while no evidence existed or exists in the supposed areas of Ancient Egyptian origins.

Nonetheless, in pinpointing the same similarities of Ancient Egyptian ideas and modern practices among a great many African people, even conceptualizing how Egyptian mythology saw the beginning, or "first occasion," Obenga (2004: 33) offers the explanation of a world and its philosophic underpinnings quite different from that seen in the Western lens, covered over in the veneer of Greek and Roman thought and practices undergirding Western culture and civilization that is actually using a false foundation and as the parade passes, the people joyfully celebrate, the king is actually naked. Here he writes: "There the creative demiurge emerges from within *Nwn*, and only after that begins the work of creation. There is no independent Creator, no Demiurge standing over and apart from Creation, born already before the birth of the universe. In ancient Egyptian mythology, it may be asserted, Idea emerges, endowed with power, from raw Matter. In the beginning there is Matter, in the form of water, apparently inchoate, obscure, abyssal. Yet it is potentially powerful, dynamic, creative, innovative, the generative source of the divinities themselves, as well as of all remaining creation. Every style and form of Life arises from that primal, uncreated water. That is the very origin of all subsequent development."

Again, and countering today's basic explanation for the existence of the universe, Obenga (2004: 33-34) negates this idea by stating, from its inception, the Egyptian creative idea "posits neither God nor Chaos-as-Darkness, but Matter, in the form of primal water." This is contrary to, "a diffuse electromagnetic mass, left over from the beginning of the universe, [that] indicate that the Universe began from masses of free elementary particles in a state of infinite density. There was no gravity at the beginning of the Universe, just matter of a nature very different from that making up our Universe now. The universe then was dominated by radiation; this was a time when the Universe was in the true sense opaque. It is supposed that at temperatures approaching 3000 degrees K, the thermal balance between radiation and matter was ruptured. Then followed an era dominated by matter produced by radiation, with consequent expansion of the universe, and the outward expansion of galaxies away from each other." In actuality, the ancient Egyptians "posited Matter at the very origins of the universe, a primordial matter very different from what was later to emerge out of it.... they posited matter prior to all else, before the demiurge and the other divinities issuing therefrom, thereafter, before heaven and earth, before living creatures and their evolving life, before the entire universe, before the cosmos as a whole."

In this evolution, Obenga (2004: 40) explained further: "Egyptian thinkers posited a state of matter before God and all his creation. Better still, God the artificer and creator himself emerged from the primal matter, itself *un-created*. The ancient Egyptians posited *un-created* matter before God the demiurge; Saint Augustine posited *con-created* matter, created by God at the same time as other creatures. Between the two conceptions, that of *un-created* matter is more materialistic than that of *con-created* matter." Therefore, in seeking to arrive at original conception of the temple, Obenga bases the emergence of the skill-set on Narmer's beginnings following Unification by development of: "A coherent organization for channeling and harnessing the waters of the Nile through systematic irrigation, accompanied by a writing system useful for regulating ceremonies and rituals, setting the calendar, and communicating Pharaoh's messages across great distances." To further concretize this idea, Theophile Obenga in *African Philosophy: The Pharaonic Period*: 2780-330 B.C. (Per Ankh, 2004: 546-47) in explaining an excerpt from a text in the Tomb of Kheti at Assyut [Assiut] (First Intermediate Period) recounts the following:

"'How greatly the god of the city loves you, Kheti, son of Itiibis! He has ordered you, thinking of the future, to renovate his temple and to construct the walls of eternity and the ground of the first day, to the depth of the soil in ancient days. This temple, which bears the name of 'Sky of The One Who Made the Sky,' which Ptah built with his own fingers, and which Thoth established for Wepwawet, Lord of Assyut.... How the great one of your time rejoice."

"How lucky are the women of your harem, your concubines! Your monuments are seen in the temple. The king says: 'Make sure that the temple is long-lasting, and its beauty touches the sky. How beautiful, then, is what was done in your time. How fortunate is the city under your rule!"

The sole companion, supreme chief of the nome of the Sycamore, who lives on earth, Kheti.'" (Excerpt from a text in the tomb of Kheti of Assyut). The author, Obenga goes on to state (2004: 547) as follows: "Egyptian temples were devoted to invocations of cosmic essence. In principle, each temple was built on the primal hill that rose from the watery abyss of Nwn, 'the ground of the first day.' And practically every object in the Egyptian temple was imbued with cosmic significance: the temple foundations, the ritual statuary, the temple wells and pylons, the sacred pool, and the orientation of the temple itself. For instance, at Abu Simbel, the sun's rays penetrate all the way into the sanctuary on the day of the equinox. Just as remarkably, at Tanis in the Delta, the axis of the temple of Anat is in exact alignment with that of the temple of Amon at Karnak, in Upper Egypt."

This connection is interesting, for, he continued: "Thus, the Egyptian thought system, which laid the foundations and erected the scaffoldings for temple architecture, was a decisive organizational influence on the construction of the pyramids. Imposing an almost abstract precision on the performance of essential rites, it was, without a doubt, a philosophy of the uncreated, conscious of itself, making of the pharaonic system a dynamic system, in the potent, complete sense of the term."

Even further and recognizing as Norman Lockyer pointed out in *Dawn of Astronomy* (1894), temples were oriented towards some heavenly body, the position of the temple and the orientation of its axial line became important; Obenga yet seems to imply all temples seem oriented towards the house of the principal god, who was himself heavenly; as for instance, Ra, the Sun God. As such, then: "The entire country, in effect, was crisscrossed with a veritable network of sacred lines. The processional axis of the burial temple of Queen Hatshepsut is at right angles to the Nile bank. Curiously enough, its projection across the river coincides directly with the main axis of the temple of Amon at Karnak. Historically, the worship of Amon, the Secret, Invisible One, like the architecture of the temple of Amon at Karnak, has lasted over 2000 years. Karnak, in Thebes, was a place of high privilege, filled with the presence of divinity."

Liberate the Temple. Ramesseum, Mortuary Temple of Rameses II. Classic image of the temple with columns of the Porch, columns of the Vestibule and columns of the Hypostyle Hall.

Liberate the Temple. Ramesseum, Mortuary Temple of Rameses II. View past the Osiride Figures against square pillars with round columns in the Vestibule and the elevation toward the Hypostyle Hall with its spreading calyx-capitals.

Liberate the Temple. Ramesseum, Mortuary Temple of Rameses II. Native Egyptian guide Showki Abd Rady beside the fallen head of the massive statue of Rameses II. Notice the nose is particularly broken.

Liberate the Temple. Ramesseum, Mortuary Temple of Rameses II. From the North, view of side columns with their bud capitals. To the left evidence of the Clerestory.

Liberate the Temple. Ramesseum, Mortuary Temple of Rameses II. Modern evidence of how massive stone is moved from place to place.

Strange, but anyone with a sense of metaphysical and spiritual consciousness can sense a higher science on any visit to the temple as if to convey millennia later there is still "soul-force" in the place.

Now, we know, once the king had decided to erect a temple to his god or himself, aided by the Goddess Seshat or the Queen impersonating that divinity, he set out to "Stretch the Cord" and "Set out the four sides of the enclosure." This was all part of a "foundation ceremony" of which Gaston Maspero, as previously indicated, found evidence at both Deir el Bahari and Luxor Temples. Even Lockyer related other scholars' comments on foundation stones and ceremonies. However, once construction was complete, the temple was consecrated in a ceremony before being handed over to the god to whose home it was to become. That is to say, after the "Consecration Ceremony," which was generally renewed annually on New Year's Day, recreating that "first time," the god in his earthly manifestation would be invited to take residence in that "God's House." Interesting how, while the temple was the "God's House;" the palace was the "King's House;"

and the tomb was the "home of the Deceased." Thus, all three had their special place of residence.

The Egyptian temple was structured in zones, each with a specific function and symbolism.

First, in the king's visit, to a worship not a mortuary temple which is generally adjacent, there is the approach to the temple after the king had disembarked from his vessel or barge onto the Quay. Here he would be greeted by persons of the sacerdotal and bureaucratic orders; musicians; nobles and princes; acrobats, craftsmen, etc. After some ceremony of welcoming, he then approaches the temple. If it is some distance from the river he would probably approach by way of a canal and onto an Avenue of Sphinxes whether by carrying chair or chariot.

Second, he then arrives at the Pylon and after, perhaps admiring the flagstaves flying temple, city and state flags, he entrances into the Great Court,

In all this, syncretism became a standard practice, whether in combining of gods or ritual practice. That is to say, there is great similarity in the ceremony of "Consecration of the Temple;" the "Opening of the Mouth" of the deceased before final burial rite; the heavenly "Lustration of the Sun God" before he begins his daily journey across the sky; and is similarly repeated for the divinity on earth as part of the daily ritual. The same is done for the king in the Per-dwet or "House of the Morning" upon his arising and again when he visits the temple as part of his "Baptism to ensure his and the temple's purity" This same ceremony is again repeated in the daily "Consecration of the Temple" to bring it to life before the ritual of the day could begin!

II. INTRODUCTION BY DR. FRED MONDERSON

While Egypt continues to remain a subject of fascinating interest to students, professional academics and tourists alike, new revealing research and new analysis of "ancient data" continues to challenge accepted notions and beliefs established in 19th and 20th Century times which were devoid of critical challenges and constructive intellectual scrutiny. Nevertheless, that goes without saying, the falsity of a "white Egypt," propagated in the "white supremacy mold" has begun to crack under the weight of its untenable structure revealing what it really is, a construct not supported by the pillars of logic. Cogently put, "the existential data contradicts the symbolic representation." In this vein, the structural foundations upon which modern understanding of the history, culture and ethnicity of the ancient inhabitants of Egypt were laid in the 19th Century by foreign experts in an era of political colonialism and intellectual imperialism was certainly devoid of constructive indigenous Egyptian involvement and critique. Hence, many false notions fabricated in the "Penny Press" age of "rapid publication" quickly became ossified in the historical record upon which many of the false contemporary views are based.

It was Mr. Zahi Hawass, former Chairman of the Egyptian Antiquities Council, who, after the recent study to determine the heritage, identity and ethnicity of King Tutankhamon, declared "King Tut is the only pharaoh whose identity we know with certainty because we found him in a sealed tomb." Subsequently, Queen Hatshepsut was identified through dental and other forms of scientific sleuthing. That is not to say the other kings and queens are not who we think they are, but unquestionably not with King Tut's certainty. In all historical inquiry, the yardstick should be akin to the American jurisprudential insistence of "beyond a reasonable doubt." Whereas, while the "King Tut Yardstick" applies to the identities of the various kings, it should also apply to all aspects of the cultural, physical and scientific history of the ancient Egyptian experience. For example, the recent Nubian Conference in October 2012 showed new research challenging some ancient accepted norms. This supports the view all aspects of the culture's interpretation are suspect; and, until we painstakingly re-examine every iota of evidence, we would not know for sure if what we have always believed is actually correct. In essence, we must extricate ourselves from ossified interpretations handed us from the German intellectual tradition and the citadels of Oxford and Cambridge as well as the discussion rooms of the Museums and societies of Europe and America. That is not to say those institutions and their experts have not supplied significant contributions but we should also rely on Ronald Reagan's dictum, "Trust but verify."

One of this writer's most cogent observations at the Temple of Mut was, despite the great archaeological effort expended to unearth the principal regions of the temple, for over a century, many statues and who knows what lies shoulder-deep in the sand. Thus, we cannot conclusively detail the temple. As such, using Dr. Hawass' "King Tut Yardstick," we must be careful about the modern interpretation of ancient Egyptian history because of the potential "rifts between the lutes" propounded by more than two centuries of falsity have failed to justify a false sense of racial superiority. What is surprising, a great many scholars and even local Egyptians had bought into unquestioned acceptance of a belief system that has begun to come apart.

That is to say, there are many inconsistencies in presentation of the history of the beloved ancient Egypt. Here, as an example, are just a few.

1.   The Ancient Egyptians were Caucasians.

2.   The Ancient Egyptians were a race of "red men," that is "red Caucasians;" yet, this contribution is actually due to the red color in image representations.

3.   The Ancient Egyptians originated in South-west Asia and migrated to Egypt, entering by way of the Isthmus of Suez and migrating up the Nile; by way of the Wady Hammamat, crossing the desert and arriving at Koptos, home of God Min; even entering the Nile Valley from the South-west desert by Caucasians who had

crossed the Mediterranean and settled in North Africa, then migrated through the Sahara entering into the Nile Valley.

4.   The Ancient Egyptians were "pastoralists."

5.   The Ancient Egyptians were "boat people."

Still, there are many more such ridiculous propositions propounded in the process of establishing Egyptology and Egyptian archaeology on a firm foundation. Such beliefs became solidified in that process that included no indigenous Egyptian experts in the field of analysis as colonial administrations channeled lucrative archaeological concessions to "favorite sons" who did wonderful work untangling the temples and tombs but were allowed to set the intellectual standards and as reward offered "choice pick" of the very best artifacts recovered. In his Introduction to Adolf Erman's *Life in Ancient Egypt*, Jon Manchip White credits Lepsius with sending 15,000 "choice pieces" to Berlin, while Gladstone Bratton in *A History of Egyptian Archaeology* (1968: 75) states more precisely: "Lepsius himself sent some fifteen thousand objects to Berlin including three tombs from Memphis, an obelisk, and a pillar from the tomb of Seti I at Abydos.... [he] rationalized his own policy by the statement that only by rescuing the antiquities and sending them to a European museum could they be preserved from destruction." Even further, Bratton (1968: 75-76) continued: "Until recently this was partly correct but a fine ethical question persists. George Ebers, his biographer, wrote naively as follows: 'With full authority to take possession of all that might embellish the Berlin collection, Lepsius appropriated what was most desirable and most interesting wherever he found it, and ventured, as we have seen, to remove whole tombs from the necropolis of ancient Memphis to the Spree (meaning Berlin). This could not be done without injury to the adjoining tombs, as they had consisted of a number of rooms collectively, and envy, ill-will and stupidity were quickly at hand to accuse the Prussian expedition of having, like impious vandals, plundered and injured the monuments in pursuit of their own purposes. But this accusation was entirely unfounded, and anyone who knows the conditions of Egypt which at that time can only rejoice that so many treasures, which were neglected and exposed to wanton destruction in their native country were at a favorable moment removed to Europe and preserved in a fine public museum." Equally, as Enos Brown recounts in "Excavations at Naga-Ed-Der, Where Prehistoric Man First Settled in Egypt" *Scientific American* (March 30, 1907) says of the American archaeologist Reisner Dr. J.C. Reisner excavated at several different sites. Rewarding his efforts: "Hundreds of cases are being unpacked and their contents catalogued. They embrace an enormous number of objects, demonstrating the gradual progress of the arts from the earliest or Paleolithic age, the age of flint, through the period of its highest development in the Cheops dynasty, up to the time when Egypt sank to the position of a Roman dependency. The rise of civilization, from a period antedating the Christian era by 7,000 years, can be unerringly traced in the flints, pottery, carvings, statues, and inscriptions, found in ancient cemeteries or sites of cities, ransacked to enrich the museum of an American university and to benefit the scholars of the new world." Mr. Brown goes on to say: "It is generally admitted that Egypt was first settled by people of Asiatic origin, and confirmation of this theory has been discovered in the graves of Naga-ed-Der, in which many skeletons of the earliest period were found. These were fortunately in perfect condition and afford splendid anatomical material for determining the racial character of the prehistoric people, which, ethnologists conclude, was Asiatic and not Nubian. Even the contents of the intestines were so well preserved that it was possible to determine, not only the food, but even the medicines which were contained in them. The disease from which the person died could be easily diagnosed. Many were resurrected who died of some kidney complaint, others of gall stones, and others of diseased bones." Naturally, Naga-Ed-Der is in the South and not the North!

What is interesting about Mr. Brown's conclusions is that later research and determinations refute his claims. Take for example, William S. Arnett in *The Predynastic Origin of Egyptian Hieroglyphs: Evidence for the Development of Rudimentary Forms of Hieroglyphs in Upper Egypt in the Fourth Millennium B.C.* (Washington, D.C.: University Press of America, 1982: 62-63) states: "There is no evidence to justify any racial identification of the ancient Egyptians. Nor should we really be concerned to know what color their skin was. It doesn't change what they did, and it doesn't change what has followed in African history or in the history of any other area. Our only concern for the origin of the Egyptian Dynastic Race should be in terms of their geographic origins and of the natural and cultural environments which produced the classic Egyptian civilization. In the opinion of tis writer, it is as impossible to determine the color of the skin of the ancient Egyptians as it is to discover their innermost thoughts."

Two things can be said in response to the above. First, the Curator Allen at the Metropolitan Museum of Art in Manhattan once informed, "Adolf Erman was the only modern man who knew exactly what the ancient Egyptians thought." Second, despite what may be said about the ancient Egyptians by Whether it is Arnett or David O'Connor that the ancient Egyptians were not "white," the preponderant propagated view is they were White. The prevalent evidence which holds all the facets of Egyptian civilization is grounded in Africa's cultural effluence is discarded and attributed to a people who left no traces of such in their place of origin.

This and much, much more as well as unending skull-duggery formed what Brian Fagan characterized as, and in his book of the same name, *The Rape of the Nile* (1975).

Liberate the Temple. Medinet Habu, Mortuary Temple of Rameses III. Entrance gateway to the temple some have labeled a "Migdol" after an Asiatic model.

Liberate the Temple. Medinet Habu, Mortuary Temple of Rameses III. Osiride Figures against square Pillars to the north of the First Court.

Liberate the Temple. Medinet Habu, Mortuary Temple of Rameses III. Round Columns to the south of the Second Court.

Liberate the Temple. Medinet Habu, Mortuary Temple of Rameses III. Round Columns and Osiride Figures against Square Pillars in the South-West Corner of the Second Court. A terrace with columns stands behind the Osiride Figures of Square Pillars.

Liberate the Temple. Medinet Habu, Mortuary Temple of Rameses III. Horus (Heru, left) and Thoth (Tehuti, right) baptize the Pharaoh before entering to officiate in the Temple.

Today, the great museums of the world particularly in Europe and America proudly boast of the splendors of their collections on Egypt acquired in an age before the Egyptian people could effectively regulate who got what. Now, in ongoing and balanced research using modern technology and more evolved methods of exploration, excavation, examination and analysis of extant knowledge such efforts are increasingly proving many "archaeological findings" to be falsely interpreted, but "old ideas die hard." As such, they linger rather than be consigned to the basement of outdated and useless information. Case in point!

An American scholar John David Wortham from his "pulpit of absolute wisdom" in *The Genesis of British Egyptology*: 1549-1906 (University of Oklahoma Press, Norman, Oklahoma, 1971: 93) has written: "Great progress was made during the nineteenth century in the study of Egyptian mummification. Augustus Bozzi Granville, a physician and a student of Coptic, undertook the earliest nineteenth-century dissection of a mummy at his London home in 1825. From his detailed dissection, he correctly concluded that the ancient Egyptians were Caucasians. He also succeeded in clearing up many erroneous ideas about the embalming process. Among other things, he proved the correctness of Herodotus' assertion that the ancient Egyptians had, when preparing a cadaver for burial, extracted the pituitary through the nostrils." He accepts this view of Herodotus who in all likelihood never visited a mummy factory, certainly not the "Mummification Museum in Luxor," ha, ha. Still, he gave no credence but discounted Herodotus' statement that the "Ethiopians, Egyptians, and Colchians had thick lips, broad noses, wooly hair and were burnt of skin!"

Now, in an interesting article entitled "Egyptian Mummy" among "Antiquarian and Philosophical Studies" in *The Gentleman's Magazine* of October 1820, pp. 349-350, in describing a mummy donated by Mr. Joshua Heywood to the Hunterian Museum at Glasgow, the writer states: "The body, shrouded in from fifty to sixty folds of coarse pale brick-red colored linen, is deposited in a strong wooden coffin, fashioned so as to bear a rude resemblance to the human shape. At the upper extremity is carved a face, the features of which (as in the case with all Egyptian sculpture) are very much of the Negro cast." We know the Egyptians loved the color red because they associated it with the sun, a solar and special phenomenon. They considered themselves special! Dr. Cheikh Anta Diop said the "Egyptians painted themselves red to be distinguished from other Africans." Even Dr. ben-Jochannan has often said, "The Egyptians painted themselves red because they were dead." They painted with the Henna plant. Even young brides, particularly Nubians, were painted red with henna." Going back to the most ancient African "Bushman Art" and even art among the "Tassili Frescoes" of the Sahara, red was the favorite color; again, like gold, it was considered to be of a divine nature!

The article continued, "Though the features were very much collapsed, the face was nowhere divested of skin. The skin itself was of a chestnut-brown color. The brow was well shaped, though, if any way defective, narrow; and to some it may be interesting to learn, the organ of music was prominent. The nose, though slightly compressed, retained enough of its original shape to be recognized as Roman." Might I also add; the original color of the mummy of Rameses II when first unwrapped in the 1880s (*Biblical World*, 1886) was of similar "brown splashed with black!" Dr. Van Sertima, however, recounted Cheikh Anta Diop's observations that "the mummy of Rameses II was exposed to so much radiation when it was being repaired in Paris, it turned white." So, if in the future people of interest are told the mummy is white understand how it got so.

Even further, the gentleman of the article continued, "One circumstance must have struck all who had an opportunity of seeing the above interesting examination; namely, the dissimilarity of the features to what we are taught to believe were those of the inhabitants of Egypt [This writer's emphasis], at the remote period at which the custom of embalming existed in that country. A moment's reflection will suffice to convince us that this circumstance can in no way throw discredit on the antiquity of the genuine character of the mummy."

The writer goes on to say, "Mr. Millar, portrait painter in Glasgow, is at present finishing a likeness in oil of the face and surrounding parts, as they appeared immediately after they were exposed; and was completely successful in the accuracy of the likeness before the exposure to the air had converted the face from a brown to a sable hue, which it did in the short period of three hours."

Scant if any attempt has been made to force the retraction of Wortham's arrogant statement. The article of 1820, five years before Granville's dissection, gets no credit; yet, young scholars, particularly from Europe and some from Egypt under the tutelage of "Professors" such as at the "American University in Cairo" know of Wortham but perhaps not *The Gentleman's Magazine* article. So, returning to my annotated list.

1. The Ancient Egyptians were Caucasians! Suppose that I acknowledge such. In 1857, an advocate for American Negro (Nubian) slavery, Samuel Cartwright argued: "The monumental record shows the Negro as nothing but slaves in Egypt from time immemorial." As a defender of slavery, Cartwright used hardly if any referents or references in his book *Slavery and Ethnology* (1857). At least he admits the Negro's existence in Egypt from time immemorial as opposed to Herman Junker (in 1924) who argued they only got there "yesterday!" He probably had not heard of Champollion, who, in a letter to his brother discussed the classification of the races of man he witnessed in the Biban el Moluk. At Oxford University, England, they never tear down any building constructed more than a thousand years ago but simply build upon these older ones. So too, in the misguided interpretation of the archaic views new edifices of falsity have assumed a prominent role in the propagation of the history of Egypt making what many contemporary young and old scholars know and profess, the falsity of Egypt is nothing but pillars cemented on a veneer of papyrus laid upon a bed of quicksand!

2. The Ancient Egyptians were a race of red men - Caucasians. While the Ancient Egyptians were painted many colors, red, black, blue, green, etc., they were never painted white to have any significance. That is, with the exception of Champollion's Biban Moluk image, as Dr. Diop pointed out, whites were below the Egyptian, African, Asiatic, on the "lowest round of the human ladder," that is, "a virtual savage!"

Henri Lhote's "Tassili Frescoes" and Mary Leakey's "Bushman Art;" both in *National Geographic Magazine* show ancient man's fascination with "The predominant Red" as choice of color in their art. Dr. Diop in *The African Origin of Civilization: Myth or Reality* (1974) stated ancient Egyptians painted themselves red to be distinguished from other Africans," viz., Libyans, Nubians, etc. Henri Brugsch in A History of Egypt of the Pharaohs indicated, "the ancient Egyptians painted themselves red to be illuminated in the blackness of the journey towards the judgment in the 'Afterlife.'"

Gay Robbins in Art of Egypt noted, in the Egyptian view, "gold and red" were associated with the sun, the gods; and as a special people they painted themselves red. In preparation for the afterlife journey those Egyptians who could not afford the luxury of lavish gold wealth in their tombs, if they had one, simply painted their coffin's image gold to symbolically represent the real thing, unfortunate for tomb robbers looking for "Ancient treasure." When the wealthy Egyptian painted trees and bunches of grapes on the ceiling of their tombs, this was to symbolically represent the fruit at their arms reach. Thus, symbolism and symbolic logic were hallmarks of ancient Egyptian thinking in the Nile Valley experience.

Everyone has acknowledged the 25th Dynasty was Nubian and Black! Yet, in their tombs these kings are pictured red!

Even more significantly far-reaching, *The New York Times* of October, 2012 printed an article on the discovery of a "paint factory" in which a pot with red paint and brush was found in South Africa dated to c. 107,000 (105,000 B.P) years ago, where evidence of the "predominant red" indicated how these ancient painters mixed their colors. The article further noted there was evidence of art material elsewhere in Africa dated at c. 150,000 but this was the first-time actual paint, red, was discovered. Even more revolutionary, the article revealed this discovery pushed modern understanding of "complex thinking among the ancients," much further back in time. Are we to believe these "South Africans" were Egyptian or White? At the recent United Nations sponsored Summit Conference on "**The Decade of People of African Ancestry**," March 8-11, 2018, it was announced the discovery of the gene from which the European mutated from the African some 8,000-years ago. Equally, in tracing the African from Eve, some 200,000-years-ago; then, for some 192,000 years only African people roamed the earth!"

Nonetheless, Dr. Diop speaks of the "absurd conclusion" based on propounded falsity that "Africans are Caucasians" which would support the contention that ancient peoples throughout Africa who painted themselves red were Egyptians and by extension Caucasians.

3.   The Ancient Egyptians were Caucasians who originated in Southwest Asia and migrated to Egypt. Either there were three waves of migration, each contradicting the other or the myth cannot be made tangible in fact. This argument of migration of the Egyptians was first and cogently stated by Von Lushan in 1896 and upheld since supported by William Flinders Petrie's "Migration" Huxley Lecture in 1911 and even later by Walter Emery, Derry and then David Wortham. Conversely, however, David O'Connor author of *Abydos: Egypt's First Pharaohs and the Cult of Osiris*, London: Thames and Hudson, 2009) has exclaimed "The Egyptians were not white" as stated in the Philadelphia Museum's "Egypt and Nubia Symposium." Adding more weight to contradicting any argument for a "white Egypt," Arnett's contention must be restated, "Diop was correct in proving the Egyptians were not white." Still, the agreed unspoken assumption is that they were white!

First, the entry via the Isthmus of Suez means upon arrival the cultural influence ascended the Nile to impact Thebes and then Aswan, if they got that far. Moret posed the view, "the Delta influenced the South" and Diop demolished this argument. He simply responded, "If so, why are the significant monuments and historic sites located in the south and not the north?"

Second, these immigrants entered Africa by way of the Horn, passing through Ethiopia, perhaps northward along the coast and through the Wady Hammamat arriving at Koptos, then sailing down the Nile. We're not sure if they first sailed southward to confer their blessing on Thebes. Possibly suffering from sun stroke in the desert they either split, some going downstream and others going upstream to Aswan then making their way again north to Memphis and points further into the Delta. Strange that the powerful Egyptian military apparatus probably stood by unconcerned while the immigrants swarmed all over their land. Equally too, if theirs has been a force of any significance, it certainly would have been recorded by a people who were meticulous in their record keeping. Unfortunately, this migrating Caucasian "man of cultural supremacy and goodwill" did not seem to have created and left any evidence in his place of origin of the cultural ideas he so graciously blest the Africans with upon his arrival. Von Lushan had argued, "For some unknown reason" he left his place of origin to migrate to Africa. We know people seldom leave their place of origin while experiencing comfort but because they are fleeing sufferable or inhospitable conditions or seeking a better way of life elsewhere; case in Point, those Englishmen who settled Australia or the Englishmen and other Europeans who settled America all seeking opportunities for a better way of life have links to the "Old Country." Importantly, they retained knowledge of their roots and still practiced their culture in the new land. However, none of this applies to Egyptian consciousness for they have no knowledge of these "migrants" of a "Superior mental attitude" who could not have invented Egyptian ideas in their native lands. Let us not forget, the ingrained falsity gained credence in the age of global white supremacy promoting "naked," "enlightened," and "intellectual" imperialism. Professor John H. Clarke did remind us, "The people who preached racism colonized history," and "When Europe colonized the world, she colonized the world's history." Nevertheless, and despite this, "Europe's claim to Egypt uses no logic!" Therefore, "African people must write African history."

In *The Gentleman's Magazine* article mentioned above and elsewhere, writers with an unbiased agenda speak of the "African mold" upon which Egyptian portraiture is predominantly molded despite later intermingling of peoples after the Hyksos occupation and imperialist adventures of the pharaohs who brought untold numbers of foreigners to settle in their land as captives and given as endowments to the temples; the mold still showed "the African imprint as late as Roman times." However, still none of the cultural traits the migrating Caucasians "blest the Africans with" have been found in their place of origin - that is, no imprint of the pyramid concept, no

Hieroglyphics, no colonnade which was invented at Sakkara by Imhotep c. 2680 B.C.; neither the Egyptian concept of the Nile boat upon which the gods first sailed across the wonderful Egyptian sky then manifest for Nile River travel. Thus, these Caucasians, not having invented the Egyptian prototypes, nor possess such, nor did they bring it with them or bequeath same to the Egyptians, can be regarded as the figment of someone's imagination.

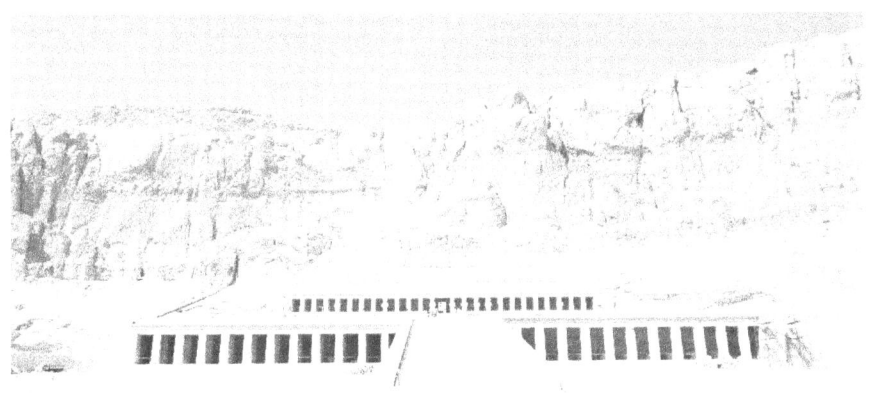

Liberate the Temple. Hatshepsut's Temple at Deir el Bahari. View of the Middle and Upper Terrace Colonnade with the mountain as its backdrop.

Liberate the Temple. Books at the author's table emphasizing Dr. Ben, Barack Obama and other books on Egypt and Black Nationalism.

Liberate the Temple. Dendera Temple of Goddess Hathor. On a Panel at the temple's entrance Hathor suckles the young pharaoh, to the right the king offers a girdle and to the left the young king in White Crown sucks his fingers.

Liberate the Temple. Dendera Temple of Goddess Hathor. On an entrance panel, while Hathor in horns and disk suckles the young, Pharaoh in Red Crown offers a sailing vessel with standard and a youthful figure with finger to his mouth stands behind the Goddess.

Liberate the Temple. Dendera Temple of Goddess Hathor. The Nile Gods bring the produce of their Domain.

Liberate the Temple. Dendera Temple of Goddess Hathor. The entrance of the Temple with its six massive screened columns with Hathor Heads are part of 24 such columns of the Great Hypostyle Hall.

We know:

1. The earliest Nile Valley art was found in Nubia and southern Upper Egypt. W. Stephenson Smith in *The Art and Architecture of Ancient Egypt* (Penguin Books, 1958, 1965, 1981: 25-26) wrote accordingly: "Art appears in the Nile valley as early as the seventh millennium B.C. The earliest productions are the rock-drawings executed on the cliffs bordering the Nile in Upper Egypt and Nubia. The most ancient of these consist principally of geometric designs such as concentric circles or half-circles and net-patterns, or abstract figurations the exact meanings of which is obscure. Represented themes appear later. There are many hundreds of drawings of animals pursued by the earliest hunters and of weapons and traps. Although the publications of these drawings are quite complete, their chronology is still problematic. Drawings of cattle and boats can be definitely associated with the developed Neolithic cultures of Upper Egypt and Nubia, and with the Egyptian Predynastic, Nubian C-Group, and later historic cultures."

2. Robert Bauval and Thomas Brophy in *Black Genesis*: *The Prehistoric Origins of Ancient Egypt* (Vermont: Bear and Company, 2011) identify people of Nabta Playa in the Western desert of Southern Upper Egypt, as the earliest scientists, who mapped the heavens [perhaps at "14,000 years ago"], invented a calendar, were pastoralists who also practiced agriculture and began worship of the "mother goddess." When their land began to dry up or desiccate, they migrated to the Nile Valley somewhere perhaps in the vicinity of Abu Simbel in Nubia.

3. Toby Wilkinson in *Genesis of the Pharaohs*: *Dramatic New Discoveries Rewrite the Origin of Ancient Egypt* (London: Thames and Hudson, 2003) discovered petroglyphs in the Eastern Desert of Southern Upper Egypt that were the actual prototype of the later fully equipped boats of the gods he identified as "1000 years before Winkler's Mesopotamians." In 1938, Henri Winkler published *Rock Drawings of Southern Upper Egypt*, then a second volume where he argued, now falsely realized, the creators of such early and geographical cultural forms of art, were from Mesopotamia. Naturally, there was no systematic "pushback to his conclusions nor

his findings. That is, until Toby Wilkinson, nearly some 65 years later after the damage had been done.

4. Bruce Williams revelation of "The World's Earliest Monarchy found in Nubia" at Qustol, was first discovered by a team from the University of Chicago, led by Keith C. Seele in the 1960 as prelude to the creation of the Aswan High Dam and Lake Nasser. He did not publish but secreted his findings in the University's Museum basement, because of the potential significance of the discovery. Published in *The New York Times* newspaper of October 1991, this is significant proof of "high culture" or civilization in the Upper Nile beyond Egypt's Aswan border. Credible arguments have sought to link this Kingdom of Ta-Seti to the Nabta Playa folks who migrated in that direction. However, unlike the "for some unknown reason" folks who failed to demonstrate in their place of origin nor upon arrival any cultural features, relative to Egypt; the Qustol find revealed incenser, Nile Boats, enthroned pharaoh, white crown, palace façade, so significant in Egypt more than 200 years later.

As a caveat to this segment two powerful ideas are raised. In the "for some unknown reason" argument, despite the above relevant data, it is stated these Caucasian migrants brought no cultural artifactual evidence except "a superior mental faculty" that "provided a great stimulus to the existing culture." Pressed for a time of this happening, during the 1896 rush to falsity, especially in the emerging "Penny Press" and other disseminating mechanisms, a date given in the Old Kingdom is all that was possible. Upon an analysis of the arrogance of the "superior mental faculty" argument in the Old Kingdom, molded in white supremacy myth, all this occurred hundreds of years after Narmer (Mena, Aha) the Theban, had mobilized an armada with all the attendant logistical ramifications of a military expedition, sailed north to conquer then establish the foundations of pharaonic rule, monarchical system of government with a multi-tiered social order supporting the status quo; a bureaucratic administrative hierarchy that maintained all the cultural trappings of trade, education, agriculture, medicine, building, endowment, mortuary practice, boat-building, mastering river navigation, quarrying and transportation of large stone over great distances, irrigation exploiting the wonders of the bountiful Nile Inundation, establishment of religious practice with the metaphysical implications of the ritualizing of the gods, astronomical observation of the heavens, the development of mathematics and invention of all the social amenities that made life enjoyable as well as possessing a powerful military that provided the society's req1uisite security. Nevertheless, and surprisingly, after all this, these peoples, possessing a "superior mental attitude," upon arrival began re-inventing Narmer's wheel! How arrogant!

Charles Finch III in *The Star of Deep Beginnings*: The Genesis of African Science and Technology (Decatur, Georgia: Khenti, Inc., 1998: 4-5) added an important explanation which can be considered a synthesis of this early time and developments. He stated: "The peopling of the Nile Valley from the Africa's Great Lakes region must have occurred over and again in waves. The population wave from the Great Lakes directly ancestral to the Nile Valley peoples probably began to settle north of the second cataract no later than 15,000 years ago. This settlement did not preempt later migrations, of course, but most of these came in from the west, that is from the Sahara, beginning about 10,000 years ago. Another line of migration apparently trickled in intermittently from the Horn of Africa along the Blue Nile from 6,000 to 10,000 years ago. The dynastic Egyptians' never-ending fascination with Punt, their name for the Horn of Africa, and clear attestations from them regarding their kingship to the people of Punt, compel us to look in that direction for an ancestral lineage of the people who created pharaonic culture. There seems to have been a touch of religious awe associated with Punt since it was also referred to as Ta-Neter, i.e., "Land of the God." We must also remember Punt is in Africa despite 19th Century attempts to extend it as far as the other side of the Red Sea to distance it from Africa. This falsity was thus, a strawman argument.

During the emergence of the 11th Dynasty consolidation, Intef organized a force and coming out of the pass at Thebes he sought to challenge Mentuhotep II. There he encountered Mentuhotep with a superior military force, ready and waiting on the field of battle. He paused and said, purportedly, "Wait a minute, brother!" Thereupon he called upon his mother to intercede with Mentuhotep's mother Queen Aam to broker a peace treaty, consolidating their forces and set about bringing the Middle Kingdom into reality. Conceptually speaking, the same thing happened to the migrating Caucasians, who upon arriving at Koptos realized God Min, the alter-ego of Amon-Ra. Some as Arthur Weigall have argued Min was a Southwest Asian; viz., Sumerian, Mesopotamian; god, brought to Koptos by the migrants. What does this mean?

Flinders Petrie discovered huge wooden statues of Min painted black at Koptos, which he dated to prehistoric times placing him among the foundation gods. Again, "new research" has argued, the statues were actually Old Kingdom; perhaps this is to coincide with the migrant's arrival. Coinciding is another strategy employed to make SWA culture complex contemporary with or superior to Egyptian. For example, the "Long Chronology" is dated more than a thousand years before the "Short Chronology," which is variously given between 3200-3000 (3050) B.C. Some critical scholars see the reality of Mesopotamian history in the Egyptian short chronological history. The image of white Egyptians is propagated in Europe and America and in Cairo Airport boutiques or bazaars where tourists transit. In Luxor and Aswan, the natives of Upper Egypt paint their images black.

All this notwithstanding, even if the Caucasians did bring Min from South West Asia, why is he painted black? Was he painted black in Mesopotamia? Is he painted black for some form of symbolism? If he is painted black as a form of symbolism, are the Egyptians painted red as a form of symbolism? Are the Nubians painted red a form of symbolism? Interesting, at this conference on the 25th Nubian Dynasty, I did not see any Nubians at the Conference? However, their images were painted red like the Egyptians. Imagine; noblemen of the "only black dynasty" were painted red in their mortuary representation! Nevertheless, Min being black means the Caucasians were worshipping black gods! Therefore, we must believe, "when God Amon instructed his public relations people" of his intent to incorporate Min into his esoteric being, he meant the black god should become the poster child of the new reality of divine worship and rule!

Liberate the Temple. Philae Temple of Isis. The Dromos or walkway to the Great Pylon with the "Western Colonnade" and its 32 Columns to the left and the "Eastern Colonnade" with its 16 Columns to the right. The doorway entrances the Court of the temple proper.

Liberate the Temple. Philae Temple of Isis. The Eastern Colonnade with its unfinished columns.

Liberate the Temple. Philae Temple of Isis. North-East view of the "Kiosk of Trajan" with its magnificent screened columns with varied capitals.

Liberate the Temple. Philae Temple of Isis. Another view of the Western Colonnade.

Liberate the Temple. Philae Temple of Isis. The Western entrance of "Trajan's Kiosk" with its magnificent architecture.

Liberate the Temple. Philae Temple of Isis. Close-up of the architectural intricacies of "Trajan's Kiosk."

Gaston Maspero insisted the origins of the ancient Egyptians, must be sought not from the east but the west. This is interesting because for a people who have had a historical record of one (26,000); two (52,000); three (78,000); possibly a fourth (104,000) years of precession stargazing have no record of their "ancestors" who arrived in the Old Kingdom when their records were very accurate. However, Maspero's argument is that they entered from the western desert but they were a Caucasian people who migrated from Southern Europe to North Africa, into the Sahara and then the Nile Valley. Keep in mind, this is an extraordinary Egyptological scholar who made the Cairo Museum place-cards and described the New Kingdom Nobleman Mahepra as "Negroid but not Negro" (Nubian). Conversely, the biographers of the musical great Beethoven, a contemporary of Maspero, described the musical genius as "Swarthy;" "Black;" "Negro;" "Negroid," etc.

Maspero's western origins bring us to the people of Nabta Playa whom Bauval and Brophy described as "Black Africans" but from misguided indigenous Egyptian "field experience" were Caucasians!

As is generally known, the question of dating is somewhat problematic. The four methods of dating are thermoluminesence, Potassium Argon, C-14 and Dendo-chronology. The first three are used in Egypt, the last in Southwest America. Nevertheless, all dates before 1750 B.C. are considered uncertain. Still, Bauval and Brophy authors of *Black Genesis*: *The Prehistoric Origins of Ancient Egypt* date these Africans of this region to 8,000-3500 B.C. but "Egyptian experts" give 8500-3500 when they migrated to the Aswan area as their habitat could no longer sustain the culture mix that developed there. We must be careful because we may unintentionally label these people, Aswan Nubians, as Caucasians and if Caucasians then the Thebans with whom these early Africans share a heritage may also be considered Caucasians and thus, as we descend the Nile, the whole Valley becomes Caucasian. We must be careful of the insidious attempts to displace Africans throughout the continent. Otherwise, we come full circle to Diop's "absurd conclusion" that "African blacks are essentially Caucasians."

In *Genesis of the Pharaohs* (2003) Toby Wilkinson identifies Min as "the earliest image of a god" discovered among Petroglyphs in the Eastern Desert of Upper Egypt. Yet, Armour identifies Min as a "black god related to the Negroes of Nubia." Those Petroglyphs discovered in the Eastern Desert, Wilkinson wrote, were "1,000 years before Winkler's Mesopotamians."

We must remember, in the slavery experience, whether the Arab Slave Trade that lasted a thousand years or the European Slave Trade that lasted four hundred years, the African was enslaved because he was "different," less than a man; not created by God; in all respects victimized by the avaricious nature of capitalist accumulation and religious bigotry. Nevertheless, there is one unmistakable fact: Even if we concede the ancient Egyptians were Caucasian, given all that was stated above, and that the whites were enslaving blacks, a la, Samuel Cartwright, "The Egyptian monuments show blacks (Negro, Nubians) as slaves from time immemorial" - the whites were painting their principal gods **BLACK**! viz., Amon-Min, Koptos and the Luxor

Museum and at Karnak beside the Sanctuary; Ptah - "a bald-headed pygmy;" Osiris - the "Great Black" (Hapi) and Amon-Ra in Blackface at Rameses II's Abu Simbel temple. In the **Papyrus of Hunefer** the nobleman states: "We came from the headwaters of the Nile at the foothills of the mountains of the moon where the God Hapi dwells." This is as clear as ever, not some mythical "unknown reason." Others argue, it is actually the **Famine Stele**. Nevertheless, this statement clearly points to Central Africa as the origin of the ancient Egyptians. Significantly, the source actually gives us the place of the origin of Osiris in Central Africa which means his wife Isis was African and also his son Horus who went north with the blacksmiths, "followers of Horus." Budge states, the great goddess Hathor, known for her "many moods" and for carrying the mummy, "was of Sudani origin."

Even further and not to belabor the example, when Ra the great creator had finished making the world, "he first made the Nubian people!" The gods liked to travel and "holiday" in Nubia or Central Africa called "God's Land." Now, all of this notwithstanding, antedating the Egyptian civilization by millennia as the Leakeys, Johansson, etc., etc., have shown - Zinjanthropus Boisie, Australopithecus Africanus, some 107,000 years ago South Africans had established a paint factory, were mixing red paint to a set and regular pattern and blazing an artistic trail as cultural expressions indicating the development of "complex thought patterns," pushing modern man's understanding of this ancient revolutionary thought process many millennia before generally such abstract processes began in places like Europe at some 40,000 years (38,000 Before Present).

One last example. William S. Arnett in *The Predynastic Origin of Egyptian Hieroglyphs: Evidence for the Development of Rudimentary Forms of Hieroglyphs in Upper Egypt in the Fourth Millennium B.C.* (University Press of America, 1982) states: "Diop was right in proving the Egyptians were not Caucasians but the bones do not prove they were Negroes." He argued, archaeology cannot prove the race of a people especially that they were Black! Of course, the "Bones of Hen Nekht" were Negroid as Myers has indicated. Certainly, David

O'Connor has argued, "The Egyptians were not white!" Nevertheless, Diop did provide evidence in "Totemism," "Circumcision," "Kingship," "Cosmogony," "Social Organization," "Matriarchy," "Kingship of the Meroitic Sudan and Egypt," "Cradles of Civilization located in the Heart of Negro Lands,' and "Languages."

Thus, to rest my case and to say no more! Critical African scholarship crying in the wilderness is becoming more vocal!

Ps. Dr. Diop has written: "While the branches of the tree of my argument could use some pruning, the trunk stands firmly planted beside the river of truth" to be watered perennially and bear fruit as part of the tremendous effort in praise of "Mother Africa" and the incorporation of Egypt into the monumental effort taking place in African Historical Reconstruction.

Liberate the Temple. Temple of Elder Horus and Sobek. Entrance doorway with screened panels with uraei on top and the magnificent columns with varied capitals supporting the architrave displaying winged sun disk and uraei above.

Liberate the Temple. Temple of Elder Horus and Sobek. Four columns of eight comprising the "Eastern Colonnade" of the "Peristyle Court" at Kom Ombo.

Liberate the Temple. Temple of Elder Horus and Sobek. On an entrance panel, Horus (Heru) and Thoth (Tchuti) baptize Pharaoh before resplendent Sobek. Notice the Uraei above the panel.

Liberate the Temple. Temple of Elder Horus and Sobek. Western view of four columns of Horus' half of the First Hypostyle Hall, with columns of the other half to the left.

Liberate the Temple. Temple of Elder Horus and Sobek. Into the deep recesses of Horus' left half of the temple with the Sanctuary area and altar visible in the rear.

LET'S LIBERATE THE TEMPLE

I.	INTRODUCTION I	4
	INTRODUCTION II	34
	INTRODUCTION III	68
II.	WHO IS DR. BEN-JOCHANNAN?	82
III.	HIS "TRILOGY"	90
IV.	THE AWESOME EGYPTIAN TEMPLE I	116
V.	THE AWESOME EGYPTIAN TEMPLE II	158
VI.	MATERIALS UTILIZED IN TEMPLE CONSTRUCTION	176
VII.	CONSTRUCTION AND LAYOUT OF THE TEMPLE	181
VIII.	ROLE AND SYMBOLISM OF THE KING	198
IX.	DECORATION OF THE TEMPLE	202
X.	THE TEMPLE AS UNIVERSITY AND COMMUNITY CLEARING HOUSE I	209

XI. THE TEMPLE AS UNIVERSITY AND COMMUNITY CLEARING HOUSE II 210
XII. THE TEMPLE AS ECONOMIC ENGINE AND MORAL TUTOR OF THE SOCIETY 213
XIII. THE SANCTUARY 214
XIV. THE KING OF EGYPT I 235
XV. THE KING OF EGYPT II 240
XVI. THE AWESOME EGYPTIAN TEMPLE III 297
XVII. EGYPTIAN ARCHITECTURE 319
XVIII. TEMPLE ORIENTATION AND DIVINE WORSHIP 324
XIX. CONSECRATION, AND PURITY IN EGYPTIAN TEMPLES 340
XX. PURIFICATION AND PURITY IN ANCIENT EGYPT 354
XXI. 10TH MEMORIAL DAY TRIBUTE TO DR. BEN - LET'S LIBERATE THE TEMPLE 374
XXII. ARGUMENT FOR EGYPT 402
XXIII. WHAT'S IN THE TEMPLE 412

LET'S LIBERATE THE TEMPLE

XXIV. ABYDOS – SITE OF ETERNAL CONSCIOUSNESS   417

XXV. CONCLUSIONS   505

Liberate the Temple. Todt. Showki Abd Rady and a friend stroll at Todt.

Liberate the Temple. Todt. Remains of the Brick wall at Todt, which goes back to the First Dynasty.

FREDERICK MONDERSON

Liberate the Temple. Todt. Showki and friends at Todt.

LET'S LIBERATE THE TEMPLE!

EXTRACTS FROM THE 8TH Memorial Day Tribute to Dr. Ben - MAY 23, 2015

III. INTRODUCTION

While the events described herein are entitled Memorial Day, they have turned out to be Memorial in Honor of the Great teacher, humanitarian and scholar. As a prolific writer and publisher, Dr. Yosef Alfredo Antonio ben-Jochannan was about research and scholarship and as the old axiom goes, "the teacher expects his students to outperform his contribution," if that is possible. The notion of the "dress-up," as we see some are doing, "is nothing but fluff," and does not seriously educate and in no-way empowers or edifies the broad masses of the African People Dr. Ben forever considered his "constituency." Therefore, in his efforts as teacher, researcher and writer, a gadfly challenging Western and American oppression of African people worldwide, he subscribed to the admonition "Publish or Perish!" That is, he instructed and encouraged his followers to research, write and teach so the fundamentals of his work of enlightenment and elevating the mind of the African masses would continue beyond his earthly existence. He also planned trips to Egypt

LET'S LIBERATE THE TEMPLE

in an effort to reinforce what he taught and wrote about, allowing visual images of the "monuments teach;" and in these expeditions his great humanitarian spirit benefitted many in that ancient land. Everywhere he went, "People got an Envelope!"

Liberate the Temple: **Abu Simbel Temple of Rameses II**. Façade of the quintessential structure with the four seated colossal statues of the monarch. The head of the second from left lies in the foreground. Statues of various queens and officials stand beside the king's legs.

FREDERICK MONDERSON

Liberate the Temple: **Abu Simbel Temple of Rameses II**. An old photo taken just before move of the temple to higher ground. Façade of the quintessential structure with the four seated colossal statues of the monarch.

Liberate the Temple. Abu Simbel Temple of Rameses II. Three of the façade's colossal heads, cut-up and ready to be hoisted in the new location as part of the Reconstruction and move of the Temple to higher ground.

LET'S LIBERATE THE TEMPLE

Essentially the great teacher spent his entire life educating African people about their greatness that, for the most part, has been hidden or omitted, generally distorted, omitted and misrepresented in recognition and understanding. This "crime to humanity" has been perpetuated through a strategy of distortion and omission and denial and demolition of efforts in order to shine light on this travesty. It has also entailed microscopically analyzing and critiquing particularly Black writers' efforts to marginalize and discredit the truths they have discovered and affirmed. This, however, has been to no avail since, "Truth crushed to earth shall rise!" Clearly it is understood, for much of the 19th and 20th Century the notion of a "white Egypt" buttressed in the garb of "global white supremacy" has misinformed the reading public, whether they be black, white or otherwise. In this crusade of falsity, many European scholars and publishers alike have, purposely denied Africa's role in the formation and perpetuation of the cultural glory of ancient Egypt, in North-East Africa, which is bad! Worse, they have mis-educated and misdirected their own people into believing the Egyptians were white and that Africans had nothing to do with Egypt! That is, this "straw-man" falsity was concocted in order to deny African origination and perpetuation of the great storehouse of knowledge Egypt and Africa bequeathed humanity. This was accomplished, because as Prof. John Henrik Clarke proclaimed, "The people who preached racism colonized the world" and "When Europe colonized the world she colonized the world's knowledge!" More important, he added, "Europe's claim to Egypt is not based on logic." Equally significant and enlightening, Mosso in *Dawn of Mediterranean Civilization* (1910) has pointed out, "The Asiatics [Caucasians, European from their places of origin] never penetrated the Nile Valley nor the Aegean area." In addition, and having shrewdly seized an abundance of artifacts from Egypt, exhibited in museums displays aided by presentations "photoshopped" with terrific trick-lighting which makes such appear European, they thus proclaim, "See, the Egyptians were white, and to support this, "See, we have the artifacts!" However, in pointing to the creation of this "straw man" myth, as stated previously, Prof. Clarke reminded and reinforced the studied observation, in attributing the cultural glory of this ancient African, Egyptian, nation to Europe, her scholars "used no logic!" Thus, in this "con" not only was the role of

FREDERICK MONDERSON

Africa in Egypt denied and Africans taken out of Egypt, but significantly the mind of Europe was culturally twisted after having been fed this false view of history promulgated from an equally false mantle of absolute wisdom, falsity became the order of the day, to this day.

Liberate the Temple. Abu Simbel, Rameses II's Twin Temple of Nefertari. Façade showing four statues of Rameses II, two statues of Nefertari and smaller images between he feet.

LET'S LIBERATE THE TEMPLE

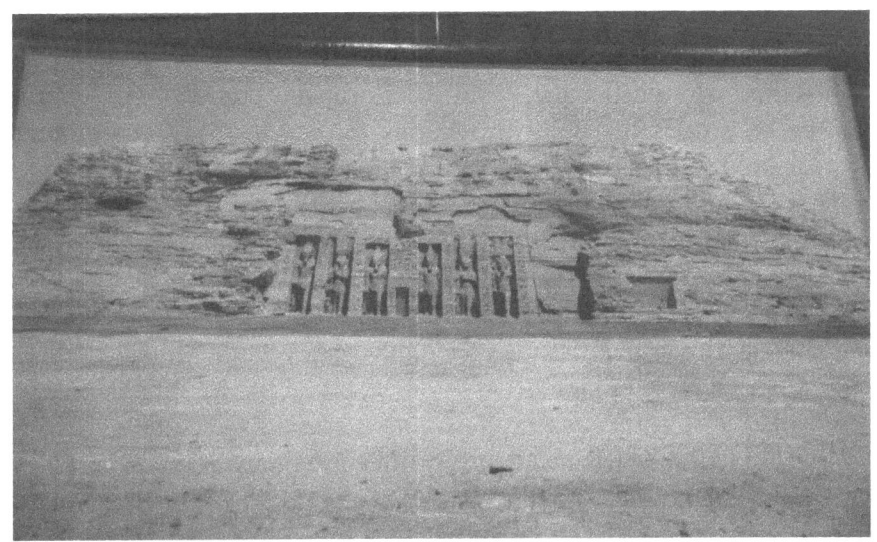

Liberate the Temple. Abu Simbel, Rameses II's Twin Temple of Nefertari. An old photo showing the Queen's Temple prior to being removed to the higher ground.

Liberate the Temple. Abu Simbel Temple of Rameses II. View of Nefertari's Temple decorated Hypostyle Hall with its 4-sided pillars as opposed to columns.

FREDERICK MONDERSON

Thus, and of significance, from the European perception, cognitive dissonance rules the day; for, despite the constructive analysis and inclusion of omissions, the prevailing or predominant mindset holds, "That's what you think!" And so, truth in history suffers because, despite what is publicly propounded, "the existential data contradicts the symbolic representation."

Of course, this has not always been the case. Whether it was classical writers who were contemporary and observed the Egyptians or early 18th and 19th Century researchers who appeared to be unbiased, they all attributed an African identity to the Egyptians. However, as the lucrative and aesthetic nature of its artifacts became more evident and appealing, especially as early archaeology revealed much of its treasure's worth, and while adventurers and collectors perpetuated what Brian Fagan named his book, *The Rape of the Nile*, the justification for the whiteness of Egypt emerged vigorously and vociferously buttressed by twin pillars of imperialism and colonialism undergirded by racism and the arrogance of discrimination. Sadly, this false "foundation of knowledge" persisted into the 20th Century and is ever-present in the 21st Century. However, in his strategy to combat the dis-information, Dr. Ben-Jochannan advised the following:

(1)   When doing research on ancient Egypt, get the earliest source materials available and "work from there!"

(2)   As often as possible write and publish the findings so all people would be more fully apprised about omission and distortion and their significance in the sphere of things.

(3)   Form "study groups" and debate the findings to further clarify the issues and correctly educate the broad masses of the people as to whom the true originators of Egyptian civilization actually were.

(4)   Visit Egypt as often as possible to get a more comprehensive understanding of the total dynamics of the ancient culture. "Let the monuments teach." For instance, and reinforcing this idea, he advised, visit the "Hypostyle Hall" in Karnak Temple some 5 or 6 times to fully

LET'S LIBERATE THE TEMPLE

comprehend its architectural magnificence, artistic beauty and religious significance.

(5). Create libraries by investing in books and become critical of their presentation through the development of Intellectual Autonomy, but also create a legacy for future generations. Speak truth to power and expand upon this through research, writing and teaching.

(6) Naturally, become more apprised of Dr. Ben's "Trilogy." Keep in mind, Prof Clarke informed "People buy Dr. Ben's books but do not read them!" Importantly, we must let these words be points of departure in future research. Equally, while knowledge of "**Dr. Ben's Trilogy**" is indispensable, knowledge of Dr. Fred Monderson's "**Trilogy on Ben**," viz., *"Celebrating Dr. Ben-Jochannan*; *Black History Extravaganza*: *Honoring Dr. Ben-Jochannan*; and the current, *"Let's Liberate the Temple"* certainly casts floodlights on the man's philosophy, his life's work and his admonitions he himself pursued or insisted his students, adherents and followers strive to educate and mentally elevate and empower African people.

Liberate the Temple. **Abu Simbel Temple of Rameses II**. Close-up of the Temple's façade, depicting the Queens between the King's feet.

FREDERICK MONDERSON

Liberate the Temple. Abu Simbel Temple of Rameses II. A further close-up of the first left statue. Notice how the faces of the Queens' statues are essentially defaced. Naturally, this far into Nubia, the faces could not be Asiatic.

LET'S LIBERATE THE TEMPLE

Liberate the Temple. Abu Simbel Temple of Rameses II. Goddess Hathor (Athor) in a boat wading through the marshes.

Liberate the Temple. Abu Simbel Temple of Rameses II. Close-up of the two left-side statues with the right one headless. Notice the Queens between the statues' legs.

FREDERICK MONDERSON

(7) Attend forums and seminars at Museums and educational institutions to more fully understand modern findings and reappraisals of either the old evidence or new archaeological revelations. That is, endeavor to understand what is being said "out there!"

(8) Pay particular attention to the architectural features in the temple and question the **Guides** vigorously to tap into their familiarity or unfamiliarity based on your own knowledge of the site and its history. However, Dr. ben-Jochannan always reminded, "60 percent of what the Guides tell you is wrong!" This realization is manifest because these "experts" hardly read but African-Americans with an interest in the ancient African culture are the best prepared, having read to be most knowledgeable of all visitors to Egypt.

(9) Adhere to a respectable decorum of dress and mannerism when visiting these holy sites. Do not enter the Sanctuary, inner sanctum of the god, for only the Pharaoh and select priests entered there in ancient times. Pay attention to your language and certainly do not have sex before you enter the temple! "Cleanliness is next to Godliness!"

(10) Remember always, the "Pilgrimage" to Egypt, the "Holy Land" is an enlightening religious, spiritual, photographic and cultural and historical adventure. If done well, it is a life changing intellectual experience and thus, the principal temple and the temple of the mind can be truly liberated. Therefore, let us remember, R.A. Schwaller de Lubicz explained the dynamics of *The Temple in Man* (1949, 1977) and so, we recognize among his great legacy, Dr. Ben-Jochannan sought to elevate humanity's knowledge of architectural, theological, scientific and spiritual dynamics of Egyptian temples and the philosophical, metaphysical and intellectual wherewithal of the human species inherent capabilities. Most important, he recognized and taught, Africa as the foundation of all Egyptian accomplishments, social, intellectual, spiritual!

LET'S LIBERATE THE TEMPLE

Liberate the Temple. **Abu Simbel Temple of Rameses II**. Close-up of two right-side façade statues. Notice the King's cartouche (Shennu) on his right forearm. Equally, his "straight beard" while the other statue is missing his beard.

Liberate the Temple. Abu Simbel Temple of Rameses II. As Amon-Ra and Mut sit enthroned, before a "Table of Offerings," Rameses offers flowers and wields a knife. Notice the Sun-Disk over his head, sporting Uraei.

FREDERICK MONDERSON

Liberate the Temple. Abu Simbel Temple of Rameses II. The King kneels to present two ointment jars to enthroned Thoth.

Liberate the Temple. Abu Simbel Temple of Rameses II. Wearing the "Blue" or "War Crown" with streamers, Rameses, in Galabieh and slippers, stands before enthroned Ra-Horakhty and two Goddesses.

LET'S LIBERATE THE TEMPLE

Liberate the Temple. Abu Simbel Temple of Rameses II. Nefertari's Temple. Magnificent view of the temple's interior, in good color, showing Rameses and Nefertari incensing and rattling before the Ark borne by priests; the king facing divinities; and before enthroned Amon-Ra.

Liberate the Temple. Abu Simbel Temple of Rameses II. Within the Sanctuary, from right to left, Ra-Horakhty, Rameses, Amon-Ra, and Ptah.

FREDERICK MONDERSON

II. Who is Dr. Ben-Jochannan?
By
Dr. Fred Monderson

Dr. Yosef ben-Jochannan, in many ways our "intellectual father," is an icon and divinity in the pantheon of Black African intellectuality and Pan-African consciousness. His has been a life of vigorous and fulfilling defense of African people and African history and culture, challenging the onslaught of imperialism, colonialism, racism and religious and other forms of bigotry. He can be considered a cultural multi-genius of the 20th Century for his work as an anthropologist, archaeologist, architect, historian, author, lecturer, publisher and Egyptologist. In 1989 Dr. Ben celebrated 50-years of taking people to Egypt to visit and study the ancient monuments of that glorious African past. I was fortunate to be part of that historic 50th Anniversary experience. He often boasted, "I took Egypt to show our people the light and foundations of knowledge!" Despite a hectic travel and humanitarian schedule, he conducted and maintained an archaeological dig on the Island of Elephantine because he believed that location held important connections to the manifested origins of the ancient Egyptians contained within and their connections with inner Africa. Alas today, that "virgin territory" is no more; but now transformed into a hotel paradise! Dr. Ben befriended the Nubian inhabitants of Upper Egypt and supported their social situation centered in the village of Daboud as the nucleus of cultural resistance against forces opposed to the Nubian way of life and history. This particularly unfolded after construction of the High Dam and creation of Lake Nasser.

Dr. Ben was betrayed by persons who conspired to derail his "Egyptian effort" in 1990. At home, he received "enemy as well as friendly fire" and survived multiple health challenges. Yet, he persevered in defense of Africa and African people while critiquing those engaged in pernicious attacks on the psychic, spiritual and historic nature of the African persona. A favorite chant of his to the

LET'S LIBERATE THE TEMPLE

African has been, "Wake up, Dead Man!" As such, he sought to raise the African from the dead level of European and American oppression, misrepresentation and miseducation oppression to an upright and conscious level of knowledge of self, of history and the development of the requisite tools of intellectual autonomy that can seriously challenge falsity and religious and cultural bigotry in order to decode their environment and problem solve all forms of social, even spiritual challenges.

Liberate the Temple. Abu Simbel Temple of Rameses II. With Colossi of the King as a backdrop, Carmen holds the "Key of Life" between two Nubian Brothers, caretakers of the Temple.

FREDERICK MONDERSON

Liberate the Temple. Abu Simbel Temple of Rameses II. Scenes within Nefertari's twin temple.

Liberate the Temple. Abu Simbel Temple of Rameses II. Rameses prepares to "Incense" the "Barque of the God" borne by priests.

LET'S LIBERATE THE TEMPLE

Dr. Ben pioneered self-publishing! Because of the uniqueness of his writing style, his exposing falsity and re-introducing truth relative to Africa's role in the history of man, and for making known, at the time, an avalanche of new and relevant historical material referents purposely missing from the known historical record, he was denied by established publishing houses. As such, he started Al-Kebulan Publishing and promoted his own works. Later much of it was adopted by Black Classics Press. In a life that opened new vistas to a great body of students and the reading public, Dr. Ben influenced many minds who began to see the world differently thus arming their minds with that tool of constructive criticism. Even further, he admonished the Black man to love the Black woman! In fact, he praised the Black woman and placed her on a pedestal that rivaled the pinnacle of the great obelisks of Egypt. He often said, "Black man love and worship your Black woman because she has done what you can't do!" He went so far as to say, "Heaven is between a Black woman's legs!" Naturally, most people did and still do not know what he meant! Thus, the African world owes a debt of gratitude to his family for sharing his time and efforts unending.

In a small chapel with a courtyard at the Temple of Dendera, the Goddess Nuit, "mother of heaven," is shown stretched across the firmament. In this depiction, she is shown giving birth to the sun in the morning and swallowing it in the evening after it has traveled across her heavenly body. She then equally gave birth to the stars which sparkle at night. Herein then is the key to the above statement. He also spoke about the sanctity and spiritual potency of sex. He explained the difference between actual and spiritual sex. He was also quick to point out the God Min, alter ego of Amon-Ra, whose creative organ is always shown prominently, but originates not from his scrotum but his belly-button. Nevertheless, it underscores the connection to and sacredness to the life-giving process and experience. The author of some thirty books who possessed an exemplary library, in the Nursing Home he confided in me, "I don't know what has happened to my books." He was referring to his extensive library as well as his published works. All I could say, "Dr. Ben, the covers of every one of your publications is represented in my praise of you entitled, *Celebrating Dr. Ben-Jochannan*." This

FREDERICK MONDERSON

exposure is more forcefully presented in *Black History Extravaganza: Honoring Dr. Ben-Jochannan*.

Liberate the Temple. Abu Simbel Temple of Rameses II. In two scenes, Rameses kneels to present objects to enthroned deities.

Liberate the Temple. Abu Simbel Temple of Rameses II. Uraeus, cartouches and deities.

LET'S LIBERATE THE TEMPLE

Thus, in Dr. Ben we have had the quintessential African scholar, intellectual gadfly, bringer of the light of knowledge and sadly the now last deceased member of the dynamic Dr. Ben and Dr. Clarke duo, that is, Yosef Alfredo Antonio ben-Jochannan and John Henrik Clarke. Dr. Ben often sat in as Guest Lecturer for Dr. Clarke in the Black and Puerto Rican Studies Department of Hunter College of the City University of New York.

Even more important, Dr. Ben implored us, "Don't fear Defeat, don't fear Death, but continue to Speak Truth to Power!" As such, in a celebrated life devoted to defending, educating and elevating Africa and African people, he planted and generated forests of constructive positive thinking Black men and women, intellectual cubs. It's been said of Marcus Garvey, when he was convicted of mail fraud and manacled on way to Atlanta Federal Prison, he raised his hands and boasted: "You have caged the lion but the cubs are running free out there! Look for me in the whirlwind!" For Dr. Ben, whose life has been one of continuous teaching and African advocacy, "While the lion may have gotten old, lost its teeth, and passed on, the intellectual cubs he helped create are indeed making a difference in all walks of professional life," particularly in distortions and omissions in Egyptian history and culture as well as in other parts of Africa.

FREDERICK MONDERSON

Liberate the Temple. Abu Simbel Temple of Rameses II. Rameses presents flowers to Khnum, god of the Cataract.

Liberate the Temple. Abu Simbel Temple of Rameses II. With Scepter raised, Rameses smites a kneeling captive before Amon-Ra as Queen Nefertari stands behind him.

LET'S LIBERATE THE TEMPLE

Because they are so intertwined, his **Magnum Opus** is his Trilogy, not because they have enlightened so many but more particularly they form a battering ram aimed at upsetting the pillars of white supremacy. It has been said, "Some books must be read and devoured; and some books must be savored and digested." Dr. Ben's Trilogy fits both these categories!

Liberate the Temple. Abu Simbel Temple of Rameses II. Rameses kneels to present two ointment jars to enthroned Ra-Horakhty.

FREDERICK MONDERSON

Liberate the Temple. Abu Simbel Temple of Rameses II. Again, Rameses kneels to present a platter to enthroned Ra-Horakhty.

III. His **"Trilogy"** comprises three of his major works entitled: **AFRICA: MOTHER OF WESTERN CIVILIZATION (1970); AFRICAN ORIGIN OF THE "MAJOR" WESTERN RELIGIONS (1971);** and **BLACK MAN OF THE NILE AND HIS FAMILY (1972)**.

These are seminal works that need be read time and time again to gain the full benefit of what the scholar intended in terms of the "journey" and the expected outcomes. Because of the complex nature of the message, of the referents, of the strategy and tactics his works offer as challenge; that many, even the avid scholar should come back to study to gain fresh insights of the message.

LET'S LIBERATE THE TEMPLE

AFRICA: MOTHER OF WESTERN CIVILIZATION
By
Dr. Fred Monderson

Africa: Mother of Western Civilization is the first part of Dr. Yosef A.A. ben-Jochannan's Magnum Opus in his "Trilogy" that includes *African Origins of the "Major Western Religions"* and *Black Man of the Nile and His Family*. This work, in fact these three, established him as thinker and historian that early projected a positive attitude regarding African people's contributions to civilization and these ideas, concepts and learning ultimately migrated to Europe through the Graeco-Roman conquest and the experience, with Egypt foremost influencing the Mesopotamian culture cluster. In his methodology designed to state his case, he presented then challenged a number of theories and positions promulgated by western writers who, in the majority, projected a negative perception of Africa, its culture, history and people; yet, despite the propagated falsity in ownership of philosophy, art, architecture, religion, we now recognize Egypt significantly influenced Greece and Rome, foundations of Western Civilization. Years ago, this writer heard the late and distinguished Dr. John Henrik Clarke declare, "People buy Dr. Ben-Jochannan's trilogy (books) but do not read them." As if to say, these are profound critical and constructive analyses on Egypt, Africa and Europe/Western scholarship and should be given the serious consideration they deserve because much that the author discusses are still relevant today. That is, the criticisms are still being leveled against Africa's dynamics despite the positive revelations Dr. ben-Jochannan and many others have emphasized.

FREDERICK MONDERSON

Liberate the Temple. Abu Simbel Temple of Rameses II. With knives in hand, Rameses prepares to carve victuals on the "Table of Offerings" before a priapic Amon as Min backed by divinities.

Africa: Mother of Western Civilization (New York: Alkebu-Lan Book Associates, 1970 (First Edition) autographed by the author and "Given" to Dr. Fred Monderson) is a massive 717-page reservoir of knowledge at the time of its publication represented new information supported by extensively copious references and referents. To many readers, the great body of information supported the author's devastating analytic dissection of; first, western writers pejoratively depicting the whole African experience. In refutation, the author painstakingly developed his arguments to show not only that Africans originated the fundamental tenets and practices that advanced the social and scientific development of humanity, but that Europe has tried to covet such, attributing it's originating in the West.

Second, he has researched and brought to the fore a reservoir of new information that had been long forgotten, omitted; thereby casting

LET'S LIBERATE THE TEMPLE

fresh light on the projected, though false representation of the historical record.

Significantly, the book is "Dedicated to the African nationalist 'Street-Corner Speakers' (deceased and surviving) who, in their own inimitable simplicity, have, from the advent of the late Marcus Moziah Garvey and the founding of the Universal Negro Improvement Association (UNIA) in 1918 C.E., kept the flame of Africa's history and culture ever present in the mind of African peoples everywhere in the 'Western Hemisphere.'" The **Table of Contents** reads: Prelude; The Nile Valley and Great Lakes; Preface; Introduction; Illustrations; The Dawn of Civilization, and the Value of a Name; (I) Prehistoric Homo Sapiens or Ancient African Man; (II) Who Were/Are the Africans of ancient Alkebu-Lan (Africa); (III) Historic Quotations and Comments About, and of, the Africans; People Who Made Middle Nile Valley History Yesterday and Today; Racism, Historians and Ethiopians; The Return of Kimit, Zimbabwe, and Nubia to the Continent of Alkebu-Lan; Nubia - "Mother of Kimit" - Gateway to the North; (IV) Predynastic and Dynastic Kimit, Nubia and Kush; The Egyptian Dynasties and Comments by High-Priest Manetho: Notes on Egyptology; (V) African Origin of "Greek Philosophy;" Arguments and Answers Relative to the African Origins of "Greek Philosophy;" Who Were the Indigenous Africans of Kimit (Egypt); (VI) Reflections on Ancient Kimit (Sais or Egypt); (VII) Chronology of Egyptian Rule Over Kush and Nubia; "Cleopatra's Needle": A Stolen African Treasure in America; (VIII) The Rise and Fall of the Africans of Khart Haddas (Carthage); The Black Man of Antiquity; What "Black is Beautiful" is Not Ready to Hear; Judaism, the "Black Jew" Or "Israelite: Roots of Biblical 'Anti-Negroism,'" etc.: A Cause for Black "anti-Semitism;" A Lecture on the Beginnings of the Christian Church in North and East Africa; The Africans Right to be Wrong is Sacred; Conclusion; Maps, Acknowledgements; Front Cover Design Description; Author's Statement on African (Black) History and Culture.

FREDERICK MONDERSON

Liberate the Temple. Nefertari's Abu Simbel Temple. Two Hathors lay hands on Nefertari, wife of Rameses II.

LET'S LIBERATE THE TEMPLE

Liberate the Temple. Abu Simbel Temple of Rameses II. Rameses offers two bouquets of flowers to enthroned Goddess Hathor in Nefertari's temple.

FREDERICK MONDERSON

Liberate the Temple. Abu Simbel Temple of Rameses II. Rameses strolls in his War Chariot holding bow and arrow and with his battle-savvy lion tagging along.

Therefore, *Africa: Mother of Western Civilization* is a unique analytic examination of Africa, its contribution to the intellectual and cultural development of human progress and western scholarship's attempts to claim such while negating the African's role in this phenomenal human development. In this, the significance of Dr. ben-Jochannan's contribution is manifold, in that, he drew attention to a number of problems posed as European and American scholars have studied African in general and Egypt and the Nile Valley in particular and they're wrongfully seeking to displace Africans from Africa, replacing them with varieties of light skinned and dark skinned Caucasian peoples, all emphasizing the superiority of the Caucasian race.

Nevertheless, the good doctor points out on page xv of "Mother" that "this work is not intended to purposely attack any person or institution, religious or secular, vindictively; but, only to cite and

LET'S LIBERATE THE TEMPLE

correct the erroneous myths about the 'inferiority' and 'primitiveness' of the indigenous African peoples and their descendants who are today, in the 21st Century, still being maligned by the archaic terms – 'Negroes,' 'Bantus,' 'Pygmies,' 'Hottentots,' 'Bushmen,' and the likes of the same misnomers, none of which the Africans created." In addition, and significantly he supplies an outstanding bibliography for independent examination of these sources and for research purposes. He was of the view, when researching Egypt especially, one need to "Get the oldest information available and work from there."

Even more important, in his efforts in the great Black-African cultural awakening, Dr. ben-Jochannan pioneered the insistence of indigenous African names regarding the various cultures and he frowned upon the use of such disgusting names as those previously mentioned as well as Negroes, Negroids, Nilotes, Semites, Hamites, etc. After all, the oppressor only uses Caucasian and white. In contradiction, however, as the Afrocentrist Molefi Asante has pointed out, "In Europe, there are no white people, only English, French, German, Dutch, Belgian, Irish, Italian, etc.!"

This great mind, Dr. Ben-Jochannan, was critical of Napoleon Bonaparte, the French Emperor, whom he explained did not come to Egypt as a tourist but as conqueror and as such he held the culture in contempt. Equally, he insisted, "Too many modern educators try to change the whole meaning of ancient history." As an example of divergent views, he compares the work of two important Frenchmen, Baron Denon who was in Egypt with Napoleon and the renowned Egyptologist Gaston Maspero. Denon, who drew the face of the Sphinx of Ghizeh with its nose intact and reported, from his observations, Napoleon's soldiers blew off the nose with their canon fire. Maspero, on the other hand, writing a century after Denon, wrongfully wrote the Mamelukes, who ruled Egypt, actually blew the Sphinx's nose off.

FREDERICK MONDERSON

Liberate the Temple. Abu Simbel Temple of Rameses II. Rameses, in Nemes Headdress, kneels to present a plant and a vessel to enthroned Ra-Horakhty.

Liberate the Temple. Abu Simbel Temple of Rameses II. Rameses kneels with both hands empty and raised before Thoth enthroned.

LET'S LIBERATE THE TEMPLE

Liberate the Temple. Abu Simbel Temple of Rameses II. Rameses tramples one enemy and about to spear the other.

Frowning on the disrespect western writers hold towards Africa and Africans, and taking to task Black Studies and African Studies Departments that parrot "racist stereotypes regarding Africa and its cultural history," he pointed to some of the following:

An Egyptian and a South African are classified as being of two separate races; whereas a Greek and a Swede are both of the same Caucasian race. He does emphasize the difference between reciting facts and the interpretation of the data.

While insisting on the "African's right to be wrong," he frowns upon the "new left" distracting African-Americans with the "rhetoric of instant revolution." Contrary to most books on Egypt which seems to erect a wall at Egypt's southern border, Dr. Ben offers a more comprehensive inclusion that connects Egypt with much of Africa far into the south, even beyond the headwaters of the Nile. Much of this was reinforced by Cheikh Anta Diop's *Cultural Unity of Black Africa*!

(1959, 1987). Even more modern and profound, Theophile Obenga's *African Philosophy: The Pharaonic Period 2780-330 B.C.* (2004) not simply and similarly conceptualized Diop's ideas but in a tour de force explication he points out that "Unity." These same ideas of ancient Egypt are still practiced elsewhere in Africa, though not in the place of the supposed origins of the "Caucasian Egyptian." As such, Dr. Ben-Jochannan insisted, "as people are criticized for being anti-Semite, Blacks must be critical of any anti-Black, anti-Negroism spewed by race haters.

Liberate the Temple. Abu Simbel Temple of Rameses II. With both hands empty and raised, Rameses kneels before enthroned Ra-Horakhty.

LET'S LIBERATE THE TEMPLE

Liberate the Temple. Abu Simbel Temple of Rameses II. Carmen and Fred pose with the Ankh key in Nefertari's temple entranceway.

Liberate the Temple. Abu Simbel Temple of Rameses II. At a gallop, Rameses shoots his arrows as he leads his chariots in battle. Notice the hawk flying over the king's head.

FREDERICK MONDERSON

AFRICAN ORIGINS OF THE "MAJOR" WESTERN RELIGIONS
By
Dr. Fred Monderson

AFRICAN ORIGINS OF THE "MAJOR" WESTERN RELIGIONS (New York: Alkebu-Lan Books, 1971) is a masterfully presented analytic discussion highlighting the role Africa and its sons and daughters have played in the development and propagation of modern religion's beliefs and practices. Dr. Yosef ben-Jochannan, in his own inimitable fashion has revealed a great body of purposely omitted information that demolished religious stereotypes stigmatizing Africa and its people, while he emphasized significant accomplishments generally absent in the sanitized portrayal of religion and who were actually responsible for these modern religious achievements.

Liberate the Temple. Abu Simbel Temple of Rameses II. Carmen Monderson of Brooklyn, New York stands with fan in hand before the façade of Nefertari's temple at Abu Simbel.

LET'S LIBERATE THE TEMPLE

Liberate the Temple. Abu Simbel Temple of Rameses II. Showki Abd Rady, Native Egyptian Guide, sits beside Carmen as they survey the view.

Liberate the Temple. Abu Simbel Temple of Rameses II. Rameses sits enthroned amidst all the excitement of the Battle of Kadesh.

Dr. Ben-Jochannan, an anthropologist, historian, Egyptologist, Black-African Pan-African nationalist, was an educator confronted by exclusion and omission across the spectrum relating to African contributions to development of religious consciousness. Because many, particularly modern writers, engage in a pejorative depiction of African religious expressions, Dr. Ben takes them to task in textual analysis by examining their statements and contrasting them with more constructive commentary in order to challenge the distortions they amplify.

In this, the second effort in his "Trilogy," he states, *African Origins* is dedicated to: "The innocently recent born and those yet-to-be-born African and African-American infants who must one day take their place in mankind's world as the inheritors of the religions their forebears created - hoping that they may become the forces of change to bring this work to its equilibrium once more."

Liberate the Temple. Abu Simbel Temple of Rameses II. The King in war chariot grasps his bow and arrow, while his pet lion runs alongside and his soldiers advance.

LET'S LIBERATE THE TEMPLE

Liberate the Temple. Abu Simbel Temple of Rameses II. View of the Temple's Hypostyle Hall with colossal figures before pillars while the Gods repose in the Sanctuary to the rear.

FREDERICK MONDERSON

Liberate the Temple. Abu Simbel Temple of Rameses II. Carmen Monderson and Showki Abd Rady, third from right, pose with local merchants at Abu Simbel Temple.

The author begins with a poem translated by Sir Richard F. Burton entitled **The Kasidah of Haji Abu el-Yezdi** which reads:

> "All faith is false, all faith is true
> Truth is the shattered mirrors strewn
> In myriad bits, while each believes
> His little bit the whole to own."

The **Table of Contents** of *African Origins* reads: Preface; Introduction; Shango: A Source of African religion; St. Augustine: African Influence on Christianity; Moses: African Influence on Judaism; Bilal: African Influence on Islam; King, Mohammed, Divine, Matthews, and Garvey: Religions New Dimensions; Conclusion; Notes and Bibliography.

LET'S LIBERATE THE TEMPLE

A symbolic glossary explains the imagery of the Cover Illustration where the author explains the compendium of nine symbols that conceptually reflects the totality of the author's message. These include: Ra: God - Sun God of the Nile - Sunburst; Symbol of the first principles of religion - Coffin Text - Pyramid with All-Seeing Eye; God: Damballah Ovedo, Voodoo - West African Rooster; Key of Life of the Mysteries - Grand Lodge of Luxor - Ankh, Nile Valley Cross; God: Jesus Christ - Christianity - Westernized Version; God: Traditional African Religions - Cross - Nile Valley and Central Africa; God: Yahweh - Hebrewism (Judaism) - Star of David; God: Al'Lah - Islam - Crescent of Tigris and Euphrates.

Liberate the Temple. Boating aboard a felucca on the Nile at Aswan.

FREDERICK MONDERSON

BLACK MAN OF THE NILE AND HIS FAMILY
By
Dr. Fred Monderson

MAN KNOW THYSELF!

BLACK MAN OF THE NILE AND HIS FAMILY (New York: Alkebu-Lan Books, (1971) 1981 is the third volume of Dr. Yosef A.A. Ben-Jochannan's **Trilogy** and in many ways, can be considered a maturing of his thoughts and a history of Egypt though it's more an analytic dissection of the Nile Valley experience. Thus, in many ways, this work defines the author, his thinking and the respectful influence he came to exert as a concerned and knowledgeable, truly indigenous, African authority struggling against the farcical portrayal of ancient Egypt and its relationship with other Nile Valley states and people.

This book is dedicated, writes the author, "To my daughter Colette Denise [Makeda] and son Kwame Edwin, both of whom represent the future African peoples everywhere. Also, to Miss Laurie Heard who passed on to an untimely death in 1969 C.E. at age 24, after having won the Pulitzer Prize with others for her story on the 'Detroit Riot' of 1968. She was an inspiration to young black womanhood everywhere."

The **Table of Contents** reads: Illustrations (727); A Special Glossary; Preface to the First Edition; Foreword of First Edition; Special Tribute: To the Mothers of African/Black Families - Past, Present, Future; Preview of the Third Edition; Chapter I: Who Were/Are the Africans?; Chapter II: Prehistoric African Homo sapiens; Chapter III: Historic Quotations and Comments About The

LET'S LIBERATE THE TEMPLE

Africans; Chapter IV: Another Look at Nubia, Meroe, Egypt, Ethiopia, Paunit, Etc.; Chapter V: Reflections on The Ancient Indigenous African and His Family of the Nile Valley; Chapter VI: A Pictorial Review of The Ancient Africans of Egypt and Other Nile Valley "High Cultures"/Civilizations; Chapter VII: The Africans of Khart/Haddas/Carthage [Its Founding, and Its Destruction]; A Chronological Outline and Data; Chapter VIII: African Origins of "Greek Philosophy" [The Myth]; Chapter IX: Mother of The Gods of Man/Woman; Chapter X: Questions and Answers About Africa; Conclusion: Orthodox and Liberal African History and Historians; Poem: "Mother African Cries of Pain" Lloyd [Boney] Thomas; General Notes; Added Bibliography; Personal Index.

Liberate the Temple. **Aswan**. The Old Oberoi Hotel on Elephantine Island is now part of Movenpick.

FREDERICK MONDERSON

Liberate the Temple. **Aswan**. An old and favorite mural no longer in the lobby of the Oberoi Hotel, replaced by Movenpick Hotel on Elephantine Island, Aswan.

Liberate the Temple. **Aswan**. Tombs of the Nobles on the cliffs at Aswan. That's where we're going next!

LET'S LIBERATE THE TEMPLE

Liberate the Temple. Aswan. Mural in a Middle Kingdom Noble's tomb on the high cliffs of Aswan.

Liberate the Temple. Aswan. A magnificent view of the Nile River from the porch of the Old Cataract Hotel.

FREDERICK MONDERSON

Liberate the Temple. Aswan. On the high cliffs at Aswan, view inside a Noble tomb.

In the **Preface**, adopted from the First Edition, the author writes: "In this volume facts of African history which have been for so long purposely withheld from the public shall be revealed and carefully explained. Africa [Alkebu-lan] will be seen from eyes which are different to the Henry Morton Stanley and Dr. David Livingston's drama; the salvation through Jesus Christ view-point; the Tarzan and Jane atmosphere; the 'Great White Father' paternalism; and last, but not least, it will not include 'the lazy Africans who did nothing in Africa before slavery,' and 'developed nothing or created nothing'

LET'S LIBERATE THE TEMPLE

historically propaganda angle of the 'Christian Missionaries.' These age-old stereotyped racist conceptions about the Africans shall not appear in this book."

He talks about deliberate suppression and distortion of true African history. This particular source represents the maturity of his thoughts and presentations. It also contains a number of objectives the author seeks to accomplish.

"This work is also an attempt to create in the young African, African-American (Black person), and all other African people, a sense of belonging in the great African heritage. For Heritage is that something which all other people are reminded of daily. And since this work is being produced in the United States of America, it is specifically directed to those who have criminally demasculinized, denuded, and otherwise debased the Africans of their cultural, economic, political, scientific, spiritual, and all other forms of their heritage and human decency. Religion and the European and European-American colonialists, for over the past three to four-hundred years, shall be shown to be two of the basic causes of Africa's downfall. Of course, there is no attempt to dismiss from guilt those African (Blacks) who contributed in the past, and in the present, to the criminal conspiracy of genocide against their African brothers and sisters for their own selfish economic gains."

Thus, the objective of this work is to present African origins of European Civilization in a manner whereby scholars can find substantial use for it in their research; as much as the layman can for general information.

Still another objective of this work is its presentation of pertinent data needed in the African people's re-identification with their great ancestral heritage. For the Black peoples have maintained that: If the European Jews can fight for an arid piece of desert; the Irish for a small Emerald Island; the British for a Barren Island of Misery; Protestant Anglo-Saxon American for their stolen Indian empire; why should the Black man [the African, African-American, African-

FREDERICK MONDERSON

Caribbean] not fight for the richest piece of real estate on the planet Earth. - His original homeland - Mother Africa [Alkebu-lan]?"

Reiterating, Dr. Ben insisted, regarding the African, "He must, persevere though the struggle seems at times insurmountable. For it is in the doing of the impossible which made the Blacks and Africa great for hundreds of centuries and it is only by the recapturing and recreation of new values by the Black man will he free his mind, then his body, and lastly – his power. The Black man must, therefore, return to his temples in Ethiopia and Egypt and read his age-old reminders, which emphatically states to him and the world these prophetic words: '**Man Know Thyself**!'"

Liberate the Temple. Aswan. Ancient images of Egyptian kings and gods painted Black, as the Nubians remember and recognize. These are no longer in place as Movenpick has replaced Oberoi as the hotel on Elephantine Island.

LET'S LIBERATE THE TEMPLE

"The Black man [indigenous African and his descendants] must once more write about himself, his cultures, and his continent [Alkebu-lan, Africa, Ethiopia, Libya, etc.]. No one cares about another's history to the point where he can feel the emotional values of the inheritors. Moreover, when a man's history is written by his master's religion or economic philosophy, such history is always distorted to suit the Master-Slave relationship, which is the only possible result from such an enforced union.

Thus, writes Dr. Ben, *Black Man of the Nile* is specifically directed to those who, "have criminally demasculinized, denuded, and otherwise denigrated the Africans of their CULTURAL, ECONOMIC, POLITICAL, SCIENTIFIC, SPIRITUAL, and all other forms of their heritage and human decency." To this we should add the intellectual heritage as represented in Egypt. As such, then "The major desired accomplishment this volume seeks to achieve is to provide anthropological research in the ancient heritage of the African and their contributions all over the world."

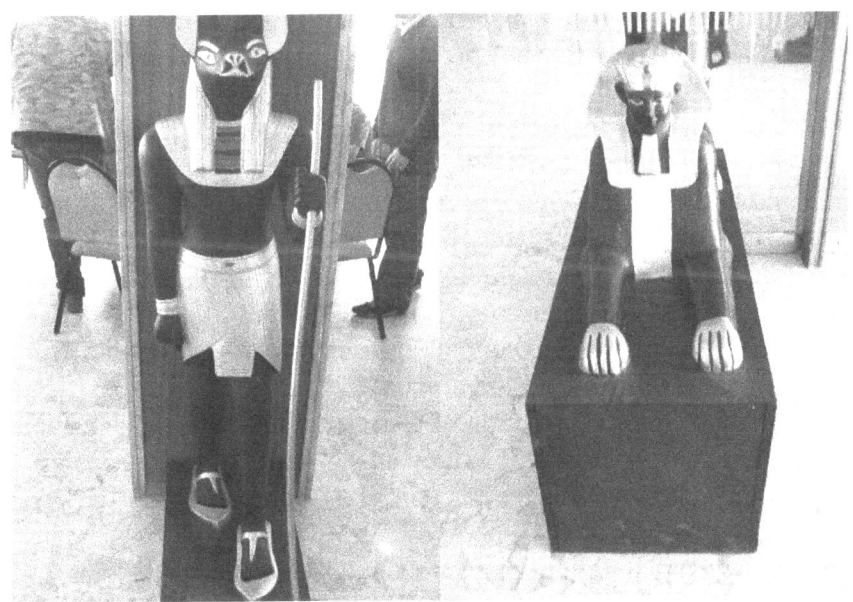

Liberate the Temple. Aswan. The images painted black as the Nubians remember and envisioned them are no longer available since Movenpick replaced Oberoi Hotel on Elephantine Island.

FREDERICK MONDERSON

IV. THE AWESOME EGYPTIAN TEMPLE I
The Egyptian Temple
By
Dr. Fred Monderson

The Egyptian temple was one of the most fascinating inventions and religious architectural constructions of the ancient Nile Valley civilization of Kemet, Tawi (the two lands), and modern Egypt. As such, the temple served many functions but essentially it was a connecting point of time and space between this world and the next where human forms were able to interact with and utilize divine power through a continuing process of ritual and worship. In this interaction, the god or gods were invited to earth to inhabit and manifest religious and spiritual power through magic and cultic symbolism while resident in the "divine house" prepared for them.

Dr. Ben-Jochannan favored two particular temples in Egypt, Karnak and Abydos. That is not to say he did not hold Hatshepsut's temple at Deir el Bahari, Luxor Temple of Amenhotep III and Rameses II's Abu Simbel as well in high regard. However, the massiveness of Karnak, home of Amon-Ra, the magnificence of its Hypostyle Hall, and for years the masterful presence of his Brother Abdul colored this as one of his most favorite places to visit and celebrate. In case of Abydos, the many gods worshipped there, the Abydos Tablet and specifically the Festival of the Resurrection of Osiris, the immaculate conception of Isis and particularly the extant and colorful reliefs gracing its interior made him appreciate this temple as well.

Nonetheless, and highlighting the metaphysical and spiritual nature of such structures, Byron E. Shafer in *Temples of Ancient Egypt* (1998: 2) provides an interesting explanation of these cosmological forces at work in temples to which he points out: "Temples and rituals were loci for the creative interplay of sacred space and sacred time. Sacred

LET'S LIBERATE THE TEMPLE

space is 'a place of clarification (a focusing lens) where men and gods are held to be transparent to one another' and 'a point of communication,' the 'paradoxical point of passage from one mode of being to another.' In sacred space, one is oriented to the cosmos and immersed in primordial order; there one experiences truth and renews life. Over time, such space appears unchanged and unchanging, 'stable enough to endure without growing old or losing any of its parts.'" Some scholars have argued for three forms of reality in this respect. There is the Book of the Dead recounting, instances in temples and on bas reliefs and the graphic recounting of Hatshepsut's experience, the actual happening of the phenomenon. For example, Amon leaving his heavenly abode to "visit" Queen Hatshepsut's mother! Second, the Queen writing about the experience; and third, photographic imagery as in her Deir el Bahari temple that graphically depicts the entire process. The power of this tri-parte depicted phenomenal experience has been so intense, so graphic in its representation, though in disuse millennia later, the esoteric and spiritual potency of the experience can still be felt by persons so psychically inclined.

Liberate the Temple. Isis Temple at Philae. Initial view of the temple from the river with the Mammisi's Colonnade and the Great Pylon further right.

FREDERICK MONDERSON

Liberate the Temple. Isis Temple at Philae. From the River, close-up view of the Mammisi's Colonnade.

(Instructions)

1. Do not touch the monuments and do not go up on the
2. Do not write and do not draw on the temple floor.
3. Do not write on the walls and on the columns, not to be punished by the law
4. Do not bring any foods inside the temple.
5. Do not smoke inside the temple
6. Do not throw any rubbish inside the temple.
7. Do not make any religious rituals inside the temple.

Liberate the Temple. Isis Temple at Philae. Instructions on being in the temple.

LET'S LIBERATE THE TEMPLE

Even further, Shafer (1998: 2) continued: "What has been said of sacred place can, for the most part, be said of sacred time as well. It is a moment, or season, or cycle of such clarification and communication, orientation and immersion, experience and renewal. Time, however, is not so stable a dimension of order as space. Egyptians experienced time as a spiral of patterned repetitions, a coil of countless rebirths. The purest moment of sacred time was the first, the moment of creation, when the existent and its order emerged from the nonexistent and its aspect of disorder. Subsequently, time, as a component of order, proved vulnerable to chaos. So, for example, the intervals between sunrise and sunset came to change from day to day and season to season, and the beginning of each new 365-day year came to rotate slowly backward relative to the seasons and the helical rising of the star Sirius. Because of order's ongoing vulnerability to chaos, Egyptians needed to conceive of creation not as a single past event but as a series of 'first times,' of sacred regenerative moments recurring regularly within the sacred space of temples through the media of rituals and architecture."

Therefore, participating and manipulating this duality through ritual and the many religious and spiritual manifestations in continuous process helped maintain the equilibrium of the Egyptian state, as practiced by king and priest. Let's not forget, the role of Ma'at in molding proper behavior whether in terms of social responsibility or conceptualizing, planning and building a temple continued to be a powerful force of righteousness. Miroslav Verner in *Temple of the World* (2013: 5) explained the relationship between the temple, the 'abode of the god,' and the exhilir Ma'at. He writes: "Above all, the temple was a symbolic primordial mound - the form that the creator god took when he emerged from the chaos of the primordial waters and started on his work at the beginning of time and the world. It was an expression of Ma'at, the order that the gods had created in the midst of chaos, and it was the point of contact between 'heaven, or the gods, the sacred place where people came to worship the god, to bring him offerings and to ask for his favor."

In seeking to establish the beginnings of architectural foundations, it was early laid down; the first architects were priests who were divinely instructed on how to construct appropriate shelter for the gods to encourage their residence on earth. Hence, the origin of the temple had to take into consideration several factors such as the geographical location, the nature of such a structure in terms of its inner and outer periphery, how to decorate it internally and externally, and what was the form of ritual, daily and ongoing.

Mann, adding more to Shafer's explanation, in *Sacred Architecture* (1993: 14) offered an even more penetrating view, when in describing several ways in which the symbolic or the spiritual is expressed in creating sacred architecture. This sacred architecture, in its own right, had to consider the best options to protect the power called in to dwell therein and because of the dynamics of this phenomenon, different layers of protection were constructed in what was constructed as the inner and outer periphery of the god's house. In Mann's view, conceptually the components are: "First, sacred architecture reflects the structure of the cosmos. Before there were buildings, humanity worshipped the stars and planets, the four elements, the earth, and its animals and plants, as gods. In our progression from caves to modern buildings, the symbolism of this early integration with the cosmos has been central, and still activates the deepest essence within us, the core of our psyche. Initially, sacred monuments were associated with a particular god, goddess, or the natural or supernatural powers they represented. They were aligned by or with the stars or planets in the sky, which represented the god or goddess. They were also geographically oriented and located in places significant to the gods. Some monuments were used by priests or priestesses as observatories to measure the movements of the planets or heavenly bodies they worshipped, while others were sited in accordance with planetary motions. Most megalithic monuments echoed some or all of these functions in their siting, design and function."

Mann continued the demonstration: "Second, sacred monuments were organized using primary geometric shapes and proportions, described by number symbolism. Mathematical mysticism or sacred geometry is a profound part of sacred architecture, and it's often mentioned in relation to the Egyptians and Pythagoreans. Pythagoras created a humanistic philosophy which utilized mathematical harmony and

LET'S LIBERATE THE TEMPLE

proportion as primary tools in daily life, including art, architecture, music, morality and history. He believed that the order inherent in numbers, a number symbolism, creates specific effects on the observer, both psychologically and spiritually. The discovery of the innate meaning of numbers is therefore a primary creative legacy of sacred architecture. The exploration of the numbers and proportions of the sacred brings a higher understanding to architecture."

Next, Mann revealed: "Third, the sacred lives in buildings or monuments in which the structure and decoration follow clear and basic patterns derived from the ancient conception of the four elements, earth, water, air, and fire, the forms of nature and from living energies and the geometries derived from them. Proportion systems amplifying natural rhythms and patterns bring a natural and organic energy and spirituality to sacred architecture – the building contains an elemental as well as a human quality evoking the spiritual."

Conversely, and elsewhere, Mann (1993: 106-07) is of the view: "The creation of sacred buildings echoes the creation of the universe, and both seek to follow similar mathematical laws. Therefore, the Golden Section (phi) is found to govern the growth of plants and animals and is also the primary proportion found in sacred buildings and monuments. In their use of numbers as a symbolic language, the Egyptians predate and influence Pythagoras and Plato. The Egyptians communicated symbolic astrological and astronomical concepts beyond the actual form of the buildings. Similarly, their hieroglyphical language used symbols instead of mere signs. A sign has a limited meaning, while a symbol evokes correspondences and widens understanding. The Egyptians used their mythology to further understanding because it was more than simple history. Their gods came from the stars, beginning wisdom, understanding and power. Their myths were cosmic myths, describing planetary movements, and brought the mathematical reality of the stars to humanity."

Consequently, we have the philosophical, cosmological and spiritual concepts of and behind the idea of the temple. Therefore, it can be not simply a repository for the god worshipped therein, but it also shaped the beliefs and practices of the culture that has impacted so heavily on

FREDERICK MONDERSON

the consciousness of man throughout history. The temple helped expand architectural designs, the extraction and transportation of stone and the ancillary crafts that decorated and made livable the enclosure. Hence the attendant great occurrences connected with the temple depended heavily on the Nile River whose gifts flowed from the bosom of Central and Southern Africa.

Even more important, in constructing the temple, the architect naturally utilized his skills but in turn demonstrated mathematical mastery and evolved a cosmological consciousness unmatched in order to complete his assignment of "giving the temple to its master." As such, this Nile Valley experience was fundamentally an African and by today's standards, Black culture, first of its kind to become conscious of its intellectual, artistic, philosophical, esoteric and spiritual creativity. Africans of ancient Kemet culture unquestionably enlightened the world through religious thought and practice, theosophy, theology, metaphysics and social and material accomplishments generated therefrom! Such has been argued by the great African intellect Cheikh Anta Diop in systematic, interdisciplinary, erudite, irrefutable and well-thought-out scholarship, entitled *The African Origin of Civilization: Myth or Reality* (1959, 1974). A similar view was enunciated by a number of dedicated African and African-American writers and scholars including Martin Delaney, W.E.B. DuBois, Carter G. Woodson, George G.M. James, J.A. Rogers, Yosef ben-Jochannan, Ben Carruthers, Leonard Jeffries, John H. Clarke, Theophile Obenga, Maulana Karenga, Leonard James, Walter Rodney, Molefi Asante and Ivan Van Sertima, among others, who, after many years of research and teaching, have asserted the exact idea. This then, is the idea to advocate!

LET'S LIBERATE THE TEMPLE

Liberate the Temple. Isis Temple at Philae. The Dromos or walkway to the Great Pylon with the Western Colonnade (left) and the Eastern Colonnade (right).

Liberate the Temple. Isis Temple at Philae. The Western Colonnade with its 32 columns lining the Dromos or walkway to the First or Great Pylon.

FREDERICK MONDERSON

Liberate the Temple. Isis Temple at Philae. The Eastern Colonnade with its 16 unfinished columns on the opposite side of the Dromos, with the Great Pylon at the rear.

First and foremost, the great achievement and gift of this North-east African culture was its theosophical, religious, architectural and moral genius embodied in the ancient Egyptian or Kemet temple. The Egyptian temple, therefore, was a divinely inspired work of art! This creation, unlike the Jewish Synagogue, Greek or Roman Temple, Muslim Mosque, or Christian Cathedral, was a unique creative experience that still evokes and exudes profound theological and cosmological spiritualism, posing thoughtful questions for scholars still seeking to define it. It was an edifice essentially erected by a king in honor of some divinity. Sometimes it was in honor of himself to be worshipped as a divinity in life but more particularly upon his death, or of a triad of divinities, to whom he wished to pay special homage. This is either in return for benefits received or for some future favors. In the sculptures and paintings on the walls and columns of various temples, the king is shown as the principal figure conducting the ritual. On the "Outer Periphery walls" he is depicted either receiving the curved sword from the God, Amon or Ra, and and/or waging war with the physical enemies of Egypt, many of whom are brought home

LET'S LIBERATE THE TEMPLE

as captives to be slaves or sacrificed. At other times of peace, in the "Inner Periphery" where he had to contend with spiritual and malevolent forces, he practiced incessant worship to ritually vanquish these forces. Equally too, we see him offering gifts and sacrifices to his god or gods and this is often depicted on walls, even on papyrus or stela, much of which has not survived. The prayers are said in his name. He leads the procession in which are carried the statues and emblem of the divinities. Therefore, whether cult, mortuary, sun, rock, valley, or processional temple, even later "Birth houses" and the much earlier "Soul houses" that deserve mention, these structures were an integral part of the Nile Valley religious and cultural sacred space embodied in ritual that helped shape the morality and social beliefs and practices of these ancient African peoples. The temple, therefore, came to play an important part in fostering much of the civilizational development, viz., religious beliefs, ethical and moral practices, and economic, medical and scientific endeavors, we have come to associate with ancient Egypt.

All this notwithstanding, the idea of the Egyptian temple is an evolved concept dating to the time of the emergence of the primeval gods who, after being invoked, needed to be sheltered on earth and so instructed their adherents, the priests, on the specifications of their homes. These priests, themselves civic and social leaders, in furthering their mission, in turn became active creators of the civilization and by the time of the Old kingdom had begun to play important roles in shaping religious, mortuary and civic and social behaviors. In fact, the origins of the priests themselves evolved from civic responsibilities. In *Religious Life in Ancient Egypt* (London: Constable, 1924: 46-47) Flinders Petrie writes to this effect: "The occupations of the priest were more often civil than religious. He was the 'Great Fowler;' the 'Great one of Medicine' or of flesh or 'limbs.' As reconstituting the dissevered body, he was the 'Builder of flesh' or limbs. Elsewhere he was the 'elder' of the community. The greatest high priest was the 'chief, commander of workmen;' elsewhere 'Over the multitude;' or the 'Great Organizer, or the 'Inundation man.' In defense, he was 'Splendid' or 'Warrior,' or 'General,' or 'Guardian who leads the Mesniu' the troops of Horus. In the prehistoric capital, El Kab, the priest was the 'Servant of the Crown.' Directly religious titles were the 'Adorer,' 'Watcher,' 'Robed,' the 'Shaved,' and the 'Sacrifice.'

FREDERICK MONDERSON

The priestly powers were 'Tongue of the God,' 'Lord of true speech,' 'Great Seer,' 'Opener of the gates of heaven,' 'Hider of sins,' 'Servant of the cow' (of Isis), and 'Guardian of the pig' (of Set)." Thus, and again, the office of the priest was more often developed from civil than from religious functions.

Women were there from the beginning as priestesses for they were the 'Nurse,' and the priest the 'Child,' or she is the 'Appeaser of the soul,' the priest the 'Favorite child.' She is the 'Protector; the 'Robed,' the 'Dark woman on the Nubian frontier,' the 'Divine mother,' or the 'Watcher.' Some of the titles come from Upper Egypt and others from Lower Egypt.

So much so, for that time, Indus Khamit Kush in *The Missing Pages of "His-Story"* (1993: 25) quoted Robert Forest Wilson in *The Living Pageant of the Nile* (The Bobs Merrill Company, Indianapolis, 1924, p. 31) who wrote by this early time, speaking of Egypt: "She had refined her system of law and government, invented taxation, developed an intricate economic system, vastly expanded the tastes and needs of her individuals, gone into foreign trade, applied state aid to agriculture, made a start with most of the common sciences, produced philosophers, erected some of the mightiest buildings the world has ever seen, discovered beauty in art, and done a thousand other things - and over the face of the rest of the earth the primeval darkness yet rested." In all this, bringing of light to humanity, the Egyptian temple played a significant role for the priests had become the great teachers, scientists, artisans and philosophers who shaped the society's cultural norms.

As the art of temple building developed, and within the sacred enclosure, no public worship was performed, the faithful did not congregate for public prayer, and no commoner was admitted into the inner portals of the temple except the high priest and his assistants; who, because of the elaborate and complex ritual, the king or his assign was in need of their assistance. Individuals high in the social echelon were welcomed into the Great Open Court, but no further! Nonetheless, and still, writes Maspero, the "Temple was built as an image of the world, as the Egyptian imagined it to be." Importantly,

LET'S LIBERATE THE TEMPLE

Erman (1907: 6) in commenting on the temple in this early age of the world or consciousness of the ancient Egyptian of Predynastic times demonstrating origins of profound spiritual and philosophic beginnings, writes: "Their temples were huts with walls of plaited wicker work, the front of the roof was adorned with projecting wooden beams. A few short posts and two high masts in front of the building were added to provide shelter decoration. The altar consisted of a reed mat, and for the celebration of festivals, simple bowers were erected."

On the other hand, and in further elaboration, Aldred (1980: 144) explained: "The Egyptian temple, 'the god's house,' had its origins in the prehistoric reed or palm-leaf both, similar to the maize-stalk shelter that the peasant even today erects in his fields to shield his beasts and himself from the cold winds of winter and the burning heat of summer. In the beginning, the god had arisen on the primeval mound above the waters of Chaos, and by magic the shrine was built around him with a fence to keep off intruders, and a rag of cloth on a pole to show that the place was sacred and taboo. As the work of creation continued and light appeared on the face of the waters, the god of the Void lifted the sky from the new marshy earth and kept it in position on its four pole-like supports. Thus, the temple as the abode of the god grew to its final form, not as an architectural concept as much as myth made tangible in stone. This finite model of the universe at its beginning is visible in the primal Egyptian temple and determines its decoration. The sanctuary, housing the image of the god, is built on the highest point of the ground, on a sort of hillock representing the primeval mound, and is a stone interpretation of the prehistoric reed hut, which is clearly discernible as a small house within larger dwelling. Except here in the elemental darkness prevailing before the First Time."

FREDERICK MONDERSON

Liberate the Temple. Isis Temple at Philae. View of "Trajan's Kiosk" or "Pharaoh's Bed" from the South-East.

Liberate the Temple. Isis Temple at Philae. Another view of "Trajan's Kiosk" or "Pharaoh's Bed" from the West.

LET'S LIBERATE THE TEMPLE

Liberate the Temple. Isis Temple at Philae. In the temple proper and from its East, the back Colonnades of the Mammisi, with Western half of the Great Pylon at its rear and columns of the Western Colonnade further on.

Sauernon in Poesner's *a Dictionary of Egyptian Civilization* (1962: 281) offers another view: "The Egyptian temple was a functional building, devoted to the most essential work of earthly life, namely, the maintenance of the creation. Obscure forces of chaos existed before the world was created, and, although they were cast away to the outer edge of the world, they nevertheless continued to threaten it; the equilibrium which maintained the visible world and the various forms of life was the fact of a creation daily renewed. Every evening, in the darkness, the world again was in danger of falling into a sleep from which there would be no awakening, the return of the sun the next morning happily drove away the risk. Only the gods, by their ceaseless efforts, preserved the precarious existence of this essential[ly] vulnerable universe. These gods, universal forces in different places under different forms, lived on earth in their "houses" - the temples. The function of this building and of its personnel was to protect the gods from attacks by hostile forces, to nourish them and keep them in perfect condition, in order to facilitate their cosmic task and to keep from them any influence which could impede their action."

After millennia of sweet communion with Deity, experimentation and daring that carried the civilization to un-believed heights of accomplishment, Aldred (1980: 145) explained how some of this process unfolded: "By the time of the New Kingdom, most of the local divinities had become solarized under the influence of the theologians of Heliopolis, and had attached to themselves the name of Re 'Horakhty, the active aspect of the sun-god, so that forms like Amon-re, Sobek-re and Mentu-re are now found. The sun god, however, was worshipped at an altar set in a colonnaded court under the open sky where he was lord. The architecture was divinely inspired and with space for the principal gods, the buildings became complex with small rooms for secondary gods, statues, dim lights, maze of halls, and arrangement of trick doors, as well as stairs to the roof. There were also side rooms for keeping garments, jewelry, and cult objects for the religious ceremonies on altars."

Equally, Adolf Erman, of whom it was said, was the only modern who knew exactly what the ancient Egyptians thought, though he had his racial bias, offered important insights into this belief system. After all, Goethe did say, "Wherever Germans went they corrupted that culture." Nevertheless, Erman's (1907: 40-41) view regarding the temple within the enclosure and having the propylon or pylon as its principal entrance is spot on. In this respect, he wrote: "Behind this gateway lay the first large space, an open court surrounded by colonnades. Here the great festivals were celebrated, in which a large number of citizens were entitled to take part. Behind this court there was a hall supported by columns, the place appointed for all manner of ceremonies, and behind this again lay the holy of holies, the chamber where the statue of the god had his dwelling. In adjoining apartments were the statues of the wife and son of the god. This was the essential part of the temple, naturally there would be various additional chambers to contain the sacred utensils, and for special purposes of the religious cults. A further characteristic of every temple is that from front to rear each apartment was less lofty and light than the preceding. Into the court the Egyptian sun blazed with

LET'S LIBERATE THE TEMPLE

uninterrupted splendor, in the halls its light was admitted to a modified extent through the entrance and through the windows in the roof; in the holy of holies reigned profound darkness."

The evidence is clear in showing every temple was commenced with a foundation ceremony of which Maspero found evidence at Deir el Bahari and again at Luxor Temple. Margaret Murray in *The Splendor that was Egypt* (1949, 1957: 232-33) says of such an undertaking: "The founding of a temple was a religious ceremony, performed by the Pharaoh in person assisted by the goddess Seshat, who was probably represented by the Queen. Each of them held an end of the measuring-cord and marked on the ground the dimensions of the temple. After the measurements had been traced out a sand-bed was made, and on this rough stone blocks were laid to form the foundations. At each corner of the building, and wherever an internal wall touched the outside wall, foundation deposits were placed under the blocks. These deposits consisted of models of all the tools and implements used in the building of the temple, modes of offerings, and scarabs or plaques bearing the name of the royal founder. Even when a temple has been completely destroyed and the foundation blocks removed, it is possible to recover the plan and the name of the founder by means of the foundation deposits. The foundation blocks were scored with lines on the upper surface, which had been smoothed, and on these lines the walls were built. As the walls rose in height earth ramps were built against them, which dragged the stones on rollers. Pillars were built in the same way with ramps. This method of raising blocks of stone to the desired level is as early as the pyramids. It is uncertain whether a temple was built from a plan drawn out by the architect before beginning the work; if so all such plans have perished. If not, then one is confronted with the fact that the architects of those early days were capable of planning a temple or pyramid completely, including the lengths of ramps required, and carrying it through to completion without even a note."

Underscoring this idea, it must be pointed out, "The architect had to be perfect in conception and completion of his task otherwise he would suffer psychological discomfort and the deity for whom the temple was being built would not come to inhabit his "home."

FREDERICK MONDERSON

Miroslav Verner in *Temple of the World* (Cairo: The American University in Cairo Press, 2013: 16) offers another view that: "Only the king could found a temple. It was his task to build a temple and deliver it to the god, so that the god could abide there. As the earthly incarnation of the sky god Horus (Hor), the king was equal to the gods, and was lord of "doing things," that is, rituals. Rituals accompanied a temple's construction from the very start. The founding of a temple, which took several weeks, would begin at the new moon with the ceremony of 'stretching the cord,' which the king was supposed to perform with the help of Seshat, goddess of writing and mathematics, and in the presence of other deities."

Building a temple upon a site carefully chosen by astronomical orientation, determining the axis – if solar, east to west, and decorating the requirements set by the calendar as prescribed by tradition and textual inscriptions as well as the nature of material, essentially stone, and the choice of decoration. Now, after these essentials are factored and a pan finalized, according to Verner who mentions 'digging the earth' and 'digging a trench right down to water, so that the building will be excellent,' he states: "The ritual also had a practical purpose, however, since the water level would at the same time define the horizontal line. The trench would then be filled with clean sand symbolizing ritual purity., the sand would soak up the groundwater, and models of work tools, bricks with magical texts, and sacrifices (a goose, the head of a bullock, and the like) would be placed at the corners of the future building. Once the temple had been built, the ritual of the 'opening of the mouth' would be performed in every temple interior so that the rooms would be magically endowed with life and ritually cleansed. At the very end of the process a cult statue of the god would be placed in the innermost shrine, and the temple thus symbolically presented to the god."

LET'S LIBERATE THE TEMPLE

Liberate the Temple. Isis Temple at Philae. Within the Court of the Temple of Isis, columns of the Second Eastern Colonnade and the western half of the Great Pylon to its rear.

Liberate the Temple. Isis Temple at Philae. Front entrance to the Mammisi with its columns with varied capitals.

FREDERICK MONDERSON

Liberate the Temple. Visitor in the Court of the Temple of Isis with front of the Mammisi to the right.

While Murray speaks of "measurements," Verner (2013: 17) is more specific by stating: "One frequent feature of the plan is the application of a right-angled triangle with a 3:4:5 ration of sides, which gave the temple harmonious proportions. The attempt to achieve symmetry and a ratio of 6:2:1 among the length, breadth, and height of the building is also evident. The towers of the pylon, reminiscent of a fortress and guard gate, and the massive, slightly slanted exterior walls separated the temple from its surroundings and emphasized that this was a sacred place, the dwelling of a god." All this notwithstanding, upon completion, the temple therefore possessed all the necessities to make it functional, self-sufficient and secure.

Libraries were an important part of any temple, for scholars congregated and even taught educational subjects in temples that were considered "Colleges." Some temples had a Well, Nilometer, Sacred Lake, granaries and dwellings for the temple staff. To help meet the needs of the daily rituals, gardens provided fresh flowers for the

LET'S LIBERATE THE TEMPLE

temple service and food for the staff. Granaries and storehouses were filled with staff-produce, looked-over by large contingents of scribes, overseers and managers in charge of administration. Significant and competing regional industries in schools of arts and crafts were developed in these structures producing memorable works of art, whether jewelry, statuary (of stone or precious metals) and colorful decorations on walls, columns, architraves, steles, etc. Temples were frequently provided with allocations of prisoners-of-wars for work on its lands. In addition, oftentimes the temples were recipients of significant kingly and noble endowments for the worship and mortuary cults they oversaw. Equally, their economic viability was enhanced as the religious body enjoyed tax-free status.

It is interesting that during the later Roman Period, the "tax free" status was revoked and in a "carrot and stick" strategy, "returned in a grant, which could be withheld, and which gave the priesthood an interest in the stability of the government." Nonetheless, while worship practices towards the gods remained predominant, the kings also came in for recognition. On this point, Aldred (1980: 146) elucidates further regarding New Kingdom mortuary or king temple building practices: "The resources that had formerly been devoted to the building of the king's pyramid complexes now went into their mortuary temples, built along the desert margin of the western riverbank at Thebes, the birthplace of their founder Amosis. These were separated from their actual burial places, which from the reign of Tuthmosis I were hewn into the rocky walls of a wadi now known as the Valley of the Kings, about a mile to the west, beneath the dominating peak of a natural pyramid. The tombs themselves were decorated in painted relief, or with walls and ceiling paintings, of scenes from the sacred books that, under the influence of Heliopolis, now governed ideas on the royal destiny...."

Emphasizing the expansion of priestly responsibilities and as regional schools of art competed and produced their outstanding pieces, we begin to see, besides representations of kings, figures of the gods, even those of exceptional private individuals are commonly found. The age also saw a growth of ideas of divinities grouped into triads consisting of a god, his consort and their child; for the most part a son. The concept of the "Holy Family" with the child was first experienced on the Nile River as an African creation.

Shaw and Nicholson (1995: 285-86) recognize the temple was "considered to be an architectural metaphor both for the universe and for the process of creation itself." However, they point to an important architectural feature in which as one ascended inward "the floor gradually rose, passing through forests of plant-form columns and roofed by images of the constellations or the body of the sky-goddess Nut, allowing the priests to ascend gradually from the outermost edge of the universe towards the sanctuary, which was a symbol of the inner core of creation, the Primeval mound on which the creator-god first brought the world into being."

In this dynamic, the seat or throne of the god rested on the highest spot in the temple affording a panoramic view of his creation. In "Temples" *The Oxford Encyclopedia of Ancient Egypt*, Donald B. Redford (Editor in Chief), Oxford University Press, Vol. 3 (2001: 366) explained this phenomenon: "The passage from the temple entrance to the chamber of the cultic image, for example, often slopes upward as either a ramp or a flight of stairs, so that the human approaches the enthroned deity from below. The up-sloping floor is often complemented by a downward slope of the roof. In the cross-section of a temple, this often produces the effect of shortening the perspective. The room that is farthest back in such a cross-section, the chamber of the cultic image, thus appears as a kind of cave, the prototype of a sacred place." Wilkinson equally believed the soil beyond the Sanctuary represented a downward slope to a lower surface.

Comparatively speaking and on the other hand, White (1980: 50-51) believed: "The temple performed the same role in ancient Egypt as the cathedral in Mediaeval Europe. It was the dual source of cultural inspiration and physical employment. As in Mediaeval Europe, with the exception of the estates of the feudal barons almost the entire ownership of land and property was concentrated in the hands of the king with his chief priests. In theory, the king held the Black Land in trusteeship for his fellow gods. His chief priests were therefore his

LET'S LIBERATE THE TEMPLE

principal tenants, although they gradually became more or less the unchallenged rulers of their own domains-in the way that the Abbot of Tintern or Rievaulx would carry out his ecclesiastic duties while superintending the agriculture, stock-breeding and building-work throughout his wide province. The main temples acted not only as the distributors of their own bounty, but of the royal bounty too. An entire population of civil servants, scribes, policemen, craftsmen, artisans, and artists was fed and clothed from the priestly granaries and storerooms. The chief priests collected taxes on behalf of the king and doled out rewards and necessities as they saw fit. They were thus the instruments and regulators of the state economy and wielded enormous power."

Interesting, this analogy underscores much in the formation of 19th Century thought about the ancient Egyptians in using European parallels while writing to an emergent "Penny Press" and European readership. On the other hand, while dr. Cheikh Anta Diop argued for and in his book, *The Cultural Unity of Black Africa* (1959, 1987), Theophile Obenga, his associate in *African Philosophy*: *The Pharaonic Period* 2780-330 B.C. (2004) throughout the entire work compares Egyptian culture with similar practices elsewhere in Africa while, no once, connecting this to anywhere in Europe.

Nonetheless, in explaining how the society's administrative mechanism changed especially under the fortunes of a lucratively imperial Egypt and the long-term effects of entities changing to meet changing dynamics, Petrie (1924: 42-43) insightfully argued: "By the time of the New Kingdom, there was in all departments a far greater centralization. The local princes who had kept up their state, even under the strong domination of the IVth and XIIth dynasties, now disappear, and every affair is under control from the capital. The priesthood did not escape this, and they were all united in general hierarchies; however, this might add to their status, it was the beginning of the end, for the priesthood usurped, and then wrecked the government." As the wealth of the priest increased from imperial plunder, splendid buildings were erected and so civil control came fully under their administration. "Grants were made, and renewed by fresh rulers, in order to secure the only organization that existed in the country. The endowments were fully regulated, as is seen at the minor temple of the out-of-the-way town of Hibeh; there the revenue was divided into 100 shares; the prophet of Amon had four, and the prophets of sixteen gods and four orders of twenty priests each, all had one share alike."

Liberate the Temple. Temple of Isis at Philae. Ra-Horakhty sits enthroned beside Bastet with Shu at their rear.

LET'S LIBERATE THE TEMPLE

Liberate the Temple. Temple of Isis at Philae.
Pharaoh presents a platter to Isis holding scepter and ankh.

Liberate the Temple. Temple of Isis at Philae.
Pharaoh makes a Presentation to enthroned Isis.

FREDERICK MONDERSON

Thus, in these explained dynamics, it is easier to speak about the ancient Kemet-Egyptian temple and its administration, rather than say what it really is, since it meant many things.

Principally however, and in one instance, Mariette-Bey explained the idea of the Trinity in the following statement: "Egyptian temples are always dedicated to three gods. It is what Champollion calls the Triad. The first is the male principle, the second is the female principle, and the third is the offspring of the other two. But these three deities are blended into one. The father engenders himself in the womb of the mother and thus at once becomes his own father and his own son. Thereby are expressed the un-createdness and the eternity of the being who has had no beginning and shall have no end." To have conceived such a concept this early in the history of the world was nothing short of brilliant consciousness. That is why Dr. Ben insisted the Black man become more knowledgeable about his heritage and the power such represents.

But who were these people, these ancient Africans resident in the Nile Valley in Northeast Africa? To answer this question, John Jackson in *Introduction to African Civilizations* (1970: 153), quotes Gerald Massey, author of *A Book of the Beginnings*, Vol. I, p. 4, who explained: "Egypt is often called Kam, the black land, and Kam does signify black, the name probably applied to the earliest inhabitants whose type is the Kam or Khem of the Hebrew writers."

Even further, Jackson (1970: 153-54) noted and essentially laid it down: "It will be maintained in this book that the oldest mythology, religion, symbols, language had their birthplace in Africa, that the primitive race of Kam came thence, and the civilization in Egypt, emanated from that country and spread over the world. The most reasonable view on the evolutionary theory…is that the black race is the most ancient, and that Africa is the primordial home." In addition, Jackson (1970: 154) continued: "The Hebrew Scriptures; among their

LET'S LIBERATE THE TEMPLE

other fragments of ancient lore; are very emphatic in deriving the line of Mizraim from Ham or Kam, the black type coupled with Kush, another form of the black. They give no countenance to the theory of Asiatic origin of Noah. Mizraim is the son of Ham, i.e., of Kam, the black race."

Now, having said that much to help further understand the scope of the temple of ancient Kemet, it can also be viewed within the context of the principle of sculptural decoration. On walls, whether within or without, pictures are arranged symmetrically, side by side. Several series of pictures are disposed in tiers one above the other and cover the walls of chambers from top to bottom. In explaining this, the role of the king is thus key as he "presents an offering (a table laden with victuals, flowers, fruits and emblems) and solicits a favor from the god. In his answer, the god grants the gift that is prayed for." Thus, decoration of the temple consists of nothing more than an act of adoration from the king. As such, a temple can be both a primordial hill or the "exclusive personal monument of the king by whom it was founded or decorated." To reiterate, as stated above, in foundation deposits, founders' emblems, tools, food, and blood from sacrificial animals were deposited to ensure blessings to the temple.

Anthony Browder in *Nile Valley Contributions to Civilization* (Washington, DC, The Institute of Karmic Guidance, 1992: 120) at a later age displays a superimposed figure of the New Kingdom, Nineteenth Dynasty monarch Rameses II on the Temple of Luxor and had this to say of the work of Schwaller de Lubicz who studied that temple with his wife and daughter Lucie. This great mind, Schwaller de Lubicz, "measured, recorded and drew every inch of the temple, including each stone, wall carving and statue." Together they wrote *Le Temple de l'Homme* (*The Temple in Man*). "Their combined research suggested that the temple was dedicated to the creation of man, and that the floor plan of the temple is representative of the anatomical structure of man. Lucie Remy superimposed the skeletal framework of a statue of Rameses II over the floor plan of the temple and discovered some interesting similarities. The open courtyard represents the legs; the hypostyle hall represents the thighs; the Peristyle court represents the abdomen and the inner temple represents the head. Within each segment of the temple, activities took place, which related to specific body functions. In the hall, the king is generally shown in the pictures on one side and one or more divinities on the other."

"The worship consists of prayers, recited within the temple in the name of the king, and above all, of processions. In these processions which the king is supposed to head, are carried the insignia of the gods, the coffers in which their statues are enclosed, and also the sacred barks which later are generally deposited in the temple, to be brought out on fete days. In the middle, concealed under a veil, stood the coffer within which lies the emblem, which no one must see. The processions are commonly held within the temple. They generally ascend the terraces and sometimes spread themselves inside the enclosure away from the prying eyes…. On rare occasions, the processions may be seen leaving the city and winding the 'Sacred Canal,' toward some other city more or less distant. Close to every temple is a lake. In all probability, the lake played an important part in the procession and the sacred barks were deposited there, at least while the fete lasted."

These ancient Africans therefore, were the "genesis of their own genius" who thought out the fundamental principles of religion that shaped social and ethical practice and other dynamics of significance for salvation and development of their people. These "houses of life," that crafted the cosmological creation of the particular cult, grew from simple beginnings into huge and complex structures of decorated stone. As such then, the temple can be seen as Maspero held, as a "royal proscynem, or ex voto that is a token of piety from the king who erected it in order to deserve the favor of the gods. It is a kind of royal oratory and nothing more."

More than two hundred years ago, in the aftermath of the American and French Revolutions, Napoleon invaded Egypt in "Carrying the war to the British." Dr. Ben-Jochannan reminded, Napoleon came to Egypt as a conqueror and so he represented an arrogance in his outlook. At the conflict's end, the Rosetta Stone was discovered and this ultimately led to the decipherment of the ancient language by the Frenchman Jean Jacques Champollion, the Younger. His work led to

LET'S LIBERATE THE TEMPLE

the birth of Egyptology and interest in the ancient culture which spawned a number of European antiquarian societies. As the discipline began to develop, the new science of archaeology significantly and systematically began the excavation establishing order in reclamation strategies laying the basis of restoration of much of the ancient Nile culture. This "scientific work" also rescued and repaired existing temples suffering from stresses of time and an abandoned culture; but more important it broadened our knowledge of their form and function. Today, these excavated and restored edifices teach much about the culture, builders, function, spirituality and ethical practices as well as the social and economic dynamics that prevailed therein.

As such, and with the expansion of knowledge in many other fields, we now know climate and geography were instrumental in dictating the types and nature of Egyptian temples. It is a given, the landscape of Egypt is one of lines, vertical, horizontal or diagonal. Columns and buildings within temple complexes were vertical or horizontal, roofs were horizontal and pylons were sloping. There was little rain in Egypt and hence the sky remained blue and this had something to do with influencing the nature of its architecture. Under Egypt's clear skies, heavenly observations, astronomy and astrology progressed significantly. For clarity, M.A. Murray's *Egyptian Temples* (London: Sampson Low, Marston and Co., Ltd., 1931: 1) explained how an aspect of climate impacted upon the psyche and nature of building and other factors within the society. In explaining this further, Ms. Murray describes Egypt as "a country of violent contrasts; the flat plain and vertical cliffs, the fertile fields and the dreary waste of desert, the brilliant sunshine and the dark shadows, the river which harbored edible fish and murderous crocodile; all these naturally had their effect on the mind of the Egyptian architect and showed themselves in the architecture." This frame of reference was not limited to religious or mortuary architecture but domestic and civic as well.

Liberate the Temple. Temple of Isis at Philae.
Pharaoh's Red and White Double Crown with Uraei and disk overhead before his *Son of Ra* and *Suten Bat* cartouche titles.

Liberate the Temple. Temple of Isis at Philae.
Pharaoh presents a platter to Osiris wearing the White Crown.

LET'S LIBERATE THE TEMPLE

Liberate the Temple. Temple of Isis at Philae. With a hawk flying overhead, Pharaoh presents a "Table of Offerings" to Isis wearing horns, disk and throne.

We now know the temple consisted of four parts such as an outer court, an inner court, a vestibule and a shrine or sanctuary. In time however, the temple of Karnak, for example, took on extra dimensions that were a result of the efforts of ruling families who vied with each other to please their god.

Essentially, and as we are aware two principal types of temples evolved from religious practices from the early age of Egyptian history. By the New Kingdom these became more clearly delineated. One temple was dedicated to the god and another was dedicated to the king. The god temple was always separate and was built in order that the god would be propitiated. The king's temple was designed to worship him when he died and became a god in the future life. However, if his reign was lengthy, he was worshipped therein while still alive. Nevertheless, through ritual practice, the king's temple, in the earliest times was attached to his burial structure as in the pyramid complex. In time, certainly for most of the New Kingdom monarchs the temple and tomb had become separate. The king's mortuary temple was built on the Plains of Thebes with an orientation generally across the river towards either Karnak or Luxor, home of Amon. The tomb, following Thutmose I's decision away from plains burial, was secreted in the Valley of the Kings, emphasizing the rock-cut, even the T-shape type of tomb.

1. Pre-Dynastic Temples

These earliest god temples were made of perishable material and are only known from illustrations. Murray pointed out (1931: 2) in regards these early god structures: "Of temples dedicated to a god none are in existence from the early periods, although the foundations of several are known; e.g., at Abydos there was a temple of Osiris in the Ist dynasty, at Hierakonpolis the temple of the sacred falcon was probably as early, at Bubastis the temple of the cat-goddess is not later than the IVth dynasty, and the shrine of the crocodile-god in the Fayum had very primitive characters." In reality, much of this has perished except for traceable foundation plans.

2. Old Kingdom Temples

The early temples dedicated to kings can be traced to the Old Kingdom and are a part of the burial apparatus. "As the primitive king or chief always had a better house than the common people, so the god who was superior to the king had a better house than the king; the original temple was then merely a finer hut than those used by human beings."

The earliest temples are those attached to pyramids and other royal burial places and were intended for the worship of the dead king. The provisioning of his repose was an important undertaking.

Petrie indicated: "At first the place of offerings was closely connected with the tomb, as shown by the large steles found at the tombs of the Ist dynasty; and such continue to be the case for the ordinary Egyptian

LET'S LIBERATE THE TEMPLE

in all times. But the place of offering to the kings was at the end of the IIIrd Dynasty..." yet, in all this, temple and tomb remained essentially together.

3. Middle Kingdom Temples

Not much has survived of Middle Kingdom temples and those that are identified can only be done so from their faint outlines on the ground. However, archaeologists Edouard Naville and H. Hall discovered the temple of Mentuhotep II of the 11th Dynasty at Deir el Bahari in 1898 and then it was excavated in 1904. It is the oldest surviving and the most complete of all Middle Kingdom temples. Hatshepsut's temple was modeled on this structure, transitional from the Old to the Middle Kingdom, during whose time, some 500 years after it was still viable. This is generally understood, given her temple, instead of being in the center of the cirque of Deir el Bahari is juxtaposed to Mentuhotep's and occupies more of the northern sector of the amphitheater. It is a wonderful structure and was richly decorated with a style that was very beautiful impacting beliefs about the art of that period generally thought to be very archaic.

4. New Kingdom Temples

With the expulsion of the Hyksos and triumph of Amon, now Amon-Ra, at the formation of the New Kingdom, temple building took on a new meaning, becoming more elaborate, complete, picturesque, and built of more varied and durable stone. Begun in the Middle Kingdom, Karnak Temple, a principal god or worship temple, experienced its greatest development in the New Kingdom, though in its present form it took nearly 2000 years to complete. Over this expansive period all the elements and dynamics of an Egyptian temple came into play. In explaining this development, the following are some features of the "vegetative" Egyptian temple such as Karnak, at Thebes in Upper Egypt.

FREDERICK MONDERSON

Now, since the temple was built by the riverside, the King would encounter the following elements when visiting:

1. A Quay for greeting, ceremony and ritual.

2. Canal connecting the river to ramparts of the temple.

3. Avenue of Sphinxes - having rams' heads as at Karnak with an image of the king between its paws.

4. Obelisk and statues in front of the entrance as well as obelisks within the structure.

5. Pylon - wall enclosure. This is a gate. The number of entrances varies. Karnak had 6, Luxor 3, Edfu had a principal and one on the side. The temple was also a refuge so that when the doors closed, it was difficult to get in. The idea was to protect the god and then the people inside its walls. On the Pylon were flagstaves that flew flags of the state, Nome and principal and subsidiary gods worshipped within. The outer periphery was extended by even greater "girdle wall," "enclosure" or even "encapsulating walls."

LET'S LIBERATE THE TEMPLE

Liberate the Temple. Temple of Isis at Philae.
Columns in the fourth room before the Sanctuary in the rear.

Liberate the Temple. Temple of Isis at Philae.
Columns in the outer room of the temple. Notice how small the base is in comparison to that of Karnak's Hypostyle Hall.

FREDERICK MONDERSON

Liberate the Temple. Temple of Isis at Philae. The height of the columns underscores the height and size of the entrance hall.

LET'S LIBERATE THE TEMPLE

6. Courts - sometimes a Great, even subsequent Courts. Here you would find:

   a. Altars - sometimes one or more.

   b. Sphinxes - sometimes original, sometimes from elsewhere.

   c. Seated and standing statues - of the king, god or some private official.

   d. steles with commemorating inscriptions.

   e. Doors and door posts - linking or entrancing an additional pylon.

   f. Jubilee or Heb-Sed Festival Court and Pavilion.

   g. Chapels or kiosks, most often dedicated to the Theban Triad of Amon, Mut and Khonsu.

   h. Columns or pillars forming a colonnade - Peristyle - Often an attached colonnaded walkway, sometimes roofed.

   i. Obelisks dedicated to the god.

   j. Portico to another Pylon

   k. Hypostyle Hall - where the processions began and also having the "Clerestory effect. Formed from a Processional Colonnade with these center columns being higher than the flanking sections given the best surviving examples are at Karnak, Ramesseum and unfinished at Luxor. James H. Breasted argued, the prototype of this new form of Egyptian architecture, with the Processional colonnade was first found at the temple of Soleb built by Amenhotep III in Nubia.

FREDERICK MONDERSON

l. Second Hypostyle Hall – While Rameses II and Rameses III, Ramesseum and Medinet Habu mortuary temples, respectively, the later Graeco-Roman temples as Edfu, Philae, and Dendera had three Hypostyle Halls.

Adjacent rooms for:

a. Clothing

b. Gold and other jewelry

c. Vessels of stone or precious metals

d. Liquid and solid offerings

e. Library with books of the ritual

f. Subsidiary gods represented in the illustration and in small temples on site.

g. Third Hypostyle Hall - Ramesseum, Medinet Habu and Dendera.

h. The Sanctuary where the God lives - This could have a single or double chamber as well as bark station for the god's ark.

i. Outside a Sacred Lake where priests washed and also provided water for storage.

j. Quarters for priests, priestesses, stewards, scribes and singing women.

k. Schools for art and learning - calendars – instruments for measurement.

LET'S LIBERATE THE TEMPLE

m. Workshops producing cotton, dyes, statuary, woodwork, pottery, painting, basketry, matting, jewelry of gold and other precious stones, etc.

n. Gardens for pleasure, flowers for the daily temple ritual and vegetables for food of the temple staff.

o. A Nilometer to measure the river's volume

p. Trees for fruit and shade

q. Chapels to other Gods

r. Decoration: Walls - Inside, Outside and some Ceilings, columns, pylon and enclosure wall within and on the outside

s. The Sanctuary and rooms adjacent to the Sanctuary.

t. Kitchens and refractory

u. Wine Cellars

v. Granaries, store-houses

w. Treasury

x. Altar in the sanctuary or outdoors in the entrance court.

y. There could be a number of halls and minor courts leading to the Sanctuary. There is generally an area or court behind the Sanctuary.

z. Calendar system for festivals, astronomy and Nile Watch to study the river's behavior.

Additionally, there may be an overseer's residence, bakeries and baker residences, boulevards, floors, pavement, gates, stelae and untold inscriptions and decorations. However, while there was residence for the permanent staff, there was also need for space for the temporary staff. Naturally there were feasts and festivals celebrated therein. Equally, there were barque stations for the ark of the deity, offering and oblation tables and furniture; as well as steles often commemorating some event, festival or otherwise. Most important, to have one's name written in the colonnade was a distinct and memorable honor. Temples possessed ships, harbors, tributary territories, towns, magazines, slaves, cattle, geese, poultry, horses, vineyards, cultus utensils, as well as guards, archers, and even much more.

The mortuary temples at Thebes were structures dedicated to the dead king who, upon reaching that state became a god in his own right. Some kings were worshipped during their lifetime! Therefore, by building his temple he was worshipped and remembered. Unfortunately, many of these, for the major kings of the New Kingdom, were dismantled after their death. However, Medinet Habu, built for Rameses III, is considered the "last major building project of the New Kingdom," and as such, no one came after to dismantle his temple. His cartouches were sometimes "8-inches" deep to preclude their being usurped by later kings. Processional Temples as the "White Chapel," "Red Chapel" and several others, as well as kiosks as at Karnak, Luxor, etc., were resting place for the god while on the move.

Temples appear to have been oriented by the river; the main direction of the stream is to the north, it naturally varies somewhat and runs occasionally east or west of north. The temples, therefore, also vary in their orientation generally along the east/west path of the sun or Sun God. The rule, however, regarding orientation is that temples lie close to, parallel or at right angles to the river, e.g., Luxor and Karnak.

In the temples of Thebes, which are almost entirely of the New Kingdom, the lighting of the hypostyle halls was by means of a clerestory. The first of these is dated to Thutmose III's *Akh Menu*, Festival Temple at Karnak and continued in Karnak's Great Hypostyle Hall and at the Ramesseum. Columns supported the nave of the hall. The temples were richly decorated on the inside and

LET'S LIBERATE THE TEMPLE

outside. On the outside the wars and struggle of the kings were depicted and on the inside the worship and ritual of the temples were showcased.

Liberate the Temple. Isis Temple at Philae. Pharaoh stands before enthroned Isis (Auset) as he holds in his hand an instrument (right) and incenser (left).

Liberate the Temple. Temple of Isis at Philae. Pharaoh presents the Red and the White crowns to enthroned Horus with Isis and Nephthys beside him.

FREDERICK MONDERSON

Liberate the Temple. Temple of Isis at Philae. Pharaoh presents a sailing boat to the Osirian triad of Osiris (White Crown), Isis (Auset in Horns, disk and throne) and Horus in Double Red and White Crown, all enthroned.

5. Graeco-Roman Temples were built by

Nubian and Egyptian architects, working with Egyptian specifications dating to the earliest times and were supervised by Greeks and Roman overlords. Edfu, Kom Ombo, Esneh, Philae, Kalabsha, were all built with new features, decorations and began to be inundated with illustrations depicting the ritual. Fortunately, this new method has helped preserve much of the cultural and religious history, thereby giving evidence of the much earlier worship and ritual practice.

E.A.E. Raymond's *The Mythological Origin of the Egyptian Temple* tells of the Edfu Documents on the History of the Egyptian Temple and this follows the work of A.M. Blackman and later Blackman and Fairman. Accordingly, on the walls of Egyptian temples as Edfu of the Graeco-Roman period are inscribed "numerous ritual texts, among which occurs a series of texts that is found only in a very abbreviated form in certain of the Pharaonic temples." These sources themselves are copies of much earlier material that go back to the earliest conception of the temple. "Those texts make it possible to reconstruct

LET'S LIBERATE THE TEMPLE

a reasonably complete history of the building of each temple concerned, a picture of the lay-out of the rooms and halls, and their ritual purpose and significance."

Here we find "The Myth About the Domains and the Temple of the Falcon." This "myth is the contents of the first and second cosmogonical record and of a part of the fifth record which seems to have been originally included in the Sacred Book of the Early Primeval Age of Gods." The Edfu myth is the "unique source that discloses the Egyptian tradition concerning the origin of the sacred domains of the Falcon and the creation of his first temple."

Another chapter of the *Mythological Origin of the Egyptian Temple* deals with the Myth about the Origin of the Temple of the Sun God.

"The 3rd, 4th and 5th Edfu cosmogonical records preserve a part of the myth described as the Coming of Re to his Mansion of Ms-nht. This myth concerns another period of the mythical age when the lands of the sacred domains were already in existence, and when the primeval houses of the gods were found in places other than the original domain of the Falcon."

Smaller and more prolific in decoration, these late period temples added the Mammisi, or birth house, where the god was born. The new form and prolific decorations took on a different format as well during this new age in Egypt.

The Egyptian Temple, therefore, represented the philosophical, esoteric, cosmological and theogonic metaphysics of the cultural history of the Nile Valley experience. In that evolution, the temple played a vital role in the development of science, building, trade, art, crafts, mathematics, mummification, astronomy, astrology and a whole lot more. Therefore, the temple was the center of the intellectual lifeblood of the society and as such, it carried forth the growth and development of the culture with its insistence on religiosity and right behavior based on the philosophical and social axiom of Ma'at, viz., righteousness, justice, balance, order, goodness, truth, straightforwardness and respect and good judgment.

FREDERICK MONDERSON

V. THE AWESOME EGYPTIAN TEMPLE II
By
Dr. Fred Monderson

I Introduction

a. The Long and Short Chronology

The "Long Chronology" can be dated anywhere from 6200 or 5701 to 3200 B.C. and the "Short Chronology" to 3200-3150! However, the prehistoric or Predynastic period, for convenience, is recognized as dating from 4241 B.C. to 3200. Some have argued the "Short Chronology" is more political aligning it with South-West-Asian history. This is in the area of the Caucasus where Caucasians are thought to originate and that they came to Egypt and ruled over the indigenous people there, "for some unknown reason" and bringing a "superior mental attitude." However, there is no precise date as to when these foreigners came and such coming is actually nothing but an imagined hypothesis. Even more important, the Egyptians have no record of any foreigners coming and impacting their culture to any extent before the Hyksos who came around 1750 B.C.

b. Temples in Time Perspective -

Temples grew from simple one room, perishable materials to complex, structures of stone, decorated and possessing enormous wealth and personnel. Some temples were built by a single individual while others were built by several people spanning several generations. Sometimes one person built while others decorated or added to the structure. Thus, temples expanded adding support facilities and decorated features as the society's wealth and fortunes of a particular god increased. Not only the building size increased but

LET'S LIBERATE THE TEMPLE

also the land space bounded by an enclosure wall. In this way, colonnades and sphinxes as well as other buildings decorated the landscape enabling the further expansion of the temple. Nevertheless, what is devastatingly significant, in *The Star of deep Beginnings: The Genesis of African Science and Technology* (1998) Charles Finch III explained and established Nile valley links with cultural developments dating to some 40,000 years.

Liberate the Temple. Temple of Isis at Philae. The "Kiosk of Trajan" never stops amazing about its beautiful yet diminutive columns atop screened walls.

FREDERICK MONDERSON

Liberate the Temple. Temple of Isis at Philae. More of the varied columns sitting atop the screen wall.

Liberate the Temple. Temple of Isis at Philae. Still more of the varied columns atop screen walls in the "Kiosk of Trajan."

LET'S LIBERATE THE TEMPLE

c. Historical Documents - Archaeology, the science of excavation, has helped clear and enabled the reconstruction of ancient Egyptian temples and in relation to its ancient civilization. The problem arose with the interpretation of the data trying to express the view, these Africans were Europeans. However, every "strawman" argument made has fallen apart.

i. The Narmer Palette - Found by Quibell at Hierakonpolis, Upper Egypt, first Capital of Egypt. This document illustrates the unification of Egypt.

ii. The Narmer Macehead - This is the King's weapon. Among other things, it shows his marriage to a Queen, claimed to be a political marriage to a Northerner but who is now believed to be a Southerner. It recounts the size of booty seized and indicates they were counting in the millions and how far mathematics had progressed at this early age.

iii. Palermo Stone -

iv. Turin Papyrus - Royal Papyrus of Turin

v. Manetho's Chronicles - He was a 2nd Century B.C. priest who had access to ancient sources. He wrote a *History of Egypt* and divided the ruling houses into dynasties. Modern scholars created Periods as Old, Middle and New Kingdoms, with attendant First, Second and Third Intermediate Periods. In the former the society flourished; in the latter, it stagnated. Though there were some minor problems or mistakes about Manetho's methods and facts, scholars have kept his "dynasties" for convenience.

FREDERICK MONDERSON

vi. **Tablets** - These are important historical documents helpful in providing names of kings and reinforced the delineation of the chronology.

a. **Abydos Tablet I** - Temple of Seti I - 19th Dynasty. Still in position or place or *in Situ*, it was discovered by Dumichen in 1864. It contained 76 kings' names from Menes to Seti I. Five names are blank. These, nevertheless belonged to Hatshepsut's because she ruled as king and later those associated with the "Amarna Heresy." These latter are Amenhotep IV or Akhnaton, Smenkare, Tutankhamon and Aye.

b. **Abydos Tablet II** - Temple of Rameses II of the 19th Dynasty. Now in the British Museum, it comes from the King's temple at Abydos.

c. **Sakkara Tablet** - found in the tomb of Thunurei (Tenroy) at Sakkara. This Royal scribe and "Chief reader" lived during the reign of Rameses II. Initially it had 58 names of which only 50 were visible at the time of discovery. Unlike most other artifacts, along with the Abydos Tablet I, it is still in place.

d. **Tablet of Karnak** - Created during the reign of Thutmose III. It had 64 names, 48 of which were readable when discovered. Its importance lies in its listing of XIth and XIII-XVII Dynasty Kings who had benefitted Karnak. It now resides in the Louvre, Paris, having been stolen by the Frenchman Prisse de Avennes.

e. **Steles/Colonnades** - These recount a king's commemoration or a person's exploits and recognition of service in the community. They also reflect a level of cultural attainment and explanations of a belief system concerning the future life. Colonnades are a decorative architectural motif that also praises an individual by "writing his name in the colonnade." Colonnades front buildings, cover vertical distances, support Kiosks (Taharka at Karnak), decorate

LET'S LIBERATE THE TEMPLE

Peristyle Courts or even have statues that seem to step-out from between such columns as at Luxor Temple. Of course, these decorate Hypostyle Halls. A Hypostyle Hall is a roofed room with columns while a peristyle is a line or set of columns in an open court without a roof.

f.   Cemeteries/Tombs - Underground disposal of the dead that contain "goods of the grave" or "mortuary furniture" that tells of the individual's life and hopes for and preparation for the future life in the next world. Cemeteries very early were violated either by animals or man. Of hillside tombs of the New Kingdom, especially, some were opened early, some remained hidden until modern times, while others were discovered, lost before being rediscovered. All depict wonderful art as part of magical provisioning for the next life.

II.   What has survived? - Much of what we know is based on speculation. For we possess no more than 20% of required data.

a.   Predynastic - Evidence indicates by Naqada times private chieftains acting as priests built primitive shrines as religious cult centers. Hierakonpolis as an early capital had a cult sanctuary. The Hunting Slate Palette, pottery evidence, the Gebel el-Arak knife, and the painted Tomb 100 at Hierakonpolis show trends toward cult practice. Palm and papyrus trees were used as support columns; an enclosed forecourt, the columnar portico and the frieze, later seen at Sakkara's Open Court and at Kom Ombo, now make their appearance.

b.   Old Kingdom - Temple and Tomb – In this early period, we see essentially grouped together, a Pyramid Complex - with Valley Temple, Mortuary Temple and Worship Temple. Texts indicate six sun temples were built during the 5th Dynasty but only two have been discovered, that of Userkaf and Nieusere at Abu Ghorab. Throughout the Old Kingdom more complex features were added. Stone was one such feature, evolving from building with mud and daub; this then gave birth to the craft of stone extraction or quarrying aided by mastery of river transportation to place of construction. The column in its many forms, first the pilaster and pillar emerged from excavated quarry supports then columns of papyrus, palm, and lotus as decorative features imitating nature now appear.

c.   Middle Kingdom - Transitional - Temple and Tomb are still together. Building materials were generally red and black granite together with sandstone. Beni-Hasan employed Proto-Doric columns. Again palm, papyrus and lotus columns persisted in use. The Kiosk and Pylon make their appearance at this time. The Osiride column was introduced at Medamud, temple of the Theban War-God Monthu.

Throughout the Old Kingdom, more complex features were added that persisted in temple building down through dynastic times. Stone became more prevalent and was aided by better coordinated river transportation especially when the river was high. The column in its many forms appear; first the pilaster and pillar emerging from quarry supports, then columns of papyrus, palm and lotus imitating nature began to be perfected.

d.   New Kingdom - Emergence of Worship, Mortuary and Processional Temples separately. - This was especially encouraged through the economic wealth of the Imperial Age that saw the building of monumental temples, both god or worship cult and mortuary temples of kings. While the palm column was used primarily in Nubia, in Egypt the papyrus and lotus forms dominated. The Osiris Pillar also played a role especially evident at Deir el Bahari, Karnak and Medinet Habu periods.

LET'S LIBERATE THE TEMPLE

Liberate the Temple. Temple of Isis at Philae. Even more varied capitals but also notice the double row of uraei.

Liberate the Temple. Temple of Isis at Philae. Still more varied columns atop the walls. Notice the Uraei to the left.

FREDERICK MONDERSON

Liberate the Temple. Temple of Isis at Philae. Another view of the colorfully magnificent "Kiosk of Trajan," called "Pharaoh's Bed."

Nevertheless, "The predominant form was the papyrus column: campaniform (open papyrus) columns lined the main axes of hypostyle halls, creating the clerestory zones in which windows to light the interior could be set, and were also used of form Processional Colonnades. By the 19th Dynasty, the papyrus-bud column had developed into a monostyle column, while the uraei surmounting the Hathor capital of the Middle Kingdom was replaced by a naos. The tent pole column of prehistoric derivation was adapted in stone in the *Akh Menu*, Festival Hall of Tuthmose III (c. 1479-c.1426 B.C.) at Karnak, which was an early New Kingdom innovation.

Kiosks - These are a small temple dedicated essentially to three gods with separate chambers for each with that of the principal male god in the center. The surviving ones are at Luxor - 18th Dynasty built by Queen Hatshepsut and dedicated to Amon, Mut and Khonsu of the Theban Triad. It was usurped by her nephew Thutmose and later Rameses II who built the "Ramessean Front" as an addition to the temple. A futile effort was made to erase her name. This kiosk was

LET'S LIBERATE THE TEMPLE

associated with the earlier temple Amenhotep III demolished to build his masterpiece.

Luxor - Built by her architect Senmut, Hatshepsut dedicated the Kiosk still, yet now located in the later "Ramessean Front" of Rameses II to the Theban Triad of Amon, Mut and Khonsu. Tuthmosis III later usurped the temple, erased her name, inserted his name and even alter Rameses II inserted his name there too.

Abydos - This Kiosk is dedicated to Seti I, Isis and Horus not Osiris. Wonderful relief paintings characterize this Kiosk as well as the general temple that is a major tourist attraction today.

Karnak - Built by Seti II of the 19th Dynasty, the Kiosk is dedicated to Amon, Mut and Khonsu and it is located in the Great Court. Karnak's and Luxor's Kiosks are separate outdoor temples while Abydos has an indoor compartment for this Kiosk.

e.   Graeco-Roman Temples at Kom Ombo, Edfu, Esneh, Dendera, Philae. Introduction of the Mammisi by Roman Times. It is the Birth place of God's son, but retain many pharaoh temple features such as layout, Nilometer and where possible a water source.

These temples are more profusely illustrated. The art becomes more sensual. These temples were built by Nubian and Egyptian architects based on the ancient plans but were supervised by Greek and Roman overlords. They preserved various aspects of the ritual and culture providing insights to the earliest practices.

FREDERICK MONDERSON

Liberate the Temple. Aswan. View of the river and surrounding area from the Old Cataract Hotel.

III. WHO IS DR. BEN-JOCHANNAN?

Dr. Yosef Antonio Alfredo was a "great light," an African intellectual, nationalist, master teacher and Egyptologist who "Took Egypt" to show African people the way! Dr. Ben always emphasized his students should pay attention to architectural features in the temple. He advised visit Karnak Temple's Hypostyle Hall 5 or 6 times to fully comprehend what it signifies in terms of architectural features, artistic decoration and ritual as represented in the visual images.

IV. THE ROLE OF THE TEMPLE

There are 2 principal temple forms, the worship or god temple and the mortuary or king temple! The Processional is another, a sort of "way side" temple designed to accommodate the Procession along the way from and to the main temple. Here the priest generally "rested" the god's bark along the journey from one sanctuary to another.

LET'S LIBERATE THE TEMPLE

a. WORSHIP TEMPLE – GOD'S HOUSE

i. The God's House - Built of stone, the God's house is a place where divinity was housed, protected, fed, nurtured and worshipped

ii. Daily practice of the ritual and worship of the god – A whole retinue of individuals were involved in preparation and practice of the daily ritual, but only a few got proximity to the god.

iii. The Nucleus of Celebration of Festivals - as the Opet Festival, Feast of the Valley, Heb Sed, Isis, Osiris, Sokar, etc., and king's coronation, first at Heliopolis and then in the National Temple. Such celebrations or "Festival," were an ongoing practice all year long.

iv. Dedication of a temple - Every temple was dedicated with a foundation ceremony. There, models of workmen's tools and a cartouche of the founder's name were placed on a bed of white sand. That is, after the king had "stretched the cord" or marked out the dimensions of the structure with a priest or queen impersonating the Goddess Seshat. Then an animal was killed in ceremony and the blood let to run. This ceremony was simply to begin the building process, preserve the identity of the builder and to bring fortune and success to the enterprise.

v. Especially in the New Kingdom, we see presentation of a King's material tribute and slaves. There the god accepts his gifts, then give the king a curved sword to conquer and scepter and whisk to rule and punish.

vi. Processions are part of the ritual -

These generally begin in the Hypostyle Hall but then parade throughout the temple. On important occasions such as the Opet Festival and the Feast of the Valley the processions leave the temple and travel towards the distant festivities.

b. Mortuary Temple - King's Temple -

It is dedicated to the dead king who becomes a god. He is worshipped therein alive if his reign is sufficiently long, but certainly when he dies, providing the requisite requirements are set in place.

i. King's Sacred Space -

There is a provisioning of the king's temple with the ritual of worship decoration on the walls and all the elements that grace the worship temple.

ii. Worship of King in life and when he becomes a god

upon death – Gone to meet his "brother gods" and becomes an imperishable star! While there is drama on earth there is also drama in the heavens and the king has to account, to his brother gods, for his actions on earth, when he returns "home." Consequently, he is held accountable for his actions as king and leader on earth.

iii. God visits Luxor Temple at the "Opet Festival."

The god leaves his abode at Karnak Temple in procession, travels by river while much of his retinue travel by canal to Luxor Temple to unite with and incubate with his wife Goddess Mut for 24 days of merrymaking and then returns to Karnak by canal and on land. There is much fanfare and joviality in the festival; all of which is depicted on the West and East Wall of the Processional Colonnade at Luxor.

LET'S LIBERATE THE TEMPLE

Liberate the Temple. Temple of Isis at Philae. Two image of Isis as Hathor, one defaced, the other betrays the "African mold" in her image.

Liberate the Temple. Aswan. One of the Hotel boats that cruise the Nile, now docked at Aswan with Memnon Hotel in rear.

FREDERICK MONDERSON

Liberate the Temple. Temple of Isis at Philae. An ape playing a stringed instrument in the "Kiosk of Hathor" at Philae Temple.

LET'S LIBERATE THE TEMPLE

Liberate the Temple. Temple of Isis at Philae. Again, two images of Isis as Hathor, one defaced, the other betrays the "African mold" in her image.

iv. The god travels by Procession and boat across the river for the "Feast of the Valley" on the west bank. There he visits the individual temples of the dead kings. This celebration can last for a number of days before the god's procession returns home from across the river.

v. God stays at Temple Palace. All New Kingdom monarchs built a Mortuary Temple, a "Mansion of Millions of Years," and each had a palace adjoining the First Court, so the King could "Visit the temple from his palace." Medinet Habu, mortuary Temple of Rameses III, has a surviving image of the king leaving his palace to enter the temple.

c. Processional Temple - A "halfway house" temple that functions as a rest area. One of the best preserved and most beautiful of these processional temples is the "White Chapel" of the 12th Dynasty Pharaoh Usertesen I, reconstructed and now on display in Karnak's Open-Air Museum.

FREDERICK MONDERSON

i. Wayside Temple or resting places used in Processions beyond the main Sanctuary. The best surviving examples are the: Kiosk in the Great Open Court at Karnak temple. The other is at Luxor in the "Ramessean Front" Peristyle Court of Rameses II.

ii. "White Chapel" - Senusert I - of the Middle Kingdom. Destroyed, it was discovered, reconstructed and now preserved in Karnak Temple's "Open Air Museum." This is a remarkable piece of art and architecture inundated with images, texts and numbers. With two opening and an elevated altar upon which the ark of the god rested when within; it is a photographic gem.

iii. "Red Chapel" Hatshepsut - New Kingdom - Also destroyed and then reconstructed and preserved in the "Open Air Museum." Hatshepsut's "Red Chapel" is thought to be Karnak Temple's early Sanctuary during the Queen's reign that was destroyed and replaced by Thutmose III in his vendetta against her rule. Thutmose's Sanctuary replaced hers and was later repaired by Philip Arredias, brother of Alexander the Great. It is now the surviving one in place.

The "Red Chapel" is richly illustrated with images of the Queen in various acts of piety and ritual praise of the god. Unfortunately, while the temple was demolished and had to be reconstructed in its present form, many of the images of the Queen were defaced, though a few have survived.

A regular dwelling was temporary but the god's house was built of stone to last for eternity. Thus, while the king's home, even palace, was built of perishable material, the god's house was built of stone and patterned after a substantial domestic structure of yard, portal, living room and bedroom. Quarrying and transportation of stone became an important industry and art.

LET'S LIBERATE THE TEMPLE

Liberate the Temple. Temple of Isis at Philae. View of "Trajan's Kiosk" from the river with the Great Pylon to the left, on the return trip home.

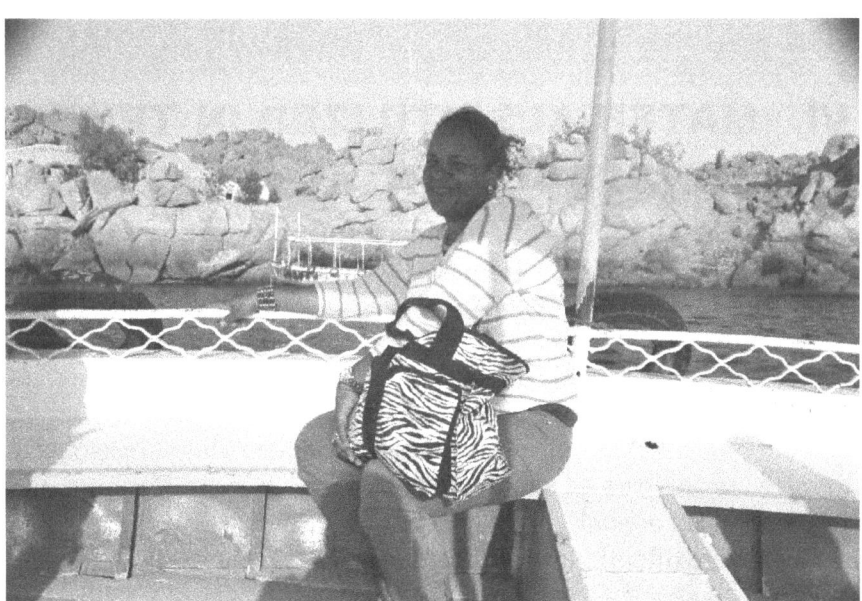

Liberate the Temple. Temple of Isis at Philae. Enjoying the boat-ride back to the taxi after an enlightening and spiritually moving view of ancient Africa at its most beautiful.

FREDERICK MONDERSON

Liberate the Temple. Temple of Isis at Philae. Some of the artifacts being sold at the boat terminal to and from Isis Temple.

VI. MATERIALS UTILIZED IN TEMPLE CONSTRUCTION

In the earliest times, temple construction utilized flimsy materials but as the culture advanced in wealth, consciousness and industry, more durable materials were quarried, transported over distances and erected as stone pillars or blocks of drums to create or work into columns, altars, statues and pedestals, walls, floors, architraves, column bases, stelae, ceilings and more. Granite, white limestone and more were all part of temple construction. Even more important, whether raised or sunk relief, images of kings and gods, the ritual and all such were oftentimes in color.

Egyptians very early mastered the art of quarrying and transportation of stone over great distances. The size of such undertakings reminds of the barge and size of Queen Hatshepsut's obelisks transported from Aswan to Karnak and depicted in her temple at Deir el Bahari.

LET'S LIBERATE THE TEMPLE

However, as early as the time of the pyramids, large stone was being transported over great distances. Significantly, in Gaston Maspero's *Manual of Egyptian Archaeology* (New York: G.P. Putnam's Sons, 1902: 47) the author offers insights to such issues. He states: "It is an error to suppose that the Egyptians employed only large blocks for building purposes. The size of their materials varied very considerably according to the uses for which they were destined. Architraves, drums of columns, lintel-stones, and door-jambs were sometimes of great size. The longest architraves known - those, namely, which bridge the nave of the hypostyle hall at Karnak - have a mean length of 30 feet. They each contain 40 cubic yards, and weigh about 65 tons…. They measure, that is to say, about 2 ½ to 4 feet in height, from 3 to 8 feet in length, and from 2 to 6 feet in thickness."

Interesting, depending on who the builder was, whether a single individual or the work done over an expanded time, sometimes one or more types of stone was used. For example, Hatshepsut's temple at Deir el Bahari, Rameses III's temple in the Great Court at Karnak, Rameses III's Medinet Habu or Rameses II's Abu Simbel, built by single monarchs generally choose one type of material, with the option of also use a variety of stone for select areas. However, temples such as Karnak, Dendera, Edfu and Philae, built over extensive periods of time, with many builders and architects, sometimes follow no particular pattern of the use of stone and so a variety may be employed. In this regard, Maspero (1902: 47-49) writes: "Some temples are built of only one kind of stone; but more frequently materials of different kinds are put together in unequal proportions. Thus, the main part of the temples of Abydos consist of very fine limestone; but in the temple of Seti I, the columns, architraves, jambs, and lintels - all parts, in short where it might be feared that the limestone would not offer sufficient resistance, - the architect has had recourse to sandstone; while in that of Rameses II, sandstone, granite, and alabaster were used. At Karnak, Luxor, Tanis, and Memphis, similar combinations may be seen. At the Ramesseum, and in some of the Nubian temples, the columns stand on massive supports of crude brick. The stones were dressed more or less carefully, according to the positions they were to occupy. When the walls were of medium thickness, as in most partition walls, they were well wrought on all sides. When the wall was thick, the core blocks were roughed out as nearly cubic as might be, and piled together without much care, the hollows being filled up with smaller flakes, pebbles, or mortar. Casing stones were carefully wrought on the faces, and the joints dressed for two-thirds or three-quarters of the length, the rest being merely picked with a point. The largest blocks were reserved for the lower parts of the building; and this precaution was the more necessary because the architects of Pharaonic times sank the foundations of their temples no deeper than those of their houses. At Karnak, they are not carried lower than 7 to 10 feet; at Luxor, on the side anciently washed by the river, three courses of masonry, each measuring 2 ½ feet in depth, form a great platform on which the walls rest; while at the Ramesseum, the brickwork bed on which the colonnade stands do not seem to be more than 10 feet deep. These are but slights depths for the foundations of such great buildings, but the experience of ages proves that they are sufficient. The hard and compact humus of which the soil of the Nile valley is composed, contracts every year with the subsidence of the inundation, and thus becomes almost incompressible. As the building progressed, the weight of the superincumbent masonry gradually became greater, till the maximum pressure was attained, and a solid basis secured."

In regards wall foundation of these temples, Maspero points to specific temples but more particularly other factors such as ceremonial practices, etc. In this, Maspero (1902: 49-50) writes: "In the Great Hall at Karnak I found them sound and firm, even after the fall of the columns in 1899. Especially from the Eighteenth Dynasty onwards it was customary at the building or rebuilding of a temple to place under the foundations of its walls deposits consisting of tiny specimens and models of the materials and articles to be used in the construction of the building, and in the service of its deity or deified builder. These foundation deposits are generally found in small pits filled with clean sand…. Among the glazed objects in this deposit were scarabs, plaques, models of offerings, besides many brilliant blue beads. The metal objects, made in thin sheet copper, include, adze, knife, axe-head, hoes and chisels. There are also many jars and little cups, an ebony cramp, model corn grinders."

LET'S LIBERATE THE TEMPLE

Liberate the Temple. Temple of Isis at Philae. With Satet at his rear, Horus (Heru) stands on a bed of trees while Isis (Auset) and Nephthys present. Unfortunately, all faces are defaced.

Liberate the Temple. Temple of Isis at Philae. Pharaoh stands before defaced enthroned figures of Osiris (Ausar), Isis (Auset), Nephthys (Nepthi) and Horus (Heru).

FREDERICK MONDERSON

Liberate the Temple. Temple of Isis at Philae. Close-up of an exquisite composite capital so characteristic of this temple.

Liberate the Temple. Gathering of Friends, Mr. Ibrahim Soliman (left) and Hammam Siddique Yosef (right) with others at Luxor. The driver (left rear) and Showki (right rear).

LET'S LIBERATE THE TEMPLE
VII. CONSTRUCTION AND LAYOUT OF THE TEMPLE

a.   Transition from perishable materials to stone Construction and decoration.

The Priesthood, an organized body of Priests with religious, economic and political power, trained architects and supervised all forms of architecture especially temple construction. As the wealth of the society increased, so too did the power of the priesthood, for they were involved in every facet of Egyptian life. They used that wealth and power to increase the dimensions, decoration and even extra-religious activities of the temple.

From reign to reign, kings endowed the temple establishment and, if we use Karnak as an example, expansion proceeded outward from the Sanctuary. The immediate Sanctuary area was beautified with supporting adjacent rooms, halls, decorated walls, columns and statues. Then pylons, courts, obelisks, altars, smaller temples, kiosks, all expanding along the central axis. So much so, we get to the final pylon and what lay beyond, whether an Avenue of sphinxes, additional temples or shrines, a further obelisk or two, and so on. If there is an important temple nearby, a second axis may be opened lining the principal and secondary temple through an Avenue of Sphinxes; sometimes even a canal. Often all is encapsulated in an Enclosure Wall, as well as a Sacred Lake, Nilometer, even a late addition Mammisi, and all may be counted within the layout of the temple. However, let us not forget gardens; flower and food; administrative buildings, housing and kitchens for staff and much more including space for teaching, perhaps a hospital, service center, art workshop, and industry factory, etc.

b.   Orientation of the Temple

i.   Axis - At first temples were generally built along the banks of the river but this changed and by Middle and New Kingdom times, the temples were then oriented along the East-West route of the sun - Important, statues along this route face the main axis. At Karnak, statues along the second axis face the first, not the second axis.

ii. Some temples have more than one axis - Karnak has 2; Luxor has 3; of which one is invisible under the floor.

iii. Individual temples have their own axis or axial line and may be oriented differently; oftentimes oriented toward some heavenly body.

iv. Mortuary temples on the West Bank at Thebes all seem oriented toward the principal axis of Karnak across the river.

c. Features -

i. This is a river culture with the Nile as the main Highway for Trade, Culture, Mortuary visits, Military ventures and Transportation of stone.

ii. A King's visit to the temple is an important occasion with great joy and fanfare surrounding such an occurrence.

d. Physical Layout of the Temple

i. **Pier at the River** where the King's entourage is greeted or the God's bark is bid farewell on some journey. On either occasion, there is much joy and celebration with music and fanfare.

ii. **A Canal from the river leads to an Avenue of Sphinxes**, then to the entrance which is part of the Enclosure Wall surrounding the temple.

LET'S LIBERATE THE TEMPLE

iii. **All temples have names** which the king generally assigns when stating his purpose for building the structure, whether it is for himself or for his god.

iv. **There are out-structures** before the entrance as part of the "Outer Periphery." Karnak had two small obelisks and ram-headed sphinxes with miniature statues of the king between the paws as well as some smaller structures. Nearby Luxor had 2 seated and 4 standing statues as well as 2 obelisks, all before the great pylon. Now only one obelisk is in place. At Luxor Temple, the entrance face of the pylon was decorated with events of the Battle of Kadesh. Hatshepsut's Deir el Bahari temple had a Valley Temple by the river's edge, a Causeway or walkway leading to the pylon with trees lining the way and "Ponds of Milk" or water pools adjacent for the god to consume.

e. Pylon or Gateway entrance - Openings on the Pylon's cornice hosts flag-staves that fly the temple, Nome and nation's flags. Again, some pylons are decorated and others are not depending on the state of completion. While Luxor was decorated, Karnak was not since it was unfinished.

f. Great Court within -

i. **Kiosk** - On the current Tourist Circuit there are only 3 surviving Kiosks at Karnak, Luxor and one within at Abydos, temple of Seti I. This architectural feature seems a New Kingdom invention that was discontinued afterwards.

ii. **Sphinxes** – These generally line a causeway or path to a temple. Karnak has sphinxes in its Court that previously lined the Avenue of Sphinxes outside, beyond the Pylon. A sphinx road linked Luxor and Karnak temples. It is now being cleared and reconstituted. There is a Sphinx Avenue linking Karnak and Mut Temples as well as another emanating from the Temple of Khonsu southward, yet inside the Karnak Enclosure. The principal Sphinx Road links Karnak with Luxor Temple, three miles away.

Liberate the Temple. Kom Ombo Temple of Horus and Sobek. View of the Columned Court, for the most part destroyed with the massive columns of the Hypostyle Hall in rear.

Liberate the Temple. Kom Ombo Temple of Horus and Sobek. Protected by Winged Hawks holding scepters and with sun-disks with uraei, Horus (Heru, left) and Sobek (right) squat holding Ankhs before two king's cartouches (Shennu) with plumes and sun-disks.

LET'S LIBERATE THE TEMPLE

Liberate the Temple. Kom Ombo Temple of Horus and Sobek. View from the north of the now generally destroyed columns of the Second or Inner Hypostyle Hall.

iii. **Altars** - For the most part there may be one or more in the Open Air First Court where invited guests could observe some ceremony. The "Holy of holies" has at least one altar.

iv. **Statues** - Dedicated to and by the temple builder. Sometimes if an official has distinguished himself he would be allowed to have a statue of himself placed in the temple. Amenhotep, Son of Hapu, one such individual who was the architect of Amenhotep III, had a statue placed in Karnak Temple's Hypostyle Hall and also permitted to build a Mortuary Temple at Thebes. In fact, several statues of him were discovered at Karnak. Deir el Bahari had more than a hundred statues of the queen. Temple of Mut had hundreds of statues of the Goddess Sekhmet placed there by Amenhotep III, the "Magnificent" of the 18th dynasty.

FREDERICK MONDERSON

**v.	Colonnades** - A line of columns of various numbers. They could be in a Hypostyle Hall or in a Peristyle Court or even fronting Kiosks. A Peristyle is a roofless structure while a Hypostyle is a roofed structure, a Hall.

**vi.	Small Temple** - "One Upmanship" as in the Case of Rameses III in Karnak's Great Court. There is another, the *Akh Menu*, Festival Temple of Thutmose III. Not only was the akh Menu built to celebrate Thutmose III's Heb Sed Festival, but it was the place where priests were trained. Karnak Temple was surrounded by some 21 large and small temples in its vicinity. These are temples built by a single king generally for a single deity.

**vii.	Obelisks** - These are placed before the pylon or in an open court within. The "good stone" for these monoliths was often quarried at Aswan, transported great distances by river to place of erection when the river was high; and then dressed and decorated at place of erection.

**g.	Hypostyle Hall** – This is where the Procession generally congregates for the ceremony or departs for an extra-temple journey. Its walls are, for the most part, illustrated.

**i.	Ritual on the Wall** - Pictures are arranged sequentially depicting the King's interaction with the Gods or the priests hoisting the God's Tabernacle. Again, as at Karnak, and elsewhere, the gods can be observed writing the king's name in the "Tree of Life." Surviving examples show Seti I having his name written in the "Tree of Life," in the northern half of the Hypostyle Hall, while on the south wall Rameses II's name is similarly written. At the Ramesseum, Rameses II's name is again written in the "Tree of Life."

**ii.	Columns** - Columns reflect the world at Creation, a sort of thicket field by the waterside. The base, shaft, capital, abacus that supports the overhead architrave, bridging the gap, are all oftentimes decorated. Sometimes the columns are undecorated. These columns

LET'S LIBERATE THE TEMPLE

are generally decorated with capitals of closed-bud, bundle papyrus or open lotus floral. At Karnak, while the processional colonnade sports open lotus, the flanking halls are decorated with closed bundle forms.

iii. Processions - Important events happen during Processions. The priests of Amon-Ra engineered the God's choice of Thutmose III to be king while he stood in line as the Procession passed by. These processions are conducted in the Hypostyle Hall, in the temple generally. The procession assembles here to begin extra-temple visits outside the enclosure wall.

h. Sanctuary – "The Bedroom of the God" where he resides in utter darkness. When the king visits the temple and sanctuary, he is said to "Open the Doors of Heaven." Only himself and the high priest may enter to conduct the god's lustration and ritual. Perhaps one or two, again higher echelon persons may assist the ceremony whether in kindling the fire, bringing water or attending to incense burning for fumigation.

i. Open Chamber - Karnak in two parts. In one part, the gods rest in darkness. The other, the god is placed there to be bathed by the rays of the sun.

ii. Closed Chamber - Luxor, Deir El Bahari, and Abu Simbel. After the Old Kingdom, when the Altar was placed in an Open Court, Closed Sanctuaries became the order of the day. The Sanctuary of Luxor Temple was rebuilt by Alexander the Great.

iii. There are Subsidiary Rooms for -

a. Liquid Offerings - Oils, unguents, perfumes

b. Solid Offerings - Food, statues, incense

c. Vestments - Clothing, jewelry, symbols

d. Bark stations for the Ark

e. Books of the Ritual

Liberate the Temple. Kom Ombo Temple of Horus and Sobek. Winged vulture wearing White Crown (top) and Red Crown (bottom) with outstretched wings decorate the ceiling of one of the halls.

LET'S LIBERATE THE TEMPLE

Liberate the Temple. Kom Ombo Temple of Horus and Sobek. Varied capitals of the columns, architrave and protective uraei.

Liberate the Temple. Kom Ombo Temple of Horus and Sobek. Native Egyptian Guide Showki Abd Rady point to image of Shu and Ma'at together.

FREDERICK MONDERSON

Liberate the Temple. Kom Ombo Temple of Horus and Sobek. Pharaoh presents a platter to Sobek, "Lord of Ombos."

f. Treasury - Storehouse of the Temple's and god's treasures and sacred emblems

g. Underground crypts safeguard temple valuables of gold and jewelry, statues, emblems. Their walls are oftentimes richly decorated.

h. Sacred Lake - for washing and other cleanliness of the priests who perform the ritual.

I. On festive nights, at Karnak especially, **sacred boats** are allowed to sail on the Sacred Lake.

1. Colonnades - a line of columns. This architectural feature was experimented with and developed in Egypt, nowhere else, by

LET'S LIBERATE THE TEMPLE

2800 B.C. The columns of the Southern Colonnade in Karnak Temple Great Court provide evidence of how these columns were erected as square slab sections before being pounded into round columns.

2.   Subsidiary Temples - for other Gods.

Seldom is a temple home to a single god. The god is always paired with a spouse and a son. Champollion called this feature the "Triad." But, in a national temple, there are other "visiting gods" who are accorded a shrine. That's why Karnak is also called "The Palaces." There were some "22 temples" of varying sizes scattered throughout the Karnak temple complex of the Northern, Southern and Central groups.

i.   Karnak had 15 gods in its Ennead

ii.   While Deir el Bahari was dedicated to Amon-Ra it also had individual Shrines to Hathor, Anubis, Ra-Horakhty, Hatshepsut and to her father Thutmose I.

iii.   Abu Simbel was dedicated to 4 Gods - Ra Horakhty, Amon Ra, Ptah and deified Rameses II.

iv.   Abydos was dedicated to 7 gods - Osiris, Isis and Horus, Gods of the Osiris Triad; Ra-Horakhty, Amon-Ra and Ptah, Great Gods of the Empire; and Seti I deified.

v.   Kom Ombo was dedicated to 2 gods, the Elder Horus or Haroeis and Sobek the Crocodile god.

Sir Gaston Maspero in *Manual of Egyptian Archaeology* (1902: 50-53) wrote:

1.   "The system of construction in force among the ancient Egyptians resembles in many respects that of the Greeks. The stones are often placed together with dry joints, and without the employment of any binding contrivance, the masons relying on the mere weight of the materials to keep them in place. Sometimes they are held together by metal clamps, or sometimes – as in the temple of Seti I, at Abydos – by dovetails of sycamore wood bearing the cartouche of the founder. Most commonly, they are united by a mortar-joint, more or less thick.

2. All the mortars of which I have collected samples are thus far of three kinds: the first is white, and easily reduced to an impalpable power, being of line only; the others are grey, and rough to the tough, being mixtures of lime and sand; while some are of a reddish color, owing to the pounded brick powder with which they are mixed.

3. The enclosure walls, partitions, and secondary facades were upright; and they raised the materials by means of a rude kind of crane planted on the top. The pylon walls and the principal facades (and sometimes even the secondary facades) were sloped at an angle which varied according to the taste of the architect. In order to build these, they formed inclined planes, the slopes of which were lengthened as the structure rose in height.

4. [Problems developed because] The mason who had inadvertently hoisted too large a block, no longer troubled themselves to lower it back again, but worked it into the building in one or other ways before mentioned. The architect neglected to duly supervise the dressing and placing of the blocks. He allowed the courses to vary, and the vertical joints, two or three deep, to come one over the other. When utilizing the materials taken from ancient ruined edifices, he would not even take the trouble to work them into fit shape for their new places; round shafts of older columns were thus intermixed with rectangular walls of the Ramesseum.

5. The rough work done, the masons dressed down the stone, reworked the joints, and overlaid the whole with a coat of cement or stucco, colored to match the material, which concealed the faults of the real work. The walls rarely end with a sharp edge. Bordered with a torus, around which is sculptured riband is entwined, they are

LET'S LIBERATE THE TEMPLE

crowned by the cavetto cornice surmounted by a flat band or, as at Semneh, by a square cornice; or, as at Medinet Habu, by a lien of battlements. Thus, framed in, the walls look like enormous panels, each panel complete in itself, without projections and almost without openings.

6.   Windows, always rare in Egyptian architecture, are mere ventilations when introduced into the walls of temples, being intended to light the staircases, as in the second pylon of Horemhab at Karnak, or else to support decorative woodwork on festival days. The doorways project but slightly from the body of the buildings, except where the lintel is overshadowed by a projecting cornice. Real windows occur only in the pavilion of Medinet Habu; but that building was constructed on the model of a fortress and must rank as an exception among religious monuments.

7.   The ground level of the courts and halls was flagged with rectangular stones, well enough fitted, except in the intercolumniations, where the architects, hopeless of harmonizing the lines of the pavement with the curved bases of the columns, have filled in the space with small pieces, set without order or method. Contrary to their practice when building in brick, they scarcely ever employed the vault or arch in temple architecture.

8.   Stone vaulting is, however, met with at Deir el Bahari, and in the seven parallel sanctuaries of Abydos. Even in these instances, the arch is produced by 'corbelling;' that is to say, the curve is formed by three or four superimposed horizontal courses of stone chiseled out of the form required. The ordinary roofing consists of flat paving slabs. When the space between the walls was not too wide, these slabs bridged it over at a single stretch; otherwise the roof had to be supported at intervals, and the wider the space the more these supports needed to be multiplied. The supports were connected by immense stone architraves, on which the roofing slabs rested.

9.   The supports are of two types – the pillar and the column. Some are cut from single blocks. Thus, the monolithic pillars of the temple of the sphinx, the oldest hitherto found, measured 16 feet in height by 4 ½ feet in width. Monolithic columns of red granite are also found among the ruins of Alexandria, Bubastis, and Memphis, which date from the reigns of Horemhab and Rameses II, and measure some 20 to 26 feet in height. But columns and pillars are commonly built in courses, which are often unequal and irregular, like those of the walls which surround them. The great columns of Luxor are not even solid, two-thirds of the diameter being filled up with yellow cement, which has lost its strength, and crumbles between the fingers. The capital of the column of Taharka at Karnak contains three courses, each about 4.8 inches high. The last and most projecting course is made up of twenty-six convergent stones, which are held in place by merely the weight of the abacus. The same carelessness which we have already noticed in the workmanship of the walls is found in the workmanship of the columns.

10. The quadrangular pillar, with parallel or slightly inclined sides, and generally without either base or capital, frequently occurs in tombs of the ancient empire. It reappears later at Medinet Habu, in the temple of Thutmose III, and again at Karnak, in what is known as the processional hall. The sides of these square pillars are often covered with painted scenes, while the front faces were more decoratively treated, being sculptured with lotus or papyrus stems in high relief, as on the pillar-stelae of Karnak, or adorned with a head of Hathor crowned with the sistrum, as in the small speos of Ibsambul or sculptured with a full-length standing figure of Osiris, as in the second court of Medinet Habu; or, as at Denderah and Gebel Barkal, where the figure of the forms fall into three types: (1) the column with campaniform, or lotus-flower capital; (2) the column with lotus-bud capital; (3) the column with Hathor-head capital."

LET'S LIBERATE THE TEMPLE

Liberate the Temple. Kom Ombo Temple of Horus and Sobek. Two entrances to the Double Temple of Horus (left) and Sobek (right). Notice the twin sun-disk with uraei above the entrance architrave.

Liberate the Temple. Kom Ombo Temple of Horus and Sobek. On a paneled wall at the entrance, while Sobek watches, Horus (Elder Horus, center) and Thoth (Tehuti, right) baptize the king before he enters the temple.

FREDERICK MONDERSON

Liberate the Temple. Kom Ombo Temple of Horus and Sobek. Pharaoh presents a platter to Sobek while Hathor "Got his back."

VIII. ROLE AND SYMBOLISM OF THE KING

i.   On Earth - The role of the king is to maintain harmony and equilibrium in the state and among his people. He does this principally by ruling within the philosophic construct of Ma'at, symbolizing justice, truth, righteousness, fairness and equality. Equally too, he also officiates in the temples through worshipping and ritualizing the gods. In turn, he is admonished, bring bounty and good fortune to the state. On the West Bank of the Nile where his Mortuary Temple is located, literary references mention the king entering the temple from his adjacent palace.

ii.   The King enters the temple as Sanctuary wearing sandals and holding a scepter, preceded by several Nome Standards and ecclesiastic individuals.

LET'S LIBERATE THE TEMPLE

iii. Every time he enters the temple, he undergoes baptism or purification at the hands of priests impersonating Thoth and Horus. We often see this depicted on a panel on the outer wall of the temple itself or pronaos or hypostyle Hall as at Edfu, Kom Ombo and Dendera.

iv. Respective goddesses present him the crowns of Upper (White) and Lower (Red) Egypt.

v. He is then led by goddesses/gods into the presence of the temple god/gods where he performs the ritual.

vi. Oftentimes he enters the Sanctuary or "Holy of Holies," alone. He breaks the door's seal, enters and converses with the god. Throughout the ceremony the king or high priest sings, praises and incenses the god. He conducts the ritual of bathing, dressing, rouging, dressing the eyes with black paint. Incense is never burned on an altar but in an incenser placed in a corner.

FREDERICK MONDERSON

Liberate the Temple. Kom Ombo Temple of Horus and Sobek. Into the deep-recesses of the temple, past the columned and succeeding halls, the Sanctuary area of God Sobek (right).

LET'S LIBERATE THE TEMPLE

Liberate the Temple. Kom Ombo Temple of Horus and Sobek. Into the deep-recesses of the temple, past the columned and succeeding halls, the Sanctuary area of God Horus (left).

FREDERICK MONDERSON

Liberate the Temple. Kom Ombo Temple of Horus and Sobek. The "Eye of Horus" as a shrine for the god's image.

vii. Then he retreats, removes his footprints with a broom; closes the door; then affixes a seal, until the next visit. Naturally, the god has to be washed, his toilet done, perfumed, lipstick and then fed his meal before the king retires until the next visit.

viii. In the Heavens - The Sun God is born on the morning around 4:00 am. Equally, the lustration of the Sun God in the heavens is mirrored in the morning baptism of the cultic image in the temple's sanctuary. The morning baptism of the king in the *Per Dwet* or "House of the Morning" follows the same lustration of the sun god's and his cultic image in the temple's Sanctuary.

ix. The red ball we see before sun-up is the god's afterbirth

x. In that daily cleansing the Sun-god's bath attendants wash, powder and lipstick and comb his hair. He is then massaged, fed and

LET'S LIBERATE THE TEMPLE

slapped on the bottom and told "Go, do your job" of sailing across the heavens to bring light, life and joy to humanity.

xi. In the morning, the sun is young; at Midday - he is mature; at evening-time he is an old man.

xii. Then he travels the underworld to arrive at the other end of the heavens to be reborn again. In that passage he meets Osiris, God of the Dead and King of the Underworld. Thus, Ra and Osiris meet, greet and strategize then part, each to continue his functions and responsibilities. At this place of purity, other gods are also born and live.

xiii. That is to say, Ra has to pass through the underworld to arrive at the eastern horizon. In this passage, the heavenly kingdom meets the earthly kingdom of the dead God Osiris. In the night realm, the sun god shines his rays for no more than an hour on and refreshes the earthly dead who earnestly look forward to this perennial but brief rejuvenation.

xiv. The god's enemies fight to hinder the boat of the sun in the night sky, but to no avail. Two fishes, Abtu and Ant swim as "outriders" who protect the boat of the Sun-God. Even the evil Seth was once said to sail in the Boat of Ra, perhaps doing a one-time act of goodness in protecting the god.

Liberate the Temple. Kom Ombo Temple of Horus and Sobek. Deface image of the King before standards.

IX. DECORATION OF THE TEMPLE

a. **Ritual** - These are found mainly in Books of Papyrus and on interior Walls. The Ritual of the temple was displayed on the walls. The Books contained more than was evident on the walls. Its contents had to be recited in the worship service and sometimes as the procession moved along.

b. **King in Adoration of the Gods on the Interior** - Some parts of the temple only the King was permitted to enter along with a few high echelon priests who assisted in performance of the ritual.

c. **Enclosure Walls** – Huge in size to afford protection for the temple occupants, helps this feature to muff sounds performed in the temple. In the external decoration, the King is shown fighting the god's and temple's enemies, moral and spiritual; that is Bad people and Bad spirits. Within the temple he is shown worshipping and interacting with the gods, even receiving their blessing.

d. **Botanical Garden** – The garden provided flowers for daily ritual and fruits for wine, beer as well as funeral garlands and bouquets. Gardens helped brighten the Egyptian spirit and its trees were used for shade. While tombs displayed evidence of gardens and flowers, the earliest Garden discovered was that of Amten who supplied flowers to temples. Evidence shows King Thutmose III being presented a huge bouquet.

e. **Deir el Bahari** - Temple of Queen Hatshepsut. The architect Senmut patterned this temple after the nearby Middle Kingdom temple of Mentuhotep II.

i. **Separated into three ascending parts**; that is, the Lower, Middle and Upper Colonnade or Terrace. These were again divided by two ramps that gave access from the first to the second to the third levels, ascended from the First and Second Courts. The

LET'S LIBERATE THE TEMPLE

Lower Colonnade is decorated with birds and fishes on the left and the Obelisk Colonnade to the right. The Middle Colonnade has to its left, from the visitors' view, the "Punt Expedition" and further to the left, the Hathor Shrine. To the right, lies the "Birth Colonnade" and still further right the Anubis Shrine. The "Punt Colonnade" is important because it depicts a voyage to the East African coast of Punt, today's Somali. It provides the earliest anthropological study of a people and culture.

ii.   The Obelisk Colonnade depicts, transport of two obelisks to be erected at Karnak. One still stands to this day. An illustration at Deir el Bahari depicts 4 obelisks. Evidence of 6 obelisks was found at the quarry in Aswan. There is also an unfinished Obelisk at Aswan. Because obelisk are single pieces of stone, when during extraction, a fissure was observed, the obelisk was abandoned and remains as a curio to this day.

iii.   The story recounting Hatshepsut's divine birth depicted in the "Birth Colonnade" is similarly shown at Luxor Temple involving Amenhotep III in which divine parentage is postulated. The concept of divine intervention in human affairs to procreate dates to the Old Kingdom when a priest's wife, Rutet, was notified three sons of her loins would become kings of Egypt. Apparently, Khufu, Khafre and Menkaure, builders of the Great Pyramids at Ghizeh were the foretold kings. However, in addition to Hatshepsut and Amenhotep III, Alexander the "Great" also had a similar revelation.

1.   The fragments of architraves and masonry bearing the name of Khafre, which were used for building material in the modern pyramid of Lisht, show that this primitive simplicity had already been abandoned by the time of the Fourth Dynasty. During the Theban period, all smooth surfaces, all pylons, wall-faces, and shafts of columns, were covered with figure-groups and inscriptions. Under the Ptolemies and the Caesars, figures and hieroglyphs became so crowded that the stones on which they are sculptured seem to be lost under the masses of ornament with which they were charged.

FREDERICK MONDERSON

2.   We recognize that these scenes are not placed at random. They follow in sequence, are interlinked, and form, as it were a great mystic book in which the official relations and responsibilities between gods and men, as well as between men and gods, are clearly set forth for such as are skilled to read them.

3.   The temple was built in the likeness of the world, as the world was known to the Egyptians. The earth, as they believed, was a flat and shallow plane, longer than its width. The sky, according to some, extended overhead like an immense iron ceiling, and according to others, like a huge shallow vault. As it could not remain suspended in space without some support, they imagined it to be held in place by four immense props or pillars. The floor of the temple naturally represented the earth. The columns, and if needful the four corners of the chambers, stood for the pillars. The roof, vaulted at Abydos, flat elsewhere, corresponded exactly with the Egyptian idea of the sky. Each of these parts was, therefore, decorated in consonance with its meaning.

4.   The bases of the columns were surrounded by leaves, and the lower parts of the walls were adorned with long stems of lotus or papyrus, in the midst of which animals were occasionally depicted. Bouquets of water-plants emerging from the water enlivened the bottom of the well-space in certain chambers. Elsewhere, we find full-blown flowers interspersed with buds, or tied together with cords; or those emblematic plants which symbolize the union of Upper and Lower Egypt under the rule of a single Pharaoh; or birds with human hands and arms, perched in an attitude of adoration on the sign which represents a solemn festival; or kneeling prisoners tied to the stake in couples, each couple consisting of an Asiatic and Negro. Male and female Nile Gods, laden with flowers and fruits, either kneel, or advance in majestic procession, along the ground level. In one instance, at Karnak, Thutmose III caused the fruits, flowers, and animals indigenous to the foreign lands which he had conquered, to be sculptured on the lower courses of his walls. Some have argued these were essentially African flora and fauna. The ceilings were painted blue, and sprinkled with five-pointed stars painted yellow,

LET'S LIBERATE THE TEMPLE

occasionally interspersed with the cartouches of the royal founder. The monotony of this Egyptian heaven was also relieved by long bands of hieroglyphic inscriptions.

5. The vultures of Nekheb and Uati, the goddesses of the south and north, crowned and armed with divine emblems, hovered above the name of the side of the lintels of the great doors, above the head of hypostyle halls, and on the [under] the king as he passed on his way to the sanctuary. At the Ramesseum, at Edfu, at Philae, at Denderah, at Ombos, at Esneh, the depths of the firmament seemed to open to the eyes of the faithful, revealing the dwellers therein. There the celestial ocean poured forth its floods navigated by the sun and moon with their attendant escort of planets, constellations, and decani; and there also the genii of the months and days marched in long procession.

6. The decoration of the architraves which supported the massive roofing slabs was entirely independent of that of the ceiling itself. On these were wrought nothing save boldly cut inscriptions, in which the beauty of the temple, the names of the builder-kings who had erected it, and the glory of the gods to whom it was consecrated, are emphatically celebrated. Finally, the decoration of the lowest part of the walls and of the ceiling was restricted to a small number of subjects, which were always similar; the most important and varied scenes being suspended, as it were between earth and heaven, on the sides of the chambers and the pylons.

FREDERICK MONDERSON

Liberate the Temple. Kom Ombo Temple of Horus and Sobek. While Isis sits on the Birth Chair (left), today's recognized medical instruments are displayed (center) and a basin for the Physician to wash his hands after the Operation (right).

Liberate the Temple. Kom Ombo Temple of Horus and Sobek. Pharaoh presents a plant to Horus with Shu and Sekhmet at is rear.

LET'S LIBERATE THE TEMPLE

Liberate the Temple. Kom Ombo Temple of Horus and Sobek. Pharaoh presents a jeweled girdle to Hathor as Isis (Ausar) with Nephthys at her rear.

7. Regarding the official relations which subsisted between Egypt and the gods, the people had no right of direct intercourse with the deities. They needed a mediator, who partaking of both human and divine nature, was qualified to communicate with both. The king alone, Son of the Sun, was of sufficiently high descent to contemplate the god in his temple, to serve him, and to speak with him face to face. Sacrifices could be offered only by him, or through him, and in his name. Even the customary offerings to the dead were supposed to pass through his hands, and the family availed themselves of his name in the formula *suten ta hotep* to forward them to the other world. The king is seen, therefore, in all parts of the temple, standing, seated, kneeling, slaying the victim, presenting the parts, pouring out the wine, the milk, and the oil, and burning the incense. All humankind acts through him, and through him performs its duty towards the gods.

FREDERICK MONDERSON

8. When the ceremonies to be performed required the assistance of many person, then alone did mortal subordinates (consisting, as much as possible, of his own family) appear by his side. The queen, standing behind him, shakes the sistrum, beats the tambourine to dispel evil spirits, or hold the libation vase or bouquet. The eldest son carries the net or lassoes the bull and recites the prayer while his father successively presents to the god each object prescribed by the ritual. A priest may occasionally act as substitute for the prince, but other men perform only the most menial offices. They are slaughters or servants, or they bear the boat or canopy of the god. The god, for his part, is not always alone. He has his wife and his son by his side; next after them the gods of the neighboring nomes, and, in a general way, all the gods of Egypt. From the moment that the temple is regarded as representing the world, it must, like the world, contain all gods, both great and small. They are most frequently ranged behind the principal god, seated and standing; and with him they share in the homage paid by the king. Sometimes, however, they take an active part in the ceremonies.

9. The sun, traveling from east to west, divided the universe into two worlds, the world of the north and the world of the south. The temple, like the universe, was double, and an imaginary line passing through the axis of the sanctuary divided it into two temples – the temple of the south on the right hand, and the temple of the north on the left. The gods and their various manifestations were divided between these two temples, according as they belonged to the northern or southern hemisphere. This fiction of duality was carried yet further. Each chamber was divided, in imitation of the temple, into two halves, the right half belonging to the south, and left half to the north. The royal homage, to be complete, must be rendered in the temple of the south and of the north, and to the gods of the south and of the north, and with the products of the south and of the north. Each sculptured tableau must, therefore, be repeated at least twice in each temple – on the right wall and on a left wall. Amen, on the right, receives the corn, the wine, the liquids of the south; while on the left he receives the corn, the wind, and the liquids of the north. As with Amen, so with Maut, Khonsu, Mentu, and many other gods.

LET'S LIBERATE THE TEMPLE

10. In Pharaonic times, the tableaux were not over-crowded. The wall-surface intended to be covered was marked off below by a line carried just above the ground level decoration, and was bounded above by the usual cornice, or by a frieze. This frieze might be composed of uraei, or of bunches of lotus; or of royal cartouches supported on either side by divine symbols; or of emblems borrowed from the local cult (by heads of Hathor, for instance, in a temple dedicated to Hathor); or of a horizontal line of dedicatory inscription engraved in large and deeply cut hieroglyphics. The wall space thus framed in contained sometimes a single scene and sometimes two scenes, one above the other. The wall must be very lofty, if this number is exceeded. Figures and inscriptions were widely spaced, and the scenes succeeded one another with scarcely a break.

X. THE TEMPLE AS UNIVERSITY AND COMMUNITY CLEARING HOUSE I

Science, education, theology, music and medicine was taught in these temple schools.

Priests were taught here and they were taught to specialize in various disciplines.

In medicine priests were taught to specialize in one organ or part of the body or in one medicine area. None trespassed on the area of specialization of the other. Whether medicine, surgery or dentistry, all were practiced as early as the Old Kingdom. In all this they were able to create a pharmacopeia of natural herbal or concocted medicines.

FREDERICK MONDERSON

XI. THE TEMPLE AS UNIVERSITY AND COMMUNITY CLEARING HOUSE II

The role of the temple and its priestly body affected all aspects of Egyptian society. First and foremost, earthly life was regulated by the moral imperative called *Ma'at*. *Ma'at* insists on everything good. It stood in opposition to *Isfit*, meaning evil. Ma'at meant order, truth, balance, justice, goodness, righteousness, you name it. The Egyptians believed their god created Ma'at and it was the moral and ethical rule to live by. Ma'at endured from the beginning of time and he who lived by Ma'at could stand confidently before his god at the time of judgment in the next life.

The Temple establishment trained craftsmen and they sold their craft. They encouraged competing schools of art and craft. They had ships which played a crucial role in domestic and foreign trade. As administrators and trainers of the government bureaucracy, these specialists conducted re-surveying of the land after the Inundation or overflowing of the Nile to pinpoint land markers so farmers could resume planting agricultural products. They collected their taxes, paid workers in-kind and reported to the pharaoh.

Persons in need of documents such as letters, wills, other papers, received legal representation paying priests who functioned from the temple as clearing-house. In temple schools, astronomy and astrology was observed and taught; science and medicine; philosophy and dance; music, art and architecture were practiced and taught; and statuary was made and art manufactured.

The temple had thousands of animals, cows, pigs, goats, chickens, so they had to practice animal husbandry. They taught farmers this craft

LET'S LIBERATE THE TEMPLE

and how to farm more efficiently so their crops would be more bountiful and in turn pay taxes which the priests collected.

So, therefore, the temple was at the heart of the culture teaching practical skills and moral and ethical beliefs while continuing to practice the religious and spiritual obligations of ritualizing the gods and bringing harmony to the state. As such, then, the temple came to play an awesome role in shaping all aspects of the society.

Liberate the Temple. Kom Ombo Temple of Horus and Sobek. Pharaoh and his alter-ego (twin) present two ointment jars and a Platter to Horus in double Red and White Crowns with Hathor in horns and disk beside him.

FREDERICK MONDERSON

Liberate the Temple. Kom Ombo Temple of Horus and Sobek. With Sobek's wife and son at his rear, Pharaoh makes a Presentation.

Liberate the Temple. Kom Ombo Temple of Horus and Sobek. Wearing White Crown and Red Crown, two Pharaoh images make Presentations to Hathor and Nephthys.

LET'S LIBERATE THE TEMPLE
XII. THE TEMPLE AS ECONOMIC ENGINE AND MORAL TUTOR OF THE SOCIETY

The Egyptian Temple was more than a religious institution engaged in art, architecture, science and even trade. Because the Priesthood was responsible for administering the wealth of the god and the state, its jurisdiction extended beyond the temple. Much of the land owned by the king and the land of the god structured as endowment was either worked by temple staff or leased to nobles who, in turn worked it and remitted taxes "in kind."

While the King commissioned the temple and oftentimes made an endowment, it was up to temple staff to parlay such, conquest booty and citizen donations into viable economic ventures that assured economic survivability. While much of grown or donated produce were either consumed, paid as wages or marketed in trade, the temples engaged in crafts and literary functions, viz., writing letters, preparing wills, and other functions as Help Centers that extended their usefulness. Much craft and jewelry were bartered, oftentimes in "International Trade" which equally spread Egyptian ideas and cultural practices. However, while t his was significant, the temple equally functioned as a moral tutor of the society particularly because of its insistence and practice of Ma'at and upheld the idea pf purity in though, word and deed. This philosophic and moral objective in admonition helped shape moral behavior across the society and ages and as such, the temple became multifunctional in its utility. Together to this we may add its instructional role as College and University that trained priests, government bureaucracy and deserving noble and other citizens. Its role in the exploration and practice of science, medicine, philosophy and naturally art and architecture, study of the Nile river's behavior and lending assistance to farmers to enhance their agricultural cultivation, all contributed to making the temple more than just a place of ritual and worship. The temple thus served many functions but more particularly it was an economic engine and moral tutor of the society.

FREDERICK MONDERSON

XIII. THE SANCTUARY
By
Dr. Fred Monderson

The especial designation ancient Egyptian Sanctuary, has been applied both to the temple itself and also to the particular spot or location within where the image of the god resides. That is, viewed from a distance, the temple is the Sanctuary of the god. Viewed from within the temple, the Sanctuary is the "Holy of Holies" where the image of the god rests in the quiet solitude of his darkened abode. In the latter instance specifically, it is unique but also the most important part of the temple.

Generally different from most other religious sanctuaries where the ceremonies are performed; the Egyptian Sanctuary has its own special peculiarities. For example, in a Christian church, the congregation gathers in the Sanctuary to hear and participate in the ceremony. However, it was not so in an ancient Egyptian Sanctuary. First, the general public never ascends into the inner regions of the temple; only members of the high priesthood do. Located beyond or adjacent to the Sanctuary itself, the "Holy of Holies," is never visited by anyone except the king and a designated high priest. Naturally, they are assisted by deputies who play the musical instruments, sing the songs, read the verses, burn the incense, carry the solid and liquid offerings, etc. Nevertheless, and except as active participants, even while the god's covered statue in the sacred bark may be observed in the Procession outside the "Holy of Holies" and within and outside the temple as seen by the general public, these people are not privileged to enter or view the divinity in his sacred realm. Still, on the holiest festivals, the god's image is sometimes bared briefly to the "Faithfull's gaze" for an instant peek! Importantly, however, it should also be pointed out, the iconic Dr. ben-Jochannan always instructed his students to never enter the Sanctuary because, he reiterated, in ancient times only the high priest or pharaoh could access the spot and behold the god, converse with him, enjoy the ambience of the chamber and even participate in the ritual dynamics of his resting place.

LET'S LIBERATE THE TEMPLE

However, having said such, a number of factors can be pointed out regarding the Sanctuary in ancient Egypt.

One of the most important purposes and intent of the Sanctuary has been as a place of shelter for the god's manifestation on earth. In addition, because the Egyptians invested their god with human attributes, lustration and sustenance became necessities on a daily basis and this was incorporated into the official liturgy of worship. Again, and as pointed out elsewhere, the lustration of the god in the heavens is the same as was done for his image in the Sanctuary; the same liturgy undergone by the king in the "House of the Morning," was equally done before he entered the temple. This was similarly done to the dead pharaoh before the burial. However, with some modification, the temple itself was baptized, every section, quarter, room, to come alive so the king could participate and lead in the daily ritual.

"The whole object of official worship, as represented in the temple reliefs, was to obtain the favor of the divinities for the Pharaoh. In return for the offering which he presents to them they provide him victory, gladness, life, stability, health, good fortune, abundance, millions of years, the duration of Re, an eternity of jubilees, etc. The very temples of the gods were erected by the king that he might receive in return the 'duration of heaven,' 'hundreds of thousands of years,' and that he might 'be granted eternity as king.' Thus, the designation of every ritual act, 'giving [var. doing] this or that to [for] his father [var. mother] NN.' Is followed by the words 'in order that he may make an 'Endowed-with-life' like Ra forever,' the 'Endowed-with-life' being the king himself."

In the beginning when the god arose from the murky depths of the primeval ocean, he stood up on a sacred mound and as the waters receded, shelter was required. It has been postulated that the first architects were priests. Consequently, in contact with divinity, they were divinely instructed on how to construct the shelter or Sanctuary. At first, this was simply a basic lean-to covering with a rag on a flag pole to indicate a sacred place. It also had a fence to keep out animals and people. As the society matured, the god's home became more sophisticated being built with more lasting materials, first brick then stone.

Though there were several versions of creation, that of the Sun-God at Heliopolis predominated in the earliest times and the king was regarded as the Son of the Sun-God and also his High Priest. Nonetheless, in syncretized coordination, his name and some of his religious features persisted throughout dynastic rule. The temple ritual also depicts the king as sole officiant. However, because he could not be in every temple, for every god across the country, he created subordinates to officiate for every god and temple throughout the land empowering them to conduct the daily ritual. These holy men, were then organized and headed an umbrella organization, the Priesthood. This is also the time when much of the religious ritual became standard practice across the land and for the duration of dynastic rule. Of significance, and given such, when the pharaoh visited the temple's Sanctuary he was accompanied by his second, the high priest, with both leading the procession containing the requisite utilities for the ritual. Then he would break the seal over the closed door and enter, offering some greeting. As this was, however, infrequent, the high priest did so several times on a daily occurrence; thus, his actions were dictated by a prescribed liturgy. There was uniformity of this practice throughout the land. That is to say, what the pharaoh did in one temple, he did in the next and the priest followed suit.

Recently, I visited Egypt and traveled to a small temple in the desert at El Kab, accompanied by my Native Egyptian Guide Showgi Abd-Rady. After the doors were opened, he said, "Let me go in first!" Once inside he then offered a greeting, "Hotep!" to the kneeling figure facing the door. Not as similarly brief, yet, this is not unlike the greeting the pharaoh or high priest would offer in salutation as they entered the God's space. Adolf Erman best explains this dynamic which occurred in approach to the god's darkened space, to begin the three occurrences of the daily ritual, i.e., incense, toilet, cleansing and feeding, then a parting greeting. He states, for example, at Abydos, in which the ritual was not dissimilar to that of Karnak; the priest began communication with the God offering incense from within the adjacent Hypostyle Hall. And accordingly, Erman (1894: 273-74)

LET'S LIBERATE THE TEMPLE

recited: "I come into thy presence O great one, after I have purified myself. As I passed by the goddess Tefnut, she purified me ... I am a prophet, and the son of a prophet of this temple. I am a prophet, and I come to do what ought to be done, but I do not come to do what ought not to be done."

Liberate the Temple. Kom Ombo Temple of Horus and Sobek. Pharaoh presents "Two Eyes of Horus" to Elder Horus with Hathor at his rear.

Liberate the Temple. Kom Ombo Temple of Horus and Sobek. Presentation of an Ape (cynocephalus) to Hathor and Bastet.

FREDERICK MONDERSON

Liberate the Temple. Kom Ombo Temple of Horus and Sobek. Principal Pharaoh makes a Presentation of a Cartouche or Shennu to Horus.

Therefore, for the most part, as an example, at Karnak the Sanctuary sits alone outdoors detached just to the rear of the Hypostyle Hall separated by one or more courts decorated with obelisks, statues, chambers, beyond the *Ouadjyt*! However, at Abydos the shrine is just atop the incline beyond the Second Hypostyle Hall within the covered temple. Nevertheless, and as such, "He then stepped in front of the shrine of the god and opened the seal of clay with these words. 'The clay is broken and the seal loosed that this door may be opened, and all that is evil in me I throw (thus) on the ground.' When the Door was opened, he first incensed the sacred uraeus snake, the guardian of the god, greeting it by all its names; he then entered the Holy of Holies, saying: 'Let thy seat be adorned and thy robes exalted; the princes of the goddess of heaven come to thee, they descend from heaven and from the horizon that they may hear praise before thee.... He then approached the 'great seat,' *i.e.*, that part of the shrine where the statue of the god stood, and said: 'Peace to the god, peace to the god, the living soul, conquering his enemies. Thy soul is with me, thine image

LET'S LIBERATE THE TEMPLE

is near me; the king brought to thee thy statue, which lives upon the presentation of the royal offerings. I am pure.'"

However, as already stated, since the pharaoh only occasionally participated in the daily ritual which dictated the god be awoken, incensed, lustrated or having his morning toilet then fed three times daily, the priest conducted the chores. Important also, because there is much to be done, procession, hymns, chanting, bringing clothing, water, food, toilet articles, etc., the Pharaoh and High Priest are also assisted by senior priests in the temple. Adolf Erman in *Life in Ancient Egypt*, translated by H.M. Tirard (London: MacMillan and Co and New York, 1894: 273) describes some aspects of this part of the ritual. He states: "The daily acts of worship performed by the priest *du jour* is known from several contemporary sources to have been essentially the same in the case of the various gods. Whether it was Amon or Isis, Ptah or the deceased to whom divine honors were to be paid, we always find that fresh rouge and fresh robes were placed upon the divine statue, and that the sacred chapel in which it was kept was cleansed and filled with perfume. The god was regarded as a human being, whose dwelling had to be cleansed, and who was assisted at his toilet by his servants. These ceremonies doubtless differed both in detail and extent at the various sanctuaries; *e.g.*, the priest at Thebes had about sixty ceremonies to perform, whilst at Abydos thirty-six were found to be sufficient. The form and object of the worship however were always the same, though the details might vary. As a general rule also, the priest had to recite an appointed formula at each separate ceremony."

Now, having opened the door and in the God's presence, Erman further states, the priest had to "kiss the ground, throw himself on his face, throw himself entirely on his face, kiss the ground with his face downwards." Then he began to incense the chamber. Important, also, while the king is often shown with a hand incenser, incensing the god, in the Sanctuary a stand-alone incenser is used. However, incense is never burned on the altar but in an incenser set in a corner on the floor.

In the *Encyclopedia of Religion and Ethics* article "Worship (Egyptian)" (Edinburgh: T and T. Clark, Vol. 12, 1921, 778), A. M. Blackman describes what he terms "The Pre-Toilet Episode" in the lustration of the god. Regarding that part of the daily ritual he writes: "Having undergone purifications in the water of the sacred pool or tank, the priest entered the temple, reciting a formula as he did so his first act after entering the temple was to kindle a fire, a blow-drill being used for that purpose, or perhaps only a spindle and 'hearth.' The priest then picked up the principal part of the censer, which was of metal, usually bronze, and in the form of an outstretched arm with the hand open palm upwards. Taking hold of the rest of the censer, the little brazier in which the incense was burned, he fixed it in its place, namely in the open hand at the end of the arm. Having filled the brazier with burning charcoal from the fire he had previously kindled, he set incense thereon, and, holding the smoking censer in one hand, proceeded to the sanctuary, the double doors of which were bolted and the bolts secured with a clay seal. The bolts seem often to have been tied with a strip of papyrus to which the clay seal was affixed. The priest broke the seal, drew back the bolts, and opened the doors of the sanctuary, whereupon the sacred boat was disclosed with the cultus-image enshrined therein."

"After the unfastening of the seal, and presumably the opening of the doors, the priest sometimes burned incense in honor of the uraeus goddess. On beholding the image, the priest made a profound obeisance, 'kissing the ground prone,' as it was said, or 'placing himself upon the belly stretched out flat.' Then, standing or kneeling, he chanted first a hymn in honor of the divinity - lifting up both his hands as he did so in the attitude of worship, or else burning incense - and after that a second hymn in honor of *R'yt*, the female counterpart of the sun-god and identified with Hathor. The priest next offered the image scented honey, or a figure of the goddess Ma'at, and then burned more incense. Having swept the floor of the sanctuary with a cloth, he was now ready to 'lay his hands upon the god,' i.e., take the image out of the boat or naos in order to perform its toilet.'" He generally requested of the god permission to lay his hands on him.

After the greeting and incensing, then next the God's toilet is done and he is dressed. Here Erman (1894: 274) described the dressing, giving an example on how the toilet of the god was performed. "He laid his hands on him. He took off the old rouge and his former

LET'S LIBERATE THE TEMPLE

clothes, all of course with the necessary formulae. He then dressed the god in the robe called the *Nems*, saying: 'Come white dress! Come white dress! Come white eye of Horus, which proceeds from the town of Nekhebt. The gods dress themselves with thee in thy name *Dress*, and the gods adorn themselves with thee in thy name *Adornment*.' The priest then dressed the god in the *great dress*, rouged him, and presented him with his insignia: the scepter, the staff of ruler, and the whip, the bracelets and anklets, as well as the two feathers which he wore on his head, because 'he has triumphed over his enemies, and is more splendid than gods or spirits.' The god required further a collarette and an amulet, two red, two green and two white bands; when all these had been presented to him the priest might then leave the chapel. Whilst he closed the door, he said four times these words: 'Come Thoth, thou who has freed the eye of Horus from his enemies - let no evil man or woman enter this temple. Ptah closes the door and Thoth makes it fast, closed and fastened with the bolt." These sequence of events, though at Abydos were no different at Karnak. However, here at Karnak, Erman states, "according to the Theban rite, for instance, as soon as he saw the image of the god he had to 'kiss the ground, throw himself on his face, throw himself entirely on his face, kiss the ground with his face turned downwards, offer incense,' and then greet the god with a short psalm."

Liberate the Temple. Kom Ombo Temple of Horus and Sobek. Nephthys (crown) presents to Pharaoh.

FREDERICK MONDERSON

Liberate the Temple. Kom Ombo Temple of Horus and Sobek. A platter for Horus in raised relief.

Liberate the Temple. Kom Ombo Temple of Horus and Sobek. Pharaoh (Notice his crown) and his Queen stand before Haroeris (Elder Horus), Hathor and their son Horus (Heru, Younger).

LET'S LIBERATE THE TEMPLE

Again, in a different spin, Blackman (1921: 778b) describes "the toilet." In this respect, he writes: "The priest's first act after 'laying hands upon the god was apparently to divest the images of the clothing and ornaments in which it had been arrayed the previous day and to remove the pat of scented grease that had been placed on its forehead. Then, placing the image on a little heap of sand, which he had previously poured out for that purpose, and having fumigated it with incense, he proceeded to sprinkle it with water, first from four *nmst* and then from four *dsrt*-vessels, or else with water from one so-called vessel. He then censed the image again, cleansed its mouth with different kinds of natron, and yet again censed it. Having thus purified the image, he began to dress it, putting on the white head-cloth and arraying it in white, green, red, and dark red cloths in succession. After decking it with ornaments, he anointed it with unguents and then painted its eyelids with green and black cosmetic. Either immediately before or immediately after this application of unguent and cosmetics the priest invested the image with royal insignia - a diadem, *uas*-scepter, crook, and whip. The toilet episode was probably brought to a close with a final burning of incense."

Naturally, after his bath and dressing then came the feeding. Again, Erman (1894: 275) offers: "Not only had the priest to dress and serve his god, but he had also to feed him; food and dress had to be placed daily on the **Table of Offerings**, and on festival days extra gifts were due." He continues (1894: 277) further: "If we leave on one side the less important items, such as honey, flowers, incense, etc., and consider simply the various meats, drinks, and loaves of bread placed on the tables of offerings, we shall find as follows: every day of the year the temple received about 3220 loaves of bread, 24 cakes, 144 jugs of beer, 32 geese, and several jars of wine. In addition to this revenue, which was doubtless chiefly used for the maintenance of the priests and the temple servants, special endowments were established for special days. There were extra offerings for the eight festivals which recurred every month. On the second, fourth, tenth, fifteenth, twenty-ninth, and thirtieth days of each month, 83 loaves, 15 jugs of beer, 6 birds, and 1 jar of wine were brought into the temple; while on the new moon and on the sixth day of the month the offerings amounted to 3656 loaves, 14 cakes, 34 jugs of beer, 1 ox, 16 birds, 23 jars of wine. Still more important were the offerings on great festival days, of which there was no lack in the ecclesiastical year of ancient Egypt. Thus, for instance, a feast of ten days was solemnized in the last decade of the month Choiakh to the Memphite god Ptah-Sokaris-Osiris; the temple of Medinet Habu took part in this festival."

Blackman (1921: 778-79), in a more explicit focusing on "The Presentation of food-and-drink offerings," writes. "The procedure observed at the presentation of food - and drink-offerings in the temple liturgy seems to have been practically identical with that observed at the corresponding part of the funerary liturgy. This is indicated among other things by the fact that in the temple reliefs depicting a divinity being fed there is sometimes inserted above the altar or offering-table, and between the divinity and the chief officiant, a so-called list of offerings identical to all intents and purposes with the lists occurring in the tomb reliefs and paintings. This is only to be expected, since every divinity was regarded for cult-purposes as an Osiris."

Before the offerings could be laid upon it, the table or altar had to be purified. The act of placing offerings on the altar or table, or else on mats spread upon the ground, was variously termed 'setting out the repast upon the altar,' 'setting down the divine offering,' 'setting down the repast.' When thus engaged the officiant either stood or knelt.

The god's meal having been laid before him, two closely connected ceremonies, the one being apparently in immediate succession, the one being variously designated 'presenting the repast,' 'presenting the divine offering,' 'performing the presentation of [or 'causing to be produced'] the divine offering,' and 'performing the presentation to, causing to be produced a great oblation for, NN,' and the other being termed 'bringing the god to his repast.'"

At the former ceremony, the officiant extended his right arm and bent the hand upwards in the prescribed manner and pronounced the formula beginning with the words 'an offering which the king gives.' When the king is depicted performing this ceremony, he is often shown holding a mace and staff in his left hand. The recitation of the

LET'S LIBERATE THE TEMPLE

formula 'An offering which the king gives, etc.,' was closely associated with, and, on the analogy of the funerary liturgy, was doubtless preceded by, the burning of incense and the pouring out of a libation of water. At the ceremony of bringing the god to his repast the officiant recited a formula calling (*dwt*) upon the god to come to his bread, beer, roast flesh, etc."

The act of consecration, by which each item of food and drink was finally made over to the god, was termed 'stretching out the arm four times.' According to the temple reliefs, it was performed in the following manner. "The king, standing before what was to be offered stretched out over or towards it four times the so-called *hrp*-baton, which he grasped in his right hand; in his left hand, he held staff and mace, or else this hand hung at his side holding the symbols of like."

In the series of temple reliefs depicting the god being fed is one representing the king in the act of 'elevating' a 'tray of offerings' 'before the face' of the divinity. Does this scene represent one special episode in this part of the liturgy; i.e., after the pronouncement of 'An offering which the king gives, etc., was a specimen of the offering elevated in the presence of the cultus-image? More probably the scene is a summation of a series of elevations; for doubtless, as in the funerary liturgy; each particular item of food mentioned in the list of food - and drink-offerings was elevated at its presentation to the accompaniment of a special formula. In the funerary liturgy, according to Utterances 108-171 of the Pyramid Texts, each item was elevated four times."

In addition to the meal laid out before the image of the principal divinity in the sanctuary and before the images of the co-templar divinities in the adjacent chambers, offerings were also laid, of course, upon the great altar in the forecourt. "If the procedure in the temple of the Aton at El-Amarna prevailed also in other Egyptian temples, it was upon this altar that the Pharaoh mostly laid his oblation."

In this manner, with the incensing, dress and feeding done, the priest began his withdrawal, never backing the god and removing his footprints from the floor and closed the door. However, even though the god had returned to his sacred abode, the festivities continued since the great offerings had to be consumed. Notwithstanding, Blackman (1927: 779b) again explained: "The removal of the footprints" thus: "The final act of the chief officiant before leaving the sanctuary, shutting the doors, and affixing the clay seal to the bolts, was to obliterate all traces of his own and his assistant's footprints. This he did by sweeping the floor with a cloth or with a besom made of twigs of the *hidn*-plant. In the sanctuary of the temple of Derr, on either side of the door, is a representation of Rameses II holding a cloth for sweeping the floor in one hand and a vase (for sprinkling it?) in the other."

With the liturgy done we now turn to the structural dynamics of the temple. In the construction of the temple, as the holiest spot in the building, the Sanctuary is generally located well into the rear of the enclosure. It sits on the highest point, so much so, in the approach inwards, the floor rises and the roof declines giving it that elevated look. The land behind the Sanctuary, oftentimes a court, is generally lower than the Sanctuary itself. A Sacred Lake is situated in close proximity so that the priests could fetch water and wash frequently to abide by that old adage, "Cleanliness is next to Godliness!" On special festivals, the barges of the temple gods are allowed to float on the lake.

LET'S LIBERATE THE TEMPLE

Liberate the Temple. Kom Ombo Temple of Horus and Sobek. On a column with cartouches, and scepter and ankh on Heb, Pharaoh presents three feathers to Sobek.

Liberate the Temple. Kom Ombo Temple of Horus and Sobek. In all his majesty, close-up of Sobek, "Lord of Ombos."

LET'S LIBERATE THE TEMPLE

Liberate the Temple. Kom Ombo Temple of Horus and Sobek. Pharaoh presents three feathers to Sobek with Hathor at his rear.

The axis or center line, another important feature of the temple, represents the orientation of the temple. In 1894, Norman Locklear argued, in the earliest times, temples were oriented towards some celestial body such as stars. This meant the temple and its axis may be north/south, east/west, or any variation therein according to a heavenly body's movement and the particular divinity resident.

Karnak Temple is oriented east to west signifying the path of the Sun God, Ra or Amon-Ra, as he traveled across the sky, over his home. In Hathor's Temple at Dendera, the Chapel of Nuit contains an image depicting the sky goddess shining her rays on the temple. This then shows how important the god's home is and its contact with or relationship with the heavens. Mentuhotep II's temple across the Nile River at Deir el Bahari was also oriented east/west to face Karnak, home of Amon, or Amon-Ra, a manifestation of the Sun God. So too was Hatshepsut's temple built alongside some five hundred years later. Amenhotep III's Luxor Temple was also built facing Karnak. When Rameses II extended the temple by adding the "Ramessean

Front," a Peristyle Court of columns, statues and altars, he re-directed the addition along a slightly different line to also face Karnak.

The axis line was thus very important for a number of reasons. Importantly it guided the construction of the structure in orientation to the dedicated divinity. Luxor temple is unique for it boasts three axes. Two axes are contained within the Amenhotep II part. However, of these two, one is an "invisible axis" beneath the floor and one rests above. Rameses II's "Ramessean Front" added a third axis in his Peristyle Court. Nevertheless, as in the case of Karnak temple, some kings or even individuals of distinction were permitted to place their statue there. While no such fixture would be placed in the Sanctuary, statues were placed in front of or in the Hypostyle Hall, a short distance away. In front of the Sanctuary at Karnak, statues of Amon and Mut, placed there by Tutankhamon and bearing his and his wife's images, represent the god and goddess and both face the center line or path of the Sun God. This is also the case of two surviving statues in the Hypostyle Hall. There are also two colossal statues of Rameses II in the Great Court just before the Second Pylon at Karnak. They too face the center line and at the entrance to the Hypostyle Hall two images of Amon and Rameses, both face the center line beginning the Processional Colonnade.

Two statues fronting the pylon of Rameses II's North/South temple in the Great Court at Karnak also face the principal East/West Center Line. However, the Osiride figures in the temple's smaller Court face the North/South axis line of that smaller temple. Even the seated colossal statues of Rameses II before the pylon and in the Court at Luxor also look out towards Karnak. All statues along these lines face the east/west center line at Karnak. Thus, from a distance Karnak is the God's Sanctuary, but once there, it is the "Holy of Holies," that is the Sanctuary! Nonetheless, as the Karnak temple expanded a second axis on a north/south path was opened linking the temple of Mut and Luxor, even farther south. Significantly, along this north/south axis, even distant in the "Ramessean Front" the seated statues do not face that extant center line but towards the principal east/west of the greater Karnak temple where the Sun God travels. Interesting, and equally at Karnak beyond the Pylon in the Great Court, the Kiosk of Seti II, the

LET'S LIBERATE THE TEMPLE

Temple of Rameses III, the Sphinxes to the north and south extent statues, even the small Sphinx of Tutankhamon all face the center line.

However, this temple of Rameses III of the 20th Dynasty is unique for a number of reasons.

(1) This is a complete temple, built by a single king and located in the Great Court, perpendicular to the principal east/west axis. In essence, it is built to face the axis.

(2) While parallel to the principal north/south axis on the extending of Karnak southward, Rameses' temple is on its own and a separate axis.

(3) Rameses' temple boasts two standing statues before the entrance. This "One Upmanship" temple consists of an Enclosure Wall, a Peristyle Court with a dozen standing Osiride Figures, six on each side, before its Hypostyle Hall that entrances its Sanctuary.

(4) Interesting and again, that the Osiride statues of this Court face this mini-temple's north/south axis line and not the east/west center line of the greater temple.

The pylon at Karnak was an important entranceway feature attached to the Enclosure Wall. This Enclosure Wall, sometimes more than twenty feet high and ten feet or more wide was designed to safeguard events within the temple from prying eyes and ears outside. It also served as a defense mechanism. Karnak itself has ten pylons. These are six on the east/west axis and four on the north/south axis.

Sanctuaries are either open or closed. Karnak is an open Sanctuary. The pharaoh looks in to worship and ritualize and his god looks out to admire and bless his creations! As the sun travels across the heavens, the god is sometimes taken out to bather in its rays. The temple of Dendera, dedicated to Hathor has a chapel on the roof. Walls of the stairs are replete with images of priests ascending and descending the stairs in the ceremony that takes the goddess to the roof to be bathed in the rays of the sun. Nonetheless, and having traveled across the sky the last rays of the sun are thrown back on the Sanctuary at Karnak. The first six pylons, from "one to six respectively" are of decreasing size and are arranged so that decreasing amounts of sunlight shines back towards the Sanctuary. That is, today's First Pylon's aperture is larger than that of the succeeding five pylons towards the smaller Sixth Pylon where the opening is very small and so the last light from the rays of the sun is regulated.

As such, the importance of the Sanctuary is underscored for, in the ancient world, when conquerors invaded, the first thing they did was attack the temple and home of the god who was viewed as the nucleus of the society. Equally, riches of gold, statues, utensils, were here and constituted a prize of seizure.

All this notwithstanding, while Karnak boasted an open Sanctuary, Deir el Bahari, Luxor, Mut, Abu Simbel, and even the late temples at Edfu, Esneh, Kom Ombo, all have closed Sanctuaries. Interesting, all New Kingdom monarchs built a Mortuary Temple across the Nile River on the West Bank. There they were worshipped in life and when they became gods after death. These "Mansions of Millions of Years" all have closed Sanctuaries and generally face the path of their father the Sun god; in a way oriented towards Karnak across the river.

Liberate the Temple. Kom Ombo Temple of Horus and Sobek. Two Horuses on a broken wall.

LET'S LIBERATE THE TEMPLE

Liberate the Temple. Kom Ombo Temple of Horus and Sobek. From the south, surviving columns of the Colonnade in the Court.

Liberate the Temple. Kom Ombo Temple of Horus and Sobek. Dates in vicinity.

FREDERICK MONDERSON

Liberate the Temple. Kom Ombo Temple of Horus and Sobek. Another close-up of the Pharaoh being baptized before he enters the temple.

LET'S LIBERATE THE TEMPLE

XIV. THE KING OF EGYPT I
BY
DR. FRED MONDERSON

The King of Egypt had 5 names but some scholars such as Dr. Ben-Jochannan attributed and emphasized nine such names to the monarch. However, while this is so, they were several other personalities he manifested that were not viewed as succinctly as his five names but more appropriately characterized the man who would be king.

Nonetheless, his principal five names were his **Horus, Two Ladies, Horus of Gold, Suten Bat** and **Son of Ra**. His personalities at first embodied in Narmer, a Southern chieftain, was as **Conqueror** who conquered the north and unified the land. As **Administrator,** he established his capitol at Memphis, reorganized the state apparatus bureaucracy and constructed the White Wall at Memphis after he diverted the Nile and reclaimed the land for the wall and his city.

No less significant, as the society matured by the time of the New Kingdom, he emerged as a **Warrior Pharaoh** who undertook military expeditions to subdue foreign adversaries and expand his kingdom. As an **Architectural Builder**, he constructed a temple to his god (worship) and one to himself (mortuary) and prepared his tomb, as well as other civil and social structures. As **High Priest** and **Son of the God**, he served a religious function but in the case of Amenhotep IV, Akhenaten, he became a religious reformer and as other pharaohs would also demonstrate, he was a **Patron of the Arts and Sciences** who planned and constructed his new city at Amarna.

While we know of Narmer the king who first united Egypt through his historic document, the **Slate Palette**, the Scorpion king as well as several others, however, preceded Narmer. We know of Scorpion from a **Macehead** on which he is depicted **Opening the Agricultural Season** in a sacred ritual that endured throughout dynastic rule. He was thus the **Chief Festival Celebrant**.

The king was the Son of God, a god himself who worshipped his father in a temple he constructed. Equally, he built a temple for himself to be worshipped. He was worshipped alive and when he died. After judgment in the heavens in which he was declared "True of Voice" and "Justified," he assumed full divinity status to exist in the Afterlife among his brother and sister gods.

Now, while there as a vizier who functioned as Prime Minister or second to the king, there was a judicial body headed by a high court judge. However, the king was the highest judge and final arbiter in judicial matters though cases seldom got to his level of arbitration. There was, however, one case that got the king's attention and this is recounted in the **Story of the Eloquent Peasant**. Apparently, the peasant was on way to the market with his produce on an ass and an official seized his property on some unlawful pretext. Seeking justice, the peasant wrote a letter to the Vizier Rensi that was laden with philosophic and moral precepts of right and wrong while explaining his predicament. Purportedly, Rensi ignored the peasant who wrote him again imploring you must demonstrate justice, for "You are the balance, do not swerve;" you are the helmsman who must pilot your ship correctly. And even more, surprisingly, these were profound philosophical thoughts from a peasant. In fact, Rensi brought this to the king's attention who "colluded" with the Vizier essentially saying "Let's see what else he has!" The peasant wrote 9 letters altogether and finally the king sent for him, then praised his intellectual courage. The king censured the thief and gave the victim all his property and position.

The question of the Heb Sed Festival always comes up when dealing with the King of Egypt. What does it mean? Some say it represented thirty years of rule and a ceremony of rejuvenation of the king. Others say it was an agricultural festival of fertility of the land and people.

LET'S LIBERATE THE TEMPLE

Still others say it was the transmission of kingship from the Queen to the king. Again, that it was a fertility festival involving marriage of the king. Since he was divine, procreation was important so he had to have a wife and harem. However, a credible argument is the question of killing of the king.

First, we have the death of Osiris. The killing of Osiris by his brother Seth is an early example of the actual killing of the King of Egypt. This, however, was done out of jealousy to seize his throne. There is a connection to water because his body was dumped into the river. Narmer was said to be drowned in the river, another legend says an alligator rescued him from drowning. Opening of the agricultural season also meant letting the waters in, as was done in case of the Scorpion king.

In addition, and however, there were plots against the king. Amenemes I of the Twelfth Dynasty initiated the Co-Regency with his son, Usertesen I or Senusert I to safeguard the throne. Then there was the Theban Revolt led by "Tety the Handsome" against the Seventeenth Dynasty kings as they were away fighting the Hyksos. Queen Teti-Sheri's daughter Aahotep was able to rally the loyal forces remaining at Thebes and put down the revolt, saving the crown for her progeny. This bravery is commemorated in a Stele at Karnak, placed there with an endowment by her son Aahmose, who married his sister Aahmes-Nefertari who possessed the royal genes. He praised his mother for her bravery and in turn he dedicated great booty of golden utensils to the Temple in gratitude to the god. There was a harem plot against Rameses III in the later ages during the 20th Dynasty, that was foiled and a trial conducted.

Females carried the royal gene and when he who would become king married the female heiress, he became legal king. That is, the queen was queen by right of birth, the king was king by right of marriage. Marriage of the queen's daughter, the princess who was the heiress, was an event of utmost importance.

Thus, the Heb Sed Festival dating back to the First Dynasty was about several things, but rejuvenation of the king after a period of thirty-years rule, as an agricultural festival, transmission of royal genes and right to rule, can be considered important among them. Some kings celebrated this festival before they had ruled for such a lengthy reign. A lengthy reign afforded the king an opportunity to celebrate a second and some did this every 3, 5, or seven years after that.

Liberate the Temple. Temple of Horus at Edfu. View of a Wall at the Mammisi to the north-west before entering the Temple Proper.

Liberate the Temple. Temple of Horus at Edfu. On an entrance wall panel, Pharaoh presents flowers to Horus (Heru), Hathor and their son.

LET'S LIBERATE THE TEMPLE

Liberate the Temple. Temple of Horus at Edfu. Visitor poses beside a surviving hawk image of Horus, a favorite photographic location of visitors.

Margaret Murray in an article, "Evidence for the custom of killing the king" in *Journal of Egyptian Archaeology* (1914: 17-23) identified in art a representation of:

1. The king is the principal figure, always represented as Osiris;

2. Before him is carried the figure of Up-Uaut, the Opener of the Ways, the Jackal-god of Siut who appears to have been a god of death;

3. The royal daughter, seated in a litter, is the most important figure after the king;

4. In most cases there are one or more running or dancing men.

"The beginning of this knowledge dates back to the translation of the Greek inscription on the Rosetta Stone, where the cycle of thirty years is mentioned. Later it was suggested - and the suggestion was accepted for many years - that the festival was the thirty anniversary of the king's accession; in 1898 this theory, being found inadequate, Sethe brought forward a good deal of evidence to prove it the thirtieth anniversary of the king's appointment as crown prince. This, however, does not cover the fact that Thutmose I had a Sed-Festival, though he was never crown-prince and did not reign thirty years; nor that Tut-Ankh-Amon had a Sed-Festival, though the sum of his predecessor's reign added to his own does not amount to thirty years."

Rameses II celebrated six Sed-Festivals. He did the extraordinary. Remember, while Ra had 14 Kas or "life forces," Hatshepsut 12; he Rameses claimed to have 30 Kas. He was married six times, three times to his own daughters, and had Nefertari as his Great Queen. He had over 100 children. A great builder who erected Abu Simbel twin temples, the Ramesseum, the "Ramessean Front" at Luxor Temple, helped finish his father Seti I's work in Karnak's "Hypostyle Hall," he built a temple at Abydos and finished and helped decorate Abydos temple of his father dedicated to Osiris. Then there was Pi-Ramesses and more, he repaired several buildings especially those damaged in the Amarna Revolution. He, however, expropriated the works of countless others. Nevertheless, very courageous, he was a warrior pharaoh and most important, a patron of the arts and sciences.

XV. THE KING OF EGYPT II
By
Dr. Fred Monderson

In many discussions, the question arises as to where and when the notion of kingship arose and what were the motivating principles of this phenomenon that has played such a significant role in statecraft and nation-building from ancient beginnings influencing modern times. Even more, whether the origin is mortal or divine, the institution's impact on civilization's progress has been unquestioned. Nevertheless, now thanks to the University of Chicago's Bruce Williams' important "Qustul discovery;" the question seems by-far settled that the notion and actuality of kingship is African in origin, or more appropriately and seeming overwhelmingly, Nubian. From the discovery at Qustul, Mr. Williams has been able to trace and date the world's earliest monarchy dating at c. 3400 B.C. or **Nile Year** 840.

LET'S LIBERATE THE TEMPLE

He showed that the paraphernalia of kingship found 200 years later in Egypt, viz., enthroned pharaoh wearing the white crown, whip and flail, falcon atop Serekh, palace facade, incense burner, Nile boat, etc., was first evident in Nubia centuries earlier. Naturally, how long this state of affairs was in the making is still unresolved.

In this respect, Charles Finch III in *The Star of Deep Beginnings* (1998: 17) writes: "A sequence of tomb affiliated with 12 pharaohs comprise Cemetery L at Qustul. This complex of royal tombs sed Bruce Williams to believe that the ruling dynasty of Ta-Seti stretched back 300 years prior to the 1st Dynasty. What Williams didn't categorically say, but what logically follows from the evidence, is that Ta-Seti represents the beginning of pharaonic civilization and is truly a founding dynasty, sequencing directly into the unification dynasties inaugurated by Aha-Menes. The lien of pre-dynastic pharaohs mentioned in certain annals must be that of Ta-Seti and therefore Ta-Seti belongs to the scheme of "proto-dynasties" that governed early Nile valley history. Bruce Williams himself implies something of the sort in the original article on the subject: apparently, the demise of Qustul coincides with the campaign of Aha in Nubia, the first king of the Egyptian First Dynasty, wo recorded the smiting of Ta-Seti. Ta-Seti was therefore brought down by its successor dynasty, that of Aha-Menes, the one that unified Egypt and inaugurated the formal dynastic era. Ta-Seti can be said to represent the transition between the late-pre-dynastic Gerzean cultural sequence and the formal dynastic period."

Certainly not far-fetched, but in analogy, perhaps Toby Wilkinson's *Genesis of the Pharaohs*' (2003) notes "One thousand years before Winkler's Mesopotamians" may be an appropriate yardstick. Nevertheless, such an occurrence therefore confirms Prof. John Clarke's classic theory of the "rehearsal stage for civilization" that originated in Ethiopia (Nubia) and manifested itself or performed on the theatrical stage of Egypt some two to four centuries or thereabouts before the dynastic period began. Therefore, the implications and ramifications deriving from theology, cosmology, monarchy even science, reinforced through religion and spirituality can reasonably be considered African, for this is where, the practiced belief holds, God first approached man in showing his unbounded love for humanity. Establishing that first divine/human compact or covenant, or a socio-religious contract, as we can gather from the Pyramid Texts that are the earliest surviving religious doctrines that have remained unchanged for millennia. In this, they reveal the Gods conferred a tremendous responsibility on the conscience of the Egyptian, Nile Valley African man, delivering the admonition to advance the cause of humanity within the construct of the fatherhood of god and the brotherhood of man.

Albert Churchward explained this task of responsibility was 300,000 years in the making of practicing "sweet communion with deity."

Placing things in context, we can examine some dates and early developments in Africa and especially along the East African Rift and into the Nile Valley.

Explain:

(1)　We date Lucy, "Denk Nesh," the most complete fossil remains ever found, at 3.5 million years;

(2)　Zinjanthropus Boisie 1.75 million years, in East Africa;

(3)　Eve is dated 200,000 years on the East African Plains;

(4)　107,000-year-old "Paint factory" discovered in South Africa;

(5)　41,000-year-old "Iron Mine" in South Africa;

(6)　Syncellus gives a literary board document of 35,000 years old recounting the history of Egyptian kings;

(7)　The Precession has been dated at 26,000 years' duration. To measure one means there must be two, possibly three; while we begin counting at one, Charles Finch begins at two, thus,

LET'S LIBERATE THE TEMPLE

possibly three and perhaps four. Therefore, 26,000, 52,000, 78,000, and 104,000 years of possible African stargazing.

In this phenomenal experience, Foucart postulated, "Ra and his friends, the Gods, organized the world; their final purpose was the reign of order and triumph of good. Egypt and its people were the land and people chosen and beloved by the gods; it was therefore, essential that the son of the gods should be able to bring the work to a successful issue, and this enterprise demanded that strangers, the ungodly, the enemies of Egypt, and all that was hostile to the ultimate triumph of the good should be destroyed or subdued."

Liberate the Temple. Temple of Horus at Edfu.
Another view of the surviving hawk image of Horus.

FREDERICK MONDERSON

Liberate the Temple. Temple of Horus at Edfu. A view of perspective on how the Egyptian artist represented groups of people, for the most part in sets of five (hands and faces).

Liberate the Temple. Temple of Horus at Edfu. Holding a Sistrum, the Queen presents to the Goddess.

LET'S LIBERATE THE TEMPLE

Providing an understanding of this interaction, R.O. Faulkner in the *Ancient Egyptian Pyramid Texts* (Oxford 1969, 1998: 1) explained the relationship between the King and the Gods in Utterance 1, 3, 6, etc. He states, in "The recitation of Nuit, 'The king is my eldest son who split open my womb; he is my beloved with whom I am well pleased." That of Geb, "The King is my bodily son." Again, Nuit, the "Great Fruitful One," noting "The King my son is my beloved; I have given to him the two horizons that he may have power in them as Harakhti. All the gods say: 'It is the truth that the king is your best-loved among your children, watch over him eternally.'"

As such, and to achieve that principal responsibility to his father, the Sun God, since he was the epitome of the nation; the king had to worship and ritualize the divinity on a continuous basis within a temple he built and dedicated the god. A significant part and first-step of this responsibility was achieved through the whole experience of baptism as part of the idea of purity and purification in order to dwell in association with the gods in the temple and more generally in this world and the next or afterlife. Further, to maintain his purity and accomplish this responsibility the king had to undergo the following purification rituals throughout his lifetime, for after all, these Africans initiated the concept of "cleanliness is next to Godliness."

(1) Baptism - The young heir to the throne was baptized at birth and much later as king. Depictions also show him being baptized before entering the temple.

(2) He was baptized at his coronation but not fully invested with all the powers of his new status until he had received the blessings and investiture paraphernalia at Heliopolis, home of the Sun-God. This is vividly depicted detailing Piankhy the Ethiopian, on his way to Heliopolis for the ceremony, where he washed his face in the "Cool Pool" as the Sun-God also had done to wash his face.

FREDERICK MONDERSON

(3) In every aspect of his earthly and heavenly existence, purification became a hallmark of the pharaoh whether in performing his ritualistic duties, visiting the temple of his god for whatever reason, being able to wage battle, actual or spiritual, or even upon his death.

(4) Before he entered the temple to perform his ritual functions for the day, even after he was purified in the "House of the Morning," he was washed again at the Temple's entrance. This is often shown on a panel on the entrance wall.

(5) In the Feast "Grace before Meat" he was washed before he participated in eating to celebrate victory over the flesh of his enemies.

(6) The altar upon which the god's food was placed had to be washed before the food could be placed on it. Naturally, this had to be done at least 3 times per day.

(7) Upon his death, the pharaoh was washed at the start of his mummification; at the end of this mummification process; and at the actual burial where he was washed and cleansed or purified in the "Opening of the Mouth Ceremony" before departing for the next world. Foucart believed the journey into the Afterlife began in a cavern in the Deir el-Bahari locale where equipped with his words of power, viz., Pyramid Texts, Coffin Texts, Book of the Dead, that is *Per-Em-Hru* or Book of Coming Forth By Day, he set out for the Hall of Two Maati, for the Psychostasia Judgment. Further, adding clarity to an important topic of color and "painted black for the funerary ceremony." Brugsch-Bey in *History of Egypt Under the Pharaohs* (London: John Murray, 1902) explained, in that "dark experience" the Egyptian painted himself red as a form of "illumination." Somewhat similarly, Dr. Ben-Jochannan argued, "he was painted red because he was dead."

(8) In route to the place of the Psychostasia he was washed by the "Tree Goddess" who poured 4 vases of *nmst* water on him

LET'S LIBERATE THE TEMPLE

before he entered the Hall of Judgment or "Hall of the Double Maati." After a successful Judgment, based on a life of righteousness prescribed by the philosophic admonition of Ma'at, and he was declared "True of Voice" or "Justified." Again, he was washed or purified to exist among the gods in their purified place of abode, where the gods are born and exist.

(9) The king was baptized before he took the field of battle in his imperial and other military exploits, whether as a protection if he fell in battle or to bring success in any such encounter.

Today, millennia later, the essence of such divine dynamics, admonitions or instructions seem the only spiritual and moral ingredient helping keep lit the flame of human existence in a world now tremendously mechanical, calculated, selfish, greedy and punitive. Yet, the responsibility of guarding the ongoing destiny of the human family is a charge well borne within the humanistic bosom of the African. It is reflective of the first act, of that "first occasion," when the African was instructed to be the religious, spiritual and philosophic shepherd of his community, nation, and *ipso facto*, given the responsibility of the future of humanity, in the interest of the divine forces that play an important role in the lives of man, then and now. In this, "we see the adaptation of the solar theologies of more ancient conceptions according to when the souls of the kings were one by one assimilated to the various solar gods, as well as to the moon and planets. In this regard, George Foucart in "King (Egyptian)" in *Encyclopedia of Religion and Ethics*, Vol. 7 (Edinburgh, 1914: 711) wrote accordingly of the: "Exclusive religious or rather divine - origin of the various elements involved in the Egyptian definition of monarchy." Even further, in respect to functions and responsibilities of the king, he stated: "Investigation shows that here also the reminisces are purely mythological in character (e.g., the alleged proto-historic wars from which the king derives some of his titles, or whose anniversaries he celebrates)."

In that phenomenal cosmogonic metamorphosis, the Gods first ruled, and then demi-gods apprenticed the king. In proper perspective, there were thus 5 levels of divine and human beings interacting in the evolving Egyptian experience of kingship. These were Gods, Demi-Gods, Manes, Kings and other rank and file Egyptians. That is ranging from divine through kingship and nobles to fellahin. In this regard, Murnane (1983: 46) has added a view to help untangle the mist of relationship and responsibility entrusted to the monarch of this Nile Valley state. He wrote: "In theory, the king's position was simple. Although born a mortal and retaining throughout his life all the human frailties, he was infused with godly power from the moment the hereditary kingship passed to him. By virtue of this office he was a god on earth, the living nexus between the divine and mortal spheres of activity. He alone could effectively worship the gods, standing before them as a son to his parents. Through him, moreover, was maintained the cosmic harmony that the Egyptians called Ma'at. Of the ritual scenes carved on temple walls, one of the most frequently encountered is the representation of the king offering Ma'at - shown as a tiny seated goddess, with her characteristic feather headdress - to the gods; and sometimes - to emphasize the king's role as the guarantor of Ma'at - the hieroglyphs that make up the king's own name are substituted for the goddesses' image. To the ancient Egyptians, whose idea of right order was a blessed un-eventfulness in natural affairs, this was the ruler's most important function."

As a result, much of these responsibilities are inherent in the king's names to which Foucart, again writes: "In fact, there is nothing in any of the attributes or denominations of the kingship (titles, costume, functions, etc.) which might be a survival or indication of the historic mode of formation or of the origins of the monarchy. Some material signs (such as the scepter [hiku] of the shepherd people, or the plaited lock, worn exclusively by gods and their royal heirs) enable archaeology to outline hypothetical theories regarding the possible origin of the masters who imposed their rule upon the Nile valley; but the texts and monuments yield no information whatever regarding these beginnings; and, as far back as we can go, we find ourselves in the presence of a conception of monarchy which is composed of purely theological elements and based solely upon the assimilation of the king to the gods who are the makers of the world and the mythical founders of Egyptian society. This explains the importance attached by the Egyptians to the power and to the exact utterance of the

LET'S LIBERATE THE TEMPLE

different names by which they designated the king. These names, taken together, form a kind of abrege of the nature of the Pharaoh, and of the royal attributes."

In support of this theological construct, a comparison in contrast was made with the other ancient nations. Here, Budge (1969, I: 3) expressed the view: "The Egyptians, however acted in a perfectly logical manner, for they believed that they were a divine nation, and that they were ruled by kings who were themselves gods incarnate; their earliest kings, they asserted, were actually gods, who did not disdain to lie upon earth, and to go about and up and down through it, and to mingle with men. Other ancient nations were content to believe that they had been brought into being by the power of their gods operating upon matter, but the Egyptians believed that they were the issue of the great God who created the universe, and that they were of direct divine origin. When the gods ceased to reign in their proper persons upon earth, they were succeeded by a series of demi-gods, who were in turn succeeded by the Manes, and these were duly followed by kings in whom was enshrined a divine nature with characteristic attributes. When the physical or natural body of a king died, the divine portion of his being, i.e., the spiritual body, returned to its original abode with the gods, and it was duly worshipped by men upon earth as a god and with the gods. This happy result was partly brought about by the performance of certain ceremonies, which were at first wholly magical, but later partly magical and partly religious, and by the recital of appropriate words uttered in the duly prescribed tone and manner, and by the keeping of festivals at the tombs at stated seasons when the appointed offerings were made, and the prayers for the welfare of the dead were said."

FREDERICK MONDERSON

Liberate the Temple. Temple of Horus at Edfu. In the "Corridor of Victory," scenes in the War between Horus and Seth. Horus and his pals. Horus (Heru) in double crown, has captured Seth disguised as a hippopotamus at the boat's bow in the water and tied to a string held by the God.

Liberate the Temple. Temple of Horus at Edfu. In the "Corridor of Victory," scenes in the War between Horus and Seth. Horus (Heru) and his pals.

LET'S LIBERATE THE TEMPLE

Liberate the Temple. Temple of Horus at Edfu. In the "Corridor of Victory," scenes in the War between Horus and Seth. Horus and his pals. Notice the damage done to the scene.

This belief is again reinforced by Robert Bauval and Adrian Gilbert's *The Orion Mystery* (1995: 180) in which the explanation holds the Egyptian, Africans, termed the time of the transition for the gods the first "golden age" or *Tep Zeti* "occasion" which translates loosely as the "First Time." Herein, the Egyptians believed, "the system of cosmic order and its transference to the land of Egypt had been established a long time before by the gods. Egypt had been ruled by a race of gods for many millennia before it was entrusted to the mortal yet divine line of pharaohs. The pharaohs were the sacerdotal connection with the gods and, by extension represented the link with the First Time; they were the custodians of its established laws and wisdom. Everything they did, every action, every move, every decree had to be justified in terms of the First Time, which served as a sort of covenant of kingship, to abide by and to explain their actions and deeds. This was true not only for the king and his court but applied to all-natural events: the movement of the celestial bodies, the unexplained phenomena of nature and the ebbing and rising waters of the Nile. It would not be an exaggeration to say that everything a pharaoh did was connected with the First Time; hence, the careful reenactment of mythical events which could be either cosmic or secular or both combined in a duality by the power of symbols and rituals. It is not surprising that this blissful First Time was invariably referred to as the Time of Osiris."

This "first time" is not something that happened once but a constantly reoccurring phenomenon throughout Egyptian history requiring unending prayer, and ritual worship linking earthly with divine reality on a daily basis. Thus, as the example given of the temple of Edfu being consecrated to "come alive," this, then, is comparable to the "first occasion" "coming alive" or starting over repeatedly.

However, regarding the totality of this cosmic drama, Mercer argued and Bauval and Gilbert (1995: 75-76) explained: "The dead king would be reborn as a star and that his soul was believed to travel into the sky and become established in the starry world of Osiris-Orion, the god of the dead and of resurrection: 'The Dog Star was identified with Sirius; Orion was identified with Osiris …. It is not surprising to find an identification of Osiris with Orion … [for] one of the central themes of the Pyramid Texts was the complete identification of the dead king with Osiris ….'" Even more of an elaboration is provided by Petrie (1923: 36) who tells of a XIIth Dynasty description of the death of the king. Accordingly, he wrote, "'the god entered his horizon, the king flew up to heaven and joined the sun's disc, and the follower of the god met his maker. The palace was silenced and in mourning, the great gates were closed, the courtiers crouching on the ground, the people in hushed mourning.' Three thousand years later, it is said: 'Upon the death of a king the Egyptians generally lament with a universal mourning, rend their garments, shut up the temples, inhibit sacrifices, and all feasts and solemnities for the space of seventy-two days; they cast dust likewise upon their heads, and gird themselves under their breasts with a linen girdle; and thus men and women, two or three hundred sometimes in a company, twice a day go about singing mournful songs in praise of the deceased king … they neither eat flesh, nor anything baked or heated by the fire, and abstain from wine and all sumptuous fare.'" That 72-day period also covers the duration of the mummification process. The end of which

LET'S LIBERATE THE TEMPLE

comes the burial. However, the time between the old king's death and the burial is the period of the Succession," where, among other things the Mystery Play of the Succession takes place. It is also the time in which the heir-apparent new king visits principal sites across the country to pay tribute to ancestral spirits and finally after the burial the Coronation takes place ending the interregnum during which time he issued his Protocol. That is, the names and their meaning by which he will be known.

Nonetheless, and adding more clarity in understanding events surrounding the king's death, McMahan (1998: 40) also states: "The Pyramid Texts make it clear that the pharaoh was expected, on his death, to become one of the stars. 'You shall bathe in the starry firmament …. The imperishable stars have raised you aloft. You shall reach the sky as Orion, your akh shall be as effective as Sothis; be powerful, having power; be strong, having strength; may your akh stand among the gods as Horus who dwells in Iru.' Sothis was the Egyptian name for Sirius the Dog Star. The brightest star in the heavens, every year it appeared below the horizon for 70 days, then reappeared in late June as the herald of the annual Nile flood."

Even more, in discussing this heavenly metamorphosis of the king upon his death, Petrie (1924: 85) says again and further, somewhat reinforcing the earlier view: "The soul of the king at death was believed to fly to heaven in the guise of a falcon. As the emblem of the king, it was always represented standing above the royal ka name; this was originally a figure of the wooden palace of a chief, with his name on the door, and the falcon-king within it was shown above, like the pattern inside a bowl being drawn resting on the top of it. The chief place of falcon worship was about the old capital of Southern Egypt, at Hierakonpolis and the neighboring Apollinopolis or Edfu. Other cities, from Philae on the south to Tentyra on the north, worshipped the hawk; below that, it was only sacred at Heliopolis in connection with the sun and Horus. Thus, the worship was essentially southern. The bird continued to be honored until the Gnostic age, when it represented the souls of the just." Interesting, this bird on the Serekh is seen in Williams' Qustol discovery but this early emblem is excluded from Lower Egypt.

FREDERICK MONDERSON

We must question authority and seek explanation of questions such as the following:

(1)   "Horus went north with the Blacksmiths."

(2)   Falcon worship was centered at Hierakonpolis in the south.

(3)   By the First Dynasty fashion was uniform throughout the country, particularly given the south was the principal power and molder of the nation's destiny.

(4)   Efforts were made to divorce Ra and Heliopolis because of this center of worship has played such a significant role in the totality of the culture. Remember this was the same falcon observed at Heliopolis, we also observed atop the Serekh at Qustol in the "World's Earliest Monarchy."

(5).   Longstanding and contemporary belief in Europe is "God is white. He made man in his own image who is white and superior. The falsity is perpetuated further in that: The African is "cursed" and inferior in the natural order. So, in the natural order, so in the social order, with its ramifications in the economic, cultural and political orders. Therefore, the "false mind game" which holds, "the white man must lord it over the black man!"

(6)   However, in contradiction; as such, since god made man in his image and an early creator God Ra, after he made the world, created the Nubians, Black People, before he made Egyptians, even Caucasians or Asiatics.

We are forced to ask: What must we believe? Evidence or Speculation? That is, particularly when the speculation was propounded during the age of colonialism and imperialism that fueled another falsity, the superiority of the white man.

Let me also add, if cows had gods their god would be a cow. The Chinese god is Chinese. The Indian god is Indian. The Asiatic god is

LET'S LIBERATE THE TEMPLE

Asiatic. The African god looks European. Dr. Ben-Jochannan remarked, "When your god and your oppressor look the same, you have a problem!"

Nevertheless, in ancient Egypt the King had 5 principal names. These are Horus, Two Ladies, Golden Horus, Suten Bat, and Son of Ra.

Liberate the Temple. Temple of Horus at Edfu. In the "Corridor of Victory," scenes in the War between Horus and Seth. Horus and his pals.

FREDERICK MONDERSON

Liberate the Temple. Temple of Horus at Edfu. In the "Corridor of Victory," scenes in the War between Horus and Seth. Horus and his pals.

Liberate the Temple. Temple of Horus at Edfu. In the "Corridor of Victory," scenes in the War between Horus and Seth. Horus and his pals.

LET'S LIBERATE THE TEMPLE

THE KING'S 5 NAMES

1.   Horus Name - Representative of Horus, the "Great God of Heaven." He was the Sun of the gods, Son of Ra. This name is written above the Serekh, the plan of a palace facade, or even within a temple or a tomb. It is where in life and death the king received the divine cult or the funerary cult. This custom of giving the king this divine name dates to the Third Dynasty.

2.   Two Ladies - The Second Name, "Two Ladies," is represented by the vulture and uraeus symbols. **Nekhabit**, goddess of the South Par Excellence, was found by Quibell at Hierakonpolis. She is always shown as a vulture, uraeus or a woman, wearing the White Crown of the South. She also wears the White Crown with feathers, or the papyrus plant, or the papyrus scepter. Of (**Oudjt**), Budge (1908: xvi) says, "Whether she appears as a serpent, or woman, she always bears or wears the symbols of the North, the red crown, the red crown on heb, or the lotus plant, or the lotus scepter." Both goddesses are shown holding the Shen ring.

3.   Horus of Gold - The third name is the "**Horus of Gold**," meaning he is of the same substance as Ra or Horus. His name is of an eternal and mystical substance. This name first appears with Sneferu, 3-4 dynasties in a cartouche preceded by both the **Suten Bat** and **Two Ladies** names and this is shown on the Palermo Stone.

4.   Suten Bat - The fourth name is the "**Suten Bat**," the sedge and bee. The first, Suten sign means, "he is king of the South" and the second, the Bee (or Bat), means "he is king of the north." Thus, the name that follows the Suten Bat title is called the "Prenomen," and written in an oval or cartouche, the Egyptians called *Shennu*.

FREDERICK MONDERSON

Wallis Budge in *The Book of the Kings of Egypt* (1908: xviii) writes: "The oldest form of the cartouche is circular, and from the scene on the vase of King Besh it is clear that the circle with a bar attached was intended to represent a ring with a flat bezel, or seal ring. This, of course, symbolized the Shen ring, or circular course of the sun about the universe, and when the king's name was written inside it, the meaning was that the king was representative of the Sun god, and that he and his name would, like the Sun, endure forever. On some reliefs, the cutting of the cartouche suggests that the name within was enclosed by a rope or cord the ends of which were tied together in an elongated knot." Cords and knots are used in magical ceremonies.

Two things can be noted. First, if we examine the Suten Bat (**Nomen**) names of certain families of kings it becomes clear that a well-recognized rule underlay their formation. Second, it seems too that the **Prenomen** of the kings of one dynasty influenced the formations of those of the kings of another.

5. **Son of Ra** - The fifth name of the king was the "**Son of Ra**," which was also written in a cartouche. Interesting that it is written inside the cartouche, after the cartouche and even before the cartouche. Thus, Budge again states, "the fourth and fifth names of the king were 'solar names,' but the fifth did not necessarily carry with it sovereignty. The fifth name of the king seems to have been his private name, or that which was given him at his birth, but though it appears to be certain that every king must have had such a name, the 'son of Ra' names of many of the early kings have not come down to us." As such, the **Nomen** is the **Suten Bat** name he gets upon coronation as King of Upper and Lower Egypt. The **Prenomen** is his birth name, his **Son of Ra** name and both are written within the cartouche.

Budge further gives "other titles which were prefixed to the cartouches of kings."

1. *Neb taui* - "Lord of the Two Lands,"

LET'S LIBERATE THE TEMPLE

2. *Nefer Nefer* - "Beautiful god" or "Well-doing god."

3. *Neb ari khet* - "Lord, creator of things," or "Lord who created the world."

4. *Ta ankh Ra ma tchetta* - "Giver of life, like Ra, forever."

5. *Nreb khau* - "Lord of Crowns."

6. *Ankh utcha senb* - "Life, strength, health, be to him."

7. *Suten Bat* - "King of the South and North."

8. *Sa Ra* - "Son of Ra."

9. *Per Aa* - "Great House," the "Pharaoh," "The "Great Pharaoh."

Therefore, in that divine, demi-god, human coming of age, lineage, the King of Egypt came to inherit many "hats" throughout his lifetime, as Prince, Pharaoh, and "God," even warrior, and his actions manifest among others. We know his protocols would later include 5 names, viz., **Horus**, **Two Ladies**, **Golden Horus**, **Suten Bat**, and **Son of Ra**. Yet, Dr. ben-Jochannan attributed 9 names to the king. The customary five; and also, when the king functioned as high priest, celebrating certain festivals, head of the army, and another, the "Prefect God." Of course, he was also father of the nation. In all this, the name "pharaoh," signifying great house (as we use "White House" to signify the US President or the government) is not found used before the New Kingdom. Nevertheless, in explaining the king's pharaonic protocol, Steindorff and Seele in *When Egypt Ruled the East* (1957: 84-85) give as an example of his five names in which, using Thutmose III, as an example, who was the: "Horus: Mighty Bull, Appearing in Thebes; the Two Ladies: Enduring of Kingship; the Horus of Gold: Splendid of Diadems; the King of Upper and Lower Egypt: Enduring of Form is Re [Menkheperre]; the Son of Re: Thoth is Born [Thutmose]." Of all these names, the last one alone was the original one which was given to the king at birth and by which he was known before the beginning of his reign; the other four were all adopted upon his accession to the throne and were often amplified by the addition of supplementary epithets in the course of his reign. In official intercourse and in letters addressed to him by foreign rulers, the king was addressed by the 'Great name' which he bore as 'King of Upper and Lower Egypt' [**Suten Bat**] and which was enclosed when written in hieroglyphic, like the personal name given at birth as the 'Son of Re,' in an elliptical cartouche. In daily life, there was a tendency to avoid the mention of the king by name; instead he was referred to by various titles or circumlocutions such as 'His Majesty' or the 'Good God,' while it was customary to say 'one commanded' for 'the king commanded.'"

In all this, because of his divine nature, the king became the embodiment of the nation, the good king, divine monarch, soul of the nation, the ancient precursor to "L'etat, c'est, moi" (the French King Louis XIV proclaimed "I am the state.") which in fact he Pharaoh was. So much so, Diop (1974: 138) in his "Argument for a Negro Origin" notes: "The concept of kingship is one of the most impressive indications of the similarity in thinking between Egypt and the rest of Black Africa. Leaving aside such general principles as the sacrosanct nature of kingship and stressing one typical trait because of its strangeness, we shall single out the ritual killing of the monarch. In Egypt, as Margaret Murray has concurred in "The Custom of Killing the King" the monarch was not supposed to reign unless he was in good health. Originally, when his strength declined, he was really put to death. But royalty soon resorted to various expedients. The king was understandably eager to preserve the prerogatives of his position, while undergoing the least possible inconvenience. So, he was able to transform the fatal judgment into a symbolic one: from then on, when he grew old, he was merely put to death ritualistically. After the symbolic test, known as the 'Sed Festival,' the monarch was supposedly rejuvenated in the opinion of his people and was once again deemed fit to assume his functions. Henceforth, the 'Sed Festival' was the ceremony of the king's rejuvenation: ritualistic death and revivification of the ruler became synonymous and took place during the same ceremony."

LET'S LIBERATE THE TEMPLE

However, and regarding this "Deification of the King" who "went to Osiris," and was sometimes worshipped alive in the Sed Festival, Petrie (1923: 16-17) explained further: "The earliest scene of it shows the king dressed in a close-fitting garment like Osiris, holding the flail and crook of Osiris, seated in a high shrine approached by steps. Before him are captives dancing in an enclosure. This is of Narmer-Mena. A little later, king Den is shown on the same high throne, and another crowned king is performing the ritual dance before him, which belongs to the coronation ceremonies. In the earlier scene is a woman seated in a covered litter. The apparent interpretation of it is that the king was deified as Osiris, and the successor married the heiress, was crowned, and performed the ritual dances. The tightly clad Osiride figures of the king are associated with Sed-festivals throughout history. The ending was that of the king's life; in African custom, the kings were killed after a term of years, as in Ethiopia and now further south; then in historic times this was commuted to the Osirification of the king at the appointment of his successor, while he lived on to his natural death, as the living Osiris."

Liberate the Temple. Temple of Horus at Edfu. In the "Corridor of Victory," scenes in the War between Horus and Seth. Horus and his pals.

FREDERICK MONDERSON

Liberate the Temple. Temple of Horus at Edfu. In the "Corridor of Victory," scenes in the War between Horus and Seth. Horus and his pals.

Liberate the Temple. Temple of Horus at Edfu. Image of Horus, Triumphant!

LET'S LIBERATE THE TEMPLE

Petrie (1923: 17-18) also identified and explained where evidence of this ceremony was found particularly in the vicinity at Thebes. "The chapel of Sonkh-ka-ra for the ceremony, with the cenotaph sarcophagus, and parts of the statue, were found on the top of one of the peaks at Thebes, and apparently another chapel, for Senusert II, stood on the highest rock at Lahun. An Osiride figure of one of the Mentuhoteps was found buried in a pit at Deir el Bahari, probably representing the burial of the king when he became Osiris. The period of this deification seems to have been connected with the end of a week of change of Sothis rising, or thirty years, and most of the dates of festivals known agree with this period. It was thus the Osirification at the Sed Feast of Hatshepsut which constituted her apotheosis, and so gave rise to the worship of her, and to her statues, while she was still reigning. Under the Ptolemies, deification began in the sixteenth year of Philadelphus. Ptolemy Soter was deified after his death. In Roman times, the emperors had their own worship as chief of the state; this, and their deification after death, was purely Roman, but it would harmonize with their position in Egypt. More Egyptian in theory was the deification of the drowned Antinous as Osiris-Antinous 'worshipped there [in his temple] as a god by the prophets and priests of the South and of the North as well as the people of Egypt.' At Arsinoe there was a temple of Jupiter Capitolinus, where the birthdays of the Emperors of Rome were kept."

Eldridge Cleaver in *Soul on Ice* wrote, "I do not use the term white man. I simply use terms like imperialist, colonialist, oppressor." Fact is, with these people when you learn dynamics of the game they change the rules.

1.   In New York City today, previously a street could be changed and named after a deserving individual. When Mayor Giuliani assumed that role and in face of African-American heroes being given such an honor for contribution to their community, he changed it so only one block and one sign was acceptable, not the entire street as in earlier times.

2.   Present all the evidence to contradict a "white Egypt, instead of a Black Egypt." They dismiss this. Yet, the unstated assumption is

FREDERICK MONDERSON

the Egyptians were white and the only evidence is, "for some unknown reason" and "They brought a superior mental attitude" to enhance the existing culture. How arrogant!

Nevertheless, it is important we consider the monarch's statement as to why a particular monument was undertaken, whether it is a temple being built, an obelisk being raised or another structure being constructed. In the following case, Queen Hatshepsut proclaimed "I sat in the palace and Amon instructed me to erect two obelisks at Karnak's Hall of Pillars." Follow me on his idea of divine communication with humans with the God leaving the heavenly realm to make union with an earthly woman which is different than erection of a monument.

(I) A priest of Ra whose wife was named Ruttet of the 4th Dynasty was told she would have 3 sons who would be kings of Egypt. These turned out to be Khufu, Khafre, and Menkaure. The Greeks called them Chufu, Chephren and Mycerinus and they are builders of the 3 great pyramids at Giza (Ghizeh). They were father, son and grandson.

(II) In order to justify her right to rule in a male-dominated world, Hatshepsut proclaimed she was the son of Amon-Ra, went about wearing male clothing, aligned with "powerful men in the kingdom," initiated and encouraged many innovative cultural practices that endured throughout dynastic rule. She even encouraged officials of her administration to travel throughout the country to view and appreciate historic monuments erected by her predecessors.

To recall, Manetho divided the 3000 years of dynastic rule into "houses of rule." Modern scholars further classified these into Old, Middle and New Kingdoms, and Late Period segments within the general framework of the Chronology of Dynastic Egypt. Before all this, we had the Predynastic Period and the Archaic Period of Dynasties 1 and 2. The Old Kingdom Comprised Dynasties 3-6; The First Intermediate Period 7-10; The Middle Kingdom 11-14; Second Intermediate Period 15-16; the New Kingdom actually began in the 17th, but more properly spanned the 18-20th Dynasties. The Later Period lasted from the 21st through 26th Dynasty, the last native

LET'S LIBERATE THE TEMPLE

dynasty. Then came Persians, Assyrian, and again Persians followed by the Greeks and Romans who were ultimately followed by Arabic Muslims. Not until the 1950s did native Egyptians rule again. Abdul Nasser followed General Naguib who overthrew King Farouk and Sadat followed Nasser. Nasser's father was Nubian and Sadat's mother was Nubian.

The Old Kingdom Pyramid Texts recognized Ra as the supreme god of the heavenly abode while Osiris emerged as God of the earthly abode, ruler of the afterlife and judge of the dead. By the Middle and New Kingdom Amon emerged victorious as the Theban god who reigned for some 800 years. So, in that era of female trailblazing as king, Hatshepsut declared her father was not Thutmose I but the God Amon, Amon-Ra, who made union with her mother "in a flash of light and perfume." This whole episode is depicted at her temple at Deir el Bahari in the "Birth Colonnade."

The mother is shown in the pregnant state being ushered by two midwives; while Khnum makes the young king and his ka on his potter's wheel. Then the two are presented to Amon-Ra for his approval. After propagandizing this experience, she built extensively to justify her right to rule as King. Retaining her youthful figure, even after two daughters, she dressed as a male, wore a false beard and went about addressed by her followers, "Her Majesty Himself." She often boasted, of her "divine figure."

Interesting, in one of the surviving images of the Queen depicted in the Red Chapel, a surprising or not surprising revelation is noticed. Upon a blow-up imagery of the Queen her facial feature is that of a purely African female. This recognition lends credence to the realization, practically all of the images of men and women represented in pharaonic art have their faces mostly disfigured. That is, with the exception of, let's list, three examples for instance:

1. On a back-wall of the Graeco-Roman temple of Kom Ombo, in glare of public view, the images of isi and Nephthys, represented in the "European mold" and these are untouched. This reality is equally found in many instances throughout the temple.

FREDERICK MONDERSON

2. At Isis' Philae Temple, the first of three temples on the Dromos, that of Harendotus, in full public view, the first encountered at the site, the "European images" are again untouched on the first wall encountered.

3. The same argument can be made about the images at the Deir el Medina Temple of Isis as well as Deir el Sherwit. That is, if it looks European it is untouched; if it looks African it is disfigured.

Liberate the Temple. Temple of Horus at Edfu. Scenes from the "Corridor of Victory" of Horus and his pals.

LET'S LIBERATE THE TEMPLE

Liberate the Temple. Temple of Horus at Edfu. Scenes from the "Corridor of Victory" of Horus and his pals.

Liberate the Temple. Temple of Horus at Edfu. Scenes from the "Corridor of Victory" of Horus and his pals.

FREDERICK MONDERSON

Such a deduction goes to the heart of the question of the African nature of the Egyptians and of the Origin of Egyptian civilization.

(III)   At Luxor Temple, Amenhotep III recorded his divine birth same as Hatshepsut did the same at her Deir el Bahari Temple. He was the son of Thutmose IV, grandson of Amenhotep II, and great-grandson of Thutmose III. As far as I know, only Bonwick in *Egyptian Belief and Modern Thought* (The London Publication Society, (reprint) 1983) informed "Amenhotep III was black."

(IV)   Young Dionysius and "Alexander the great" claimed to also be sons of the Egyptian great god.

Still, Bruce Williams' discovery aside, and equally the image of the Scorpion King opening the agricultural season, one of the earliest pictorial representations of Egyptian kingship comes from the Narmer Palette. Here Narmer is shown as a conqueror from Upper Egypt, or the South.   Diop described him as Theban, meaning similar in surviving evidence of ethnicity and color as Mentuhotep, Aahmes-Nefertari, her husband-brother and son, Aahmes and Amenhotep I, Thutmose I, Amenhotep III, Tutankhamon, and the rest. In his first significant recorded act, the monarch subdued the North, Lower Egypt, and in a process of creating national harmony, united the two lands under one kingdom. On the Narmer Macehead we see the king enthroned with his wife, Queen Neithhotep, nearby. Their son Aha followed his father to the throne as Pharaoh. Narmer's victory ended the divisive and destructive pre-dynastic internecine wars, established protocols of the monarchy and laid the groundwork for subsequent economic pursuits and other forms of harmony that encouraged constructive development in the state.

In awe of reverence and with his inherited powers, Narmer set up the monarchy as the form of government. It seems he continued the monarchial system Bruce Williams revealed as originating at Qustol, more than 200 years before Narmer's reign. Perhaps, as Charles Finch

LET'S LIBERATE THE TEMPLE

III indicates, the Pre-Narmer kings discovered by Petrie are possibly linked to Ta-Seti, based at Qustol. Next, the administrative system that characterized such parameters throughout dynastic rule. Evidence seems to show, from as early as the First Dynasty, fashion was uniform throughout the land, from Aswan or Elephantine to the Delta, reinforcing this view. E. Jefferson Murphy in *Ancient Civilizations of Africa* provides a very colorful description of the Pharaoh's regalia. As conqueror who led the army from the South, he also defined the nature and role of the army in internal and external relations. Strange still, as late as the 17th Dynasty, Petrie identified this dynasty as "coming from Nubia, held Thebes as its capitol…." Again, is this a continuation of the earlier monarchy of Nubia at Qustol? It is believed King Narmer also defined the type of weaponry the army used, and especially, the weapons and emblems we came to associate with the king. In addition, the Bull Palette and the Libyan Palette are artifacts relating to the person and activities of the king in this early age.

More particularly, however, the evidence for Egyptian kingship, besides the Narmer Palette and Macehead comes from the various **King Lists**. Not that many, but those that have survived in conjunction with other evidence, provide significant information enabling scholars to practically account for every ruler from Narmer to Cleopatra. While the lists for the most part, relate to the early dynasties, the later periods have sufficient corroborative evidence that the entire history of the kings is clearly established. Ian Shaw and Paul Nicholson in the *Dictionary of Ancient Egypt* (1995: 152) mention: "Several such lists exist, although only that in the temple of Sety I (1294-1279 B.C.) at Abydos, listing seventy-six kings from Menes [Narmer] to Sety himself, remains in its original context. A second list, from the nearby temple of Rameses II (1279-1213 B.C.), is now in the British Museum, and an earlier example from the temple of Amun at Karnak, listing sixty-two kings from Menes to Thutmose III (1279-1425 B.C.), is now in the Louvre. The **Sakkara Tablet**, an example of a private funerary cult of the royal ancestors, was found in the tomb of a scribe called Tenroy; it lists fifty-seven rulers from the 1st Dynasty until the reign of Rameses II. Another private example of a king list was found in the tomb of Amenmessu at Thebes (TT373;

c. 1300 B.C.), where the deceased is shown worshipping the statues of thirteen pharaohs."

Even further, Shaw and Nicholson (1995: 53) continued: "The hieratic papyrus known as the **Turin Royal Canon**, compiled in the 19th Dynasty, and the basalt stele known as the **Palermo Stone**, dating from the end of the 5th Dynasty, are valuable records, although both are incomplete, much of the Turin Canon having been lost in modern times. There are also a few much briefer king lists, such as a graffito at the mining and quarrying site of **Wady Hammamat**, dated paleographically to the 12th Dynasty (1985-1795 B.C.), which consists of the names of five 4th Dynasty rulers and princes." To this must be added the work of the Greek-Egyptian priest Manetho (323-245 B.C.) who wrote a **History of Egypt** that has only survived in fragments commented on by ancient writers. His most lasting contribution however, has been the division of the History of Egypt into dynasties or rule by houses or families of kings. In modern times, Alan Gardiner (1974: 46) provides insights into **Herodotus** who was, of course, an earlier commentator on Egypt in his book, *The Histories*, c. 450 B.C., with Book II, *Euterpe*, devoted to Egypt. After Herodotus came **Diodorus Siculus** and the Jewish historian **Josephus** who flourished around A.D. 70, and together with **Sextus Julius Africanus** (early 3rd century A.D.), and **Eusebius** (early 4th century A.D.) as well as the compiler **George the Monk**, known as **Syncellus** (c A.D. 800), who all have helped in the transmission of **Manetho's** works through their commentaries.

Nonetheless, at the early time of the Archaic Period of Dynasties I and II, the regalia of pharaonic protocols were many. These included crowns and insignia, the sacred symbol of the Uraeus upon the king's brows, as well as whip, flail, crook, scepter, mace, sickle-shaped sword, and pectoral. Some pharaohs carried a bow and arrows. Also, part of the pharaoh's protocol included a talisman, amulets, precious stones, magic jewels, necklaces, tunic, girdle, beard, tail, and sandals. His jewelry included rings, arm-bands, ankle-bands, necklace, a breast

LET'S LIBERATE THE TEMPLE

plate, and much more. Explaining this phenomenon, Erman (1894: 61) noted: "The royal insignia were very complex even in the time of the Old Empire; in later times, they were essentially the same, though more splendid in appearance. In the later period, special importance was attached to the front piece of the royal skirt, which was covered with rich embroidery, uraeus snakes were represented wreathing themselves at the sides, and white ribbons appeared to fasten it to the belt. If, according to ancient custom, the Pharaoh wore nothing but this skirt, it was worn standing out in front in a peak, which was adorned with gold ornamentation. Usually, however, the kings of the New Empire preferred to dress like their subjects, and on festive occasions, they put on the long transparent dress under as well as the full over dress, the short skirt being then worn either over or under these robes."

However, not only did the king dress like his subjects, he often interfaced with and rewarded them for loyalty and service. Foucart in Hasting's *Encyclopedia of Religion and Ethics*, (1914: 714), in commenting on this king and subject relationship wrote: "For the living and the dead the assurance of royal approval is the supreme recompense. The episode of a dignitary summoned to the palace, arriving at the royal audience, and receiving the eulogy or honorific distinctions (such as the collar of gold, from the divine monarch), is the culminating point of his whole career and the crowning moment which he wished to have depicted on the walls of his 'eternal abode.' When he appears before the tribunal of Him who is the ancestor of pharaoh that will be the decisive proof of his merit for worthy service to the gods." Thus, all this notwithstanding, the crowns of Egypt were the embodiment of power. There were about 5 principal crowns, each for a specific purpose or region. In fact, there were actually 3 sets of surviving lists of 23 crowns depicted at the temple of Hathor at Dendera. One each is on the eastern and western outer face of the temple and another on a column on entering the Pronaos to the right. The crowns of Egypt included the Red Crown of the Lower Kingdom with its traditional religious capital at Behedet near Tell-el-Bel-Amon. Its heraldic plant was the papyrus.

FREDERICK MONDERSON

We must be careful of misinformation in fact disinformation designed to lead us astray. **Gary Byrd,** the New York City radio personality admonished we must have all the information. In this he stated: "The information we don't have could kill us." The Red Crown was built up to symbolically elevate the north and supposedly encompass Heliopolis and Ra worship to improve their status. However, the earliest evidence of the Red Crown is found in the southern Upper Egyptian Eastern Desert depicted in Petroglyphs as reported by Toby Wilkinson in his book *Genesis of the Pharaohs* (2003).

On the other hand, the White Crown represented the Upper Kingdom with the royal residence at Ombos near modern Naqada. Let's not forget, Williams' discovery of the White Crown at Qustol in Nubia before dynastic rule. It is generally thought the heraldic plant was the lotus. At unification, the red and white crowns were united in the Red and White Double Crown, though they were worn individually at different times and occasions. Nonetheless, the entire repertoire of the king's insignia with the crowns remained constant throughout dynastic rule. Steindorff and Seele (1957: 84) explained the difference between the principal crowns worn by the king, each with its respective designation. "The royal headdress consisted of a whole collection of crowns: the white crown of Upper Egypt; the red crown of Lower Egypt; the double crown, a combination of the red and white crowns, which symbolized in the person of the king the 'uniter of the Two Lands' and therefore the ruler of all Egypt; the blue crown, a cap of cloth or leather which the king often wore on the battlefield; the linen kerchief which covered the head and extended in front over the shoulders and chest in two broad lappets, while it ended behind the head in a sort of queue hanging below the back of the neck."

LET'S LIBERATE THE TEMPLE

Liberate the Temple. Temple of Horus at Edfu. Scenes from the "Corridor of Victory" of Horus and his pals.

Liberate the Temple. Temple of Horus at Edfu. Scenes from the "Corridor of Victory" of Horus and his pals.

FREDERICK MONDERSON

Liberate the Temple. Temple of Horus at Edfu. Scenes from the "Corridor of Victory" of Horus and his pals.

All these items of royal paraphernalia represented the full panoply of pharaonic symbolism, each contributing to the esoteric, magical mystique of the King of Egypt, who was both man and god. Foucart further writes, "Even under the 1st dynasty, there appeared scenes of that distant epoch similar to those found in the Greek period upon the walls of the temple of Edfu or other sanctuaries built in Egypt by the Ptolemies." As such, "The king, then, is a being constituted by all that, in this world, religion could know of divine forces, governing powers, magic resources, and inter-terrestrial science."

In addition, the king had his personal priests and his family, viz., mother, sons, wives, daughters, harem, and noble companions who all had a role to play in the dynamics and totality of the king's responsibilities to the nation and the gods. The issues of these "players" surrounding the king were such, Erman (1894: 53-54) provides an interesting description of the challenging dynamics of kingship amidst intrigue and statesmanship. He pointed out: "Around the king were the old counselors who had served his father, and whom the clerks and officials were accustomed blindly to obey, as well as

LET'S LIBERATE THE TEMPLE

the generals with the troops in their pay, and the priesthood with their unlimited power over the lower classes. In the small towns the old rich families of the nobility, residing in their countryseats, were nearer to the homes of the people than the monarch dwelling in his distant capital. The king was afraid to offend any of these powerful people; he had to spare the sensitive feelings of the minister; discover a way of gratifying the ambition of the general without endangering the country; watch carefully that his officers did not encroach on the rights of the nobility; and above all keep in favor with the priests. It was only when the king could satisfy all these claims and understand at the same time how to play off one party against another, that he could expect a long and prosperous reign. If he failed, his chances were small for their lurked close to him his most dangerous enemies, his nearest relatives."

This is interesting, for Erman (1894: 54) continued further: "There always existed a brother or an uncle, who imagined he had a better claim to the throne than the reigning king, or there were the wives of the late ruler, who thought it a fatal wrong that the child of their rival rather than their own son should have inherited the crown. During the lifetime of the king they pretended to submit, but they waited anxiously for the moment to throw off the mask. They understood well how to intrigue, and to aggravate any misunderstanding between the king and his counselors or his generals, until at last one of them, who thought himself slighted or injured, proceeded to open rebellion, and began the war by proclaiming one of the pretenders as the only true king, who had wrongfully been kept from the throne. The result was always the same; the others admired the boldness of their rival and hastened to imitate it, until there were as many pretenders as there were parties in the kingdom. It made little difference who won in the fight; he made his way to the throne through the blood of his opponents, and then began a struggle with those who had helped him. If he possessed good luck and energy he was able to clear them out of his way; otherwise he became a tool in the hands of those around him, who, at the first sign of independence, would cause him to be murdered and place a more docile ruler on the throne in his place."

There were also others with whom he had to contend. For example, this is highlighted by Rawlinson (1898: 288-89) who pointed out, the kings were particularly fearful of their subjects, the priests. He states: "The kings lived always in a considerable amount of awe of the priests. Though claiming a certain qualified divinity, themselves, they yet could not but be aware that there were diverse flaws and imperfections in their own divinity - 'little rifts within the lutes'- which made it not quite a safe support to trust to, or lean upon, entirely. There were other greater gods than themselves - gods from whom their own divinity was derived; and they could not be certain what power or influence the priests might have with these superior beings, in whose existence and ability to benefit and injure men they had the fullest belief. Consequently, the kings are found to occupy a respectful attitude towards the priests throughout the whole course of Egyptian history, from first to last; and this respectful attitude is especially maintained towards the great personages in whom the hierarchy culminates, the head officials, or chief priests, of the temple which are the principal centers of the national worship - the temple of Ra, or Tum, at Heliopolis, that of Phthah at Memphis, and that of Ammon at Thebes. According to the place where the capital was fixed for the time being, one or other of these three high-priests had the pre-eminence; and, in the later period of the Ramesside, Thebes having enjoyed metropolitan dignity for between five and six centuries, the Theban High-Priest of Ammon was recognized as beyond dispute the chief of the sacerdotal order, and the next person in the kingdom after the king." In fact, Herihor, the High Priest of Amon-Ra during the 22nd Dynasty had himself depicted in Karnak's Hypostyle Hall as equal in size with the reigning pharaoh. Even more important, Herihor would seize the throne and declare himself pharaoh, *Pontifex Maximus*. That is, king and high priest.

The dynamics of such intrigue aside, on the Narmer Palette, the king is shown with his sandal bearer. He is also shown smiting the enemy with his mace and as a true conqueror, with captives. The raised relief sculpture of the palette shows him as a colossal figure in relationship to his subjects. This colossal representation of the kingly person remained an art form throughout Egyptian history. Important, however, on the Narmer Macehead, numbering of captives of men,

LET'S LIBERATE THE TEMPLE

goats, and cattle show they were counting in the millions this early in time.

Once again, Williams' discovery notwithstanding, perhaps underscoring his relationship with the divine, Narmer established a shrine for the God Ptah at Memphis and began the official practice of religious worship and ritualization of this divinity. Much of this became well established by the first and second Thinite Dynasties coming from This, near Abydos in Upper Egypt, also site of the "tomb of Osiris." Abydos is where Flinders Petrie discovered 10 successive layers of temples and where he found the only image or statue, al be it miniature, of Khufu, builder of the Great Pyramid at Ghizeh, during the 4th Dynasty.

While Budge describes Hathor as of "Sudanic origin" and she appears significantly on Narmer's palette; Bauval and Brophy in **Black Genesis** credits the people of Nabta Playa as initiating worship of the "cow goddess" among other creations as early as Predynastic times and such may date several millennia into that past.

Next, the king's role as builder was shown with several projects, beginning with the major "white wall," Narmer built at Memphis. After unification, for economic and strategic reasons, this city was chosen as the nation's new administrative capital. As Pharaoh, he was responsible for the inspection of public works such as irrigation projects consisting of canals, basins, embankments, wells and lakes all important conduits in an agricultural society. These contained the much-needed waters essential in Egypt in preparation for the Inundation season had ended. In addition, records depict the king, after the first dynasty, inspecting the frontier and establishing his authority by "going around the wall" and "uniting the lands of Upper and Lower Egypt." At the beginning of the dynastic period, King Scorpion was also depicted as breaking ground to open the agricultural season after the waters of the Inundation had receded.

Consistent with his divine heritage and cognizant of the existence of good and evil both internally and externally, the head of the Egyptian state assumed the function of head of the army, chief administrator, and high priest who performed religious functions on behalf of the state's responsibility to the god. As chief and principal priest, he, however, could not be in every temple to perform the three daily ritual responsibilities to the god. So, he appointed a Chief Priest for each temple, though the reigning god's chief priest headed the national priestly priesthood bureaucracy. Of course, only after Coronation could he officiate and worship the god in his temple.

Liberate the Temple. Temple of Horus at Edfu. Scenes from the "Corridor of Victory" of Horus and his pals, with Pharaoh before the God and his consort.

LET'S LIBERATE THE TEMPLE

Liberate the Temple. Temple of Horus at Edfu. Scenes from the "Corridor of Victory" of Horus and his pals.

Liberate the Temple. Temple of Horus at Edfu. Scenes from the "Corridor of Victory" of Horus and his pals depicting the King before the enthroned God and his consort.

FREDERICK MONDERSON

According to the religious beliefs, nonetheless, these rituals were especially important. J. Manchip White's *Ancient Egypt* (1970) offers commentary that explains one of the philosophical and spiritual roles as a function of the king. He wrote: "The enemy whose onslaughts Pharaoh resisted was not only the host of Libyans, Nubians, Beduins and Asiatics who lurked on Egypt's physical boundaries, but also the spiritual enemy in the shapes of Seth and Apophis." This cosmological belief held, the "powers of darkness, though constantly vanquished, attempted ceaselessly to overthrow Egypt by blighting the crops, obstructing the flow of the Nile, causing floods or preventing the sun from rising." As such, the pharaoh unceasingly worshipped and ritualized the Gods or was in turn ritualized as their earthly manifestation to help maintain a balanced universal order. He was "the Gods' man on the ground," who did the earthly work for the divinities in combating these cosmic powers of evil intent.

To accomplish such an assignment by the king; or his assignees or subordinates; of placating the gods, and in comparative analogy, Petrie (1924: 25) comments on Clemens' view of "a temple in living order." In this description he wrote: "The porticoes, vestibules and groves are constructed with great splendor; the halls are adorned with many columns; the walls are perfectly splendid with rare stones and brilliancy of color; the sanctuary shines with gold, silver and electrum, and with a variety of glittering stones from India or Ethiopia, and the adytum is hung with curtains of gold tissue. If you enter the circuit of the holy place, and, hastening to behold what is worthiest of your search, you seek, the statue of the deity, one of the priests, who performs the rites there, steps forward to introduce you to the object of his worship, looking upward with a grave and reverent face, as he chants the paean hymn in the native tongue."

The ritual of the temple generally practiced several times per day, in practically all temples with slight variation, remained essentially traditional and unchanged throughout dynastic rule. Again, Petrie (1924: 28-29) explained how the ceremony was conducted throughout the day, with the king officiating as part of his functions as the Gods' representative on earth, or as a god worshipping himself as well as the

LET'S LIBERATE THE TEMPLE

other gods. "The whole course of daily service began with the series of actions each carried out with a long speech. This may not have been entirely aloud, as there are long prayers and adorations recited inaudibly by the priest in the Coptic service. So, anciently, much may have been recited mentally, or by 'intention.' First the incense was offered, to perfume the whole sanctuary. Then the priest opened the chapel and saluted the god with many protestations, and chanting hymns. Sand was sprinkled on the floor. Then the sacred vessels were taken, and the daily toilet of the god performed. Twice, water was sprinkled over the statue, which was then clothed in linen bands, white, green, red, and brown. Then the statue was anointed, and painted with green paint under the eyes, and black on the eyelids. Then the food was placed before the god. The food and the linen could next day be offered to the statues of dead persons, which were placed in the temple. Thus, a man often secured his own offerings, and insured his own benefit by making an endowment to the god, which could not be revoked. The copying of domestic service is obvious. The house was fumigated, the floor sanded; then the master was awakened. He was washed, dressed, had the preservative eye paints put on, and then partook of his morning meal. Processions were the great external part of the worship. The barque of the god was carried, just as a noble was carried, on a stand supported on two long poles, which rested on the shoulders of the two rows of priests. At other times, it might be the emblem of the god, such as the sacred head of Osiris that was carried."

The idea of the king worshipping himself is generally considered a New Kingdom phenomenon. Perhaps it is Ramesside! We look for this at the Temple of Seti I at Abydos that is dedicated to multiple gods. In fact, the temple's seven shrines are for the seven deities worshipped there such as, from right to left as the visitor looks inward, Horus, Isis, Osiris, Ra Horakhty, Amon, Ptah and Seti deified. These were the gods of the Osiris cycle; the three great gods of the Egyptian Empire; and a deified Seti. This is one of the first such surviving temples principally dedicated to multiple gods. Hatshepsut's temple at Deir el Bahari is dedicated principally to Amon and secondarily hosts Shrines to Hathor and Anubis, as well as having an altar to Ra-Horakhty and a shrine for herself and father Thutmose I. Equally,

FREDERICK MONDERSON

Thutmose III is also represented within. However, Rameses II's temple at Abu Simbel is dedicated, again, to the three great gods of the New Kingdom, Amon, Ra-Horakhty, Ptah and that deified king Rameses II. Later, during Graeco-Roman times the surviving temple at Kom Ombo was dedicated to twin deities, the Elder Horus and Sobek, the Crocodile God. This latter and several other temples are dedicated to particular gods or may have shrines to other deities but not the king. Karnak is a good example. It is a worship temple dedicated to the Theban Triad of Amon, Mut and Khonsu, though each had their own temple. There are a host of other deities worshipped at Karnak and that is why it is called the 'Palaces' as a place where the gods "Visit." Still, though the kings built there at Karnak, no one king is worshipped at this shrine. Still, we know Thutmose III built his *Akh Menu*, festival temple beyond the Middle Kingdom Court at the rear of and east of the "Holy of Holies;" Rameses II built the "Temple of the Hearing Ear" beyond the *Akh Menu* and Taharka, who had erected a Kiosk in the center of the great Court at the Western end of the temple, place another between Rameses II's "Hearing Ear" temple and Nectanebo's eastern gate. Rameses III built his temple on an axis perpendicular to the main center line in the Great Court at the other or western end entrance to Karnak. However, some scholars believe Seti I considered the Hypostyle Hall at Karnak, which he for the most part built and decorated, to be a mortuary temple within a worship temple. How interesting!

Even more, prior to Ramesside times, no king is shown being worshipped as deified. Nevertheless, Petrie (1924: 103-04) does, however, supply surviving Ramesside evidence of clear-cut examples of the king being worshipped asa god at this time. He states: "The best evidence for the worship of the living king before Osirification is in the Harris papyrus where Rameses IV represents Rameses III as enjoining people to bow to Rameses IV, serve him always, adore him, implore him and magnify his goodness, as they do to Ra. As Rameses IV was under thirty years old at the time, he cannot yet have been Osirified, even as co-regent. There was a lesser claim of divine descent; this was enforced by each generation claiming direct divine paternity, by the father impersonating the god. The idea still

LET'S LIBERATE THE TEMPLE

continued to Greek times, as seen by the tales of their divine paternity of Alexander from Zeus Ammon, quoted by Plutarch and others and elaborated into a tale. The Persian conquerors were naturally disliked, yet Darius, 'while he was alive, gained the title of a god, which none of the other kings ever did; and when he was dead, the people allowed him all those ancient honors due and accustomed to be done to the former kings of Egypt after their deaths.'"

Further, records indicate, the "spiritual potency of the king, on which the well-being of his subjects depended, was enhanced by the purity of his breeding. Theoretically the actual blood of the sun god had been transmitted by Horus into the royal veins." This caused the priesthood, one of whose realms of concern was succession, to take great pains in ensuring prolific procreation for the Pharaoh. However, and as far as possible, they permitted few marriages outside the royal family. This way divinity was kept "all in the family."

The Pharaoh ruled by Ma'at, a philosophy and social practice of order in the society through truth, justice and righteous behavior. In the afterlife and in front of Osiris, Thoth, Anubis, Isis, and Nephthys, he was judged based on his actions while on earth. So, he structured his rule to bring about the ideal - "Justice was defined as 'what Pharaoh loves,' wrongdoing as 'what Pharaoh hates.'" He was the rule of law in the state and the final refuge of appeal. Few cases, however, reached this level of litigation.

FREDERICK MONDERSON

Liberate the Temple. Temple of Horus at Edfu. King and Queen and God and Consort.

Liberate the Temple. Temple of Horus at Edfu. Holding Hathor's rattle, the Queen stands behind the king to present two crowns to Horus and Hathor.

LET'S LIBERATE THE TEMPLE

Liberate the Temple. Temple of Horus at Edfu. From the Pronaos, observe two visitors in the Peristyle Court (left) with its three rows of columns, each with a different capital.

In time, Pharaoh Amenemhat III ruled in the Twelfth Dynasty, during the Middle Kingdom. A high official in his service spoke to his children and summed up what was a universal belief throughout Egypt regarding his master, as well as the symbol of Pharaoh. "'He is the God Ra whose beams enable us to see. He gives more light to the Two Lands than the sun's disc. He makes the earth more green than the Nile in flood. He is the Ka (i.e. the guardian spirit). He is the god Khnum who fashions all flesh. He is the goddess Bast who defends Egypt.'"

Further, continued this source, "... whoever worships him is under his protection. But he is Sekhmet, the terrible lion goddess, to those who disobey him. Take care not to defy him. A friend of Pharaoh attains the rank of Honored One, but there is no tomb for the rebel. His body is thrown into the river. Therefore, listen to what I tell you and you will enjoy health and prosperity.'"

FREDERICK MONDERSON

Therefore, in order to understand how the king came to enjoy this status, respect and engendered such awe, we need to create a framework to examine why the Pharaoh came to epitomize the lifeblood of Egypt and Nile Valley cultural and philosophical experience. First, the religious character of the king is indicated in Hastings *Encyclopedia of Religion and Ethics*, Vol. VII (1914: 711-715) entitled "King, Egyptian," wherein is discussed the "conception of monarchy which is composed of purely theological elements and based solely upon the assimilation of the king to the gods who are the makers of the world and the mythical founders of Egyptian society." Taken together, therefore, the names of the king in their totality, "constitutes the nature of the pharaoh and of the royal attributes."

The king's divine lineage extends deep into the prehistoric period. In this examination, we find "the old 'sky-god' source of life and death, of rain and heavenly fire. Among his names that of Heru symbolized conventionally by the hawk, has given rise to the so-called 'hawk names,' which appear among the most ancient forms of royal names with which we are acquainted - viz., the series of names from the monuments belonging to the Thinite period (1st and 2nd dynasties). These show, when set in order, that the reigning king is a form or emanation upon this earth of the Supreme Being - or, more exactly one of the 'souls' of that being." In the theological evolution of the religious thought and practice, "the 'sky god' was replaced by the 'sun god.'"

"When the king is called 'the two Horus,' or the 'Horu-Siti,' we see a reminiscence of the system which divided the world into two halves, each with its Supreme God, in heaven and on earth. Similarly, the religion of the sky-goddess Nuit, who was believed to have produced the world, first by her own activity and later by union with the earth-god Sibu, gave the king the name of 'son of Nuit,' or 'eldest son of Sibu.' This prepared the way for the assimilation of the Pharaoh to Ra, then to Osiris, according to the successive theologies reversing the order of the first cosmogonies, have made Ra the son of Nuit, or, on the other hand, the father of Sibu and Nuit, and the grandfather of Osiris. In the last form, the Pharaoh is the successor of Osiris, as the direct descendant of Horus, son of the pair Isis-Osiris."

LET'S LIBERATE THE TEMPLE

Even further, we learn an "outstanding characteristic of the king has always been that he was either an incarnation of the god who made the world or his son (in the literal sense of the word, not symbolically, or by a mystic adoption, but by real dilation). The king of Egypt has thus never been merely a representative or interpreter of the Supreme God, or his 'vicar;' either he is the god himself, manifest upon the earth in human body in which is incarnate one of the souls of the god, or he is the god's own son." The article continued: "This form of the affiliation best known to us is the title of Sa Ra, 'son of the sun,' which was inaugurated as early as the middle of the Vth dynasty, under the influence of the priesthood of Heliopolis, and persisted as long as the Pharaonic protocol was in existence."

"This divine descent was, as a rule, proved by the ordinary genealogy. From ancestor to ancestor, the reigning king was able to trace back his lineage to the fabulous Menes, or Mini, the legendary founder of the first human dynasty, and from him he went back through the mythical reigns of Menes as far as Horus, son of Isis, and son and avenger of his father Osiris, the first king-god of the valley of the Nile."

But in certain exceptional cases of which we possess three or four historical examples the king boasts of being procreated directly by the god. It's stated, "in order to establish legitimacy indisputably, the Pharaoh seems to have claimed the testimony of a more direct and recent intervention of the Supreme God. Thus (1) in the temple of Luxor for Amenhotep III, (2) in the temple of Deir-el-Bahari for Hatshepsut, and (3) at Erment for Caesarian, the bas-relief tells how the god himself descended to the earth in order to have union with the queen and himself beget the little prince who should one-day reign over Egypt. They also show the birth of the divine scion, the magic charms which accompanied him, and the benediction of the god upon the new-born child when it was presented to him."

"They felt that the kingship must be the final result of all that legendary Egypt had known of divine domination or, rather, that it meant the total heritage of all that the world contained of the forces belonging to the beneficent gods. Hence the walls of the temples show the king as heir and adopted son of all the great deities of the national pantheon in succession - the great feudal gods of the Nile Valley and the chief elementary or starry gods."

So, in winding down, we recognize:

The king is well-beloved son
He addresses the gods 'father'

"In the case of the goddesses, they make the young king their veritable son by giving him milk from their breast in token of adoption. Even this accumulation of divinity seemed insufficient to the Egyptians to constitute their god-king completely."

Still, the philosophical transformation is another issue facing the new king. Even more we are told correctly: "The true Pharaoh does not exist, theologically speaking, until he has received at Heliopolis, all the magico-religious consecrations which transform him into a living incarnation of Ra, the sun-god, creator of the world. The elaborate series of ceremonies employed to accomplish that transformation is well known to us today through: (1) the historical inscriptions, such as that of the celebrated Ethiopian conqueror Piankhy, (2) the ritual published in the Pyramid Texts, (3) the bas-reliefs and special enactments of the solar temples of Abusir, (4) the extracts from anointing and coronation scenes sculptured in the great temples, chiefly at Thebes, (5) the statues and statuettes commemorating coronations (notably at Karnak), and (6) the descriptive scenes telling of the 'jubilee' feasts of habsedu. Finally, the Thinite monuments discovered at Abydos provide evidence that the whole of this ceremonial was already established, in its essential elements, at the Thinite period. Even under the 1st dynasty there appeared scenes of that distant epoch similar to those found in the Greek period upon the walls of the temple of Edfu or other sanctuaries built in Egypt by the Ptolemies." We must remember uniformity of culture as early as the First Dynasty was widespread across the country. Therefore, these ideas are as southern as Narmer and we must be reminded, according to Amelineau and Diop. "The Anu, a Black race of Africans, founded

LET'S LIBERATE THE TEMPLE

Heliopolis and thoughts emanating therefrom. That is, particularly the "doctrine of Ra."

Liberate the Temple. Temple of Horus at Edfu. Columns of the First Hypostyle Hall with their thin bases.

Liberate the Temple. Temple of Horus at Edfu. One of the varied columns with its delicate intricacies.

FREDERICK MONDERSON

Liberate the Temple. Temple of Horus at Edfu. Showki Abd Rady and Carmen Monderson "Mug for the Camera" in the temple's Court.

As such, then, the king was lord of all order and truth and after his spiritual and philosophical roles, the next most important role was defender of the realm from actual and spiritual forces.

This makes him, the heir to the power and qualities of the Good Gods, whose powers are symbolized by, and materialized in the various names. He also has access to the accumulated power of his brother and sister gods from which he may replenish his own power.

THE ROYAL TITLES

The king, then, is a being constituted by all that, in this world, religion could know of divine forces, governing powers, magic resources, and super-terrestrial science.

LET'S LIBERATE THE TEMPLE

"The king of Egypt had at least five names in the classical period: (1) 'birth-name,' which is his human name, expressing the relation of the reigning dynasty to one or another of the great provincial gods of Egypt (e.g., Thutmose = 'Thoth had fashioned him;' Amenhotep = 'he is united to Amen'); this is the name which is preceded by the epithet 'son of the sun' (Sa Ra) in the inscriptions; (2) the coronation name, preceded by the affirmation of kingship over the world of the north and world of the south by the heraldic figuration of the Reed and the Bee; this name (chosen by the astrological colleges of priests according to horoscopic indications) materialized, somehow or other, the aspect and attributes of the particular solar soul that came to transform the young prince into a god on the day of his anointing; it was sometimes a long motto expressing the role or the energies of Ra in this world (e.g., 'Ra is the lord of the cosmos,' 'Great are the successive becomings of Ra'); (3) the hawk name (i.e. sky-god name; this was enclosed in a kind of panel or rectangle representing a facade of a palace, and surmounted by a hawk, divine Horu; (4) a name called in archaeology 'name of the vulture and uraeus,' which reached to the extreme frontiers of Egypt, from El Kab to Buto; (5) a name, often incorrectly called 'golden hawk name,' which, preceded by the figure of a hawk perched on a sign of gold (nub), declares in reality that the king is the heir to the stellar powers who share the two astrological halves of the universe."

Other names

Heir of the war-like gods, he is called 'Powerful Bull' (*Nib iri khitu*), or 'Resplendent in his glorious appearings' (*Nib khau*). Some of these names expressing the virtues or forces of the kingship bear a curious resemblance to those which describe (or designate) the kings of certain monarchies in Black Africa (e.g. the sovereigns of Dahomey or Benin) and it would be worthwhile to draw up a list of the possible comparisons. None of these epithets should be regarded (as they too often are) as arising from vanity or grandiloquence, for each corresponds theologically to a very precise definition of a function or force belonging to one or other of the great gods of Egypt."

FREDERICK MONDERSON

"Good God"

"Double Palace"

"Sublime Gate"

"Great Dwelling" (= the royal Residence), the equivalent of which is found in the royal title-list of certain Black monarchies of West Africa. The Egyptian term pir-ao has become the word 'Pharaoh,' which served throughout the classical world to designate the king of Egypt."

EARTHLY COUNTERPART OF THE GODS

The sovereign is a singularly complex person, whose body contains even more souls (*biu*), doubles (*kau*), and 'shadows' (*haibit*) than that of ordinary men.

These are frequently figured beings formed by the gods in heaven, or beings suckled at birth by the fairies, or accompanying the king (but distinct from him) in coronation and procession scenes.

The king is a living epitome of all that is divine in the Nile Valley.

"First, he is in every function an earthly image of the various gods and performs their legendary activity on the earth. In his justice he is Thoth, in his power he is Ra; like the first divine masters of the divine valley, he destroys the enemies of the work done by the ancient gods when they assisted Ra in the conflict against darkness and in the organization of the world. This view, the very beginning of dualism originated in the primitive cosmogony and was later transformed by the Osirian legend into the myth of the conflict between the partisans of Horus and the bad spirits who were the friends of Set. The Pharaoh

LET'S LIBERATE THE TEMPLE

is thus heir to the powers and qualities of the good gods, whose powers are symbolized by, and materialized in, the various names."

The organized theologies ascribed to the royal person a thousand different roles, implying a thousand traditional moral duties and magical powers. Some of these duties concern war, and perhaps may seem somewhat brutal for our taste; others are as noble as modern thought could desire. Scenes and texts display the king 'as some bull young, ardent, and resistless, which tramples down under its hoofs the enemies of Egypt' (Hymn of Thutmose III), the 'rebels.' Some of the other names are, 'accursed;' the 'children of ruin;' as a 'devouring lion;' as a Sudan leopard; or as a hawk which tears and rends the foreign nations with beak and claws (The Thinite palettes). To each of these representations there is attached a role formerly played by the national gods, which the king assumed when he ascended the throne of Horus. The lion, the griffin, the bull, the hawk, and the sphinx are all aspects of powers he possesses.

The King is therefore, "Lord of all order and truth" and after his spiritual and philosophic roles, the king's next most important role was as defender of the realm. From the time of Narmer when he conquered Lower Egypt and established unification, all through the Archaic Period, the Old Kingdom actions against the Asiatic Bedouins, the Middle Kingdom unification, consolidation and expansion with punitive actions against enemies north and south; in the War of Liberation to expel the Hyksos and establishment and maintaining the New Kingdom; wars of Thutmose I, III, Amenhotep; the Ramesside kings, Seti, Rameses II, Rameses III; the Ethiopians, Piankhy, Shabaka, Taharka, etc.; the king was always a warrior pharaoh. Here he defended his nation against internal and external tangible enemies as opposed to the role he performed in his spiritual responsibility to the gods and country. Therefore, the Kingship of Egypt was quite a responsibility in ancient times when the world was just coming into vogue, and the Nile Valley was aflame with the thoughts, aspirations and accomplishment of ancient Africans with noble aspirations in Egypt, northeast Africa.

FREDERICK MONDERSON

In conclusion, the King of Egypt was both man and god. He possessed extraordinary powers when rightfully ordained. His principal function was worshipping and ritualizing the gods, defending Egypt from natural and spiritual forces, keeping the country in equilibrium and reigning as a good king who ruled in truth, justice and righteousness. He had to be a statesman, politician, diplomat, warrior, artistic patron and astute and generous. Only then was he able to subdue the forces that threatened his nation, domestic and foreign, material and spiritual, ecclesiastic and secular. When able to do all these things, the nation prospered and great national projects were undertaken, arts and crafts, science and medicine, building and engineering, theology and cosmogony and astronomy and astrology as well as learning, were pursued and thus the culture has left us great evidence of its accomplishments. Without question, the temple played a major role in bringing about the success of all these factors.

This and more is the legacy of Africans, the projected falsity notwithstanding, we must defend Egypt as African and Black.

Liberate the Temple. Temple of Horus at Edfu. Uraei in Red and White Crowns stand before two defaced images of Hathor.

LET'S LIBERATE THE TEMPLE

Liberate the Temple. Temple of Horus at Edfu. While Horus squats before an image of himself, an ape and jackal and the number ten represented several times depict this "Procession."

REFERENCES

Bauval, Robert and Adrian Gilbert. *The Orion Mystery*. New York: Crown Trade Paperbacks, (1994) 1995.
Budge, E.A.W. *Gods of the Egyptians*. Vol. I. New York: Dover Publications, Inc., (1904) 1969.
Foucart, George. "The King" in *Encyclopedia of Religion and Ethics* Vol. 5. New York: C. Scribner's Sons, 1915.
Erman, Adolf. *Life in Ancient Egypt*. New York: Macmillan, 1894.
Gardiner, Sir. Alan. *Egypt of the Pharaohs*. New York: Oxford University Press, (1961) 1974.
McMahan, Ian. *Secrets of the Pharaohs*. New York: Avon Books, 1998.
Murnane, William J. *The Penguin Guide to Ancient Egypt*. New York: Penguin Books, 1983.
Petrie, Sir Flinders. *Social Life in Ancient Egypt*. Boston and New York: Houghton Mifflin Company, 1923.
_____. *Religious Life in Ancient Egypt*. London, Bombay, Sydney: Constable and Company, Ltd., 1924.

FREDERICK MONDERSON

Rawlinson, George. *Ancient Egypt*. New York: G. P. Putnam's Sons, 1893.
Shaw, Ian and Paul Nicholson. *The Dictionary of Ancient Egypt*. New York: Harry N. Abrams, Inc., Publishers, 1995.
White, J.E. Manchip. *Ancient Egypt*. New York: Dover Publications, Inc., (1952) 1970.

Liberate the Temple. Gathering of Friends. (left to right) Hammam, the Driver, "the Wedding Dad," Showki and Ibrahim Soliman.

LET'S LIBERATE THE TEMPLE

XVI. THE AWESOME EGYPTIAN TEMPLE III: A Summary
By
Dr. Fred Monderson

I Introduction
    a. The "Long" and "Short Chronology"
    b. Temples in Time Perspective
    c. Historical Documents

i. **The Narmer Palette** - Found by Quibell at Hierakonpolis, Upper Egypt, first Capital of Egypt. This document illustrates the unification of Egypt.

ii. **The Narmer Macehead** - This is the King's weapon. It shows his marriage to a Northern Queen, now thought to be a Southerner.

    iii. **Palermo Stone**
    iv. **Turin Papyrus - Royal Papyrus of Turin**
    v. **Manetho's Chronicles**
    vi. **Tablets**

a. **Abydos Tablet I** - Temple of Seti I - 19th Dynasty. Still in place or *in Situ*.

b. **Abydos Tablet II** - Temple of Rameses - 19th Dynasty. Now in the British Museum.

FREDERICK MONDERSON

Liberate the Temple. Esneh Temple of Khnum. Façade of the Temple, some 50-60 feet buried below street level. This shows how the land has risen from the Inundation over the millennia.

Liberate the Temple. Esneh Temple of Khnum. The king offers a platter to Bastet with figure in Double Crown at her rear.

LET'S LIBERATE THE TEMPLE

Liberate the Temple. Esneh Temple of Khnum.
Khnum offers symbol of many Sed-festivals or "years" to the king as a youngster (with hands to his mouth) stands behind the God.

Liberate the Temple. Esneh Temple of Khnum.
Offering a boat vessel and ointment jars to Horus.

c. **Karnak Tablet** - Thutmose III - 18th Dynasty. Now in the Louvre, Paris, stolen by Prisse De Avennes.

d. **Sakkara Tablet** - Old Kingdom. Still in place at Sakkara.

e. **Steles/Colonnades** - These recount a king's commemoration, establishment of a person's exploits and recognition of service in the community. They also reflect a level of cultural attainment and provides explanations of a belief system concerning the future life. Colonnades are a decorative architectural motif, particularly in temples, a marker or recording that also praises an individual by "writing his name in the colonnade."

f. **Cemeteries/Tombs** - Underground disposal of the dead that contain "goods of the grave" or "mortuary furniture" that tells of the individual's life and is hopes and aspirations for existence in the Afterlife. They also exhibit, especially tombs, pictographic and material evidence of the society's accomplishments.

II. What has survived?
- Much of what we know is based on speculation. For we possess no more than 20% of required data. Still, a lot has been recovered in terms of material evidence. For instance, the Cairo Museum of Egyptian Antiquities has a purported collection of 120,000 pieces. There are other pieces in museums throughout Egypt. Consider, however, Britain has 128 Museums with Egyptian collections; the United States has 29; and there are numerous museums scattered across Europe. However, while there are 54 countries in Africa, only Sudan, beside Egypt, has an Egyptian collection. Much more significant and devastating, for example, among all the people – archaeologists, artists, linguists, anthropologists, scientists, who worked to unearth and interpret Egyptian ancient knowledge, and there were literally thousands over two centuries, not to discount tourists, etc., Lepsius shipped 15,000 pieces to Berlin and Reisner unloaded "several hundred boxes" as a gift to the University of California. Now, multiply these numbers by

LET'S LIBERATE THE TEMPLE

the workers who took home artifacts, adventurers who collected and sold to public and private collection and we thus have some understanding of the notion of "a culture in captivity" or as Brian Fagan named his book, *The Rape of the Nile*.

Liberate the Temple. Mentuhotep's 11th Dynasty Temple at Deir el Bahari. View of some of the rubble of this "Oldest Temple at Thebes" and "best preserved of the oldest temples."

Liberate the Temple. Mentuhotep's 11th Dynasty Temple at Deir el Bahari. View of some of the rubble of this "Oldest Temple at Thebes" and "best preserved of the oldest temples."

FREDERICK MONDERSON

Liberate the Temple. Mentuhotep's 11th Dynasty Temple at Deir el Bahari. View of some of the rubble of this "Oldest Temple at Thebes" and "best preserved of the oldest temples."

a.   Old Kingdom - Temple and Tomb Together - Essentially a Pyramid Complex - with Valley Temple, Mortuary Temple and Worship Temple, Pyramids and more.

b.   Middle Kingdom - Transitional - Temple and Tomb still together – Beginning of Processional Temple – Mentuhotep II's temple at Deir el Bahari (11th Dynasty) and Sesostris I's **"White Chapel"** (12th Dynasty).

c.   New Kingdom - Emergence of Worship, Mortuary and coming of age of the Processional Temples separately. - This architectural breakthrough was encouraged through the economic wealth of the Imperial Age.

c.   Kiosk - These are a small temple dedicated to three gods. The surviving ones are at Luxor - 18th Dynasty built by Queen

LET'S LIBERATE THE TEMPLE

Hatshepsut, dedicated to Amon, Mut and Khonsu, the Theban Triad. It was usurped by her nephew Thutmose II and later Rameses II who built the "Ramessean Front," as an addition to the temple.

Abydos - This is dedicated to Isis, Horus and Seti I.

Karnak - Seti II of the 19th Dynasty, dedicated to Amon, Mut and Khonsu. Karnak and Luxor are outdoor separate temples while Abydos has an indoor compartment for this Kiosk.

d.   Graeco-Roman

i.   Introduction of the Mammisi - Birthplace of the God's son.

ii.   Temples were now more Profusely Illustrated. The art becomes more sensual. These temples were built by Nubian and Egyptian architects based on the ancient plans but were supervised by Greek and Roman overlords. These temples preserved various aspects of the ritual and culture. Nevertheless, with Greek and Roman temple building innovation these structures became graphically illustrated. Thus, was preserved much of the ancient ideas for modern bases of knowledge that helps enlarge the picture and an understanding of the dynamics of African mind in the ancient Nile Valley.

III. The Role of the Temple.

a.   Worship Temple - God's Temple

i.   The God's House;

ii.   Practice of the ritual and worship of the god;

iii.   Celebration of Festivals;

iv.   Dedication of a temple;

v.   Presentation of a King's tribute, slaves;

vi.   Processions are part of the ritual, generally in the Hypostyle Hall but also throughout the temple.

vii.   Place of the Coronation of the King.

b.   Mortuary Temple - King's Temple

i.   King's Sacred Space

ii.   Worship of King in life and when he becomes a god upon death - Gone to meet his "brother gods."

iii.   God visits Luxor Temple at the "Opet Festival." The god leaves his abode at Karnak Temple in Procession. The god and king on separate boats, travels by river and others on land to Luxor Temple to unite with and incubate with his wife Goddess Mut for 24 days of merrymaking. Then he returns to Karnak by canal and land. There is much fanfare and joviality; all of which is depicted on the West and East Wall of the Processional Colonnade at Luxor.

The god travels by Procession and boat across the river for the "Feast of the Valley" on the west bank.

iv.   The God stays at Temple Palace. All New Kingdom monarchs built a Mortuary Temple, a "Mansion of Millions of Years" and each had a palace adjoining the First Court, so the King could "Visit the temple from his palace."

c.   Processional Temple

i.   **Wayside Temple used in Processions** beyond the main Sanctuary. The best surviving examples are the:

ii.   **"White Chapel"** - Senusert I - of the Middle Kingdom. It was reconstructed and now preserved in Karnak Temple's "Open Air Museum."

LET'S LIBERATE THE TEMPLE

iii. "**Red Chapel**" Hatshepsut - New Kingdom –

iv. Also reconstructed and preserved in the "**Open Air Museum**." Hatshepsut's "**Red Chapel**" is thought to be Karnak Temple's early Sanctuary during the Queen's reign that was destroyed and replaced by Thutmose III but later repaired by Philip Arredias, brother of Alexander the Great and now the surviving one in place.

III. Construction and Layout of the Temple -
A regular dwelling was temporary but the god's house was built to last for eternity. Thus, while the home, even palace, was built of perishable mu brick material, the god's house was built of stone. Quarrying, transportation and decoration of stone became important and picturesque.

a. **Transition from perishable materials to stone Construction** - The Priesthood, an organized body of Priests with religious, economic and political power, trained architects and supervised all forms of building especially temple construction.

b. **Orientation of the Temple**

i. Axis - along the East-West route of the sun - Statues along this line face the main axis. At Karnak, statues along the second axis face the first, not the second axis.

Some temples have more than one axis - Karnak has 2; Luxor has 3;

iii. Individual temples have their own axis or axial line, and may be oriented differently; oftentimes oriented toward some heavenly body.

iv. In 1894, Norman Lockyer's *Dawn of Astronomy* indicated, "Egyptian temples were oriented towards some heavenly body.

FREDERICK MONDERSON

c. **Features** -

This is a river culture with the Nile as the main Highway for Trade, Culture, mortuary visits, Military ventures and Transportation of stone

Liberate the Temple. Mentuhotep's 11th Dynasty Temple at Deir el Bahari. View of some of the rubble of this "Oldest Temple at Thebes" and "best preserved of the oldest temples."

LET'S LIBERATE THE TEMPLE

Liberate the Temple. Mentuhotep's 11th Dynasty Temple at Deir el Bahari. View of some of the rubble of this "Oldest Temple at Thebes" and "best preserved of the oldest temples."

Liberate the Temple. Mentuhotep's 11th Dynasty Temple at Deir el Bahari. View of some of the rubble of this "Oldest Temple at Thebes" and "best preserved of the oldest temples."

FREDERICK MONDERSON

v.   A King's visit to the temple was an important occasion with great joy and fanfare surrounding such an occurrence.

d.   Physical Layout of the Temple

a.   Pier at the River where the King's entourage is greeted or the God's bark is bid farewell on some journey.

b.   A Canal leads to an Avenue of Sphinxes to the entrance which is part of the Enclosure Wall surrounding the temple.

c.   Pylon or Gateway entrance - Openings on the Pylon's cornice hosts flag-staves that fly the temple, Nome and nation's flags.

d.   Great Court within – With a number of architectural and statuary features.

i.   **Kiosk** - On the current Tourist Circuit there are only 3 surviving Kiosks at Karnak, Luxor and Abydos. In addition, there is the "Kiosk of Trajan" at Isis's Temple and a small "Kiosk to Hathor" there also. They seem a New Kingdom invention and discontinued afterwards.

ii.   **Sphinxes** - Generally line a causeway or path to a temple. Karnak has sphinxes in its Great Court that are some of those previously lined the Avenue of Sphinxes outside, beyond the Pylon. That is, at Karnak Temple these Sphinxes stand before both the northern and southern colonnades in the Great Court.

iii.   **Altars** - For the most part there may be one or more in the Open Air First Court where invited guests could observe some ceremony. The altar in the Sanctuary is upon which the daily ritual is performed. Like every other part of the temple that has to be consecrated, the altar has to be washed before the ritual ceremony

LET'S LIBERATE THE TEMPLE

could begin and especially before the god's food was placed before him.

iv. **Statues** - Dedicated to and by the temple builder. Sometimes if an official has distinguished himself he would be allowed to have a statue of himself placed in the temple. Deir el Bahari had more than a hundred of the queen. Temple of Mut had hundreds placed there by Amenhotep III. The French Archaeologist Legrain recovered thousands of statues out of the "Cachette Court" at Karnak/ This is the area just north of the Seventh Pylon. Amenhotep Son of Hapu, Amenhotep III's architect was permitted by the king to put his statues in the temple. Aahmose, after the Hyksos had been expelled and he begun the 18th Dynasty, he placed a stele in Karnak Temple area in what became the Hypostyle Hall, praising his mother and creating an endowment in perpetuity for the queen.

v. **Colonnades** - A line of columns of various numbers. They could be in a Hypostyle Hall or in a Peristyle Court or even in Kiosks. A Peristyle is a roofless structure while a Hypostyle is a roofed structure, a Hall of columns.

vi. **Small Temple** - "One-Upmanship" as in the Case of Rameses III in Karnak's Great Court. There is another, the *Akh Menu*, Festival Temple of Thutmose III which lies perpendicular to the east/west axis line. Karnak Temple had some 22 Temples surrounding it.

vii. **Obelisks** - These are placed before the pylon or in an open court. Hatshepsut erected two obelisks at Karnak that we know of; an illustration at Deir el Bahari indicated there were actually four obelisks; her father Thutmose I erected two and Thutmose III erected two and one remained prone between the Seventh and the Eighth Pylons. There is an inscription relating that Thutmose IV later erected it but it later disappeared.

e. **Hypostyle Hall** - Where the Procession generally congregates and its walls are illustrated. The concept of the columns and colonnade therein represents "a forest as at creation" of the world.

FREDERICK MONDERSON

i. **Ritual on the Wall** - Pictures are arranged sequentially depicting the King's interaction with the Gods or the priests hoisting the God's Tabernacle and the king generally shown either incensing the barque of the god or following it.

ii. **Columns** - Columns reflect the world at Creation, a sort of thicket field by the waterside. Colonnades generally line Open Court areas. It was an honor to "have one's name written in the colonnade." Beside the round columns, there were also square pillars fronted by Osiride figures that also formed colonnades as in the First and Second Courts at Medinet Habu, mortuary temple of Rameses III. Rameses II's temple at Abydos consists of square pillars but no round columns.

iii. **Processions** - The priests of Amon-Ra engineered the God's choice of Thutmose III to be king while he stood in line and the procession passed by. The king generally leads the god in procession to such places as Luxor Temple to celebrate the Opet Festival and across the river for the Feast of the Valley.

f. **Sanctuary** - The "Bedroom of the God." This is where the ritual is performed and the god resides there in utter darkness.

i. **Open Chamber Karnak** – This is an Open Sanctuary with both east and west entrances penetrated by the rays of the sun in the morning and with its last rays at evening time.

ii. **Closed Chamber** – Luxor, Deir El Bahari, Abu Simbel, etc. After the Old Kingdom, when the Altar was placed in an Open Court. By Middle and New Kingdom times, Closed Sanctuaries became the order of the day.

iii. Subsidiary Rooms for -

a. Liquid Offerings - Oils, unguents, perfumes

LET'S LIBERATE THE TEMPLE

b. Solid Offerings - food, statues, incense

c. Vestments - clothing, jewelry, musical instruments

d. Books of the Ritual

e. Treasury - Storehouse of the Temple and god's treasures and sacred emblems

f. Sacred Lake - for washing and other cleanliness requirements of the priests who perform the ritual.

g. Sailing of sacred boats at times of festivals

h. Colonnades - a line of columns. This architectural feature was discovered and developed in Egypt, as early as 2800 B.C., and nowhere else. Columns are generally quarried square stone blocks, transported to place of erection and set up in place, then pounded round before decoration.

i. Subsidiary Temples for Gods. Seldom is a temple home to a god. The god is always paired with a spouse and a son. This Champollion called the "Triad." But, in a national temple, there are other visiting gods who are accorded a shrine. That's why Karnak is also called "The Palaces." It is the place where the gods "stay."

FREDERICK MONDERSON

Liberate the Temple. Mentuhotep's 11th Dynasty Temple at Deir el Bahari. View of some of the rubble of this "Oldest Temple at Thebes" and "best preserved of the oldest temples."

Liberate the Temple. Mentuhotep's 11th Dynasty Temple at Deir el Bahari. View of some of the rubble of this "Oldest Temple at Thebes" and "best preserved of the oldest temples."

LET'S LIBERATE THE TEMPLE

Liberate the Temple. Mentuhotep's 11th Dynasty Temple at Deir el Bahari. View of some of the rubble of this "Oldest Temple at Thebes" and "best preserved of the oldest temples." This now blocked-up entrance led to the Sanctuary and tombs deep in the mountain.

j.   Karnak had 15 gods in its Ennead.

ii.   While Deir el Bahari was dedicated to Amon - it also had Shrines to Hathor, Anubis, Ra-Horakhty, Hatshepsut and her father Thutmose I.

iii.   Abu Simbel was dedicated to 4 Gods Ra Horakhty, Amon Ra, Ptah and deified Rameses II

iv.   Abydos was dedicated to 7 gods - Osiris, Isis and Horus; Ra-Horakhty, Amon-Ra and Ptah; and Seti I deified.

IV.   Decoration of the Temple

FREDERICK MONDERSON

a.   Ritual – Contained in Books of Papyrus and on interior Walls. In the later Graeco-Roman Period, the Ritual of the temple was profusely displayed on the walls. The Books contained more than the walls. Its contents had to be recited in the worship service as the Procession proceeded.

b.   King in Adoration of the Gods on the Interior - Some parts of the temple only the King was permitted into accompanied by a few high echelon priests who assisted in performing the ritual.

c.   Enclosure Walls - King is shown fighting the god and temple enemies - Bad people and bad spirits

d.   Botanical Garden - Flowers for daily ritual and fruits for wine, beer as well as funeral garlands and bouquets. Gardens helped brighten the Egyptian spirit. While tombs displayed evidence of gardens and flowers, the earliest Garden discovered was that of Amten who supplied flowers to temples. Evidence shows King Thutmose III being presented a bouquet. Nakht was also a gardener.

e.   Deir el Bahari - Temple of Queen Hatshepsut. The architect Senmut patterned this temple after the nearby Middle Kingdom temple of Mentuhotep II.

f.   The Punt Expedition depicted at Deir el Bahari shows a voyage to the East African coast of Punt, today's Somali. This expedition provided the earliest anthropological study of a people and culture. Fruits, plants, animals and incense trees were brought from Punt; incense trees were planted alongside the Avenue of Sphinxes stretching from the river's edge Valley Temple to the main temple's entrance. Evidence remains today indicating two incense trees were planted before the Pylon entrance to the First Court.

g.   Transport of two obelisks on flat-bottomed boats by Hatshepsut's architect, Senmut, to be erected at Karnak. One still stands to this day. Another lies beside the Sacred Lake.

LET'S LIBERATE THE TEMPLE

V. Role and Symbolism of the King

a.   On Earth - The role of the king is to maintain harmony in the state and among his people. He does this by officiating in the temples through worshipping and ritualizing the gods. In turn, the gods bring bounty and good fortune to the state. On the West Bank of the Nile many references mention the king entering the temple from his palace beside his mortuary temple.

b.   The King enters the temple Sanctuary at the head of a procession as he wears sandals and holds a scepter. Several Nome Standards are evident in the procession.

c.   Before he enters the temple, he undergoes baptism or purification at the hands of Thoth and Horus or priests impersonating these gods. In this case, the priests dress in appropriate masks to impersonate these gods.

d.   Respective goddesses present him the crowns of Upper White) and Lower (Red) Egypt.

e.   He is then led by goddesses/gods into the presence of the temple god/gods where he performs the ritual.

f.   Oftentimes he enters the Sanctuary alone. He breaks the door's seal, enters and converse with the god; He sings, praises and incenses the gods. Incense is never burned on an altar but in an incenser placed in a corner.

g.   After the lustration, dressing, perfuming and feeding, further incensing, he then retreats, removes his footprints in the sand with a broom, a branch of the *hidn*-tree. He then closes the door; then affixes a seal, until the next visit.

h.   In the Heavens - The god is born on the morning around 4:00 am. He then receives his lustration, vi., bath, incense, dress, food; the same of which is also provided for the statue of his divine presence in the Sanctuary's Naos.

FREDERICK MONDERSON

i.   The red ball we see before sun-up is his afterbirth. The lustration the god undergoes in the heavens is the same his counterpart on earth receives. It is the same as the king undergoes, either in the Sanctuary or in the Per-dwet or "House of the Morning," even when he visits the temple or any other time he must be purified.

j.   In the heavens, the god's bath attendants wash, powder and lipstick and comb his hair. He is then fed and slapped on the bottom and told "Go, do your job" of sailing across the heavens to bring light and life to all creation.

k.   In the morning, he is young; at Midday - he is mature; at evening-time he is old.

l.   Then he travels the underworld to arrive at the other end of the heavens to be reborn again.

m.   He has to pass through the underworld to arrive at the eastern horizon. There the heavenly kingdom meets the earthly kingdom of the dead. In the night realm, the sun god shines his rays and refreshes the earthly dead.

n.   The god's enemies fight to hinder the boat of the sun in the night sky.

VI. The Temple as University and Community Clearing House

a.   Science, education, theology, music and medicine were taught in these temple schools

b.   Priests were taught here and they were taught to specialize in various disciplines

LET'S LIBERATE THE TEMPLE

c. In medicine priests are taught to specialize in on organ or part of the body or in one medicine area. None trespasses on the area of the other.

Liberate the Temple. Mentuhotep's 11th Dynasty Temple at Deir el Bahari. View of some of the rubble of this "Oldest Temple at Thebes" and "best preserved of the oldest temples." Stumps of the eight-sided columns that lined the Hypostyle Hall.

Liberate the Temple. Mentuhotep's 11th Dynasty Temple at Deir el Bahari. View of some of the rubble of this "Oldest Temple at Thebes" and best preserved of the oldest temples. From within, close-up of the column bases.

FREDERICK MONDERSON

Liberate the Temple. Mentuhotep's 11ᵗʰ Dynasty Temple at Deir el Bahari. View of some of the rubble of this "Oldest Temple at Thebes" and best preserved of the oldest temples. Now we see two entrances sandwiched by the eight-sided columns.

Liberate the Temple. Mentuhotep's 11ᵗʰ Dynasty Temple at Deir el Bahari. View of some of the rubble of this "Oldest Temple at Thebes" and best preserved of the oldest temples.

LET'S LIBERATE THE TEMPLE

XVII. EGYPTIAN ARCHITECTURE
INTRODUCTION
By
Dr. Fred Monderson

Egyptian architecture has been, perhaps, the most fascinating invention emanating from the mind of man. Whether religious, mortuary, domestic, civic or military, Egyptian architecture has endured, set standards and been most innovative in its features enabling and benefitting mankind. However, while its various modes have been tremendously beneficial to the outward posture of human endeavor, religious architecture has penetrated the inner man, influencing his soul and psychic being. Because of man's inherent desire to interact with cosmic and divine forces, whether praise or mortuary architecture, no other field has so influenced the alpha and omega experience of the human spirit. Thus, from his earliest consciousness, Churchward says some 300,000 years, man has enjoyed "sweet communion with deity" and this interaction has been so significant in humanity's psychological and spiritual pageantry, it has laid the basis for and innovated in many a field benefitting man's march of development along the historical continuum of mankind's wonderful journey.

In the emergence of man's religious consciousness along the Valley of the Nile, religious architecture was born to shelter and protect the divine essence that contacted and contracted with the ancient African being. In essence, divinity explicated, "You protect and worship me and I will benefit you with the spirit and creativity to bring you joy, happiness and industry beyond your greatest expectations." According to the new Kingdom *Instruction of Ani*, it's been said of the god, "Song, dance and incense are his foods. Receiving protestations are his wealth." As such, then, temple or religious architecture was born to house and protect the deity who could be evoked to manifest his presence among humanity. In that

FREDERICK MONDERSON

manifestation, many points of divine contact were established of which the temple became the principal loci.

Because of the structure of the society of king, "Servants of the God" or priests and other citizenry, the first two enjoyed an access to divinity not shared by the last. The Egyptian belief system has shown, the gods first ruled Egypt and the king, later pharaoh, was a direct descendant and heir to the throne they vacated. This meant, the king as the son of God was himself a god on earth and can and did have access to his father and brother gods. However, while his holy person enjoyed a divine aura and spiritual potency, wherever he was could be considered holy, yet it was only in the temple he could invoke and worship his god and which was a ritual created for this purpose.

Just as today we call god by a multitude of names, so too disparate groups of these early Africans worshipped their own separate god but based on the same principle of a universal and beneficent father god. In time, the god's representatives we called theologians sorted the disparities and fused the various strands of divine worship into a syncretism establishing harmony throughout a hierarchical structure that enabled all to be part of the conjoined whole to enjoy the blessing of the divine beneficence.

Sacred Egyptian texts representing the codification of oral beliefs reaching back into the remotest millennia indicated there was a time when nothing existed. Yet, from this nothingness the divine essence emerged and made manifest first creating everything including man and giving specific instructions on how things were to be. In *The World of the Pharaohs: A Complete Guide to Ancient Egypt*, Christine Hobson (1987: 128) explained what she calls "The first occasion." As stated, she wrote: "There was once a time, Egyptian legend said, when the earth was filled with a watery emptiness, without shape. From these waters, called Nun, there emerged a mound of land, and upon this mound, all that exists came into being. According to which group of priests told the story, either a plant emerged that served as a perch for the first life [manifesting as] the falcon Horus; or, a lotus plant grew and blossomed, from which the sun emerged. The outpouring of energy that created mankind on this, called the First Occasion, was

LET'S LIBERATE THE TEMPLE

revered by the Egyptian as the tangible manifestation of divine power. The first temple came into existence on this mound in the form of an outer enclosure wall, designed to separate the god and its power from everything outside. Inside, a reed-mat shelter was placed over the very source of creation – the perch or plant – to protect it and mark it as being sacred." As such, "every Egyptian temple" was "built as a copy of the first temple" encouraging the god to return to earth lured by the familiarity of the structure.

From this early time the god's shelter, made of the flimsiest material, together with ritual and intonation served to invoke the divine presence and as time passed more durable material was used to build the temple. Contrary to the muddle as to who were the ancient Egyptians, the earliest surviving examples of Egyptian temples date to one for the god Min at Koptos in Upper Egypt. Another on the Island of Elephantine, Aswan, stood at Egypt's southern border. Both the God Min, a black god, and the island of Elephantine were more closely linked to inner Africa. However, two interesting points are raised in the above scenarios. Addressing this controversy presented here has been the life's work of Dr. Ben-Jochannan.

The Englishman Flinders Petrie, the "father of archaeology" found large intact pre-dynastic statues of God Min painted black at his temple in the city of Koptos. These are now safely preserved in the confines of the Ashmolean Museum, Oxford University town. In the rush to falsely claim foreign origin of the ancient Egyptians scholars first discounted the statues' age assigning them to the Fourth Dynasty of the Old Kingdom. Next the god's statues were said to be of Mesopotamian origin from whence the Caucasian originators of Egyptian civilization supposedly began. Yet, the first contradiction is that these Caucasians were painting their important god statues black! Now, as with the 11th Dynasty king Mentuhotep II whose statue was found in his temple at Deir el Bahari wearing the Red Crown of Lower Egypt and wearing the Heb-Sed Cloak, and the 18th Dynasty statues of King Tutankhamon both were yet said to only be painted black for the funeral service. Now, Min was a living god and no need to have camouflaged his color. In addition, and in analogy contrast, one of Mentuhotep's Queens Kemsit was painted black in her tomb yet she was called a Negress, but he painted black was said to be so for the funeral service. In Elliot Smith's *Egyptian Mummies* (1905) he explained, "The black coating on Egyptian mummies was simply to protect the mummy but the brown skin could still be observed beneath." Again, while the two guardian statues of Tutankhamon in the Cairo Museum are also painted black and wearing royal regalia, on a wall in the Hall of Tutankhamon the king is shown as a bronze sphinx trampling other Africans painted black and called Negro! Yet the king is said to be neither Negro nor black! Prof. John H. Clarke insisted Europeans claim the heritage of Egypt but use not logic!

Liberate the Temple. Hatshepsut's Temple at Deir el Bahari. View of the temple with the mountain as a backdrop.

LET'S LIBERATE THE TEMPLE

Liberate the Temple. Hatshepsut's Temple at Deir el Bahari. View of the three levels of Colonnades, the two Ramps (center) and the Shrines of Hathor (left) and Anubis (right) on the Middle Colonnade.

Liberate the Temple. Hatshepsut's Temple at Deir el Bahari. These two incense trees, brought back from the Queen's Expedition to Punt, East Africa, were planted in this spot before the temple's pylon.

In a recent book of the last decade entitled *Black Genesis* by two authors Robert Bauval and Thomas Brophy (Rochester, Vermont, Bear and Company, 2011) discuss a people who occupied the region of Nabta Playa from 7500-3500 B.C. were the first scientists who mapped the heavens, crated a calendar, were agriculturalists and pastoralists who first began worshipping the cow goddess. When the region began to lose rainfall and dry-up, the people migrated towards the Nile River settling in the Aswan area near Elephantine Island. They argue these black people were the predecessors of ancient Egypt.

XVIII. TEMPLE ORIENTATION AND DIVINE WORSHIP BY DR. FRED MONDERSON

In 1894 Sir Norman Lockyer in *Dawn of Astronomy* (1894) indicated Egyptian temples were essentially oriented towards some solar body; that is a star, or planet or moon. He even identified a temple to Hathor which stood in the mountain vicinity of Deir el Bahari as early as 10,000 B.C.

Nevertheless, in seeking to cultivate a well-rounded understanding of Ancient Egypt in its many manifestations, we must, however, be careful in our acceptance of the record as presented, for, as Dr. Leonard James taught regarding this historical phenomenon, "The existential record contradicts the symbolic representation." Dr. Cheikh Anta Diop of *African Origin of Civilization*: *Myth or Reality* (1974) fame, indicated, in European hijacking of Egypt they made it so complicated, so confusing, we are forced to accept the white man's version as presented with its glaring falsity and contradictions. In clarifying this belief and its reality, we must purposefully understand there was an "Africa before the white man."

Nevertheless, as we have come to understand, in Nile Valley religious beliefs, two forms of religions or beliefs were emerged and was practiced in Egypt, one celestial, one terrestrial. That is, one sky or

LET'S LIBERATE THE TEMPLE

heavenly and one earthly. In this we have the Ra religion which is sky and centered at Heliopolis, a city founded by the Black Anu race. Heliopolis, like so many other temple sites were founded by the Anu, and the religion they started, these practices remained paramount throughout dynastic rule. Some books teach the Egyptian mythology, its religion, came from the heavens and so in Hollywood distortion we got **Battlestar Galactica**, the TV Series. Remember, this view purported, aliens brought religion and the workings of the mind, from the deep blue beyond, for Black men to ritualize and worship the notion of divinity.

We know and science has affirmed, Zinjanthropus Boisie, Lucy, Eve, all East African forms of humanity, essentially gave birth to the human race who migrated therefrom to people the earth. It is thus easy to recognize these forms of early/ancient man descending rather than ascending the Nile River

A popular aphorism has been, "Swim or Sink" and "walk or Ride" and in this case, even "Sail." So, in his dispersion utilizing one method of movement man descended the Nile River, the prominent highway at the time. He settled in Thebes and along the Nile in small communities. Thus, in that early emergence, what we know as Upper Egypt extended from beyond Aswan to the Delta in which 22 Nomes of 42 mini states or Nomes were demarcated. The other 20 to make 42 were later set. So, we have Upper Egypt with 22 beginning in the South and Lower Egypt with 20 beginning from the Delta peak northwards towards the Mediterranean Sea. There was no Middle Egypt in the earliest times of Dynastic beginnings. Though the land was there, occupied by people, yet incorporated in Upper Egypt, the term Middle Egypt essentially got prominence under the Amarna revolution during the Eighteenth Dynasty and onward.

We know evidence of stone tools were found at Thebes and dated to 300,000 years or thereabouts. So African craftsmen were working for the longest. Albert Churchward says equally these people were practicing their religion, having "Sweet communion with deity," as early as the 300,000-year mark in time. Let us not forget *The New York Times* articles:

FREDERICK MONDERSON

1. A 43,000-year old Iron Ore mine discovered in South Africa.

2. A "Paint Factory" and paint pot artifact containing red paint and a brush dated at 107,000 years.

3. The Katanga Bone with mathematical markings dated at 25,000 years old.

4. Censorious mentioning an Egyptian historical tablet dated at 35,000 years.

5. The Great Precession of 26,000-years wherein to measure one means you must have two or three and Dr. Charles Finch implied the possibility of a fourth; meaning 26,000, 52,000, 78,000 or even 104,000 years of African star-gazing.

6. Bauval and Brophy in *Black Genesis* (2011) mentioning the "Black People of Nabta Playa" in the Western Desert of Upper Egypt were the first people to map the heavens dating to a period from 20,000 to 7500 to 3500 B.C.

7. Toby Wilkinson in *Genesis of the Pharaohs* (2003) noted, in the Eastern Desert of Upper Egypt he found Petroglyphs depicting cultural practices of boats-full of "Gods" and other features that became crystallized later in Dynastic Egypt which he dated to "1000-years before Winkler's Mesopotamians." It is interesting how, in 1938 when henry Winkler published his *Rock Drawings of Southern Upper Egypt* (1938) which he attributed to "Mesopotamians" he received tremendously glowing reviews; yet, Wilkinson's correction of the record has done little to "move the needle" in terms of the great mountain of distortion inundating the particularly Western record on Egypt.

Norman Lockyer did say in the particular regard, there was a Temple of Hathor on the Mountain at Deir el Bahari vicinity dated at 10,000

LET'S LIBERATE THE TEMPLE

and many believe this may have had a connection to the chapel to the goddess in the later Hatshepsut Deir el Bahari temple at 1500 B.C.

Now, Karnak Temple of God Amon of the Theban Triad of Amon, the Sun-god; his wife, Mut, the Earth Goddess; and their son, Khonsu, the Moon god, was oriented East to West, the path of the sun. What is not stated, the temple of Hathor was possibly oriented towards the Temple of Amon across the river. We know the Middle Kingdom, 2000 B.C. Temple of Mentuhotep II (11th Dynasty) and the Temple of Hatshepsut (18th Dynasty) some 500 years later, 1500 B.C., were both oriented in a line established through survey towards the Karnak Temple. Therefore, it stands to reason Hathor's temple in the same location, may very well be similarly oriented. This being the case, Karnak may very well have been in existence much longer than we generally ascribe to it. Such temple triangulation is consistent and reinforced through the people of Nabta Playa studying the heavens and creating their star map.

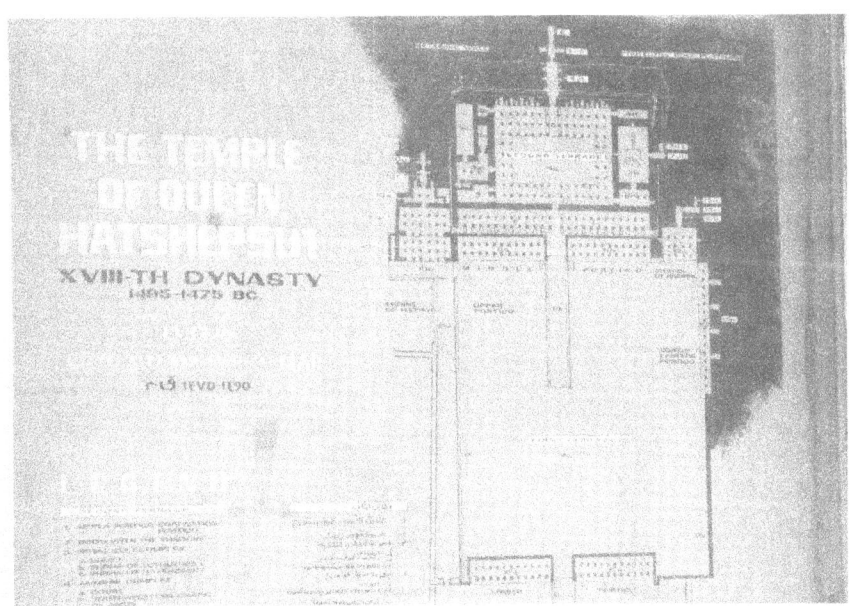

Liberate the Temple. Hatshepsut's Temple at Deir el Bahari. Plan of the essential part of the Temple famously built by Senmut for his Queen.

FREDERICK MONDERSON

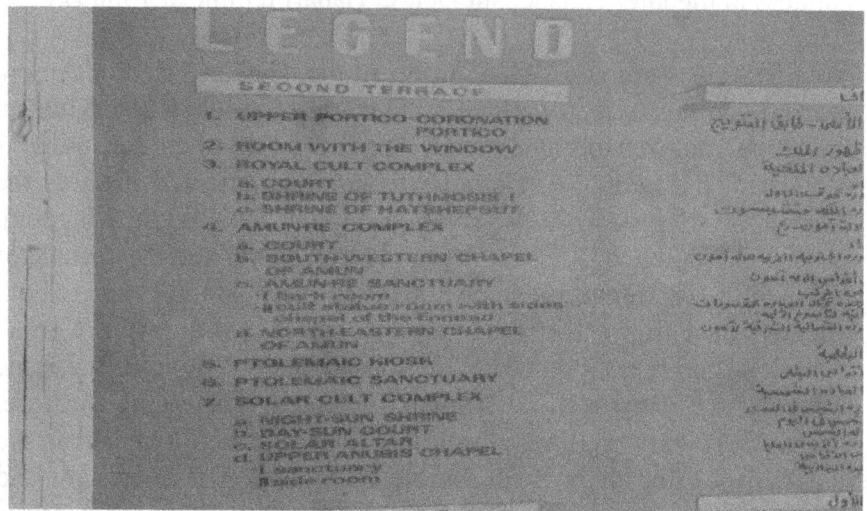

Liberate the Temple. Hatshepsut's Temple at Deir el Bahari. The **Legend** explains the principal part of the temple from the Second Terrace and Upper Court.

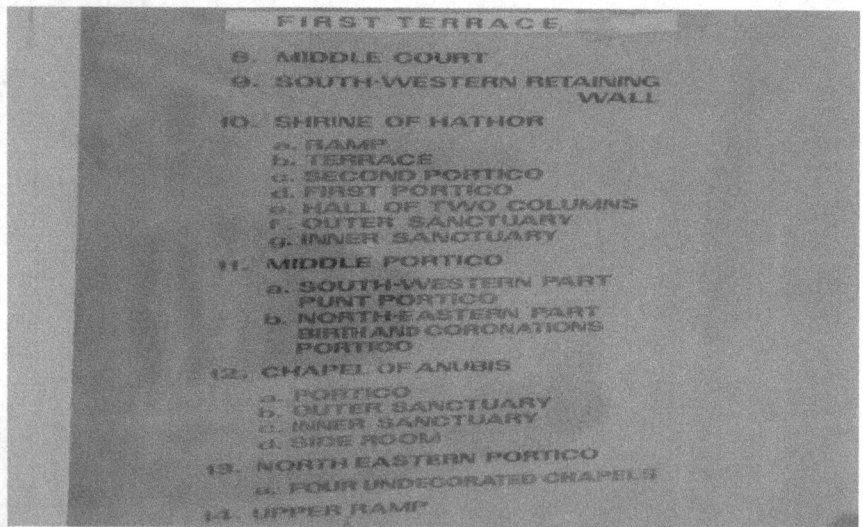

Liberate the Temple. Hatshepsut's Temple at Deir el Bahari. Again, the **Legend** explains features of the First Terrace.

LET'S LIBERATE THE TEMPLE

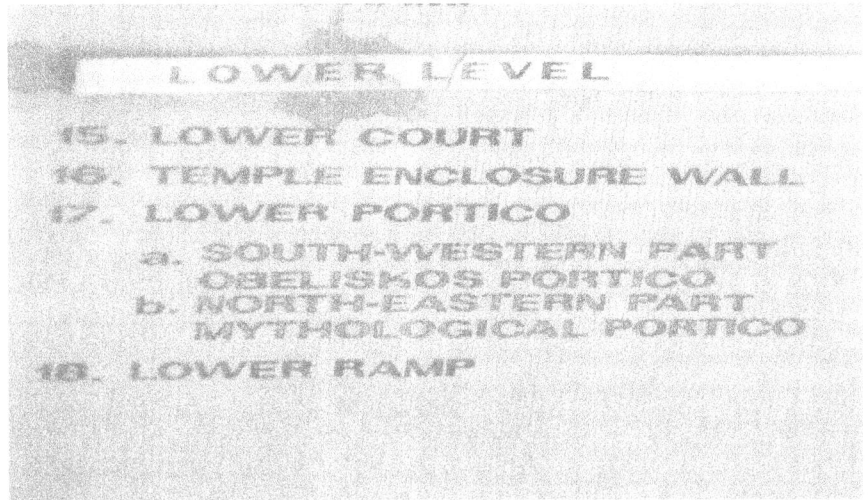

Liberate the Temple. Hatshepsut's Temple at Deir el Bahari. The Lower Level is actually the first or entrance part of the temple.

Equally too, the location of Luxor Temple, facing north, was also oriented towards Karnak. But more particular, when Rameses II (19th Dynasty) added a Peristyle Court called the "Ramessean Front," the axis was turned towards Karnak. Some have said it was to avoid the river but more particularly it was probably oriented toward the main temple. Again, triangulation towards the Sun-god Amon, home as the principal point is certainly credible.

Luxor Temple is unique. Not only was it essentially built to celebrate the "Opet Festival," but it is the only temple with three axes, so states Schwaller de Lubicz in his *Temple in Man* (1949, 1977). In this important structure, there is an invisible axis beneath the original temple's floor; the above ground axis of the original temple of Amenhotep III; and of course, the axis of Rameses II's Peristyle Court addition, the "Ramessean Front."

Now, how does all this play out in a discussion on Axis orientation which actually has to do with divine action and placement!

FREDERICK MONDERSON

We know the people of **Nabta Playa** in the Western Desert of Upper Egypt were considered the "predecessors of the pharaohs." They vigorously occupied this region from about c. 7500 B.C. to 3500 B.C.

1. They were the first astronomers. Star-gazing, they mapped the heavens and used the heavenly bodies as directional points of location moving their cattle back and forth. In this practice, they were also pastoralists. Rainfall was plentiful in the region at this time. So, they practiced agriculture and kept cattle as the source of all their wants. They created the first calendar and began worship of the "Cow Goddess." Why a cow? The cow gave blood, milk, meat, leather and philosophically reinforced the "mother concept" of nurturing humanity. When the land began to dry-up from lack of rainfall, around 3500-3400 B.C. or so, the Nabta Playa Africans migrated from the desert and settled on the banks of the Nile, perhaps in the Qustol area, somewhere south of Aswan towards Abu Simbel. They probably founded or were influential in developments recurring in the kingdom of Ta-Seti. This historic location was highlighted in this vicinity in which *The New York Times* newspaper has described "The world's earliest monarchy found in Nubia." There we see what later became pharaonic paraphernalia, viz., enthroned pharaoh, palace façade, white crown, sailing boats, incense burner, cows and other animals, etc., at c. 3400 B.C. that emerges in Egypt by Unification at c. 3200-3100 B.C. according to the "Short Chronology." Remember the Hathor Temple at Thebes 10,000 B.C., well these people were probably worshipping her which may prolong their existence even further.

Given there was probably no southern political border at Aswan, Upper Egypt lands may be connected to Qustol and Nabta Playa inhabitants. This may very well be where Narmer honed his administrative and logistical know-how in equipping his armada's descent of the Nile and ultimately military success that brought about unification and the subsequent orchestrated social dynamics of dynastic rule.

LET'S LIBERATE THE TEMPLE

Still significant, the "five souls" accompanying Narmer on his Palette are Southern remain so throughout dynastic rule following the pharaoh and are never replaced or added to by elements from the north. In clearer identification, we also see the Goddess Hathor Narmer's Palette. Hathor was the daughter of Ra, the principal deity of the sky religion throughout dynastic rule which places father and daughter at an early time in history. We must also remember, accordingly, soon after Ra created the world, he made the Nubian, Black, people even before the made Egyptians. This is not surprising, since Ra worship dynamics and his center of worship at Heliopolis were founded by the Anu, a Black African people. The terrestrial religion, that of Osiris, centered at Abydos was later syncretized with Ra to create complementarity rather than conflict. Some have argued, the Ra religion was for the intellectual, literate Egyptian; while Osiris worship was for common folk who understood and grappled with the fact that the body was deposited in the earth. Through this process they would experience the quest for eternal existence with hopes for justification and resurrection as did Osiris.

A few things we know:

1. Hathor is shown "coming out of the mountains" and she carried the deceased into the "Afterlife."

2. When the deceased began the journey into the Afterlife, purportedly he entered a cavern in the Deir el Bahari area. Perhaps this is why the "Deir el-Bahari Cache of Mummies" were secreted in this area and discovered in 1881-82.

3. Brugsch-Bey in *A History of Egypt* (1902) argued the Egyptian painted himself red for illumination in the darkened journey into the "Afterlife" towards the Hall of Judgment presided over by Osiris.

Strange but modern man prides himself with a unique ability that seems to know more than ancient man about ancient man's own ancient cultural practices and surroundings. Naturally, racist bigotry played an important role in this, oftentimes misguided arrogance. Nevertheless, and more significant, at the temple of Luxor in the

FREDERICK MONDERSON

"Ramessean Front" Peristyle Court, on a back wall to the southwest, there is an interesting scene. The façade of the later temple is pictured with its seated and standing statues, obelisks, flagstaves, etc., before the Great Pylon and the sons of Rameses II lead a procession of fat cows to be sacrificed for the ceremony. A fascinating depiction shows a Nubian lady coming out of the head of one of the fat cows. This is Hathor, a Black woman pictured in the position. Most books and even guides, even those who take tourists to this particular feature show the temple but remain silent on significance of the Nubian lady, the Cow and the Hathor connection. Thus, what is the message of all this? Perhaps they don't know! So, the question then becomes, 'Why is this Nubian, Black, woman, depicted in such a prominent place in this important procession and again her connection to Hathor, the cow symbol?'

1. Heliopolis was founded by the Anu, Black people from Upper Egypt which was essentially Nubia, Ethiopia across the broad swathe of land, from Aswan but more particularly Ethiopia, down to the Apex of the Delta. In association, Ra worship was established.

2. Hathor was the daughter of Ra, and as a cow she was worshipped in long-standing.

3. The Black African people of Nabta Playa of the Upper Egyptian Western desert whom, in *Black Genesis* (2011), Brophy and Bauval describe as the "precursors of the pharaohs," believed they initiated "cow-goddess" worship. These people and their cultural and religious practices played an important role in the evolution of Nile valley culture.

4. The first significant recorded historical document, the Narmer were southern, depicts this "cow goddess" Hathor in a prominent position.

5. By the time of Thutmose III's 18th Dynasty rule, Amon, fused with Ra as depicted in the Luxor Museum wears a "Black face." In this period also, he is often fused in syncretism with Min, the Black

LET'S LIBERATE THE TEMPLE

or Nubian God, as Amon-Min. We must remember, this is what has survived!

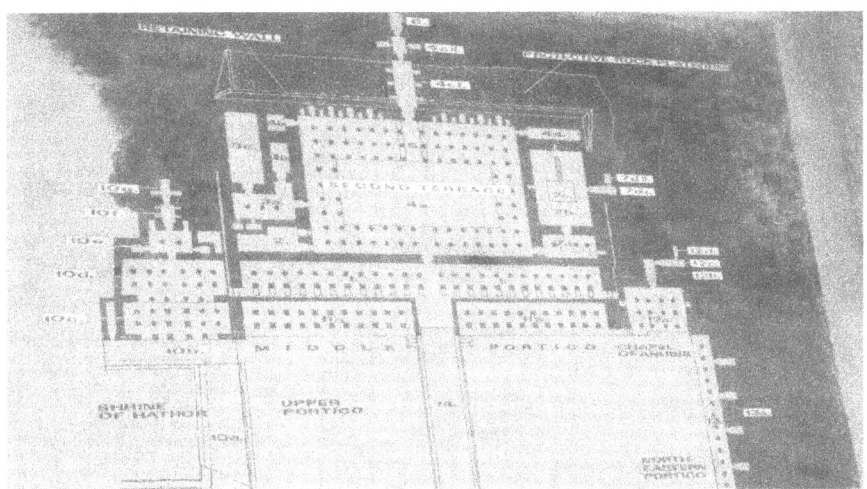

Liberate the Temple. Hatshepsut's Temple at Deir el Bahari. Close-up of the upper portion of the Temple and the extensive display of alternating Column and Pillar Colonnades.

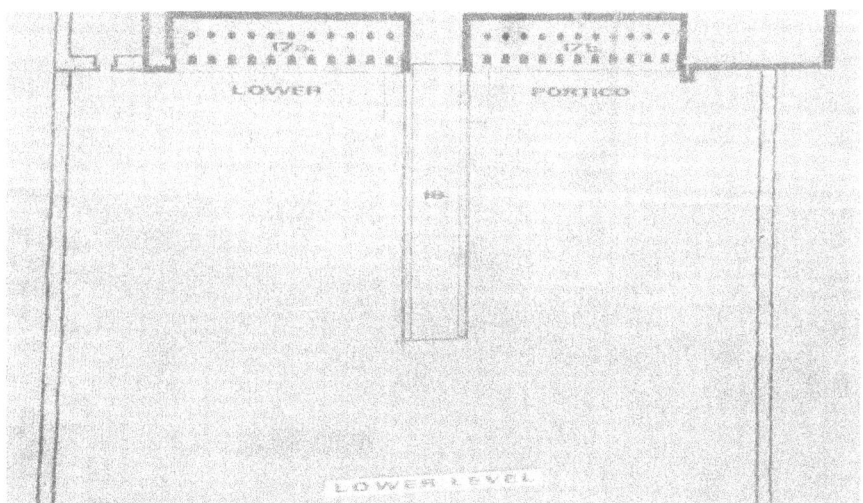

Liberate the Temple. Hatshepsut's Temple at Deir el Bahari. The Middle Terrace in the Lower Level's Court boasted Pillars and Columns.

FREDERICK MONDERSON

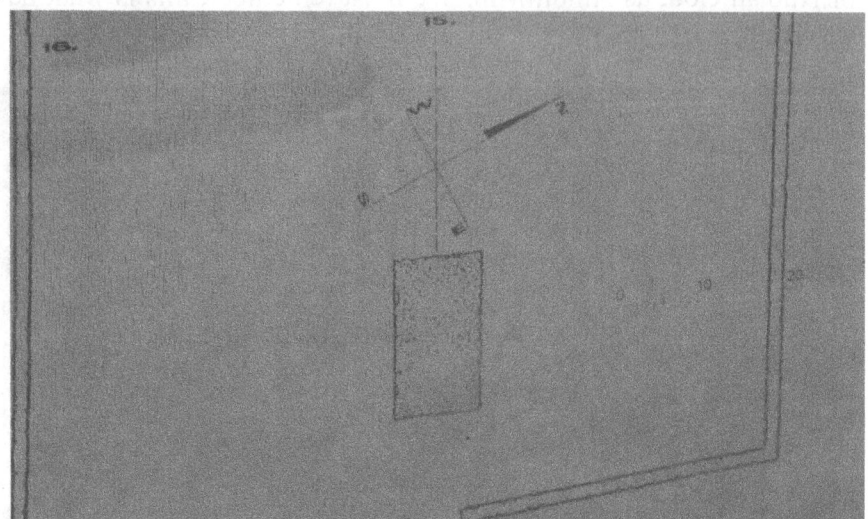

Liberate the Temple. Hatshepsut's Temple at Deir el Bahari. The lower Level's Court boasted a Lake or Pond.

6. This same Amon-Min is pictured in the 19th Dynasty of Rameses II in "Black-face" where the associated temple to his wife Nefertari, he Nubian, is dedicated to Hathor. Though both Abu Simbel temples are located in Nubia, "Hathor-land," perhaps it was a male thing, that his own temple was dedicated to Ra-Horakhty, Ptah, Amon and himself, deified, as was that of his father Seti I at Abydos where the gods were those of the Osiride cycle, Osiris, Isis and Horus; the great gods of the Empire, Ra-Horakhty, Amon and Ptah, and finally, Seti I, himself deified. This same Amon-Min is pictured in the 19th Dynasty of Rameses II in "Black-face" where the associated temple to his wife Nefertari, the Nubian, is dedicated to Hathor. Though both Abu Simbel temples are located in Nubia, "Hathor-land," perhaps it was a male thing, that his own temple was dedicated to Ra-Horakhty, Ptah, Amon and himself, deified, as was that of his father Seti I at Abydos where the gods were those of the Osiride cycle, Osiris, Isis and Horus; the great gods of the Empire, Ra-Horakhty, Amon and Ptah, and finally, Seti I, himself deified.

7. Full of controversy, there is this "Syrian thing" the racists trot out and propagate ever so often. For example, the parents of Tiye, the

LET'S LIBERATE THE TEMPLE

18th Dynasty Queen who wielded significant influence during her husband Amenhotep III's reign and that of her son Amenhotep IV, Akhenaton's reign. Yuya and Tuya were thought to be "Syrian" though this was proven to be false. Even Rameses II, the 19th Dynasty monarch was once described as Syrian. The interesting thing, at the *Battle of Kadesh*, battling Syrians, Rameses exclaimed in requesting assistance from God Amon in his time of challenge; in admonishing the god the king extolled, his ancestors had worshipped Amon from time immemorial. Consider that Rameses' father, Seti I who built the surviving Temple of Osiris at Abydos inscribed a significant feature, the Tablet of Abydos. This important document lists kings from Narmer to himself Seti I, deified, as ancestor kings. This is as potent evidence for Rameses' ancestors but nowhere are Syrians mentioned. So, we have the falsity exposed wherein Dr. Leonard James' admonition states, the "existential data contradicts the symbolic representation.' Explained! Rameses II "the Syrian" calls upon Amon-Ra, the African god in blackface whom his ancestors had worshipped from time immemorial. Wow! Falsity, yes. Confusion. Certainly!

A.   Thus, we have Dr. Cheikh Anta Diop's charge, in their creation of the "true Negro," European scholars have reduced all the other Negroes of the world to be "fake Negroes."

B.   So, again we realize, in their seizure of Egypt, Europeans have made the presentation of history tremendously confusing.

8.   Through his erudite studies and understanding, Prof John Henrik Clarke made us aware, "Europe's claims to Egypt is not founded on logic." But more important, Dr. Clarke stated, "the people who preached racism colonized history" and "when Europe colonized the world, she colonized the World's knowledge." That is why, at the end of the 19th Century the prevailing intellectual imperialist view held, "for some unknown reason," Caucasians left South-West Asia and "seeking to found a new fatherland in the West," arrived in Egypt bringing "a superior mental attitude" that gave a particular "impetus to the existing culture." However, as Mosso has shown, Asiatic people "never penetrated the Nile Valley nor the Aegean." Nevertheless, and if so, arrogantly this is after Narmer set out from

FREDERICK MONDERSON

Abydos and effectively reorganized the Southern Kingdom whose capital was Hierakonpolis, though Diop Says he was Theban.

In so doing, he unified the land, founded dynastic rule, built a temple and established Ptah rule at Memphis his chosen administrative capital. Thereafter, he determined the nature of bureaucratic service, recognized and reinforced a viable nobility in support of the new dispensation, encouraged the furtherance of art and architectural developments, determined the nature of military hardware, even encouraged active internal and external trade in art, ideas and religious expression, some of which among other resources, were slated for export. Despite these indigenous creative accomplishments, the aliens arrived to "reinvent Narmer's wheel." Perhaps the new wheel was of a square type. Nonetheless, this reinforces and highlights the end of the 19th Century view that is consistent with and seeks to reinforce Dr. Jacob Carruthers' contention, "Hegel took Africans out of Egypt and Egypt out of Africa at the beginning of the 19th Century." In this they created and placed Egypt in the "Middle East" or "Nearer East." Again, this geographical dispensation is consistent with the concentric idea belief, Europe is the center of the world and that culture and cultural values diminishes the further one moves from this center of gravity. Therefore, such areas must either be conquered and exploited or rechristened according to the whims of European in name of dispensation. Conversely, Runoko Rashidi held, Africans were moved from the center of world leadership to the fringe or periphery as meaningless actors.

9. In his "Egyptian Religion" published in Hasting's *Encyclopedia of Religion and Ethics* Vol. 5 (Edinburgh: T. and T. Clarke, 1912), Flinders Petrie wrote, "The Seventeenth Dynasty, coming from Nubia, held Thebes as its capital…." Yet, no modern book, certainly not the *Cambridge Ancient History* (1970) has reported on this consistent with its significance for the New Kingdom and the glory of ancient Egyptian history and culture.

10. Now, contrast all of the above factual evidence with "for some unknown reason" and "a superior mental attitude" boast in which we equate the European (Caucasian) propensity to perpetuate the

LET'S LIBERATE THE TEMPLE

barbarity of slave trade and slavery; the exploitative nature of colonialism and imperialism; and in modern times, the harsh and practical aspects of political disfranchisement, systematic and horrendous prison incarceration; perpetuation of sub-standards in orchestrated ghetto enclosures and conditions as in Apartheid South Africa; and concerted efforts in education shortcomings in order to deny the intellectual autonomy of African people in a false and justifiable argument African people are inherently inferior in the natural and social orders. This state of affairs flies in the face of existential evidence that Africans, particularly through Egypt, Nubia and Ethiopia have been in the forefront of lifting the veil of ignorance in humanity's development of consciousness and material accomplishments certainly and earlier than Europe's emergence.

11. Despite the propagated inconsistency, contradictions, distortions and omissions of some of current historiography, G.H. Richardson in "The World's Debt to Egypt," in *Open Court*, 24 (1914: 303-317) provides an argument applied to European nations and culture.

A. "Our modern civilization is the outgrowth of that of the Mediterranean, and this can be traced back to the Nile valley, where, if the antiquity of the monuments is a safe guide, we find an advanced civilization many centuries before we find it in Babylon. In fact, it is in the Nile valley that we find the first civilization."

B. Additionally, in a note on p. 303, he writes, "Dr. Naville, in a personal note to the writer, after reading this wrote, "the relative antiquity of Egypt and Babylon is very much discussed between Egyptologists and Assyriologists. It is undeniable that the civilization of Babylon goes very far back though I do not agree with Hommel and others who pretend that Babylon was the mother of Egypt. Still it seems to me that Babylon's birth is in a very remote past." The Predynastic discoveries made since this note was sent seem to justify the statement of the text. Mosso (*Dawn of Mediterranean Civilization*, 1910) wrote: "Many still believe that our civilization comes from Asia, but anthropology has decided the controversy and we know that the Asiatic race never penetrated into Egypt or into the isles of the Aegean. Although the origin of man is wrapped in mystery, naturalists are agreed in admitting the preponderating influence of Africa upon the population of Europe." In 1924 Raymond Dart argued as much and in 1959 L.S.B. Leakey discovered Zinjanthropus Boisie in Olduvai Gorge, East Africa and whose remains were dated at 1.75 million years old.

Interesting and in the wider understanding of the dynamic force of history this early at the beginning of the 20th Century, men of intellect and courage were nor opposed not afraid to propose Africa as being the home of humanity and essentially the dynamic force that laid the foundations for much of the world's intellectual, scientific and cultural beginnings and growth.

Liberate the Temple. Hatshepsut's Temple at Deir el Bahari. Close-up of the temple's front seeming to blend the First and Second Ramp.

LET'S LIBERATE THE TEMPLE

Liberate the Temple. Hatshepsut's Temple at Deir el Bahari. Pillars front the Middle Terrace to the South.

Liberate the Temple. Hatshepsut's Temple at Deir el Bahari. Pillars front the Middle Terrace to the South and to the rear, columns form the pillar and column alternation.

FREDERICK MONDERSON

XIX. CONSECRATION AND PURITY IN EGYPTIAN TEMPLES
BY
DR. FRED MONDERSON

When the god emerged from the watery abyss of the universe that preceded this universe, the first requirement was that there be shelter to protect the divine essence on earth. This shelter became the temple that evolved from the simplest structures to temples built of stone to last for eternity. Pharaoh's palace was built of mud-brick but his god's temple and that of his own was also built of stone.

Because we're studying a complex culture whose beginnings are shrouded in the mist of time, much relating to such beginnings are lost through the obliterating nature of time and the destructive hands of man. We are fortunate, however, for as the art of building evolved with particular changes occurring in the later periods, especially in the XXVth and XXVIth Dynasties and later which brings us to the Graeco-Roman temples, we look to the temple of Horus at Edfu as a crucially informative force in recounting early temple conception, construction and consecration. While Manetho in ancient times and Maspero in modern times, even Raymond emphasize its interior decoration, the temple depicts the drama in the formation of cosmological dynamic beliefs when the gods ruled Egypt and equally their successors the Manes and finally earthly kings succeeded them. That is, after a lengthy time of reign by Ra, Osiris, and finally his son Horus, the mortal king succeeded on the throne and hence we have the first, and Horus, title as the god's successor.

Benjamin Carruthers pointed to five centers of creation and divine worship, viz., Ra at Heliopolis; Ptah at Memphis; Osiris at Abydos; Thoth at Hermopolis; and Amon at Thebes, manifesting at Karnak and Luxor temples. Then there was Khnum on Elephantine Island, Aswan.

LET'S LIBERATE THE TEMPLE

Here and elsewhere reality was the requirement of temple building which was in full-effect. Again, in reflecting back upon the initial requirement of providing shelter for the god, we must first remember, again as Dr. Carruthers has explained, "the five centers of creation do not represent conflicting points of religious worship but complimentary versions of the same as seen through the same lens but from different perspectives." Nevertheless, we know both Ptah and Thoth were creator gods, architects and patrons of the arts and artisans. As such then, Thoth and his wife or daughter Seshat, were the original builders of temples "stretching the cord" within the mythological realm. Practically, on the earthly plain, the king built the temple in honor of his god and so, he impersonated Thoth and his wife, the queen, that of Seshat.

According to the time and place, and the significance of the god in question, the temple constructed by the king to his divine father depended on several factors, such as: what time of year its building would begin, what is the country's economic condition at the time, where the temple would be located, what heavenly body it would be oriented towards, what type of stone would be used in its construction, the actual size of the temple, the nature of its decoration, viz., pylons, courts, altars, statues, columns, sphinxes, flagpoles, sacred lake, walls (enclosure and compartment), distance from the Nile as the principal waterway, intervening canals, avenue of sphinxes, the name given the temple and most important the dedicatory inscription as to why he did it. "I constructed this temple for my father, as a dutiful son, etc.," as an example. Naturally, the nature of stone to be used in the temple's construction, and whether it would be single or multiple stones, was a serious consideration.

Without question, there would be support facilities within the temple and in its proximity such as gardens, flower and vegetables; housing for staff; magazines for storage of essential equipment and so on. Beyond its religious function, some temples were schools of instruction, medical institutions, help centers, artistic schools competing with other areas in creating art, whether statues, gold jewelry, books, ideas to be exported, items for trade and the administration of lands owned by the temple rented out and income generated therefrom. To this we may add tribute from vassal states and booty from foreign plunder, much of which was donated in gratitude to the temple for their expansion and decoration.

Whether it's after the temple was built or a visit from the king, consecration was a principal factor that had to be undertaken. Explaining tis important ceremony and how it was conducted, Awkward M. Blackman and H.W. Fairman in "The Consecration of an Egyptian Temple" in *Journal of Egyptian Archaeology* Vol. 32 (December, 1946: 75-91) writes, "probably the main requirement of the Master of the Ceremonies, for whom the architype of the two Edfu texts was drawn up, was a list of the various ceremonies comprising the rite arranged in their proper sequence so that all might be performed in an orderly manner and the solemn progress of the ritual not marred by mistakes or hesitations."

TEXT I

EXCERPTS FROM THE DIRECTORY OF A MASTER OF THE CEREMONIES

1. Supervision of the rite by the Lord of Hermopolis. 2. Asperging with the *nmst*-ewers and red pitchers. 3. Substance of the god. Incense on the fire. Touching the mouth and eyes; arraying in the head cloth. 6. Presenting oil. 7. Putting on the holy raiment. 8. Proffering the broad-collar. 9. Salutation with the *nmst*-ewer. 10. Censing the Uraeus-goddess and the gods and goddesses. Adoring Ra. Summoning the gods. Reciting the htp-di-nsw-formula. 11. Setting the meal in order upon the altar. 12. Purifying the sanctuary and cleansing the temple. 13. Rewarding its craftsmen from the oblation and gladdening their hearts with largess. 14. Ceding the Great Seat by His Majesty to its Lord.

LET'S LIBERATE THE TEMPLE
TEXT II

Long live the Good God, who fashions [a memorial] in *Mesen*, brightens the Great Seat with its beauty, constructs [the Mansion-of-the Falcon] the Falcon of Gold, and confers the benefactions on the Lord of the Sky [even he] the Son of Re (Ptolemaeus-may-he-live-forever-beloved-of-Ptah)] given life.

Liberate the Temple. Hatshepsut's Temple at Deir el Bahari. Sixteen-sided, "Proto-Doric Columns."

Liberate the Temple. Hatshepsut's Temple at Deir el Bahari. The Author, Dr. Fred Monderson leaves Hatshepsut's temple.

FREDERICK MONDERSON

Liberate the Temple. Hatshepsut's Temple at Deir el Bahari. A double row of pillars matching the double row of columns of the previous image.

LET'S LIBERATE THE TEMPLE

Liberate the Temple. Hatshepsut's Temple at Deir el Bahari. Pillars and the back-wall of the Middle Terrace of the "Birth Colonnade."

FREDERICK MONDERSON

EXCERPTS FROM THE DIRECTORY OF A MASTER OF THE CEREMONIES - (Continued).

1. Purification by the Lords of Purification. 2. Ptah takes his chisel to open the mouth and Seker uncloses the eyes. 3. Taking the Sorcerer. 4. Presenting the finger of fine gold. 5. Proffering the Copper Adze of Anubis. 6. Ushering in the Courtiers: opening the eyes with their adze and touching the mouth with the four slabs. 7. Beheading a *smn*-goose and decapitating a goat. 8. Pointing at an Upper Egyptian male ox. 9. Slaughtering long-horned cattle with strangling geese. 10. Presenting a great oblation of bread, flesh and beer. 11. Opening the Mouth of Throne-of-the-Protector-of-his-Father. 12. Censing its cult-chambers and purifying its chapels. 13. Seker feeds the priesthood from the oblation: gladdening their hearts with their largess. 14. Ceding Wetjset-Hor to its Lord by His Majesty.

With the Behdetite, great god, lord of the sky, may he show favor to his beloved son, the King of Upper and Lower Egypt (Heir-of-the-Beneficient-God-and-of-the-Goddess-Who-Loves-Her-Mother-the-Savior-Goddess-Chosen-of-Ptah-Judiciar-of-Re-Living-similitude-of Amun, and reward him with life, stability, and happiness upon the Throne of Horus, at the head of the living for-ever.

The temple is beautiful
Girdle wall on all four sides
Beautiful ambulatory
Sacred enclosure
His majesty is venerated in the names of her temple. The sacred enclosure, how happy is he who enters it, to see it is like seeing the horizon or Re.
The cord was stretched by Seshat
The temple is nobly set upon its four corners
Participation of Ptah in the construction of temples
The king directs the ceremonial like the Lord of the *hidn*-plant
Role of the Creator gods

LET'S LIBERATE THE TEMPLE

Task of celebrating

Purification of the mouth with ten pellets of natron and five of incense
Five pellets of Upper Egyptian natron
Five pellets of Lower Egyptian Natron.
Five pellets of incense

The Sem-priest, when preparing the statue with the head cloth, is bidden to touch its mouth and eyes four times

Opening the Mouth and in the daily temple-liturgy the correct place for this ceremony is after proffering the broad collar.
Presenting oil
Application of the green and black eye-pigments
Light blue cloth
Green cloth
Red cloth
Dark-red cloth
Light blue cloth

The time for consecrating the temple and 'ceding' it to its Lord was the night of the New Year and furthermore that at the beginning of every New Year a temple was re-hallowed and handed over once more to its divine occupant

Building inscriptions

Horus, Geb, Thoth, and *Dwn-cnwy*

Geb having taken the place occupied by Seth in the earlier versions of the lustration formula

In some versions of the Opening of the Mouth no mention is made of an adze of the Courtiers nor of their opening the mouth of the statue with it. Furthermore, the four slabs (*cbwt*) are not manipulated by them but by the *si-mry-f*, who 'wipes' or 'touches' the eyes and mouth of the statue therewith, and so opens them.

FREDERICK MONDERSON

The sacrifice of a bull, which precedes the offering of the beheaded goose and goat is the normal version of this rite, constitutes along with that offering and the above-mentioned 'touching' of the mouth and eyes with the four *cbwt* the main part of Ceremony XXIII

CONCLUSIONS

Horus the Behdetite and the co-Templar divinities made and female, the various parts of Horus' body, the ornaments or emblems which he wore or carried, his temple with its halls, chapels, the boat-shrine in the holy of Holies, and all the other furnishings 'are called upon to rouse themselves from slumber, being clearly regarded, one and all, as separate animate being who sleep during the hours of darkness, but 'awake in peace' as soon as the sun appears on the horizon and sheds its light upon them.' That the Egyptians believed that divinities could become immanent at will in the figures depicting them in the temple wall-reliefs, which thus became alive and active, was clearly demonstrated by Herman Junker.

"From the representations showing them to us in progress we really learn nothing of how they were actually performed, for the pictures have a purpose on their own. They not only serve to decorate or illustrate, but stand in close relationship to the rite. In their own selves, everything that they depict is carried out, seeing that the divine spirit of the god and of his retinue enters into the figures.

Thus, the same conception that we meet with in regard to the sculptures in the tombs is here transferred to the temple reliefs, or rather the same idea underlies them both. In the latter as in the former, in that the divine spirit (der Geist), enters the figures and really eats and drinks what is set before him, whether painted or named in writing. With the temple and its sculptures, the king has fashioned for the god 'a monument for his ka' which is not only to proclaim his deeds and his might and depicts his cult but is to carry on in itself;

LET'S LIBERATE THE TEMPLE

beside the service the priests and other officiants, a continuous actual cult the indwelling of the divine ka."

Liberate the Temple. Hatshepsut's Temple at Deir el Bahari. In the Anubis Shrine on the Middle Colonnade, Thutmose III offers to Sokar, a one-time "God of the Dead."

FREDERICK MONDERSON

Liberate the Temple. Hatshepsut's Temple at Deir el Bahari. Ra-Horakhty stands in colossal size in the Anubis Shrine.

LET'S LIBERATE THE TEMPLE

Liberate the Temple. Hatshepsut's Temple at Deir el Bahari. Fanciful ceiling decoration in the Anubis shrine with cartouches (Shennus) of Thutmose III.

FREDERICK MONDERSON

Egyptian belief that Divinities and the dead could become immanent in the representation of them sculptured or painted on temple and tomb-chapel walls and naturally also in their statues is long standing. This belief, he maintained, accounted for erection of cenotaphs and memorial stelae at Abydos.

As is well-known, the "Opening of the Mouth" was regularly performed on behalf of the statues of all divine and human beings, statuettes used for magical purposes, and even on behalf of the heart-scarab, to imbue them with life and identify them with the beings or creatures they represented. Of our two texts, with the significant word quoted at the beginning of the article meant a version of the "Opening of the Mouth," the sequence and character of the ceremonies composing the rite suggesting that first of all it was performed on behalf of the cultus-statues and that then the 'Mouth of the Temple' itself was opened. The idea evidently was that not only the cultus-statues were enabled to become alive and active through the due performance of this rite, but the figures in the wall-reliefs also and the entire edifice with all its appurtenances.

The "Opening of the Mouth" and the daily temple-liturgy are, apart from a number of ceremonies essentially peculiar to the former, practically identical rites. Both comprise an elaborate toilet followed by a meal, which, indeed, except for preliminary ceremonies, are the main features of the temple-liturgy.

The mysterious life originally imparted to the whole temple and its occupants by the "Rite of Consecration" would perpetually be renewed, that is to say as long as the two texts remained intact.

The actual performance of such ceremonies and the recitation of the accompanying formulae were naturally regarded as more efficacious than sculpture representations and mere written words.

Having asperged or sprinkled the statues of Horus and the co-Templar divinities with holy water and presented them with pellets of natron

LET'S LIBERATE THE TEMPLE

and incense for the purifying of their mouths, the officiants censed them.

One official opens the mouth, one opens the eyes of the statue
We mention the adze used in the ceremony

Sacrifices of the animals

The mouths wiped or touched

After the chanting of hymns and praises to Ra, the gods were summoned to their repast and then the image of Ma'at was presented to the sun-god.

After the ceremonial repast, the "Opening of the Mouth" of the temple was enacted, probably as the ceremony unfolded, the officiating priest visited each hall and chapel separately, censing and Asperging them, and, it may well be, making mimetic gestures with their ceremonial adzes and other implements. It is presumably by means of these performances that not only the temple as a whole, but all its individual parts and furnishings became alive and active. The divinities could now become immanent at will in their figures appearing in the reliefs, while the inanimate objects depicted therein became the actual equivalents of what they represented. That is, food, vessels, floral offerings, and the like.

When the service of consecration was over and, so one would suppose, the statues of the divinities had been carried in solemn procession to their respective sanctuaries, the craftsmen who had participated in the building and decorating of the temple were given a meal consisting, it would seem, of bread, meat and beer, and the members of the temple priesthood were similarly entertained, but probably separately, entertained.

With the ceding of the sacred edifice to its divine owner, a proceeding which the Pharaoh himself was supposed to take the leading part, the consecration solemnities came to an end.

FREDERICK MONDERSON

XX. PURIFICATION AND PURITY IN ANCIENT EGYPT
BY
DR. FRED MONDERSON

While righteousness is a hallmark of Egyptian Ma'atian ethics manifesting in truth and justice, Purification is just as paramount in religious beliefs and practice, but equally in the social realm particularly as to how individuals, viz., priests, nobles, bureaucrats, laity and common-folk, behave but more especially how they relate to the king, the Son of God who functioned as the principal dispenser of truth and justice. Notwithstanding, purity and purification are more pronounced in relationship to worship in temples through the methods and practices of ritual and liturgy; and equally secondarily in mortuary temple dynamics in preparation for the journey into the Afterlife where the king as a deceased representative hoped to meet destiny in the final executed divine practice of justice. That is, the judgment or Psychostasia where, unlike normal humans, he is judged by his brother gods to determine whether he had lived up to his true and admonished responsibilities as dictated by Ma'at.

Purity is a requirement in the place where the council of the gods are born, dwell and administer justice among themselves and where both king and commoner are subjected to the same standards divinity required of themselves; for, after all, when an individual is declared "true of Voice," or "Justified," he or she is allowed to exist into eternity in that place of purity among the gods. This place of heavenly bliss, solemnity and sacredness must be the epitome of purity since and those who dwell therein represents the essence of divinity, justice and purity. Still, no one mortal can conceptualize what heaven is like, a place of eternity, until one gets there. That is why Egyptian belief held individuals must subject themselves to the most rigorous and resolute moral and spiritual preparation undergirded in practices of purity in thought, word and deed, in order to attain and manifest the

LET'S LIBERATE THE TEMPLE

prerequisites to guarantee immortality in such an existence of everlastingness.

Liberate the Temple. Hatshepsut's Temple at Deir el Bahari. Cartouches of Thutmose III in Hatshepsut's Temple!

Liberate the Temple. Hatshepsut's Temple at Deir el Bahari. Another image of the author leaving Hatshepsut's temple.

FREDERICK MONDERSON

Liberate the Temple. Hatshepsut's Temple at Deir el Bahari. Colorful image of Hathor, tutelary goddess of the temple.

LET'S LIBERATE THE TEMPLE

Liberate the Temple. Hatshepsut's Temple at Deir el Bahari. Nubian-Egyptian personnel who provide security and were on hand to greet the returning Punt Expedition.

In that sphere of the just where the gods dwell in spirit and truth, the good are rewarded for having lived a life of justice and service to humanity; while the evil, short-lived at judgment, are dispatched to the infernal regions for destruction, perhaps, penance; but, nevertheless, they never share in the beatific vision and experience as examples of worthiness. Still, it is possible there is redemption. That is, probably only after an extensive period of rigorous cleansing to acquire that purity necessary for eternal life. For, having been given the sacred opportunity of life such persons seem to undergo, yet never giving credit to standards of moral and spiritual purity, their lot ultimately become punishment in a lake of fire. Nevertheless, we recognize in ancient Egypt there were two existing, not competing but complimenting belief systems, that of the Sky-Religion of the Sun-god Ra and the terrestrial religion of the Earth-god Osiris, judge of the Afterlife. Disparate yet together, they both laid down the law and requirements for membership into eternity.

FREDERICK MONDERSON

In exploring the potent ancient Egyptian conception of purity and purification we begin in the heavens with the rise of the Sun-god before he begins his trek across the heavens. We equally encounter the king, as Son of the Sun who undergoes his purification in the *Perdwet* or "House of the Morning" in preparation for his daily activities, perhaps after his visit to the temple. The same requirements of cleansing for the sun-god in the heavens, duplicated on the image in the Sanctuary and the living king is also required of the dead king or person in preparation for the next life experience. However, and notwithstanding, while the king does not generally reside in the God's temple, evidence indicates many of the New Kingdom kings' mortuary structure at Thebes, their "Temple of a million years," had an adjacent palace in which surviving illustrations of a few but specifically at Medinet Habu and Ramesseum, there the king is depicted leaving the palace to enter the temple. In many instances and places, analogy is used to explain an act or fact at one place relative to another. In this respect, while there is an example on Rameses II's "Girdle Wall" at Karnak, at Dendera, Kom Ombo and Edfu, the king is seen on the outer portal being baptized by Horus and Thoth who bathe him in streams of ankh on the outside before he enters the temple. Given that though we know so much about ancient Egypt, in contradiction so little has actually survived the passage of time and the destructive nature of man. As such, then, on the other hand, and while still reinforcing this idea of baptism, on a wall in a room adjacent to the Sanctuary within the temple of Karnak, on the northern side, Hatshepsut is depicted being baptized by Horus and Thoth but in this case, her image is systematically chiseled out of the baptism and purification rite. This seemingly spiteful act of desecrating the queen's image is blamed on Thutmose III and his adherents engaged in the reaction as retribution for the queen depriving him of kingly rule for some two decades. One scholar, however, mentions an image depicting Thutmose III leading the Queen's cortege at her funeral.

However, just as the Sun-god was lustrated upon his arising in the heavens on the morn, his earthly counterpart dwelling in the sanctuary's naos was subject to the same treatment. This time, however, while the Sun-god's lustration was theoretical in the minds

LET'S LIBERATE THE TEMPLE

of man, lustration of his earthly manifestation was more practical, constantly on a daily basis being performed by the king or high priest. Thus, and in order to perform that function both king and high priest also had to undergo purification. That is, the same as was done for the king upon his arising in the palace, a cleansing he was subjected to in the "House of the Morning," that same cleansing was again rendered at the temple; again, for both him and the priest.

Blackman and Firman, using Edfu as an example, have shown the temple itself; not the consecration which was done at the completion of the holy place prior to being handed over to its owner, the resident god; this entity had to be baptized or purified on an equal basis in order to come alive; the whole temple, that is, so that the day's ritual could commence. In this perennial ritual, the god's servants, the priests and their helpers also had to be purified in order to successfully execute their functions in administering their responsibilities, no matter ow small a part each played. Even the instruments employed in the execution of the ritual, viz., incense burner, ointments, vessels for water, even in singing, playing musical instruments and certainly the other support personnel engaged in assisting the day's events which generally occurred three times per day.

In similar fashion in all his earthly manifestations the king was subject to the rigorous and unending purification. As Crown Prince he was purified at birth; at his Coronation; on way to wage battle with Egypt's enemies; when visiting before he enters the temple; before he officiates in procession and temple ritual; at his death; in mummification preparation; at the tomb's entrance; on way to the Hall of Judgment in the Afterlife, the "Tree Goddess" pours four pitchers of water on him; before entering the Hall of Judgment; and once declared "true of Voice," having survived the Judgment, he had to be purified once more in order to live within the company of the gods in that place of purity.

Normally there was more to the whole purity and purification idea; for even in modern times, Dr. Yosef Ben-Jochannan instructed his students to not simply dress properly before entering the temple, demonstrate a temple decorum with respect for the culture of the holy place and don't enter the Sanctuary, for, in ancient times, only the king and his high priest designate could enter this inner sanctum where the god resided. Thus, Dr. Ben was big on the purity idea and so repeatedly stressed proper behavior in the temple. Heeding his admonition and painting a picture of temple restriction, we must remember, using Karnak Temple as an example, even nobles invited beyond the Pylon entrance were prescribed from proceeding beyond the Great Court. Only the priestly procession could assemble and proceed within and without the Hypostyle Hall. In a note of clarity, the temple procession, as part of some festivity within the temple or on a distant visit, for example, to celebrate the Opet festival at Luxor Temple or the Feast of the Valley across the river at the West Bank, were different to the Sanctuary procession to administer to the god. That is, while the Sanctuary Procession was more involved, the "visiting procession" traveled "light." Nevertheless, there was that rare yet solemn occasion, when in procession, the image of the god was bared and the faithful was rewarded with an instant peek of the subject of their worship and veneration.

The area beyond the Hypostyle Hall that entrances the Sanctuary or "Holy of Holies," is called the Wadjit. Decorated with pylons, spacious halls filled with statues, obelisks, colonnades, the ritual depicted on the walls, and more, only the Sanctuary Procession enters this location and beyond. The temple in general; yet, this structure is sort of equated with a domestic "bedroom" where only the family members could enter. Important, while the support personnel carry the utensils, sing and play songs on musical instruments, read from the holy books, burn incense, fetch the food and flowers and water for sprinkling and washing, only the king and high priest among this purified body can "Open the doors of heaven." There to enter to view, ritualize and serve the resident divinity. Upon completion of his task, done three times per day, serving a heavy breakfast and lunch, then a light snack at evening-time, on those three occasions the servant, having fulfilled his mission, "brings the foot." That is, as the worshipper, king or high priest, withdraws facing, never backing, the god he uses a particular instrument, a branch of the *hidn* tree, to erase all footsteps from the sandy soil before the god. Then he closes and secures the door until the next occasion for awakening and disturbing the divinity's rest and to repeat the ritual again and again.

LET'S LIBERATE THE TEMPLE

Liberate the Temple. Hatshepsut's Temple at Deir el Bahari. Frontal view of the entrance to the Sanctuary in the Upper Court of the Upper Terrace.

Liberate the Temple. Hatshepsut's Temple at Deir el Bahari. From the south of the Upper Court, columns of the Colonnades and niches for the Queen's statues.

FREDERICK MONDERSON

Liberate the Temple. Hatshepsut's Temple at Deir el Bahari. View of the sanctuary's entrance and remaining statues in the niches.

The use of sand is important in the area of the sanctuary before the god's naos.

In a wonderful article entitled, "Purification (Egyptian)," Aylward Blackman in Hasting's *Encyclopedia of Religion and Ethics* Vol. X (Edinburgh: T. and T. Clarke, 1918: 476-482), details with succinct clarity the full panoply of events, individuals, materials and process in the experience of creating the divinely acceptable state of purity through purification in order to execute the responsibilities to protect the god and make him comfortable.

I.   **Purification Materials** were:

1. Water -
2. Natron -
3. Incense -

LET'S LIBERATE THE TEMPLE

4. Sand -
5. Food -
6. Fire -

Vessels for washing both hands and feet were made of gold and silver but more especially copper. Earthen pitchers were used for bathing or sprinkling purposes and even a metal vase was employed.

II. Purification of the Whole Person.
This was accomplished through:

1. Bathing -

2. Purification of the mouth -

3. Washing of the feet -

4. Cleansing of the nails -

5. Shaving of the -

    a. head -

    b. face -

6. Depilation -

7. Purification before a meal -

III. Purification to be part of a community

1. Circumcision -

2. Purification at birth -

3. Purification after sexual intercourse -

4. Purification for women -

5. Sometimes the entire body -

    a. During menstruation -

    b. After childbirth -

IV. Religious Purity - is designed to purify the priest, even the Pharaoh before officiating in the temple in praise and ritualization of the god.

1. Purification of the living pharaoh -

a. In infancy -

b. Before Coronation -

c. At Coronation -

d. Before officiating in the temple -

e. At a Sed-Festival –

f. Before he takes the field of battle

2. Purification after death –

a. before and during mummification;

b. on way to the tomb;

LET'S LIBERATE THE TEMPLE

c. at the tomb;

d. completion of the ceremony;

e. In the next life by the gods.

Liberate the Temple. Hatshepsut's Temple at Deir el Bahari. Through the mesh view of the inner chamber of a Sanctuary in the temple.

FREDERICK MONDERSON

Liberate the Temple. Hatshepsut's Temple at Deir el Bahari. Historic surviving Altar with its nine-steps for worship of Ra-Horakhty, the Sun god.

Liberate the Temple. Hatshepsut's Temple at Deir el Bahari. Thutmose III kneels to present ointment jars to enthroned Amon-Ra.

LET'S LIBERATE THE TEMPLE

Liberate the Temple. Hatshepsut's Temple at Deir el Bahari. Another look at the Porch through which the Sanctuary is entranced and the surviving statues in the Niches.

Thus, purity was the only guaranteed passport to posthumous happiness; that is, a purity upon which the welfare of the dead depended. Accordingly, "more than physical purity or cleanliness was expected of the pharaoh" and as time passed from the Sixth Dynasty onward, "the claims made by the dead to moral integrity and purity became more and more prominent where in the Books of the Dead's Negative Confessions the deceased declared he as not guilty, among other sins, of fornication, masturbation and adultery." Notwithstanding, the "Confessions" he had to work and maintain the purity he would so finally boast of. In that respect, "There were several ways of attaining that purity upon which the welfare of the dead so entirely depended."

a. Ceremonial acts performed by the deceased in his lifetime.

i. Bathing in Sacred waters or pools -

ii. Participating in the Osirian mysteries -

b. Spells asserting "that these acts had been performed" and "That all impurities had been avoided."

c. Ablutions performed after death by the deceased himself.

d. Ceremonies performed for him by the gods;

e. Ceremonies performed for him by the living at preparation of the mummy and at the burial before the tomb.

3. Significance of Posthumous Purification -

The funerary washing, sprinklings, fumigations, etc., possessed, therefore a secondary, what we might call sacramental, significance; they both helped to reconstitute the deceased and, together with the food and drink-offerings, supplied him with nutrient which enabled him to continue his existence and to maintain unimpaired all his reconstituted faculties and powers.

According to Blackman (Edinburgh: T. and T. Clarke, 1918: 479) who writes as follows:

i. The water with which the corpse or statue was washed or sprinkled not merely cleansed the deceased from his impurities but brought together the head and bones and made the body complete (tm) in every particular. Accordingly, either stream of water that flows about the figure of the dead User terminates in a large symbol of life. With the offering of libation-water to the deceased is associated the giving to him of his spirit (ib) and his power (shm), and at the same time he is bidden to stand upon his feet and to gather together his bones.

LET'S LIBERATE THE TEMPLE

ii.   Incense-smoke had the same effect, cleansing the dead from all the evil appertaining to him, and making him 'strong and powerful above all gods.'

iii.   For the mysterious virtue of the food and drink-offerings

iv.   The deceased was also, of course supposed to be similarly reconstituted by the purifications that he underwent to be reconstituted in the other world. After ablutions in the Field of Earu he received 'his bones of metal' and 'stretched out his indestructible limbs which are in the womb of the sky-goddess.' By the washings of Horus and Thoth and other divinities the dead was cleansed from all impurities, moral and physical, his body came together again or was entirely refashioned, and he was fit to enter heaven or the Tie, i.e., underworld.

V. Purity and Purification of Offerings to Gods and the Dead.

1.   All offerings made to gods and the dead had to be purified. "The doorposts of temples often bear the following or a similar inscription: 'The offerings and all that enters the temple of such-and-such a divinity - it is pure.' The living pray that the mortuary equipment of the dead may consist of every good and pure thing."'

2.   Purification of Offerings - These were purified by pouring libations over them and by fumigating them with incense. The testing of all funerary victims was customary as far back as the Old Kingdom.

VI. Purification of Temples and building used for religious ceremonies.

1.   Consecration of a new temple or shrine -

2.   Renewal of purification -

FREDERICK MONDERSON

3. Purification before the day's proceedings –

VII. Purity and Purification of the Priests - The Web priest meant he was "the pure one." As such, a number of measures were taken to assure his purity.

Liberate the Temple. Temple of God Amon at Karnak. Visitor stand before the entrance to the "Avenue of Sphinx" and the Great or First Pylon with the inner reaches beyond the "Processional Colonnade" in rear.

LET'S LIBERATE THE TEMPLE

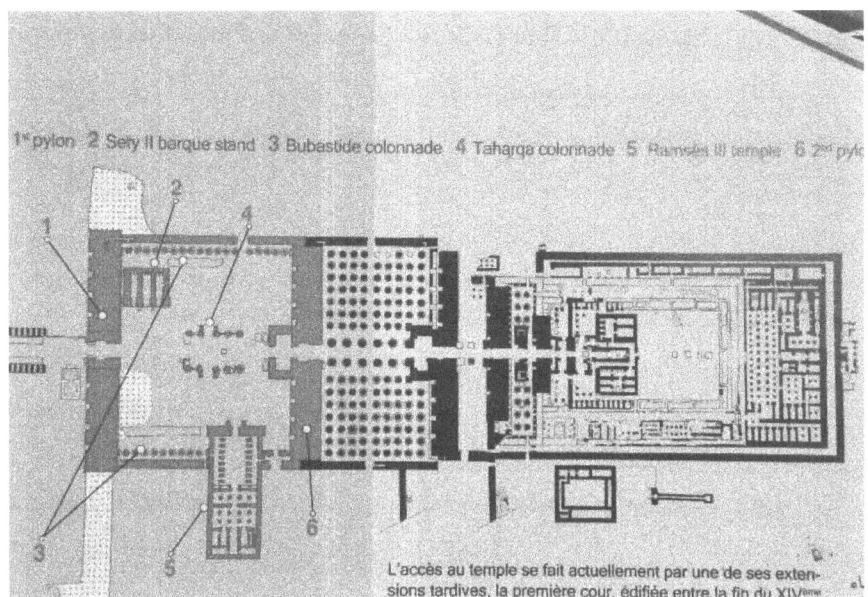

Liberate the Temple. Temple of God Amon at Karnak. Plan of the temple with the First Court highlighted.

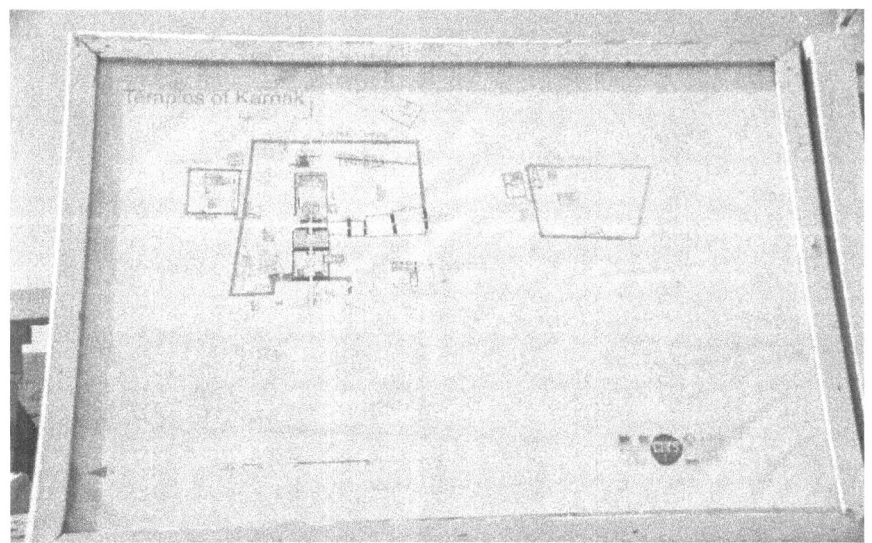

Liberate the Temple. Temple of God Amon at Karnak. Plan of the Karnak Temple of Amon with temples of Mut (right) and the War-God Monthu (left).

1.	In Graeco-Roman times a priest had to purify himself for several days before he performed his functions.

2.	Priests had to always wash or sprinkle themselves before entering a temple. At its entrance, every temple had a pool or tank, maybe a basin set aside for this purpose. This is a carry-over in today's church practice with a basin of "Holy Water" at the entrance.

3.	The priests also perhaps fumigated themselves with incense before they performed the daily ritual.

4.	Great emphasis was laid on the purity of the priest's hands.

    a.	Pairing the nails -

    b.	Depilation -

    c.	Shaving -

    d.	Dress -

    e.	Circumcision -

## VIII.	Purity and Purification of the Laity.

1.	The laity must undergo purity and purification before entering a temple or sacred place.

2.	Purification in practice or effectuated by "sacred water" or in pools. Near the Khercha stood a pool in which the Sun-god washed his face. This also benefitted humans who did the same. Perhaps this is where Piankhi washed his face on way to Heliopolis to be recognized by the Sun-god, to be blessed and declared Son of Ra. This

LET'S LIBERATE THE TEMPLE

was part of the ceremonial ritual in which the pharaoh received the protocols and paraphernalia investing with full power and divinity status.

3. Two great pools stood at Heracleopolis manga, the "Pool of Natron" and the "Pool of Ma'at."

4. The waters of the First Cataract, the traditional source of the Nile, was believed to be endowed with special cleansing properties and therefore used (or supposed to be used) for all the lustrations and libations offered to the gods and the dead. The fact that, the dead go there to be bathed by the goddess Satis meant that the living also performed ablutions there.

Liberate the Temple. Temple of God Amon at Karnak. Open Air Museum. The 12th Dynasty art and architectural gem of Senusert I, known as "the White Chapel."

FREDERICK MONDERSON

XXI. 10ᵀᴴ ANNUAL MEMORIAL DAY TRIBUTE TO DR. YOSEF BEN-JOCHANNAN

FREE   FREE   FREE   FREE   FREE

DR. FRED MONDERSON INVITES TO 10ᵀᴴ ANNUAL MEMORIAL DAY TRIBUTE TO DR. YOSEF BEN-JOCHANNAN

CELEBRATING AND HONORING DR. BEN-JOCHANNAN

BROOKLYN, NEW YORK 11216
DATE: Saturday June 10, 2017
TIME: 4:00 TO 6:00 pm

THEME:

LET'S LIBERATE THE TEMPLE

WHAT YOU WILL LEARN:

LET'S LIBERATE THE TEMPLE

1. **WHAT IS DR. BEN'S TRILOGY**

2. **TEMPLE ORIENTATION**

3. **PURIFICATION AND PURITY**

4. **RITUAL DECORATION**

5. **DRAMA IN THE SANCTUARY**

6. **SOURCES FOR FURTHER READING**

7. **UPDATE ON THE CHRONOLOGY OF ANCIENT EGYPT**

"Trilogy" *Africa: Mother of Western Civilization*; *African Origins of the Major Western Religions*; and *Black Man of the Nile*, later, *Black Man of the Nile and His Family*.

Dr. YOSEF A. A. BEN-JOCHANNAN
A TRIBUTE
By
Dr. Fred Monderson

It is with great sorrow that I announce the death of my mentor, friend and world renowned African historian, Egyptologist and humanitarian

FREDERICK MONDERSON

DR. YOSEF ANTONIO ALFREDO BEN-JOCHANNAN. At this time, AFRICAN PEOPLE HAVE LOST A CHAMPION OF GREAT MAGNITUDE, wisdom and intellectual fortitude. LET US WISH HIM A WONDERFUL RECEPTION INTO THE PANTHEON OF GREAT AFRICAN ANCESTORS who have never compromised in quest of the best for African people.

Liberate the Temple. Temple of God Amon at Karnak. Open Air Museum. Sign indicating door of Amenhotep I in two languages.

Liberate the Temple. Temple of God Amon at Karnak. Open Air Museum. Another chapel in the Open-Air Museum.

LET'S LIBERATE THE TEMPLE

Liberate the Temple. Temple of God Amon at Karnak. View from north of the Court, the "Taharka Column" and inner and southern face of the First or Great Pylon. Notice (1) the Mud-ramp that enabled scaling to heights and (2) end two columns, how they were first erected (right) and after dressing how they end up (left).

Liberate the Temple. Temple of God Amon at Karnak. What a Triad! Amon-Ra, Rameses II and Carmen Monderson at the entrance to the Hypostyle Hall.

LET'S LIBERATE THE TEMPLE

Liberate the Temple. Temple of God Amon at Karnak. From within the Hypostyle Hall, view of Hatshepsut's father Thutmose I's Obelisk.

Among his many accomplishments, Dr. Ben has placed the Black Woman on the HIGHEST PEDESTAL to be admired and respected in the hope she will continue to do what no Black man can ever do!

FREDERICK MONDERSON

DR. BEN HAS been a LIGHT and he has shown us the LIGHT!

LET US ALSO HOPE PEOPLE, YOUNG AND OLD, WILL CONTINUE TO READ HIS BOOKS AND FOREVER DRINK FROM THE FOUNT OF HIS ENLIGHTENMENT EFFORTS as Tour Guide, archaeologist and nationalist spokesman whose 97 years on earth have been a tremendously wonderful and enlightening experience. He possessed a vision that looked far into the future. His efforts HAVE KNOWN NO LIMITS in quest for the very best for AFRICAN PEOPLE! Again, his books should be introduced into the schools to let young people understand the man and forces at work!

GOD BLESS DR. BEN-JOCHANNAN AND MAY HIS EFFORTS AND MEMORY CONTINUE TO BE AN INSPIRATION AND GUIDE TO US ALL!

Dr. Ben was an extraordinary man of many talents, but principally a man who held the African woman in the highest esteem. He taught us in the beginning was the African woman! Creation came out of the African woman's womb! As the obelisk is a small pyramid on a tall base, this is the pedestal upon which Dr. ben-Jochannan placed the African woman. He honored the Black Woman who is the source of the Black Family! He taught us the Black Woman is a Goddess! He also led the light to the Nile Valley. He "took Egypt to challenge and destroy white supremacy!" It's like Marcus Garvey said, "Though you have caged the lion, the cubs are running free out there," and thanks to Dr. Ben, intellectual cubs are challenging the distortions, omissions and putting Africa in its proper place in world civilization history given its accomplishments in Nubia and Egypt, Nile Valley cultures that point to inner, Central and Southern Africa, as well-springs of intellectualism, that gave so much to the world.

The Twentieth Century has been blessed with great African and African-American writers and historians. These include Dr. W.E.B. DuBois, Dr. Carter G. Woodson, Dr. Kwame Nkrumah, Dr. Ivan Van Sertima, J.A. Rogers, Cheikh Anta Diop and Dr. Leonard James,

LET'S LIBERATE THE TEMPLE

Emeritus Professor of New York City Technical College of the City University of New York, among others. This enormous collection of brainpower equally extends into the Twenty-First Century. However, none of these giants singularly surpass the literary production, commitment, tirelessness, and sincere dedication of Dr. Yosef Alfredo Antonio ben-Jochannan. Outspoken visionary, iconic symbol and before his time; controversial and not afraid to take an iconoclastic and individual if a somewhat idiosyncratic point of view; Dr. Ben was always prepared to defend his position, irrespective. His friends and students, affectionately call this father, teacher, historian, friend and Egyptologist, "Doc Ben."

In fact, back there in the early 1970s when even "Black folks" did not readily accept "Dr. Ben," ever wonder how he got his name? It was a young man named "Barney" and myself, Fred Monderson, who first started calling him not "Dr. Ben" but "Ben Jo" and the name stuck among us; and finally when a fellow student Curtis Dunmoodie picked it up and said we must be more respectful, we began calling him "Dr. Ben" in defiance of those "feather bedders" who said "Dr. Ben has no Ph. D!"

Ever cried for Dr. Ben? This odious statement once made me cry at New York City (Community) Technical College. I hurriedly took the A-Train to 125th Street to their second-floor office on Lennox Avenue across from the **Choc-Full-O-Nuts** Coffee Shop in Harlem, before Prof. George Simmonds calmed me down, showing me Dr. Ben's **Doctorate in Anthropology** on the wall. That is what some of the "false prophets" still do today in academia to him and others! And so, you ask them to match their literary production with their in-clandestine vituperativeness and they cannot! Period!

Here was a serious scholar, Dr. ben-Jochannan, who spent a lifetime researching, writing, and defending the integrity and intellectual capabilities of African people worldwide. Dr. Ben pioneered in indigenous ancient African terminology. Imagine a European-American scholar discovered the bones of a fossilized African woman in Ethiopia which was dated several million years old. He named her

"Lucy" after an Englishman's song "Lucy with Diamonds," then playing on the radio in camp. Dr. Ben said "No! Her name is *Denk Nesh* not Lucy!"

Liberate the Temple. Temple of God Amon at Karnak. The Ark at Rest in the northern section of the Hypostyle Hall. Above, the Gods Thoth (left) and Horus (right)

Liberate the Temple. Temple of God Amon at Karnak. Open Air Museum. Hatshepsut's "Red Chapel."

LET'S LIBERATE THE TEMPLE

Liberate the Temple. Temple of God Amon at Karnak. Seti I approaches the Shrine of the Theban Triad of Amon-Ra, Mut and Khonsu. Interesting that all four are on a different plane.

Liberate the Temple. Temple of God Amon at Karnak. Sphinxes before the Northern Colonnade of the Great Court of the Temple.

FREDERICK MONDERSON

Liberate the Temple. Temple of God Amon at Karnak. Sphinxes before the Southern Colonnade in the Great Court of the Temple.

In 1989, Doc Ben celebrated fifty years of visiting ancient Kemet, Ta-Merry (Egypt) and the Nile Valley cultures. This prolonged involvement has under-girded and strengthened the basis of his researches, speeches, writings and educational tours revealing much and enlightening many. Equally, he began and for some time maintained archaeological digs on the Island of Elephantine and elsewhere. Alas, these have been discontinued.

This writer was happy to be a part of that epoch-making tour that marked Doc Ben's Fiftieth Anniversary visiting the ancient African "holy-land" and the next year for the First Nubian Festival. More importantly, I met "Doc Ben" in early 1972. This was right after the publication of his seminal works, his "Trilogy," which were, *Africa: Mother of Western Civilization* (1970), *African Origins of the "Major" Western Religions* (1971), and *Black Man of the Nile* (1972), later *Black Man of the Nile and His Family*. The style of his writings, copious nature of referents employed to defend things African was an instant attraction to young nationalists contending with the unfolding

LET'S LIBERATE THE TEMPLE

realities in the 1970s. More importantly, however, his Afrocentric pioneering approach made "Doc. Ben," a very well-respected scholar and elder, and in his later years a sought after speaking attraction, a man who "Tells it Like It Is especially on Gil Noble's show of the same name, Like It Is." Equally and intellectually stimulating, the preponderance of his included bibliography and illustrations helped simplify his message but also stimulated and encouraged more interest in Egypt and African history.

In his life's work, Dr. ben-Jochannan (he asked for a small "B" meaning "Son of Jochannan) has compiled an impressive thirty-odd publication of books. These I am intimately familiar with, having bought most of these books in first edition format which the author subsequently autographed. He helped set the stage for a whole new approach in interpreting Africa's contributions to civilization and its legacy. There was that 'great trio" consisting of Dr. Leonard James, Dr. John Henrik Clarke and Dr. Yosef Ben-Jochannan, champions of the classroom, insistence on development of a resolute research methodology and resulting enlightenment as essential tools for problem solving skills and cultivation of intellectual autonomy. Important, they all helped show me the way, as they did to so many others. Thus, as the "Point man," Dr. Ben lit the fire of intellectual and cultural consciousness in Africans worldwide as he pursued teaching, self-publishing and continuous trips to Egypt carrying thousands, so the monuments could teach them. The Diasporan style of dress with an Afrocentric flavor is also credited to him. Establishing connections between Africans in America, the Caribbean, Africa, Asia and Europe are all attributed to Dr. ben-Jochannan, a man of vision, a seer, a literary and intellectual giant. Many of his books challenged the distortions of Europeans in writing, publishing and disseminating knowledge about the arts, sciences, religion, etc., of the ancient people today called Egyptians. Dr. Ben has rightly included omissions and corrected distortions systematically implanted and perpetrated by racist Western, European and American historiography that has falsified the historical past with a prejudiced interpretation against African people. Many of his books challenged the distortions of Europeans in writing, publishing and disseminating knowledge about the arts, sciences, religion, etc., regarding origins in ancient Africa as represented in modern interpretation. Dr. Ben dared to expose the hypocrisy of western scholarship. He attacked the foundational pillars upon which this false legacy rests. Like the other two giants, his work made manifest, "the existential data contradicts the symbolic representation." Naturally, he paid a price!

Very early, he also expressed the view some scholars are confused because they were taught from a wrong premise. This view is similar to Dr. Leonard James' insistence in educating his students regarding the proper methodological approach to studying and understanding historical evolution utilizing the 8-major social sciences, viz., geography, archaeology, anthropology, history, sociology, economics, political science and psychology. Within this methodological construct, students acquire the skills to correctly engage in critical comparative historical analyses into the cognitive areas of reasoning and learning, forcing new and more complete analyses of the data, thus arriving at more thorough and effective generalizations of any and all historical phenomena. As such, then, and utilizing this approach, it becomes more readily apparent, that "The existential data contradicts the symbolic representation." In his own right, and as a result of his teachings, Dr. Ben-Jochannan had no choice but to produce, publish and distribute his works without the aid of major publishing firms. He was thus a pioneer in self-publishing, launching Alkebu-Lan Publishing Company and appealing and winning the support of many upcoming nationalists as "they purchased his books in first edition form!"

Initiating that new approach to viewing and analyzing history, the end result was an exposition and critical analysis of dynamic forces of Europe and Africa in struggle to claim heritage of the ancient and modern historical record. Dr. Ben addressed professionals, scholars, laymen, clergy, students and educators. He stressed vitality, resilience and creative expressions that shaped the modern African personality and worldview. Such an approach found ready ears among a people yearning for enlightening factual information about their illustrious African past in effort to free their minds from the shackling oppression and aggression of slavery and colonization. These young and old minds were enthused by the positive nature and realization of the

LET'S LIBERATE THE TEMPLE

potency of their cultural African heritage as "Ben" outlined it. He also took great pains to explain that there were lusterless pages in Africa's past, but these must be remembered but discarded. Nevertheless, his concern fueled their emerging aspirations. This outlook brought Dr. Ben the adulation and respect of a grateful people, he for long deserved. They understood and welcomed his contributions among the litany of great African-American literary artists.

Dr. Ben's writings, lectures and educational tours over the years, have stressed two essential themes. The first is that the "emergence of civilization, viz., science, religion, government, architecture, agriculture, philosophy, and the arts, began in Africa." The mouth of these utterances became the conduit of today's Egypt and the Nile Valley. In his approach, Dr. Ben has shown how the structural foundations of western civilization developed from discoveries and scientific applications in this ancient African land. Lastly, he took great pains to show the writing and teaching of modern history has been distorted to elevate Europe and denigrate Africa, which is clearly wrong and must be rectified. This fundamental view helped establish the need for African historical reconstruction and interpretation particularly as we navigate this new century and millennium.

Liberate the Temple. Kurneh Mortuary Temple of Seti I. Seti presents his name as Ma'at to the enthroned Amon with Mut as his rear.

FREDERICK MONDERSON

Liberate the Temple. Kurneh Mortuary Temple of Seti I. Remaining 8 of 10 columns of the temple's façade.

Liberate the Temple. Kurneh Mortuary Temple of Seti I. Seti in regal splendor.

LET'S LIBERATE THE TEMPLE

Liberate the Temple. Kurneh Mortuary Temple of Seti I. On a block of stone in the Outer Court, an enthroned Amon sits with Mut at his back.

The second of Dr. Ben's themes has been that "Africans worldwide should be proud of their ancestors' accomplishments. The arts and sciences that today govern the world are Africa's legacy. African-Americans should show great pride and dignity in their history and heritage." They must respect themselves and carry themselves with dignity and pride. Those who know can and should teach the young how to identify with Africa. In so doing, they must form study groups and visit Africa. Yet, they must also be aware of the machinations of cultural imperialism and cultural genocide constantly at work with tits devastating detriment as a prime goal. Further the young must learn to and immerse themselves in an African-centric perspective and in process research, write and teach others in turn. They must study languages such as French, German, Swahili, Greek, Latin, Coptic, Arabic and Medu Netcher or Hieroglyphics. This is where the knowledge of Ancient Africa lies, in the temple, tombs and cemeteries because scholars from these language places of origination did the research and their museums "hold" great reservoirs of artifactual "culture in captivity." They must become conversant with the Archaeology of Egypt and how anthropology shaped its interpretation to write its history. They must struggle to correct the recent distorted history of Africa's past. In this way, future leaders would help to better the lot of humanity and save the world from its impending moral, spiritual and scientific destruction. To accomplish these objectives, the good doctor has supplied a reservoir of information from his life's researches in the arsenal of published works he has created. Of course, these works must be read, ingested and digested and returned to time and again. This is important, for as Dr. John Henrik Clarke once pointed out, "People buy but never read Dr. Ben's books." Herein then is the dilemma!

The author's major thesis of his *African Origins of the Major "Western Religions"* is that African religious practices were denigrated and called "fetishism" and "paganism." In fact, these early thought processes he showed are the fundamental bases of Judaism, Christianity and Islam. He argued that these ideas were first developed and nurtured in Central Africa among indigenous peoples and then migrated and extended throughout the Nile Valley. Echoing Cheikh Anta Diop's *Cultural Unity of Black Africa*, Theophile Obenga in *Egypt and Black Africa* and *African Philosophy: The Pharaonic Period: 2780-330 B.C.* equates Punt to similar thoughts and practices, religious and scientific, among many peoples and cultures spread across Central and Southern Africa. The foundations and connections of these ideas are not to be found in Asiatic places of origin of "White Egyptians." After all, Mosso in *Dawn of Mediterranean Civilization* noted, "Asiatics did not penetrate the Nile Valley nor the Aegean region." Evidence indicates and conversely, the cultural bonanza of Ethiopia and Central Africa found greatest fruition in Kemet (Egypt) and were preserved by its civilization advances and the nature of its geography.

After decades of oral recording and practice, the early knowledge was first written down in such selections as the "Book of Gates," "Book of Knowing Ra," etc. These were part of the earlier "Pyramid Texts"

LET'S LIBERATE THE TEMPLE

(Old Kingdom); then "Coffin Texts" (Middle Kingdom); and the later *Book of the Dead* or *Book of Going Forth By Day* (New Kingdom); and the "Mysteries of Sais" (Egypt). Thus, the fortunes of geography enabled Africa's second cultural daughter, Kemet, to rise to greater prominence than did the eldest, Ethiopia, Dr. Ben explained! He stressed and still maintain to his later age, despite all the "new evidence," that civilization began to the south of Egypt! However, despite modern falsification of history and the insistent propagation of such falsity, his thesis is as credible as ever. That is because much of this was subsequently made manifest by *The New York Times* publication of Bruce William's "The World's Earliest Monarchy found in Nubia" at Qustol; reinforced by the revelations of Brophy and Bauval's *Black Genesis* (2011) regarding people of Nabta Playa; the discoveries reported in Toby Wilkinson's *Genesis of the Pharaohs* (2003) which show petroglyphs of Egypt as cultural beginning was "1000-years before Winkler's Mesopotamians;" and William Arnett's *The Predynastic Origin of Egyptian Hieroglyphs: Evidence for the Development of Rudimentary Forms of Hieroglyphs in Upper Egypt in the Fourth Millennium B.C.* (1982) where among his many claims, the ne most profound has been, "Diop was correct in proving the Egyptians were not white!" All of which was eloquently argued in Diop's *The African Origin of Civilization: Myth or Reality* (1974). Even more, Theophile Obenga has elaborated further in his own penetrating analysis, supporting Dr. Diop where *African Philosophy: The Pharaonic Period*: 2780-330 B.C. (2004) and again in **Egypt and Black Africa** have very eloquently reinforced continental universality of much we see and understand about Egypt.

Another of Dr. Ben's seminal works is *Africa: Mother of Western Civilization*. Its major thesis holds that the "fundamental laws, principles, philosophies, ideas, arts and crafts that educated the west, are indigenous to Africa through the Nile Valley cultural experience." For critical teachers who face this dilemma he has some advice. As such, he wrote: "The only credentials necessary in the experience of African history, otherwise misnomered 'the Black Experience' and 'Black Studies' are the documented proofs and the sources from whence they are taken."

FREDERICK MONDERSON

For this reason, *Africa: Mother of Western Civilization* is an enormous compendium of facts, sources, illustrations, and analyses that challenge laymen and scholars alike. It suggests all educators and lay persons alike become involved in reclaiming the stolen heritage of Africa. This *magnum opus* opens new vistas for historical investigation and provides a wide array of references relating to the significance of Africa in world civilization.

Black Man of the Nile and His Family marks the third in the "trilogy of Dr. Ben's seminal works." This particular source represents the maturity of his thoughts and presentations for it focuses on the role Black men and women have played in bequeathing science, religion, arts, metaphysics, agricultural method, boat building and Nile River navigation to the world through Africa's conduit in Nubia and Egypt. It also contains a number of objectives the author seeks to accomplish.

The first of these objectives is, "an attempt to create in young African, African-American (Black person), and all other African people, a sense of belonging in the great African heritage." It is, writes Dr. Ben "specifically directed to those who have criminally demasculinized, denuded, and otherwise denigrated the Africans of their **CULTURAL, ECONOMIC, POLITICAL, SCIENTIFIC, SPIRITUAL**, and all other forms of their heritage and human decency." To this we should add the intellectual heritage as represented in Egypt; that is, through "acquisition methods," and other mechanisms of stealing as well as teaching, writing and mis-representation of the artifactual evidence.

It also presents: "**AFRICAN ORIGINS OF EUROPEAN CIVILIZATION**" in a manner whereby, "scholars can find interesting use for it in their research and intellectual endeavors; as much as the layman can for processing information."

Dr. Ben views his role as gadfly presenting, "pertinent information needed in the African peoples' **RE-IDENTIFICATION** with their great ancestral heritage." Lastly, he continued, the "major desired

LET'S LIBERATE THE TEMPLE

accomplishment this volume seeks to achieve, is to provide anthropological evidence in the ancient heritage of the Africans" and their contributions all over the world.

Liberate the Temple. Kurneh Mortuary Temple of Seti I. Looking back towards the entrance walkway to the temple proper.

Liberate the Temple. Kurneh Mortuary Temple of Seti I. Cartouches and uraeus on Heb surround squatting image of a hawk sporting a feather. Below the Cartouche or Shennu of Men-Ma'at-Ra, Seti I

FREDERICK MONDERSON

Liberate the Temple. Kurneh Mortuary Temple of Seti I. Seti offers two ointment jars to the Moon God Khons or Khonsu, of the Theban Triad.

Abu Simbel to Ghizeh: *A Guide Book and Manual* (1989) is in itself another useful piece of writing. But, there are other books.

Regarding the acquisition of knowledge, Sir Francis Bacon (1561-1626) noted: "Some books are to be tasted, others to be swallowed, and some few to be chewed and digested." This much can be said of the trilogy of Dr. ben-Jochannan's works, *Black Man of the Nile and His Family*, *Africa: Mother of Western Civilization* and *The African Origins of the "Major" Western Religions*. The others are equally interesting! Everyone must buy and read these books and pass them on to others particularly their sons and daughters and nephews and nieces.

Finally, as a student of his, and based on observations and analytic critique, this writer would like to add a 20-point summation of how we can view Dr. Yosef Alfredo Antonio ben-Jochannan's contribution

LET'S LIBERATE THE TEMPLE

as an unselfish and fearless elucidation of the historical record systematically distorted to elevate Europe and denigrate Africa while wrecking psycho-social debasement of the African spirit and persona, especially in America and globally.

In this manner, whether through omission, distortion and even false presentation, the urban youth across America have most seriously been victimized in the systematic alienated educational process they have been subjected to. As such, the potent cultural lifeline Dr. Yosef Alfredo Antonio ben-Jochannan has provided is today critical in rescuing these young people adrift in the academic and intellectual cosmos of these modern times going forward. The prescription therefore is as follows:

1. We must praise and show thankfulness for the man who, for more than half a century challenged the behemoth of western intellectual oppression of Africa and her offspring while enlightening many to the wonders of a creative African cultural heritage.

2. We must commend Dr. ben-Jochannan for the humanitarian work he did among the Nubians in Egypt and Sudan, viz., Aswan, Daboud, Wadi Halfa, Dongola Province and Fashoda.

3. We must recognize his call to action to combat the cultural genocide in the African-American studies curriculum predating the Afrocentric insistence on multi-culturalism.

4. We should continue to emulate his style of critical analysis of contemporary developments, whether it was historical omissions in Alex Haley's *Roots*; misrepresentation in King Tut's exhibition that has taken place several times in America; taking to task T. Eric Peet's "The Problem with Akhenaton;" Criticism of Father Temple's *Bantu Philosophy*; challenge to another writer's description that Rameses II had "badly abscessed teeth," and so forth. We must importantly emphasize "New World tobacco" found in the intestines of the King Rameses' mummy and its implications that Africans were in the New World some 3000-years before Columbus' arrival.

FREDERICK MONDERSON

5.   We can appreciate his identifying *"They all look Alike, All,"* thus linking African peoples across the globe who were victims of religious bigotry, racial hatred and cultural aggression.

6.   His early clarification of the differences between *The Black Nationalist and the Black Marxist* was very timely and inspiring and still is.

7.   First to outline the *History of the Bible*, he challenged *The Black Clergy Without a Black Theology* and offered *A Black Bible for Black Spiritual and Religious Consciousness.*

8.   We must acknowledge as a human, he may have made some mistakes; miniscule, as they were outweighed by the foundational reservoir of ethical, intellectual and cultural Ma'at he Dr. Ben implanted in the consciousness of African people worldwide.

9.   His insistence that all African-Americans visit the Nile Valley to imbibe in the cultural heritage and grow from the intellectual exposure, but more particularly their dress code and mannerism among the people must not be construed as the "arrogance of Ugly Americans," was and is still timely and insightful.

10.   His outspoken nature, love for *Marcus Garvey* and his *Philosophy and Opinions*, praise of Black Goddesses, critique of Academics who are "fifth columns" made him anathema to people with ill-intentions, Black and White, toward African people.

11.   Dr. ben-Jochannan had little respect for people in high positions who never promoted the aspirations of their Black subordinates. He pointed to many in academic, business enterprise and even the military who never advanced the positions of their fellow Africans as did other cultural and ethnic groups in similar situations.

12.   A staunch Pan-Africanist, he aspired to see accomplished sustained and measurable economic, political and educational empowerment for people of African heritage worldwide.

LET'S LIBERATE THE TEMPLE

13. He said, "I took Egypt to show our people the proper way" and to challenge its misrepresentation, racism and religious bigotry inherent in teachings related to this ancient African culture.

14. He insisted we not just read books and do research on Ancient Egypt in Africa, but also form study groups that debate and discuss these important issues raised by him as well as personally critique status quo's positions. He also insisted we must visit Egypt and observe and let the monuments teach.

15. He asked us to standardize our learning and take responsibility for our own history. He stated: "Until African (Black) people are willing, and do write their own experience, past, and present, we will continue being slaves, mentally, physically, and spiritually to Caucasian and Semitic racism and religious bigotry." This latter we must never allow to happen, for as Dr. John Henrik Clarke has admonished, "African people must write their own history" because the "People who preached racism colonized history" and as a result, "When Europe colonized the world, she colonized the world's knowledge."

16. Today more than ever young people, their parents, even grand-parents need to be enmeshed in the wisdom and enlightenment of the ancients as Dr. Ben-Jochannan revealed in his efforts and literary contributions.

17. Dr. Ben's "Wake Up Dead Man" mantra is just as relevant today, even more so, in many respects our young lave lost their way, being ignorant of their own history.

18. Today, African people must realize, we are in no way, "Out of the Woods;" in fact, we are "deep in the Woods." Since most young people don't know who was Rosa Parks, even "Malcolm the Tenth?

19. Parents must become more involved in their children's education. They must query who is teaching their children; what are they teaching them; what is the relevance of today's educational curriculum and they must remain committed for educational excellence and advancement of their children.

FREDERICK MONDERSON

Liberate the Temple. Kurneh Mortuary Temple of Seti I. Profile view of Seti I in seriousness.

Liberate the Temple. Kurneh Mortuary Temple of Seti I. In Red Crown and holding two libation bases, Seti dances before an enthroned Amon-Ra with his wife Mut at his rear.

LET'S LIBERATE THE TEMPLE

Liberate the Temple. Kurneh Mortuary Temple of Seti I. Two ointment jars for a "Traveling Amon-Ra."

FREDERICK MONDERSON

Liberate the Temple. Kurneh Mortuary Temple of Seti I. View from deep within, the Sanctuary area, of the depth extending to the trees beyond.

LET'S LIBERATE THE TEMPLE

20. Today more than ever we need an avalanche of reading, writing, listening and speaking skills to remain competitive in a fast-paced and changing world. The work and teachings of Dr. James, Dr. Ben, Dr. Clarke, Tony Browder, Maulana Karenga, Molefi Asante, **CEMOTAP**. Dr. Monderson, Runoko Rashidi, Cheikh Anta Diop, Theophile Obenga, Ivan Van Sertima, coupled with and reinforced by *The Philosophy and Opinions of Marcus Garvey* New York: Atheneum, 1971), the works of Kwame Nkrumah, the insights of Malcolm X, the love and vision of Dr. Martin Luther King, and the contributions of the great Black Pantheon consisting of Frederick Douglass, Harriet Tubman, Henry Highland Garnett, Martin Delaney, Langston Hughes, Claude McKay, W.E.B. Dubois, Thurgood Marshall, Arthur Schomberg, Sonny Carson, Elombe Brathe, Jitu Weusi, Mary McLeod-Bethune, Rosa Parks, Percy Sutton, Queen Mother Moore, Nelson Mandela, Winnie Mandela, Rev. Shuttlesworth, Rev. Herbert Daughtry, Rev. Cleveland, Julius Nyerere, Sekou Ture, Kwame Ture, and so many more. Only then, reinforced in the knowledge of the work and experiences of these ancestors will African people resist the "Move from the Center to the Fringe."

For, if today our children begin at the Periphery, who knows where they will end up. This and more is why Dr. Ben-Jochannan's work is so crucially important at this time. The courage and contributions of these great Blacks should never be forgotten!

MAN KNOW THYSELF!

Therefore, we must recognize that Dr. Yosef Alfredo Antonio ben-Jochannan has made a major contribution to African intellectual growth and consciousness. He created a cosmological vision over time that allowed us to see the light. His work has been seminal! In fact, he was our light! He taught us how to persevere to persevere! He asked that we establish and maintain a standard for our behavior, and "Don't fear, don't fear defeat, don't fear death!"

FREDERICK MONDERSON

XXII. ARGUMENT FOR EGYPT BY DR. FRED MONDERSON

Significantly, the reason for the great hunger for Egypt is best explained in a quote from W.J. Perry in *The Growth of Civilization*, Penguin Books (1924) (1937: 48-49) where he quotes G. Elliot Smith in *The Ancient Egyptians* (1911) who stated: "The Egyptians did a great deal more than merely invent agriculture and devise the earliest statecraft and religion. Not only did they devise the methods of working wood and stone and the art of architecture, they seem also to have been the inventors of linen and of the craft of weaving, of the use of gold and copper, and the making of metal tools and implements. They were the first people to measure the year and to devise a calendar, and later on to substitute for the rough calculation based upon the date the observation of the sun's movements. They also invented shipbuilding and constructed the first sea-going ships. In a thousand and one of the details of our common civilization the originality of Egyptian civilization is revealed. The art of shaving, the use of wigs, the wearing of hats, the invention of the kilt and of the sandal and subsequently of a variety of other articles of dress, many of our musical instruments, chairs and beds, cushions, jewelry and jewel-cases, lamps - these are merely a few of the items picked at random out of our ancient heritage from the Nile valley."

Interestingly, however, when he uses the term "our" he means Europeans, not all of humanity or Africans. This, then, is what is at stake and must be corrected in unrelenting challenge!

In the reality of the "Slave Trade and Slavery," the western world could not admit at the back of their civilizations of Greece and Rome, were the creations of the people they were enslaving. In fact, this is what Count Volney affirmed in his *Ruins of Empires*, p. 16.

LET'S LIBERATE THE TEMPLE

Notwithstanding, commenting further on the significance of ancient Egyptian contribution to civilization, Margaret Murray in *The Splendor that Was Egypt*, New York: Hawthorn Books, Inc., (1949) (1969: xvi) wrote the following, reinforcing the view previously expressed and attributed to G. Elliot Smith: "For every student of our modern civilization Egypt is the great storehouse from which to obtain information, for within the narrow limits of that country are preserved the origins of most (perhaps all) of our knowledge. In Egypt are found the first beginnings of material culture - building, agriculture, horticulture, clothing (even cooking as an art); the beginnings of the sciences - physics, astronomy, medicine, engineering; the beginning of the imponderables - law, government, and religion. In every aspect of life Egypt has influenced Europe, and though the centuries may have modified the custom or idea, the origin is clearly visible. Centuries before Ptolemy Philadelphus founded his great temple of the Muses at Alexandria, Egypt was to the Greek the embodiment of all wisdom and knowledge. In their generous enthusiasm, the Greeks continually recorded that opinion; and by their writings they passed on to later generations that wisdom of the Egyptians which they had learnt orally from the learned men of the Nile Valley." Arnett's denial nevertheless, and contrary to Murray's mentioning "the Greeks," Diop names these people and enumerates their views!

Further, in her explanation, Murray (1969: xvii) confessed: "Egypt was the supreme power in the Mediterranean area during the whole of the Bronze Age and a great part of the Iron Age; and as our present culture is directly due to the Mediterranean civilization of the Bronze Age, it follows that it has its roots in ancient Egypt. It is to Egypt that we owe our division of time; the twelve months and three hundred and sixty-five days of the year; the twelve hours of the day and the twelve hours of the night are due to the work of the Egyptian astronomers. The earliest clocks, the clepsydra, were the invention of Egyptian physicists. The earliest known intelligible writing is the Egyptian, so also are the earliest recorded historical events. It is due to the passion of the Egyptians for making records that so much has been preserved of their history and their literature, of their religious beliefs and their religious ritual. This passion for writing made them invent the first actual writing materials - pens, ink, paper - materials which could be packed in a small compass, were light to carry, and easy to use."

Liberate the Temple. Kurneh Mortuary Temple of Seti I. Date trees line the immediate entrance into the temple.

LET'S LIBERATE THE TEMPLE

Liberate the Temple. Kurneh Mortuary Temple of Seti I. Another view from deep within the temple, beyond the Pillared Hall before the Sanctuary. This temple has columns and pillars in alternation.

Liberate the Temple. Kurneh Mortuary Temple of Seti I. Seti offers his name as Ma'at to "Traveling Amon-Ra," Horus and Mut.

FREDERICK MONDERSON

Thus, it is reasonable to argue, "this passion for writing" evolved from the simplest art, through the emergence of hieroglyphs and thus the invention of the tools to express the ideas and concepts generated therefrom.

However, and having scored a home-run, Murray (1969: xvii) continued highlighting Egyptian contributions even more, by contrasting this earliest culture with subsequent civilizations in the human drama and pointing out how Egyptian accomplishments have left them in the distance. She wrote: "The splendor of Egypt was not a mere mushroom growth lasting but a few hundred years. Where Greece and Rome can count their supremacy by the century, Egypt counts hers by the millennium, and the remains of that splendor can even now eclipse the remains of any other country in the world. According to the Greeks there were **SEVEN WONDERS OF THE WORLD**; these were the Pyramids of Egypt; the Hanging Gardens of Babylon; the statue of Zeus at Olympia; the Temple of Diana at Ephesus; the Tomb of Mausoleum; the Colossus of Rhodes; and the Lighthouse of Alexandria. Of all these great and splendid works, what remains to the present day? Babylon and its gardens are a heap of rubble, as ruined as a bombed city; the statue of Zeus was destroyed long ago; the Temple of Diana is utterly demolished, leaving only a few foundations; fragments of the Mausoleum are preserved in museums where they are a source of interest to experts only; the Colossus of Rhodes survives only in legend, so completely has it disappeared; the Lighthouse of Alexandria has perished almost without a trace.

Of the **Seven Wonders**, the Pyramids of Egypt alone remain almost intact, they still tower above the desert sands, dominating the scene, defying the destroying hand of Time and the still more destructive hand of Man. They line the western shore of the Nile for more than a hundred miles, and are the most stupendous and impressive as they are the most ancient of all the great buildings of the world." It is interesting, all of these wonders built by Caucasians

LET'S LIBERATE THE TEMPLE

in Europe have disappeared but the most significant one built in Africa, Egypt, has survived and is yet claimed by Caucasians. Equally too, the one surviving, has no counterpart from whence the Caucasians came. There is no prototype of the pyramids and sphinx in Asiatic lands. This means they not only had no knowledge of the pyramids, yet they came to Egypt to build them. Thus, "the superior mentality" argument is nothing but arrogance on the part of the European man! More important, not only are there numerous pyramids in Nubia as well (South of Aswan), human made and naturally formed over thousands of years, but Dr. Ben-Jochannan spoke of "silt pyramids" predating the man-made ones. Let us also further recognize Hatshepsut's mortuary temple at Deir el Bahari, today considered an architectural and artistic masterpiece even after surviving the ravages of time and also the hands of man; yet it was never given the designation "Ancient Wonder," still, it has survived all but the one such glorious monument.

Nonetheless, and even more penetrating, Lester Brooks in *Great Civilizations of Ancient Africa* (1971: 28) confirms: "From the cemeteries dating back before 3200 B.C., anthropologists have identified remains they label 'Eurobond' (indicating those of Cro-Magnon types), "Negroid" and some Asian types, with the 'Europoids' predominating in the north and the 'Negroids' predominating in the south. As one expert puts it, 'the races were fused on the banks of the Nile well before Pharaonic civilization came into being. These people were black by the operating definition of skin color as well as by the general physical characteristics they had then.'" Even more, Brooks (1971: 28-29) continued: "The Greeks were surprised twenty-five hundred years ago to discover that the Egyptians were the darkest-skinned peoples of the so-called Near East. Typically, they were - and are today - not homogeneous. Their skin color ranges from red-black to yellow. Their hair is black and wavy, curly or wooly; their eyes are bright and black; their bodies are lean and muscular, generally tending to tallness. Egyptian noses usually are large and straight, but frequently aquiline; their jaws generally tend to thrust forward with fleshy lips, often curled back. We can say without the slightest hesitation that the ancient Egyptians would have been considered Negroes by American standards, and

FREDERICK MONDERSON

until the passage of the **Civil Rights Act of 1964** not one of the Egyptian Pharaohs could have bought a cup of coffee in a white drug store in the southern states of the U.S.A."

Still, and again, contrary to Arnett's contention of not sufficient evidence for his position; in his "Argument for A Negro Origin" in *The African Origin of Civilization: Myth or Reality*, Cheikh Anta Diop (1974: 134-155) utilizes "Totemism," "Circumcision," "Kingship," "Cosmogony," "Social Organization," "Matriarchy," "Kingship of the Meroitic Sudan and Egypt," "Cradles of Civilization Located in the Heart of Negro Lands," and "Languages," as evidence for his position. On the other hand, the postulated position for an Asiatic Caucasian origin is that "for some unknown reason," these people left their homes and brought "a superior mental attitude" that essentially reinvented Narmer's wheel is nothing but white supremacy arrogance! Diop's two-cradle theory for "ice" and "sun" environments and their influences, and patriarchy as opposed to matriarchy, viz., Europeans in the North and Africans in the South, were equally very convincing. Using as an example, cultural influences including costume and dress, Brooks (1971: 29) also sheds even more light on this situation: "What African elements can be discovered in the extremely sophisticated civilization of Egypt? Among others, the complicated religious beliefs wherein tribalism, animism and taboos had extraordinary force - with special rites for the major activities such as planting, harvesting, fishing, hunting and war, in addition to the rites du passage - birth, marriage, death." Even further he points out: "We think of African witch doctors with fantastic, colorful costumes. Look again at a formal portrait of a Pharaoh. Note that, he wears an enormous headdress. From his 'double crown' sprout the head of a vulture and the 'fire-spitting' flamed head of a female hooded cobra, supposedly capable of consuming rebels in flames. The pharaoh was the son of the falcon-god, and was considered a falcon himself, endowed with magical powers and an all-seeing eye. From his waist hangs an animal tail; on his shaven chin, he wears a false beard, which is, itself, considered a god. In his hand, he carries a scepter with the head of the god Seth atop it - recognizable in the curious curved snout, long, straight ears and almond-shaped eyes."

LET'S LIBERATE THE TEMPLE

There is so much more that can be added to the argument for Egypt.

Liberate the Temple. Seti's Temple to Osiris at Abydos. Seti offers a plant to enthroned Osiris in his shrine. Notice the hawk flying over the King's head.

FREDERICK MONDERSON

Liberate the Temple. Seti's Temple to Osiris at Abydos. Enthroned Isis suckles Seti. Here she wears horns and disk above the "Vulture Headdress."

LET'S LIBERATE THE TEMPLE

Liberate the Temple. **Seti's Temple to Osiris at Abydos**. Seti offers a vessel to enthroned Amon-Ra. "Amon was so black, he was blue!"

FREDERICK MONDERSON

XXIII. WHAT'S IN THE TEMPLE BY DR. FRED MONDERSON

The temple possessed a magical, mystical, esoterically metaphysical significance that was brilliant in its conception and execution. In its multi-faceted dynamic religious and philosophic belief, temple architecture came to embody many outstanding and artistic features as an Avenue of Sphinxes, along with gates, pylons, propylon, with flagstaves and flags, an axis or two, enclosure walls, forecourts or great courts and inner courts, doorways, portals, stelae, walls, doors, columns and colonnades, stone drums, capitals, architraves, pavements, floors, roofs having spouts to drain off water, shrines, statues, kiosks, a sacred lake, obelisks, decorations, gardens, trees, halls, chambers, the "Holy of Holies" or Sanctuary, altars, Nilometers, sphinxes, standards, libation vases, incense-burners, and other vessels for liquid and solid offerings, vestments for the god, musical instruments to entertain the god while he was being administered to, as well as animals, viz., - cattle, geese, chickens, pigs, horses, donkeys, lions and the implements used by the priests, stewards, priestesses, their kitchens, vine cellars, crypts, bakers and cooks, confectioners, store houses, as well as gold and other precious stones, treasury, a library, craftsmanship, gardens and even more as reflected in the wealth of the state and priesthood. To this we may add industrial crafts for temple decoration and trade that encouraged flourishing and competing schools of arts and crafts that produced jewelry and other statuary masterpieces. Land holding was an important part of temple wealth. Most temples were considered a "House of Life" that doubled as schools, practiced medicine and served as "Service Centers" for persons in need of literary documents as letters, wills, and other correspondence.

This naming of things as in the personality of the individual was very important to the ancient Egyptian. Among the nine parts of the soul, the name was really considered very important for without it the

LET'S LIBERATE THE TEMPLE

individual did not exist. In similar fashion, as Badawy states: "The temple is usually 'like heaven, beautiful, pure, glorious and excellent.' Its pylons 'reach heaven and the flagstaffs the stars of heaven.' They are 'of real cedar, wrought with Asiatic copper, their tips of electrum, approaching heaven.' 'Two mighty obelisks of red granite, with pyramidions of electrum, rise at the double façade of the temple.' The columns 'wrought with electrum,' usually in stone, but originally in wood. The shrines 'of sandstone, ebony or enduring granite, lined inside with electrum, or gold of the best of the hills, are placed upon a base of alabaster from Hat nub.' Doors are 'of new cedar, of the best Terraces (Lebanon), mounted in real black copper and wrought with inlaid figures in electrum or gold, representing the great name or the shadow (of the god),' 'like the luminous mountain-horizon of heaven.' The 'shadow' of the god is the representation of the deity on the copper lining of the door as if coming out of his temple. Pavements are covered with silver or gold, and offering tables are of silver, gold, bronze, or Asiatic copper. One boasts of using the 'beautiful stone of Ayan, fine white sandstone, every splendid costly stone,' or finally 'that never was done the like since the beginning.' In the description of restoration work the building is said to have been in ruin. The walls were rebuilt in stone and brick, ruined doors replaced by new ones, and wooden columns by stone ones."

As such then, the name is important, not simply because it is a part of the personality of the man, but for the purpose of building the temple and the temple itself. Equally, everything, living and inanimate was named, had a name, and this, therefore, made naming important; for without a name something did not exist. Take for example, "John Doe."

Even further, Badawy (1968: 155-156) mentions: "The names of the temples can express a quality of the building or of its lord: 'Shining-in-Truth (Temple of Amenhotep III at Soleb), 'Most-Splendid' (Temple of Thutmose III at Deir el Bahari, 'Splendor-of-the-West' (small temple at Medinet Habu). 'Splendid-is-the-Seat-of-Amun' (small temple at Medinet Habu), 'Heat-which-is-in-Aten' (Sanctuary of Harakhte at Karnak built by Akhenaten). Sometimes the name clearly expresses ownership: 'House-of-Nib-mare' (temple of Amenhotep III at Memphis), 'Temple-of-the-Son-of-Seti-Meryamon-

FREDERICK MONDERSON

in-the-House-of-Amon northern part of the Hypostyle Hall at Karnak, by Seti I), 'House-of-Usermare-Meriamon-in-the-House-of-Re' (temple of Rameses II at Derr), 'Temple-of-Ramses-Meriamon-in-the-House-of-Amon' (temple of Ramses II at Luxor.) Or the name may designate the deity to whom it is dedicated: 'House-of-Amon-on-the-West-of-Thebes (mortuary temple of Amenhotep III), 'Temple-of-the-Spirit-of-Seti-Merneptah-in-the-House-of-Ptah,' 'Temple-of-the-Spirit-of-Seti-Merneptah-in-the-House-of-Amon-on-the-West-of-Thebes' (Mortuary Temple of Seti I). Parts of the temple such as shrines and doors are also named: 'Amon-has-received-his-divine-barque' (pylon in the mortuary temple of Amenhotep III), Amon-Mighty-in-Wealth" (door of Thutmose at Karnak), 'Menmare-is-rich-in-food' (door of Rameses II in the temple of Seti at Abydos), 'Usermare'-is-splendid-in-strength' (door in the temple of Rameses II at Serre), 'His-Great-Seat-is-like-the-Horizon-of-Heaven' (Holy of Holies of Thutmose III)."

Liberate the Temple. **Seti's Temple to Osiris at Abydos**. With Isis (Auset) at his back, Seti approaches divinity.

LET'S LIBERATE THE TEMPLE

Liberate the Temple. Seti's Temple to Osiris at Abydos. Seti offers a golden necklace.

Liberate the Temple. Seti's Temple to Osiris at Abydos. Holding scepter, Seti reaches for gift from enthroned Ra-Horakhty in his shrine as Isis stands at his rear.

FREDERICK MONDERSON

Liberate the Temple. Seti's Temple to Osiris at Abydos. Façade of 14 pillars fronting this masterpiece's entrance.

Liberate the Temple. Seti's Temple to Osiris at Abydos. Isis (Auset) and Seti Set up Osiris' (Ausar's) Tet or Backbone.

LET'S LIBERATE THE TEMPLE
XXIV. ABYDOS - SITE OF ETERNAL CONSCIOUSNESS

I. INTRODUCTION

II. WHO WORKED AT ABYDOS

III. A PLACE OF BURIAL - CEMETERY

IV. TEMPLES UPON TEMPLES

V. TEMPLE OF SETI I

VI. OSIRIS - UNIVERSAL GOD

VII. CONCLUSIONS

VIII. FURTHER READING

FREDERICK MONDERSON

I. INTRODUCTION

Abydos, capital of the 8th or Thinite Nome, is today one of the most visited cities in Egypt. There are a number of reasons it achieved righteous immortality throughout the lengthy of its history; but particularly, today's tourists come to see the Temple of Seti I dedicated to the god Osiris. Whereas, in days of old, the forts, cemeteries and even the Temple of Rameses II also attracted their share of attention. Still and even more important, people, living and dead, came to celebrate the drama or festivals of Osiris, to erect a stele or be buried nearby where the god's head was buried and be part of this important site that benefitted tremendously from royal patronage throughout its history. However, to accomplish the modern visitor's itinerary and because of current realities, tremendous precaution is undertaken by security personnel, via, convoys and armed personnel, to ensure tourists view the temple with the slightest inconveniences. Notwithstanding, as visitors today come to Abydos, so too have visitors been coming, for four, five, perhaps six thousand, and more years, and for a multiplicity of purposes.

It is interesting, Albert Churchward in *Signs and Symbols of Primordial Man*, Buffalo, New York: Eworld, Inc., (1993) (1994: 263) extends this even more in stating: "At Abydos, Professor Petrie has been excavating and found remains, well preserved, of ancient cities, which he dates at least 15,000 B.C. and which show clearly that the people practiced the Osirian religion at that time in its full forms and ceremonies. This is the so-called birthplace of the Osirian religion, which came after the doctrines of Amen-Ra, practically the same, developed under different names, and before there was the Stellar Mythos of Horus: thus, we see how old this country is." Even further, Churchward (1994: 263) continued: "The remains in the immense tomb, discovered by Professor Petrie, prove that these very ancient people lived here, and by their 'rude marks' it is seen that they had made considerable progress in their evolution, and that they certainly may have existed here long before the last glacial epoch,

LET'S LIBERATE THE TEMPLE

when every place was frozen and uninhabitable, from the North Pole to 53 degrees or 56 degrees latitude (south of France)."

Even more significant, Continued Churchward, "The conclusion he arrives at by summarizing the characters of these ancient people and comparing them with those of the Egyptians of the time of Pharaoh, shows how much progress these latter had made by working out their own evolution. Their civilization was anterior to that of the Pharaohs in its definite and well-known form, and the whole of the arguments brought forward by Petrie, De Morgan and Wiedemann really furnish the proofs that these were all one people of African origin, and that time and evolution had worked the different advancements we find amongst the Pharaohs."

Liberate the Temple. Seti's Temple to Osiris at Abydos. Seti with curved beard as a divinity wears side-lock, a wig and necklace.

FREDERICK MONDERSON

Liberate the Temple. Seti's Temple to Osiris at Abydos. The enthroned Isis holds a Sistrum and Menat in her right hand and dangles the Heb-Sed symbol hanging from the notched palm-branch.

Liberate the Temple. Seti's Temple to Osiris at Abydos. Seti gestures before Ra-Horakhty in his shrine. Notice how the king's face is defaced.

LET'S LIBERATE THE TEMPLE

Liberate the Temple. Seti's Temple to Osiris at Abydos. Seti presents a platter to enthroned Isis sporting red, white and blue.

FREDERICK MONDERSON

In *The Encyclopedia of Egyptian Art* (The American University of Cairo Press, 2003) the author informs, at Abydos: "At least 12 royal cult complexes are attested to either archaeologically or from other sources, dating from the 12th to the 26th Dynasty ("house of millions of years," places where the king was re-united with Osiris)." Important, however, Margaret Bunsen in *The Encyclopedia of Ancient Egypt* (1991: 3) refers to one scene in the temple [that] depicts Rameses adoring the gods Isis, and Osiris as well as Seti deified.

The modern tourist visitors come to enjoy the masterful art and architectural beauty of the temple as a religious mecca and to bask in the significance of this holy place, while the ancients came for even more important reasons. Even before Seti's time, particularly kings of the Twelfth Dynasty came to repair or build temples, worship the god of the city and temple, enact the "Passion Play of Osiris" unfortunate experience, even to be buried at Abydos, home of Osiris. Still, while other persons came to Abydos as the world's earliest site of pilgrimage; they also came to worship and be buried, particularly for the wealthy, who could afford costs the "prime real estate" of the site represented. Those who could not afford the burial erected a stela recounting their deeds of service to the state, even if they were buried elsewhere. Others still came for the "passing boat trip" and this was often depicted as decoration in their tombs more frequently in the Theban area. Still, others sent a token of earthenware pottery to simply establish a philosophical, religious and spiritual link to be with the god Osiris who sits by the stairway to heaven. This latter was so profound, the site Umm el Ga'ab (Qa'ab), "Mother of pots," got its name from the mountain of discarded earthenware in the vicinity. Nevertheless, according to Adolf Erman in *Handbook of Egyptian Religion* (London: constable, 1907: 35), that thing that attracted most persons: "It is the human element of Osiris, the wifely devotion and motherly love of Isis and filial piety of Horus." Thus, Osiris came to dominate the site of Abydos as "Universal God." These characteristics he notes, "captivated the Egyptian nation at a period which must have been very remote. At the same time, they formed the people's conceptions of the future life, teaching them that after death the just and upright were

LET'S LIBERATE THE TEMPLE

more valued than those who had possessed authority and power on earth."

James Baikie in *The Life of the Ancient East*, (New York: The Macmillan Company, 1923: 19-20) puts it best in the statement: "There were three places where the devout Egyptian hoped to secure for himself after death the blessing of immortality. The first was his tomb, with its images and offerings, and the services of the tomb-priests; the second was one of the temples where he had worshipped in life, and where, as a special reward from the king, he might be allowed to place a statue of himself, that it might share in the offerings which were made to the god. But these two were essentially for the great and the rich of the land; the third was open to the humblest and the poorest. At Abydos was the tomb of Osiris, the great god of the Underworld, - to be buried near him was infallibly to secure all the blessings which the god could bestow; if your circumstances made such a thing impossible, it was still possible to keep the channel of blessing open by erecting a stone on the staircase of the great god; while, if even this was beyond the means of the devout aspirant, he could in the last resort send a piece of votive pottery to be laid as near as possible to the holy place, and so establish the much-coveted link between himself and the lord of eternal life."

In explaining this Abydos dynamic further, Baikie (1923: 20) continued: "Accordingly, from a very early period in Egyptian history, it became the custom for the great and wealthy of the land to have a tomb at Abydos. Often the Holy City was preferred for this purpose even to the capital, where the dead noble might rest beside his king; or, if it was necessary for him to accompany his liege-lord in death as in life, it was still possible for him to erect a cenotaph at Abydos and to furnish it with all that might be needed for his soul when it visited the abode of the great god. During the Middle Kingdom, it was more customary to secure the advantages of Abydos by the erection of a stele or memorial slab; and multitudes of these votive steles are to be found in the museums. But all through, and especially during the earliest period, and again from the XIXth to the XXVIth Dynasty, when there was apparently a great revival of the cult of Osiris, the common folk of the land pinned their faith to the efficacy of the ex-voto piece of pottery, laid as near as might be to the sacred site. The result is that Abydos is simply a wilderness of broken pots of all sorts and ages, from the earliest period down to the time of the Saite revival. It is impossible to move about the site of the ancient sepulchers without crushing into yet smaller fragments of some of the potsherds which litter the whole ground; and the modern Arab name for the place does no more than justice to its chief characteristic - "Umm-el-Ga'ab" - "the Mother of Pots."

All this reverence notwithstanding, the site of Abydos meant more than as temples of worship. The cemetery at Abydos also played as important a role, for the archaic kings chose to be buried there and this must have added to the luster of the holy city. Working for the Egyptian Research Account, A Caulfield, in *The Temple of the Kings at Abydos* (London: Bernard Quaritch, 1902) shows the connection between the Temple of Seti I and the cemeteries of his ancestor kings. Caulfield (1902: 1) tells, first of all, regarding the king's choice of the site and the ultimate layout, of this temple to Osiris: "Seti I wanted a temple with a priests' dwelling-house and store-rooms attached to it. The temple required large halls and a high roof; the priests only required rooms big enough to live in, and the conventional theory of sacred building required the sanctuary to be on a higher level than the entrance."

Regarding this architectural majesty, Paul Brunton in *A Search in Secret Egypt,* New York: Samuel Weiser (New York: Samuel Weiser, 1935, 1980: 167) says of Abydos, today's magnificent attraction, the Temple of Seti I: "It rose up in its white simplicity, with twelve shattered square pillars to guard its frontal line; a plain, narrow doorway giving entry to it. How different, and how grand, it must have looked in its heyday! Architecture in Egypt was a hieratic art. Religion was the thread upon which its craftsmen and artists slipped the threads of their beautiful work." Quoting its builder who boasted, Brunton continued, "'The palace within it is much embellished with fine gold true and fresh from the workings. When it is seen, hearts exult and all people make obeisance. Its nobility is that which gives it splendor. Its gates, exceeding great, are of pine of the forest, their bodies are gilded with fine gold and bound with bronze at their back parts. The great

LET'S LIBERATE THE TEMPLE

pylon-towers are of stone of Anu, the head-pieces of granite, their beauties reach Ra in his horizon."

Liberate the Temple. Seti's Temple to Osiris at Abydos. Seti assists Isis to raise the Tet or backbone of Osiris.

Liberate the Temple. Seti's Temple to Osiris at Abydos. Seti presents a platter to two divinities in a shrine.

FREDERICK MONDERSON

Liberate the Temple. Seti's Temple to Osiris at Abydos. A defaced Seti presents flowers to equally defaced images of Osiris and Isis.

"Here then was a place fitted by nature to fulfill these three conditions. The natural slope of the desert surface beneath one horizontal roof was fit for (1) a temple whose floor was to rise from front to back; for (2) high courts and halls for an entrance and approach to the sanctuary; and (3) a convenient hill on which smaller halls for sacristies and offices could be built, adjoining the main temple and still under the same roof, without having to make an unsightly break in the line of the roof."

And even further, "Instead of the temple being altered to suit the position, I should say that the position was specially selected to suit the necessities of the design, and particularly the purpose for which the temple was built."

The second and perhaps more important reason Caulfield's *Temple of the Kings* (1902: 1-2) gives for the purpose of the temple at Abydos,

LET'S LIBERATE THE TEMPLE

linked the contemporary worship of the temple's god in a mortuary relationship with the ancestor kings buried within distance from the building. He also importantly makes us realize there was a west or back pylon in addition to the east or front pylon of the monument. In addition, he provides graphic evidence of how he arrived at his early deductions, particularly about the exterior regions of the temple.

"To the westward of the temple is the desert pylon in the Temenos wall. A mile and a half further to the westward are the royal tombs of the Ist dynasty. At first sight, the whole temple and enclosure walls are parallel; none of the angles are right angles. The desert pylon is not in the middle of the Temenos wall, and there seems to be no correspondence between the pylon and the temple. Now the temple itself is practically hidden by the mounds of rubbish thrown out from it by Mariette's excavations; so that the surveying of the general plan meant establishing sighting points on the top of these rubbish mounds, and setting out the relative position of walls and temple by a somewhat complicated system of cross-bearings. For instance, the desert pylon is invisible except from the highest point of the temple roof; and from the North-West corner of the Temenos the only part of the temple that is visible is part of the roof about 10 meters back from the North-West corner of the outer court; so, while I was drawing the plans I failed to see any symmetry at all in the arrangement. However, when Plan No. 1 was finished, I showed it to Mr. Petrie, remarking sadly on the painful lack of symmetry. Mr. Petrie looked at it for a bit; suddenly he seized a piece of string, stretched it across my drawing, and behold the string passed through the desert pylon, the center door of chapels, the center door of the main court, the main east door and the courtyard pylon. Thus, the axis of the main temple produced to the West passed through the desert pylon. This was tested by hanging plumb-bobs from the centers of the temple doors, and sightings along them from the center of the pylon gate to a mark on the North rubbish heap; a hole in the chapel wall enabled a thorough sight to be got from the rubbish heap mark to the pylon mark to the temple roof. These sightings were carefully carried on till the temple axis was marked out on the roof itself, and the marks then pointed to a spot a little to the right of the center of the desert pylon; and a mile and a half to the westward the axis of the temple produced passed over the offering mound just to the south of the royal tombs of the Ist dynasty. We found traces of a sunk causeway leading in this direction, just outside the desert pylon, but failed to find any traces of it further out in the desert; so, it was possible only an approach to the gateway."

Caulfield (1902: 2) then makes a rather compelling argument regarding the construction of this structure. He writes: "Here then is another reason for building the temple in such a position, namely, ancestor worship. In one of the temple passages is a list of all the kings, and out in the desert are the tombs of some of them. As a mark of respect, the temple was built so that those who were celebrating commemorative services in the sanctuary should face the tombs of the early kings. The idea of worshipping an invisible power in a definite form or position is no new one. The Zoroastrian looked - as the Parsee looks - to the rising sun, the Muhammedan turns his face to Mecca, the western Christian faces the east or Jerusalem, and the XIX dynasty Egyptian king turned his face to his ancestors' tombs as the most obvious revelation of the One Unknown."

Further, he ends this line of argument by stating, "there seems no reasonable doubt that the temple was used for commemorative services of the early kings." This being the case, it is also interesting that of all the king lists, commemorative documents, etc., that help establish the chronology of Egypt, based on the life and times of the kings, none perhaps with the exception of the Sakkara List, has remained *in situ* as the Abydos List, with a specific intent of continuing its original purpose.

Beyond being the most complete list of its kings, Abydos has also been kind to scholars of Egyptian history by providing evidence of the beginnings of mortuary architecture; the nature of "mortuary furniture;" the "Forts" provide evidence of earliest military fortification; the beginnings of hieroglyphic writing; the beginnings of Egyptian art; some of the most beautiful art surviving in all of Egypt, and much more. In combination, all this has contributed to the mystique that draws the many modern visitors to this ancient yet significant site of religious worship. It needs be underscored so as to dispel notions about threats to travelers in the ancient land; the Tourist Police make an extraordinary effort to provide protection to visitors

LET'S LIBERATE THE TEMPLE

ensuring the safety of those who go to their country to view the ancient monuments.

II. WHO WORKED AT ABYDOS

A number of people worked at Abydos being involved in excavations, reading inscriptions, taking photographs, doing drawings, even making reproduction of the images, doing "squeezes" and making maps. In his *A History of Egyptian Archaeology* (New York: Thomas Y. Crowell Company, 1968: 128-129) Fred Gladstone Bratton presents a list including, "Belzoni, Mariette, Petrie, Caulfield, Quibell, Amelineau, Mace, Garstang, McIver, Peet, Naville, Margaret Murray, Frankfort and Whitmore." However, since that time, work has continued uninterrupted at the site.

From the time David O'Connor began his work at Abydos in 1962, as indicated in his book *Abydos: Egypt's First Pharaohs and the Cult of Osiris*, (London: Thames and Hudson, 2009), a number of institutions such as - The Pennsylvania-Yale-University of Fine Arts; the New York University Expedition; Liverpool University; Oxford University; University of Pennsylvania Museum; and Suhag University; as well as individuals besides David O'Connor, such as William Kelly Simpson, Barry Kemp, Amice Calverly, Omm Seti, David Silverman, Stephen Harvey (1993), Matthew Adams (1991), David Anderson, Joseph Wegner (1994), David Patch (1982-83), Janet Richards (1986(, (1987), Mary-Ann Pouls Negner (1996), Laurel Bestook Michelle Barlar, Harold Dribble, Deborah Otszlwski, Shannon McPherson, John Baines, Sneve Snape, Ahmed Issawy, Bahai Issawy, Jenner Westerne, and more.

Toby Wilkinson in *Genesis of the Pharaohs* (London: Thames and Hudson, 2003: 76-77) adds even further to understanding of the work at Abydos. He states, "Some of the most spectacular Egyptological discoveries of recent years have been made at the site of Abydos. Here, on the west bank of the Nile in Upper Egypt, German archaeologists have been excavating a huge Predynastic cemetery, spanning ten centuries from the Nagada I period to the First Dynasty. Toward the end of the predynastic period, it is clear that the cemetery had become the exclusive burial-ground of the local ruling class. The graves of this period are large, brick-lined constructions with several chambers and a wealth of burial goods. Earlier, however, the Abydos cemetery seems to have been used by a much greater cross-section of the population. There are simple pits cut into the surface gravel with no more than a few pots. There are also burials which, although by no means wealthy, nevertheless hint at the sophistication and social complexity of the local community in early Predynastic times."

Liberate the Temple. Rameses II Temple at Abydos. With the Osireion in the center and the surrounding desert in the background.

LET'S LIBERATE THE TEMPLE

Liberate the Temple. Rameses II Temple at Abydos.
Rameses offers a vase as enthroned Thoth does his mystical writing.

Liberate the Temple. Rameses II Temple at Abydos.
Rameses offers two ointment jars to Osiris in White Crown and holding scepters.

FREDERICK MONDERSON

Even more striking, though, than the tomb-owner's identity was one of the objects buried alongside. It is a bowl of the red-polished hand-made pottery so typical of the Nagada I period; but nothing is typical about its decoration. For around the rim stand eight women, modeled in clay and stuck to the inside of the vessel. Each figure has been given individual features; all are shown wearing white-painted skirts; and all hold hands in a ring around the top of the bowl."

There were broken ware showing male figures.

U-502

A petroglyph in the Wadi el-Atwani, north of the Wadi Hammamat, certainly suggests that the motif of a group of skirted women holding hands held some particular meaning in prehistoric Egypt. The petroglyph is one of the most intriguing in the whole corpus of Eastern Desert rock art. It is also one of the most difficult to record, being close to the back of a boulder lying close to the cliff on the southern side of the wadi. The rock face is permanently shaded, and its inaccessibility further hampers photography. Yet the subject matter is not hard to discern: seven skirted women, standing in a line, holding hands. It is an exact parallel, but in two dimensional rather than three, of the bowl from Abydos tomb U-502. So precise is the correspondence between pottery vessel and petroglyph that there can be no doubt whatsoever that both were made at the same time. The excavations at Abydos have therefore provided us, quite unexpectedly, with a firm date for at least this Eastern Desert petroglyph: The Nagada I period of Predynastic Egypt, in other words 4000 B.C. or a little later.

"Another grave in the same cemetery at Abydos produced an equally unexpected and important discovery. Tomb U-239 may well have been robbed in antiquity, for the sole surviving object was a tall vase of C-ware. A single pot it may have been, but again there was nothing ordinary about its decoration. In a complex scene which wraps around the vessel, a ruler wearing plumes in his hair and an animal tail

LET'S LIBERATE THE TEMPLE

attached to his waist-band brandishes a mace next to a group of bound captives. This is the earliest known example of what was to become the quintessential motif of Egyptian authority: the king smiting his enemies. It is repeated down the centuries, from the ceremonial palette of King Narmer at the dawn of Egyptian history to the walls of Ptolemaic temples some 3,000 years later. Here it is, on a humble pot from 1,000 years before the formation of the Egyptian state. The image of the ruler with mace in hand is also found in the Eastern Desert, at one of the many remarkable rock art sites in the Wadi Aby Wasil. Here the 'mace man' stands in a boat, his superhuman stature emphasizing his exalted status. Until the discovery of the Abydos vase, the earliest known example of the smiting motif came from the Painted Tomb, dating to the Nagada II period. Now, we know for certain that the ideology and imagery of political power were being actively developed at an earlier phase of Egyptian prehistory."

III. A PLACE OF BURIAL - Cemetery

The above, notwithstanding, from time immemorial, certainly from the start of dynastic rule, Abydos has been a place of burial for kings, nobles and in some respects, the common man.

Beginning with Narmer or Menes, first and second dynasty kings were buried at Abydos. Evidence indicates, kings before Narmer of Dynasty "0" were also probably interred there. Nevertheless, excavations at Sakkara also revealed burial sites of these Archaic Period kings with a few exceptions. As such, a controversy developed as to which site, Abydos or Sakkara, actually contained the bodies of these kings and which were cenotaphs, "dummy tombs," or simply symbolic internments.

FREDERICK MONDERSON

The problem is simply stated as such. One of the names of the king of Egypt, presiding over a united land has been his **Suten Bat** title as King of Upper and Lower Egypt. He assumed this name or title upon his coronation. This **Suten Bat** title and his **Son of Ra** title, which he got at birth, his **Prenomen** and **Nomen** names are represented in cartouches or **Shennu** as the Egyptian named them. The Step-Pyramid at Sakkara contains a Heb-Sed Court for the King to run the race of rejuvenation and nearby two buildings representing his sovereignty over the North and South,

Nevertheless, a controversy has raged as to which site held the body. And a controversy it is because modern man (analysts) projects that he knows more about the ancients than they themselves did. Keep in mind, it's been said of the German scholar Adolf Erman, "He is the only modern man who knew exactly what the Egyptians meant." Notwithstanding, a number of actors can help us focus attention on the question as to where the earliest kings were buried and right offhand, Abydos comes to mind.

First, Narmer was buried at Abydos and his son Aha built a much larger tomb for Narmer's wife and his mother Merneith. No tomb was discovered for Narmer at Sakkara, that came into prominence as a burial site after the founding of Memphis as the state's administrative capital. Other kings of both the first and second dynasty chose to be buried at Abydos, the place of the origin of their founder and where he was buried. These later kings built a second tomb at Sakkara and this site, worked by Walter Emery, opened the question as to where the kings were actually buried.

Despite Narmer's founding of Memphis as his administrative capital and this for strategic geo-political, even symbolic reasons; Sakkara, as a burial site really came into prominence with the building of the Step-Pyramid by Imhotep for king Zoser in the third dynasty. This cemetery later developed as a burial site for the capital of Memphis and as a capital burial site. With the society's building of the pyramids, there emerged "urban planning in the city of the dead;" the Pyramid Texts and development of building practice, arts and craft,

LET'S LIBERATE THE TEMPLE

science, river transportation, etc., that fueled trade, endowments; and a now focused belief in the Afterlife; all the glories of the Old Kingdom's "Golden Age" came to bear upon the society with Memphis playing a greater part. Let us not forget, though "culture was uniform through the land from south to north! Still, by the end of the Old Kingdom, Abydos was considered the "gate to the South," then the great edifice of the god-king belief system came crashing down in the First Intermediate Period.

Countering the claim Asiatics from South-West Asia, Proto-Europeans, are the founders or originators of Egyptian civilization, we must remember Mosso in *Dawn of Mediterranean Civilization* indicated "Asiatics never penetrated the Nile Valley nor the Aegean area." Still, "Semitic peoples" never came into historical record and certainly prominence before 2000 B.C. Nonetheless, and again, given the first dynasty onward there was a "uniformity of culture throughout Egypt from south to North," and this pretty much represented the status quo until the Greeks and Romans came and imposed their rule on the Valley. However, as the king's **Suten Bat**, King of Upper and Lower Egypt title indicated, the South always predominated in culture, religion, science, art and wisdom. So much so, when Alexander Moret argued, "By whom was Upper Egypt influenced but by the North?" Cheikh Anta Diop in *The African Origin of Civilization: Myth or Reality* (1974), countered, "If this is so, why are all the great monuments, viz., temples, tombs, prehistoric sites, etc., located in the south."

FREDERICK MONDERSON

Liberate the Temple. Rameses II Temple at Abydos.
Rameses offers a pyramid to Ra-Horakhty.

Liberate the Temple. Rameses II Temple at Abydos.
Rameses offers a plant as Thoth writes his magical words.

LET'S LIBERATE THE TEMPLE

Liberate the Temple. Rameses II Temple at Abydos.
A Nile God bringing the fruits of his harvest.

Nevertheless, before the 11th Dynasty consolidation and formation of the Middle Kingdom; that is, after the Old Kingdom and during the

First Intermediate Period, Abydos was considered the "Gate to the South." However, when Intef and Mentuhotep consolidated their power, founded the Eleventh Dynasty and set out to unify the county to begin the Middle Kingdom, Abydos then became the "Door to the North." Naturally, in the emergence of a unified state in the Middle Kingdom after the collapse of the Old Kingdom that ushered in First Intermediate Period, while the 12th Dynasty moved their capital north to Lisht and Rameses II of the 19th Dynasty built his palace in the Delta and moved his capital there, it was because the ancient world had awoken to its new geo-political possibilities, trade and artistic and economic enterprise, diplomatic coordination and strategic military defense and other forms of engagement became the order of the day. Still, the South, Abydos and Thebes retained its economic, religious and artistic-cultural viability and leadership.

An equally important realization is that while culture, dress, religious practice, was essentially uniform from the Delta to Syene (Aswan/Elephantine), the people who lived in the respective areas never moved. Recognizing Diop's refutation of Moret's Delta claims; in 1905, Randall McIver produced his study, *Eureka* in which he argued, "Two peoples, one white, one black, lived side by side in Egypt with whites predominating in the North and Blacks, predominating in the South." Therefore, and given Narmer went north, founded the Dynastic Period, that ultimately laid the foundation for the Old Kingdom; and Mentuhotep and Intef founded the Middle Kingdom; and later, Ahmose founded the New Kingdom; these uniters of the two lands were all from Upper Egypt. As such, we need not overlook, Flinders Petrie "Letting the cat out of the bag," in stating in "Egyptian Religion" in Hasting's *Encyclopedia of Religion and Ethi*cs, vol. 5, (Edinburgh: T. and T. Clarke, 1912) "The 17th Dynasty, coming from Nubia, held Thebes as its capital...." Therefore, we can easily argue, north and south of Abydos from Nubia to the Apex of the Delta was one unit, where the Black population predominated.

IV. TEMPLES UPON TEMPLES

LET'S LIBERATE THE TEMPLE

Abydos is the world's earliest holy place and site of pilgrimage. A hallmark of Egyptian temple building is that once a site has been sacralized, it is continually used by subsequent generation of builders who recognized and revere this early reality; that is, once a king has chosen a location to raise a temple to his god, he either chooses a site adjacent to an existing structure or dismantles the existing structure found there, that in most cases had begun to decay. There he builds, sometimes, a larger, and depending on the economic and decorative accomplishments, a more beautiful, more modern structure, generally of equal size or larger and of more durable material.

In his archaeological work at Abydos, Flinders Petrie discovered "Ten Temples at Abydos," reported in *Scientific American Supplement*, No. 1514 (January 7, 1905: 23258-59), where he states, "dating from the beginning of the kingdom and ending with almost the last of its native kings - from Mena, about 4700 B.C., to Nekht-hor-neb- 372 B.C. History is here laid before us in strata, from which the past can be read as we lift them away one from another."

Emphasizing the knowledge gained from the pottery, the filings, the beads, etc., which show each the age to which they belong, Petrie reported in the following article:

"The Ten Temples of Abydos" by Prof. W.M. Flinders Petrie, in *Scientific American Supplement* No. 1514 (January 7, 1905: 24258-59).

"For the first time, the whole history of one of the great national sites of Egypt has been opened before us; dating from the beginning of the kingdom, and ending with almost the first of its native kings-from Mena, about 4700 B.C., to Nekht-hor-heb 370 B.C. History is here laid out before us in strata, from which the past can be read as we lift them away one from another.

In order to read, however, one must know the alphabet of the subject; and that has only lately been learned, from the pottery, the flints, the beads, which show, each the age to which they belong. Excavation on a site with a long history is mere destruction if each stratum is not read

FREDERICK MONDERSON

and interpreted intelligibly as it is opened; unfortunately, this has never been done before on any such site. On the earliest sacred site of Abydos, the first capital of Egypt, temples had been piled one on the ruins of another, until ten ages of building stood stacked together in about twenty feet depth of ruins. Each temple had become partly ruined after a few centuries, and then at last was pulled down, leaving a foot or two of the walls and foundations; and a new temple of a different plan was then erected on the ground. America is not old enough for this to be done even once; but London stands on a mound of over twenty feet of ruins, from which its past will someday be read as we now read that of Egypt.

The earliest temples were all of mud brick. Stone first appears for the doorways of the fourth temple, that of the sixth dynasty, about 3400 B.C. Sculptured stone walls are found of the eleventh dynasty, about 2700 B.C., and in the later temples. These buildings of the well-known historic times are, however, of much less importance to us than the earlier temples, which yield us fresh views of the civilization to which they belong.

About the middle of the second dynasty, say, 4300 B.C. a clearance of the temple offering was made, and hundreds of small objects more or less injured were thrown into a disused chamber, which served as a rubbish hole and was later buried under fifteen feet of ruins. The contents of this chamber were old and disregarded at that time; and as the first king has been found close by at the same level, it seems that we should refer the contents of this limbo to the first dynasty.

LET'S LIBERATE THE TEMPLE

Liberate the Temple. Ramesseum Mortuary Temple of Rameses II. Classic view of the temple with Osiride Figures against square pillars before massive columns and the Hypostyle Hall in rear with its Clerestory for letting light into the structure.

Liberate the Temple. Ramesseum Mortuary Temple of Rameses II. From the Court view of the Massive Osiride Figures before Square pillars before the vestibule toward the Hypostyle Hall in rear. Notice the stairs to the next level of elevation.

FREDERICK MONDERSON

Liberate the Temple. Ramesseum Mortuary Temple of Rameses II. From the North amongst the storage magazines, the ruins of the original temple with its massive columns and Clerestory.

Groping in the thick brown organic mud of this rubbish hole, I lifted out one by one the priceless examples of glazed work and ivory of this earliest age of great artisan art of which we had never understood the excellence from the traces hitherto known. The ivory was sadly rotted, and could scarcely be lifted without dropping asunder in flakes. So, when I found that I had touched a piece, it was left, until at last a patch of ground was left where several pieces of ivory had been observed. Cutting deep around this, I detached the whole block of sixty or eighty pounds of earth, and had it removed on a tray to my storeroom. There it dried gradually for two or three weeks; and then with a camel-hair paint-brush I began to gently dissect it and trace the ivory figures. Not a single piece was broken or spoiled by thus working it out, and noble figures of lions, a large ape, and several boys came gradually to light. Suddenly a patterned robe and then a marvelous face appeared in the dust, and there came forth from his six-thousand-year sleep one of the finest portrait figures that has ever been seen. A single photograph can

LET'S LIBERATE THE TEMPLE

give but little idea of the subtlety of the face and the expression, which changes with every fresh light in which it is seen.

Wearing the crown of Upper Egypt and clad in his thick embroidered robe, this old king, wily yet feeble with the weight of years, stands for the diplomacy and statecraft of the oldest civilized kingdom that we know. No later artist of Egypt, no Roman portrait-maker, no Renaissance Italian, has outdone the truth and expression of this oldest royal portrait, coming from the first dynasty of Egypt. The simplicity and lack of pretension are almost baffling; it does not claim any idealism or beauty, it scarcely seems to intend to be so fine or powerful, and yet it appeals equally to the first artists and to the ordinary man. No other object has so generally compelled the admiration of visitors in any of our annual exhibitions.

That this did not stand alone as a stray phenomenon is seen by the group of other ivories, of which we may instance a very small one of a woman, which shows the same character of work in simplicity and directness, and in the perfectly natural expression of the statuettes. Among other figures discovered, those of the boys, standing, walking, and seated, are all true and unconventional in form, and show firm and accurate modeling. A little bear seated on the ground and couchant lions and a mastiff show that animals were studied and understood as well as men. We must now grant in future that a complete art had risen nearly seven thousand years ago, and that it has seldom been equaled and hardly ever surpassed in the five fresh births of arts which have occupied the course of human history.

Nor was the skill of technical work reflected. The abundance of vases and bowls, cut from the hardest and most refractory materials-granite, syenite, porphyry, rock-crystal, and obsidian-which we found in the royal tombs of this age, show a taste and ability for fine material and work which was never equaled in later times. And the mastery of glazing provided large vases with the royal name inlaid. This was part of a globular vase, eight inches wide, with purple glaze. Here we have the property of the oldest king in the world whose name is preserved in history - M-na, the first king of the first dynasty of Egypt. This vase must have been handled by this figurehead of all monarchy, and

FREDERICK MONDERSON

almost certainly was dedicated by him in the primitive temple of the capital.

Strange, indeed, it is to look on so personal a link, and to think that the whole sum of what we know as human experience has come and gone since this was last worthily handled; the pyramids, the Northman, all were unthought-of when this last saw the light.

The use of colored glazes was also carried out on a great scale for wall decoration. Thick tiles, a foot high and a half as wide, were made, fully glazed in green on both sides, and provided with a deep keying on the back, and groves to hold thick copper wires to thread them together, so that one could not be lifted without moving those on either side. The surface was ribbed to represent papyrus stems; and there was a band of tiles of papyrus heads along the top of the stem tiles. This glazed tiling was also made in a great variety of sizes and patterns- some ribbed, some fluted, some plain, some inlaid with inscriptions, and others copied from mat-work design. Another light on the architecture is given by the glazed vases copied from the lotus capitals, showing that such a form was already in use. The complete capital is of green glaze with purple spots, the same polychrome as the Mena vase, and probably from the same factory. The form of the top, with a slightly raised disk, is evidently copied from the architectural detail of a capital. The other work in glazed pottery is of great variety. Figures of men, women and children, captives and servants; figures of baboons innumerable, of various quadrupeds and birds; model vases and shrines; toggles for fastening the dress, and beads of many forms-all subjects came alike to the ready hand of their early potter. He modeled the forms in the siliceous paste, and then covered them with the hard coat of glaze which binds the material firmly together, and which has in many pieces ever kept its color after thousands of years in wet ground.

An entirely new class of glaze work is the tile with relief designs and inscriptions. One whole tile I picked out of the mud, which has a figure of an aboriginal negro chief, and his name and locality. This proves of particular interest, as he belonged to the "fortress of the Anu," a people with whom the early Egyptians were continually at war, and

LET'S LIBERATE THE TEMPLE

the day of whose destruction was a yearly festival down to late times. From this tile, we now know that the Anu were the negro races of the southern border, which the Egyptians had some difficulty in holding back. The Sudan question is as old as the beginning of history.

In another chamber, we found a large number of sacred figures, which had been carefully put away when thought too rude for the devotions of more civilized times. Few, if any, were as late in style as those which I had taken out of the mud in the great rubbish pit; and judging from that, and their resemblance to figures found some years ago at Hierakonpolis, it is probable that these are as early or earlier than the age of Mena, and so touch the close of the prehistoric time. The most curious, and probably the oldest, objects here were some very elementary figures of baboons, and other purely natural stones. The figures of baboons are very slightly worked. Rude lumps of limestone had been picked up, having a slight resemblance to the form of the animal; and then a little pounding away on the surface had improved them into an unmistakable connection, helped in some cases by a few scores scraped with a flint. The first of these is only pounded, like an Easter Island idol; the second is the most improved, by scratching a mouth and eyes; the third and fifth have only a broad groove hammered to divide the head from the body and mark the snout. And we see in the fourth a natural flint selected for its resemblance to the baboon, and slightly improved by knocking off a few awkward projections; there can be no question as to the intention of placing this flint with the other elementary figures; they were all alike kept in honor of the sacred cynocephalus baboon. But with these figures, which are seven or eight inches high, there were too much larger flints, two or three feet high. They were set upright in the chamber, and had evidently been selected, out on the desert, a mile or more away, and brought into the temple, associated with the very primitive baboon figures, and placed on end with them. All this attention to them is only explained by looking at their resemblance to animal forms. In the first one we see a quadruped on its hind legs, the head having been lost at the break on the top. In the second stone, there is the baboon form tolerably evident.

We cannot but see here the primitive fetish stones, such as the Papuan will now collect and reverence. Thus, we touch the Egyptian behind

FREDERICK MONDERSON

all art and civilization, back in the time when the stray resemblances of nature caught the attention of the mind as yet untrained to disentangle the connection of things. That mind is by no means now extinct; the coat of arms of cardinals are quoted in telegrams as forecasts of their probable papacy, in accord with a supposed prophecy, and the name of a ship is supposed to link its fate with that of its namesake. Most men pick up their fetish stones by the wayside in life, and imagine connections which strike their fancy.

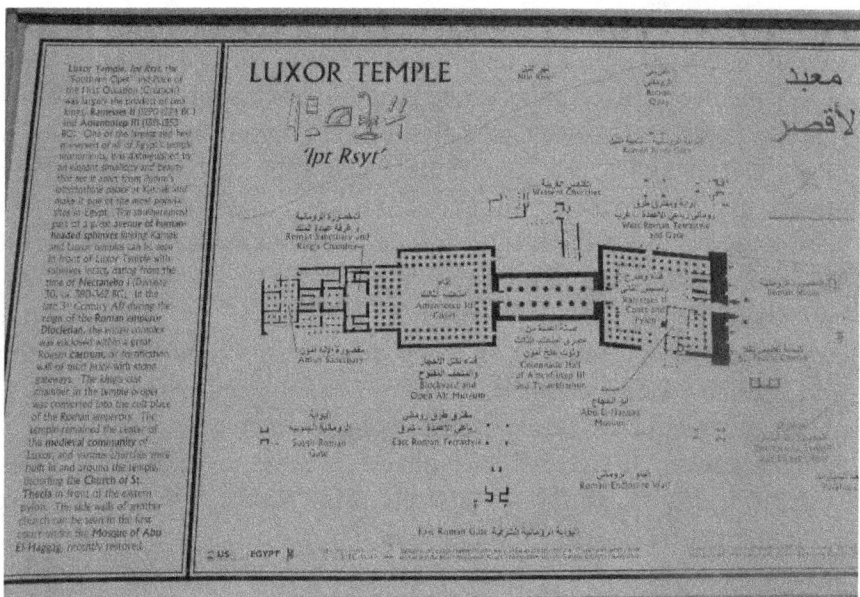

Liberate the Temple. Luxor Temple of Amenhotep III and Rameses II. Plan of the Temple with explanation at left.

LET'S LIBERATE THE TEMPLE

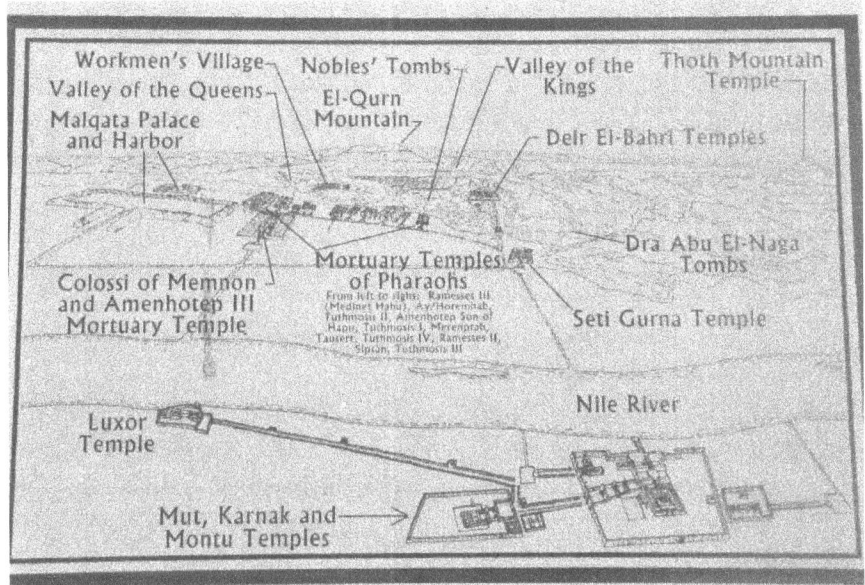

Liberate the Temple. Luxor Temple of Amenhotep III and Rameses II. Identification of the principal monuments on both sides of the river in the Luxor area.

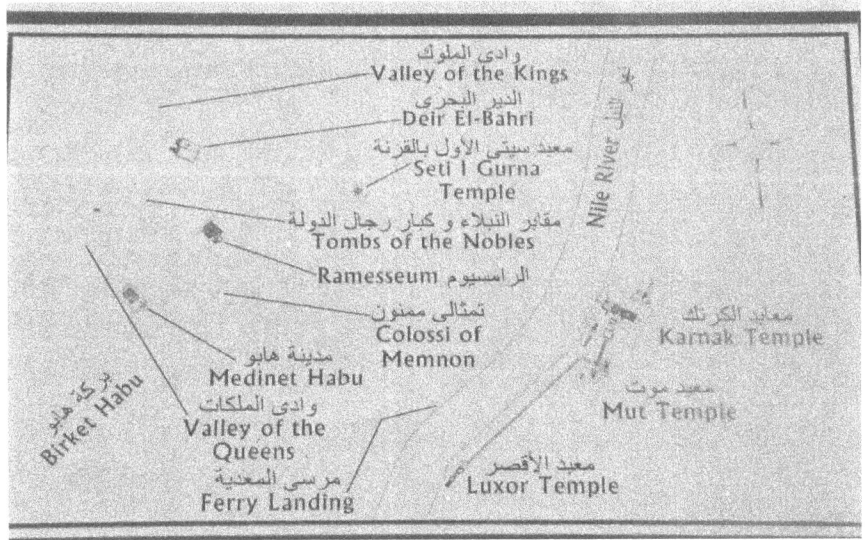

Liberate the Temple. Luxor Temple of Amenhotep III and Rameses II. Arabic identification of the principal monuments on both side of the river at Luxor.

FREDERICK MONDERSON

But these stones, found far below the polished statues of an Egyptian temple, open our eyes to the source of sculpture. We see here that man did not first sit down with a block of stone and determine to carve some figure, but he picked up some strange, weird form that seemed as if it must be something else than all the rest of the stone around; he treasured it, venerated it, improved it so as to piously help nature; and little by little he became bolder, until the finished statue did not even need the least resemblance of the block to start with. I envy the glow of the first man who say that any stone would do, and that he need not be the servant of nature and only adopt what was indicated to him. Such are the glimpses of the rise of art which these stones give us; but these were by no means the earliest examples of such notions, as prehistoric man in Egypt had long existed, though here we touch a survival of the primitive ideas in these rude untouched fetish stones set up in the first temple of Abydos.

In the same chamber with these early sculptures we found also a modeled pottery head of a camel. So far, this animal was unknown in early times in Egypt. Not a single figure of or allusion to the camel is found there before Greek times, although familiar is Syria from the days of Abraham. Here we find that at least in the first dynasty the camel was known to the Egyptians.

A similar throw-back in history occurs when we find a piece of iron in a bundle of copper tools of the sixth dynasty, or before 3400 B.C. Hitherto not a scrap of iron had been found which could be certainly dated before 1000 B.C. in Egypt, and it was not in familiar use till Greek times. But we see now that in some way the Egyptians got a bit of iron, apparently only worked into a wedge, two or three times earlier.

It is not only the history of Egypt that we recover deep down in its ruins, but also that of Europe. Some years ago, I found foreign pottery in the prehistoric time, and the earliest stage of painted Greek pottery in the royal tombs of the first dynasty. Now, of the same age, we find in the temple a whole class of black pottery which is not Egyptian and is clearly Greek in its forms. I took a piece of it in my vest pocket to

LET'S LIBERATE THE TEMPLE

Crete; and there, on the terrace of Dr. Evans' house at Knossos, I picked up the exact parallel to it, undistinguishable in color, material, and polish. Unfortunately, the Cretan pieces are much broken, and the forms have not been yet restored for comparison with the amphora and bottle which I found; but more than a dozen black bowls from the temple are like those of Crete. As to the age, this pottery belongs to the late Neolithic period in Crete, which must be of 4000 B.C., or earlier, in good accord with the Egyptian date of about 4500 B.C. for this class of pottery. It is only by thus connecting the early dawn of Europe with the more complete history of Egypt that we can recover more of our own past, and trace surely the various steps by which our present civilization has been built up. To understand the action of the present time, to grasp the meaning of the tendencies of its religion, its politics, and its life, without knowing the stages by which it has grown, is as ineffective as to look at geography of the past, and have formed and will yet regulate in future the surroundings of mankind, so the past civilizations have formed the social present, and will yet control the future of man.

We come down from this beginning of the high civilization, which is only now brought before us, and some eight centuries later we meet at 4000 B.C., a name which has never fallen into oblivion, but, has kept its place as that of one of the leading figures of history. By the pen of Herodotus, the personality of Cheops has passed over from the reach of Egyptian literature, safe and sound into the Greek world, and so to our days. The character of this great and masterful ruler is the oldest that has been handed down in the memory of every generation since his time. In all ages to offend a priesthood is a sure title to infamy; and whether it be Cheops or Manasseh, Leo the Iconoclast or Henry II., the result is the same. In this light must we read the history of Cheops, who is said to have "abandoned himself to every form of depravity. He closed all the temples, forbade the Egyptians to offer sacrifices, and ordered them all to work for himself," as Herodotus records. Manetho likewise says that "he was supercilious to the gods," but adds, strangely, that he "wrote the sacred book which is greatly valued by the Egyptians." This apparent contradiction shows how we are to read the abuse which precedes it. Of the depravity, there is no evidence beyond a confiscation of religious endowments; of his real religion, there is the proof that he edited or wrote a work which was

FREDERICK MONDERSON

valued in ages afterward, and the temples of Bubastis, of Koptos, and of Denderah, all show him as a religious founder. Hitherto we have no portrait to enable us to judge the man as an acquaintance, to estimate his abilities, his ideas, and his nature; and he has remained an enigma which no historian has fully understood.

At last we can look into his character face to face. In one of the storerooms of the temple of Abydos many figures had been thrown aside, probably in the sixth dynasty. Those of wood had entirely decayed, and more films of painted stucco were left in the earth; but one little figure of ivory about three inches high had preserved its original polish almost complete. The workmen in digging had broken the head off, and brought me the figure headless. When I cleaned it, and found the Horus name of Cheops (Khufu) upon the throne, it was evident that no trouble was too great to recover the head-the only portrait of one of the greatest kings. I anxiously inquired of all the boys where they had thrown the earth, and marked out the possible limits of our search; and then began a sifting of every morsel, in order to find a piece no bigger than the tip of the little finger. A whole day the boys sifted, and day after day they went on sifting a great bank of earth; one week passed, and then another; but at end of the third week of incessant sifting the precious face was found in perfect state, and the next day the back of the head completed the figure, and Khufu once more sat in all his dignity before us.

We can now study the nature of this great monarch. The first thing that strikes us is the enormous driving power of the man, the ruling nature which it seems impossible to resist, the determination which is above all constraint and all opposition. As far as force of will goes, the strongest characters in history would look pliable in this presence. When we analyze it, we see the ideality of the upper part of the face- the far look in the eyes, and the high cheek-bone; the expression of conception and construction and the attaining of great ends. And when we look below, to the mouth and jaw, we feel the terrible force which carried forward his ideals, the all-compelling power to which no man could say nay. There is no face quite parallel to this in all the portraits we know - Egyptian, Greek, Roman or modern.

LET'S LIBERATE THE TEMPLE

Face to face with Khufu we can better understand the record that we have of his acts. No doubt such a man, with great ideals and unlimited strength of will, did many unpleasant things; but the sight of such a face wipes away any such notion of personal baseness or evil nature. And this reform and economic revolution was the step toward the resumption of the wealth of the country by the state. The king was all in all to the Egyptians-lawgiver, administrator, organizer, general, high priest; and after putting an end to the wasteful service of the religion, "he made they all work for himself." The name of Khufu still remains at some of the great temples, at a vast quarry of alabaster, on the rocks of Sinai, and above all at the Great Pyramid of Ghizeh, which is the greatest mass of masonry and mountain and contains some of the most accurate work that has ever been put together by mortal man. Such were the triumphant results of this ruling will, of which we now see the living expression set before us.

Liberate the Temple. Luxor Temple of Amenhotep III and Rameses II. Visitor stands in the walkway to the temple's entrance with lying, seated and standing statues in the rear.

FREDERICK MONDERSON

Liberate the Temple. Luxor Temple of Amenhotep III and Rameses II. Classic view of the Temple's entrance Pylon with remaining Obelisk (2), seated statues (2), standing statues (4). To the left in foreground, one crumbled standing statue and into the Temple beside the Processional Colonnade, one of two seated statues in the Peristyle Court.

LET'S LIBERATE THE TEMPLE

Liberate the Temple. Luxor Temple of Amenhotep III and Rameses II. Looking out from the temple towards the "Avenue of Sphinxes" heading towards Karnak Temple, three miles away.

The accounts of the reign of Khufu have been slighted by some writers as improbable. But this year an entire confirmation was found in excavating the temples of Abydos. At the bottom of all was a temple of the first dynasty; above that another temple of the second dynasty; and then at the fourth dynasty there was a blank in the ruins, with no great walls or buildings, but only a hearth of vegetable ashes, among which were hundreds of little pottery offerings, without a single bone of a sacrifice. Here we actually saw before us the abolition of the temple and the sacrifices, and the substitution of the clay models of no value, in place of the costly offerings which had sustained the priesthood. After that the system of temples revived, and increased in cost and grandeur to the end of the history. But the political economy of Khufu stood revealed, and Herodotus was vindicated.

Rows of pits are sunk, and the earth thrown out, until buildings are reached, and then each wall is followed and traced, and one structure below another is cleared, until all the past history of the series of temples is exposed, and every fragment has been transferred to the plans which permanently secure the facts.

More than four thousand measurements and a thousand levels were taken to unravel the history of these temples of Abydos; and every day I was cutting sections of the earth with trowel and knife to trace in the mud soil the course of the mud-brick walls. The pillager merely in search of antiquities would find only two or three dozen inscribed stones and much worthless pottery; but for the historian and archaeologist there was the history of the land for four thousand years in that twenty feet of ruins. I have to thank England and America equally for enabling these discoveries to be carried on by means of the Egypt Exploration Fund, in the publication of which the detailed results are given.

James H. Breasted in *Ancient Records of Egypt* (Chicago: University of Chicago Press, 1906:

TEMPLE OF OSIRIS

Inscription of Mentuhotep 12th Dynasty

"I conducted the work in the temple, built his house, and dug the lake. I masoned the well, by command of the majesty of Horus."

Sehetepibre says:

"A tomb at the stairway of the great god, lord of Abydos recording all the offices and all the pleasing things thou didst."

Elaborating further on Middle Kingdom work, Arthur Weigall in *A Guide to the Antiquities of Upper Egypt*, New York: The MacMillan Company (1910: 4-5) writes: "Under the great King Senusert IIIrd extensive works were carried on at Abydos. This king, desiring to be buried beside the archaic kings of Egypt, and their chief Osiris, and yet feeling it incumbent upon him to erect a pyramid at Memphis,

LET'S LIBERATE THE TEMPLE

resolved to be interred at both places. He therefore constructed a huge rock-cut tomb for himself at Abydos, and here it is probable that he was buried for a short space of time, his body afterwards being removed to the northern pyramid. The officials whom he sent to superintend the temple works have left some records of themselves. We read of one who erected a statue of the king. Another tells how he was sent to adorn the secret places of Osiris with gold obtained in the king's Nubian wars. A portable shrine of gold, silver, lapis lazuli, carob-wood, meru-wood, and other costly materials were made."

"King Amenemhat IIIrd of the XIIth dynasty sent an official to Abydos to assist at some such festival as the above and this personage also conducted work on the sacred barge, 'fashioning its colors;' and, by virtue of his office as Master of Secret Things, he clothed the statue of the god with its ceremonial robes. In the XIIIth dynasty Sobekhotep IIIrd built onto the temple of Osiris, and also restored the tomb of Osiris."

Aahmes Ist, the first king of the XVIIIth dynasty, restored the ruined temples of Abydos, and also erected a pyramid here for himself in order that he might be buried temporarily beside his ancestors before being interred at Thebes. He also constructed a mortuary chapel near this pyramid for his grandmother Tetisheri. The next king, Amenhotep Ist, build a temple in honor of his father Aahmes. Thothmes Ist, the succeeding Pharaoh ordered a barque to be built for Osiris, made of cedar, the bow and stern being of electrum. A portable barque was also made, being decorated with gold, silver, black copper, lapis lazuli, and other precious stones; and he ordered statues to be erected, their standards being of electrum. He further presented the temples with offering tables, necklaces, censers, and dishes. The names of Thutmose IInd and Thutmose IIIrd are found together in the temple.

Thothmes III, "took much interest in Abydos, and built largely onto the ancient temples, setting up also the statues of Senusert IIIrd, his ancestor. The high priest of Osiris at this time named Nebuana, states that he conducted many works in the temple of Osiris, using gold, silver, malachite, lapis lazuli, and 'every splendid and costly stone' in the decorations. 'I was summoned,' he writes, speaking of himself, 'to the god's golden house, and my place was among his princes. My feet strode in the splendid place; I was anointed with the finest ointment; and a wreath was around my throat.'"

King Thothmes IVth appears to have taken great interest in Abydos. He presented 1200 stat of land to the temple, and regulated the supply of cattle, poultry, etc., for its altars. He also made endowments for the tomb of Aahmes Ist. Amenhotep IIIrd erected a large temple in Thinis; but this was abandoned during the heretical period which followed on the death of this king."

King Rameses Ist of the XIXth dynasty, and King Sety Ist restored some of the buildings within the Thinis enclosure; but the energies of the latter were mainly given to the erection of his splendid temple in Abydos proper, dedicated to Osiris, Isis and Horus, and also to other gods not closely connected with the district."

The Chancellor Bey, on behalf of King Siptah of the XXth dynasty, left is name at Abydos. King Rameses IIIrd built a temple in Thinis for the god Anhur, and seems to have erected a palace for himself in or near it. He speaks of having built a large enclosing wall also, with ramps and towers, and with doors of cedar fitted unto doorways of stone.

King Paynezem IInd of the XXIst dynasty is stated to have sent a statue of a great Libyan chieftain named Namlot to be erected at Abydos.

Inscriptions of Kings Takeloth Ist and IInd have been found in the Thinite enclosure. During the reign of Taharka the vizier Menthuemhat visited the royal tombs at Abydos, and inscribed his name on the rocks nearby by. King Haabra of the XXVIth dynasty undertook some building works here, as did his successor Aahmes IInd. The latter king sent an official named Pefnefdeneit to superintendent the work, and this personage records that he restored the ruins of earlier temples, re-established the priestly revenues, planted arbors of date palms, and made vineyards.

LET'S LIBERATE THE TEMPLE

Kings Nectanebo Ist and IInd also turned their attention to Abydos, and the former Pharaoh erected a temple of some size."

Liberate the Temple. Luxor Temple of Amenhotep III and Rameses II. Visitor relaxes in shade before the left-side seated colossal. Notice another seated statue beside the Colonnade in the Court.

FREDERICK MONDERSON

Liberate the Temple. Luxor Temple of Amenhotep III and Rameses II. On the seated statue, the Nile Gods unite the land under Rameses II.

Liberate the Temple. Luxor Temple of Amenhotep III and Rameses II. A Procession of the sons of Rameses heading to Luxor Temple.

LET'S LIBERATE THE TEMPLE

Liberate the Temple. Luxor Temple of Amenhotep III and Rameses II. Fat cows in the procession to Luxor Temple. Notice the Nubian Lady coming out of the head of the cow (top left).

V.   Mortuary Temple of Seti I

Margaret Murray called it: "The most beautiful temple in all Egypt" and Breasted concurred.

1.   This Seti I Temple to Osiris at Abydos is "the most complete of all Egyptian temples even though the first pylon and first court are destroyed."

2.   It was discovered by Mariette in 1864 who partially cleared it and this is when he discovered the **Abydos Tablet**. His efforts probably prevented the list from being stolen like the **Second Abydos List** of Rameses II (Now in the British Museum) and the **Karnak List** of Thutmose, (now in the Louvre, Paris)

FREDERICK MONDERSON

3.   Flinders Petrie discovered Archaic kings at Abydos in 1898 and published his findings in 1900-01.

4.   In January 1901-02 Petrie arranged for St. G. Caufield to survey the site of Abydos. The temple area, including the Cenotaph was excavated from 1900-1930 by the Egyptian Exploration Society staff which included Petrie, Quibell, Margaret Murray, Frankfort, Naville, and Whittemore, according to Bratton, *A History of Egyptian Archaeology*, 1968: 185.

5.   The temple is built of fine-textured white limestone and is excellent in its technique and artistry.

6.   The temple was begun by Seti I but finished by his son Rameses II. Generally, the visitor sees the temple looking in, while the god experiences the temple looking out. That is to say, the first part of the temple should be the Sanctuary. Here the god resides, and it is built out. Now, there are two Hypostyle Halls in this temple. The First one, from the visitor's view, is actually the second, but it is furthest from the god. This was completed and decorated by Rameses II and depicts an inferior style of decoration. The second Hypostyle Hall, completed and decorated by Seti I himself which the visitor encounters but is closest to the god possesses some of the finest sculptures characteristic of Seti's other works at Karnak and Kurneh. We see this arrangement again in the Hypostyle Hall at Karnak. The northern half was completed and decorated by Seti while the southern half was done by Rameses. Clearly the decoration of the northern half is superior to the southern. We can theorize, two sets of artists decorated both structures. This as indicated occurs at Abydos.

7.   There is a wing added to the south-west corner of the temple. Normally this set of building or chambers would be at the rear of the structure. Perhaps because of the Osireion behind the main temple, this was as is.

8.   The Osireion is considered a Cenotaph. It is a unique structure, the only one of its kind, surrounded by water.

LET'S LIBERATE THE TEMPLE

9.   The temple of Seti I is dedicated to Seven deities - Horus, Isis, Osiris, Ra Horakhty, Amon-Ra, Ptah and Seti, deified. As I said, two Hypostyle Halls, an outer (first) and an inner (second). The inner Hypostyle Hall sits on a raised platform that entrances to the shrines of the seven deities. These shrines have corbeled roofs and false doors.

10.   The Hall of Osiris in the rear of these shrines which the visitor enters from the Eastern end, spans their distance and its roof is supported by 10 columns.

11.   In this temple, Amon is shown as Amon-Ra and as Amon-Min.

12.   Father, son and grandson are shown in this temple. That is, Seti I, Rameses II and his son Amenherkhepshef, throwing the bull.

13.   The **Abydos Tablet of Kings** is here, *in situ*, and lists 76 kings from Narmer to Seti I. Five cartouches are blank and represent Hatshepsut and the Amarna Revolution monarchs, Akhenaten (Amenhotep IV), Smenkhare, Tutankhamon, and Aye. However, Hatshepsut, ruling earlier than these kings, was proscribed because as a woman she chose to rule as the Son of God. A list of 300 gods is also shown nearby in this western end.

14.   The resurrection of Osiris, the impregnation of Isis assisted by Nephthys, Thoth and Anubis is also represented in this western part.

15.   In the Hall of Osiris, on the opposite eastern end; in a Kiosk Isis, Seti and Horus are the deities depicted. In other words, Seti takes the place of Osiris in this Kiosk in the Hall of Osiris.

Osiris' name is associated with the Nile - death and rebirth of the land. As some commentators have asserted, this is a form of ancestor-worship by his followers.

Equally too, as Kamil in *Upper Egypt and Nubia* (1986) (1993: 15) has pointed out:

FREDERICK MONDERSON

"A large Macehead excavated at Nekhen records a military victory of an Upper Egyptian king (known as the 'Scorpion King') over the chieftains of the Delta (symbolically depicted as dead birds hung from Upper Egyptian standards), the main theme of this Macehead is agricultural; the central register shows the king wielding a hoe in both hands and breaking ground amidst scenes of rejoicing."

Liberate the Temple. Luxor Temple of Amenhotep III and Rameses II. In the Peristyle Court, statues come out from between the columns, the Kiosk of Hatshepsut to the Theban Triad and the Western Half of the Great Pylon in rear.

LET'S LIBERATE THE TEMPLE

Liberate the Temple. Luxor Temple of Amenhotep III and Rameses II. Statues coming out from between the Columns in the Peristyle Court.

Liberate the Temple. Luxor Temple of Amenhotep III and Rameses II. Rameses' Suten Bat, King of Upper and Lower Egypt Cartouche or Shennu.

FREDERICK MONDERSON

Liberate the Temple. Luxor Temple of Amenhotep III and Rameses II. Defaced alabaster statues of Tutankhamon and his wife because they "Look so African."

VI. Temple of Seti I - The Sculptures

The Temple of Seti I is a magnificent structure with some of the best-preserved images in all of Egypt. Its significance is even more highlighted because of its dedication to Osiris, situated at Abydos and was constructed at a place where some of the greatest pharaohs left their mark. This Temple of Seti I to Osiris at Abydos is a principal site of tourist attraction today and has been so down through the ages.

LET'S LIBERATE THE TEMPLE

Arthur Weigall, *A Guide to the Antiquities of Upper Egypt*. (New York: The Macmillan Company, 1910; 12-20) has provided an extensive description of the illustrations within the temple. As such, he states and though somewhat early, such a description is wonderfully made and still viable.

"The Pylons and Forecourt of the temple are still buried under the houses of the village, and the visitor first enters the open Second Court, of which only the southern end is now preserved. At this end, there is a raised terrace, approached by a gently graded stairway; and on this terrace, rise the stumps of twelve square pillars, built, like the temple, of limestone, but having sandstone bases. These pillars supported a roof which has now disappeared, and thus a kind of portico or pronaos was formed along the front of the main building. The reliefs on the pillars, show Rameses IInd embraced by the principal gods of Egypt. On the outer walls of the main temple there is at the east end a long inscription which tells how Rameses IInd came to Abydos and, finding the temple unfinished, decided to continue the building. Farther along (1) one sees a large figure of the king offering the symbol of truth to Osiris, Isis, and his father Sety Ist. Next (2) there are the figures of Horus, Isis, and Sety Ist, after which (3) Rameses is shown standing beside a sacred tree, on the leaves of which Ptah writes his name, while Thoth records the number of his years. He is presented at the same time with the royal crook and flail by Harmachis, behind whom Osiris stands. Rameses is next (4) led forward by Horus (?) and Khnum, preceded by the standards of the Jackal which represents Wepwat of the south, and that of the uninterpreted emblem of Thebes. The king then (5) addresses Osiris; and on the west wall (6) there is a damaged scene in which he is shown slaughtering Asiatic prisoners before Amen-Ra.

The First Hypostyle Hall

One now enters the First Hypostyle Hall, the roof of which is supported by two rows of twelve columns. To obtain some idea of the magnificence of this hall, the visitor should look at it from the extreme east or west end, allowing the eye to travel down the whole length of the rows of columns. In the original plan, the hall was entered from the Second Court through seven doorways but all but two were later blocked by Rameses IInd. Seven corresponding doors led from this hall into the Second Hypostyle Hall, from which again seven shrines open. These shrines from west to east are dedicated to Sety Ist, Ptah, Harmachis, Amen-Ra, Osiris, Mut, and Horus; and thus, the two Hypostyle Halls are also divided into seven sections, each dedicated respectively to one of these gods. The visitor, however, will find it best to examine all the main reliefs in this first Hypostyle Hall without regard to these divisions. Commencing from the first scene on the east side of the main entrance (7) one sees Rameses between Amen-Ra and Tum of On, who throw over him the signs of 'life' and 'stability.' Above the king is shown offering vases before a ram-headed form of Amen-Ra. Next (8) Rameses holds a religious standard before the shrine of Ptah; and above this scene he kneels upon the symbol of the union of Upper and Lower Egypt, while the stems of the papyrus and lotus plants, emblematic of the two countries, are interlaced by Wepwat and Horus (?). Rameses is then (9) shown worshipping Min, behind whom are the mystical insignia of his cult; and above this the king draws by a rope the sacred barque of Seker, which rests upon a sledge. On the east wall (10) Rameses is purified with the water of life by Thoth and Horus; and above this he performs a ceremonial dance before a seated figure of Ptah, behind whom stands the lion-headed consort of that god, Sekhmet. Next (11) he is suckled by Hathor of Per-Kau, Hathor of Albastronpolis, Hathor of Diospolis Parva, and Hathor of Denderah; and he is dangled by Isis (?). This scene is intended to demonstrate the divine up-bringing of the king; and the next scene (12), which represents the god Khnum, who made man on a potter's wheel, presenting the newly-fashioned child to Ptah, is intended to show his divine origin. On the south wall between the doorways, the reliefs continue. First (13) Rameses is introduced by Mut to Ptah and Sekhmet, and Ptah records his royal name. Above this he stands before a shrine containing the barque of Seker. Then (14) he is blest by Harmachis, while behind him stand two goddesses, one of which is Hathor. Above this he offers a figure of truth to Amen-ra and Hathor. Next (15) he makes an offering to Amen-Ra and Mut; and above there is a variation of the same subject. Next (16) he offers kneeling statuettes to Amen-Ra and Khonsu. He is then (17) seen

LET'S LIBERATE THE TEMPLE

receiving the symbol of Jubilees from Osiris, and behind him stand Harsiesis and Isis. Above this his name is inscribed upon his shoulder by Thoth, in the presence of Osiris. He next (18) receives the royal cobra, the Hathor symbol, and a necklace from Isis, and the double crown from Horus. Above this he is sucked by Isis in the presence of Harsiesis. On the west wall (19) Rameses offers various golden symbols to Osiris, Isis, Harseosiris; and above this his name is written on the sacred tree by Thoth, he himself kneeling amidst the foliage. He is then (20) led by Wepwat of the south and by Harendotus to Hathor of Denderah; and (21) he is purified with the water of life by Thoth and Harsiesis; while above this he dances before a god and is embraced by other deities. On the north wall (22) he performs one of the well-known but little understood foundation ceremonies before Harsiesis, who projects towards him the symbols of 'power,' 'stability,' and 'life.' Above this he worships Harsiesis. He then (23) performs the foundation ceremony of pegging out the limits of the temple in the presence of Osiris, the goddess Safkhet, the patron deity of archive and records, assisting him. Above this he breaks ground with a hoe before Osiris. Finally, he receives life from Amen-Ra, while Osiris stands behind him; and above this he offers incense and a libation to Amen-Ra.

THE SECOND HYPOSTYLE HALL

The visitor has now seen the main reliefs in this hall and should pass through one of the seven doorways into the Second Hypostyle Hall. The roof is supported by three rows of twelve columns, of which the third row stands on a raised platform or terrace, which forms the threshold of the seven sanctuaries. The reliefs on the east and north wall of this hall do not attract one's attention. Those on the west wall, however, are perhaps the most beautiful temple reliefs now preserved in Egypt. From this point, onwards practically all the workmanship is that of the reign of Sety Ist, and the superiority of these reliefs over those of Rameses IInd which have already been seen, is at once apparent. Under Sety Ist, Egyptian art reached one of its highest levels; and the delicate cutting of the stone displayed here, and in his tomb and temple at Thebes, is worthy of the best periods of the old kingdom. The scenes on this west wall have lost their original color, but the white limestone only serves to increase their beauty. We first see Sety Ist (25) burning incense and pouring a libation before Osiris and Harendotus. Above this he kneels before a god. He next (26) presents offerings before (27) a shrine containing Osiris seated between the goddesses Maat and Rennet on one side, and Isis, Amentet-Hapet, and Nephthys on the other. Above this he pours a libation before Osiris and Isis. He then (28) offers a figure of Truth to Osiris, Isis, and Harsiesis; while above this he kneels before Horus and Isis, receiving the curved sword, the crook, and the flail from the former.

Liberate the Temple. Luxor Temple of Amenhotep III and Rameses II. Inscriptions on the still standing Obelisk before the Pylon.

LET'S LIBERATE THE TEMPLE

Liberate the Temple. Luxor Temple of Amenhotep III and Rameses II. Columns of the Eastern half of the Peristyle Court with the wall supporting the Mosque of Abu Haggag in the rear.

FREDERICK MONDERSON

Liberate the Temple. Luxor Temple of Amenhotep III and Rameses II. Columns of the Hypostyle Hall. Notice the elevation ramp from the Peristyle Court to the next level of location.

Liberate the Temple. Luxor Temple of Amenhotep III and Rameses II. From the lower level of the Processional Colonnade, columns of the Peristyle Court.

LET'S LIBERATE THE TEMPLE

Liberate the Temple. Luxor Temple of Amenhotep III and Rameses II. From the elevated Court, the lower avenue of the Processional Colonnade.

FREDERICK MONDERSON

Liberate the Temple. Luxor Temple of Amenhotep III and Rameses II. From the East beside the "Open Air Museum,' the Processional Colonnade, Abu Haggag Mosque and Great Pylon to the right.

One should now enter the first sanctuary at the west end, which was dedicated to Horus. On its walls Sety is shown worshipping that god; and especially noticeable are the beautiful reliefs on the east side (29), where one sees the sacred barque of Horus standing in its shrine, the king burning incense before it, while below he makes various offerings to Horus and Isis. At the end of the sanctuary is a false door which was heavily inlaid with metal, as is shown by the deep cutting between the ornamentation. One may notice the grass mats rolled up at the top of each panel of the door, as was the custom in the case of real doorways. Between the entrance of this sanctuary and that of the next there is a recess in which the deities Isis, Unnefer, and Harseosiris are shown; and above this there is a large relief (30) showing the king receiving emblems of royalty from Horus and Isis. The second sanctuary is dedicated to Mut, and on either wall, one sees the sacred

LET'S LIBERATE THE TEMPLE

barque of the goddess, before which the king burns incense. The rest of the reliefs show him making various offerings to Mut. The recess between this and the next sanctuary contains figures of Nut, Osiris, and Isis; and above it (31) the king is seen kneeling and burning incense between Osiris and Isis. The third sanctuary is that of Osiris, and through it one passes into the chambers specially dedicated to his worship, which will be described later. On the east wall (32) the king is seen burning incense before a shrine containing the emblem of Abydos; the wig and head of Osiris raised upon a pole. In front of the shrine are five standards, namely the Jackal Wepwat of the south, the Jackal of the north, the Ibis of Hermopolis, the Hawk of the Horus tribes, and the figure of Anhur of Thinis. On the opposite wall (33) there is the sacred barque of Osiris; and one may here notice the rich and elaborate ornamentation; the colored fans and plumes, the head of Osiris above the shrine in the barque, and the fruit of offerings of grapes, pomegranates, figs, etc. Between this and the next sanctuary the recess in the wall is decorated with the figures of Mut, Amen-ra, and Khonsu; and above it (34) the king is seen kneeling between Amen-Ra and Osiris, bedecked with the magnificent insignia of royalty. The next sanctuary, which lies in the axial line of the temple, is dedicated to Amen-Ra, the great god of the empire. In the reliefs, he is sometimes shown in the form of Min, as at the Luxor temple and elsewhere. One sees the sacred barque of the god, accompanied by those of Mut and Khonsu; and again, one observes the gaudy fans, plumes, and insignia. Fruit and flowers are heaped before the barque: grapes, figs, pomegranates, trailing vines, festoons of flowers are shown; and jars of wine, golden statuettes, etc., are seen here. Outside this sanctuary the next recess in the wall contains the figures of Harmachis, Amen-Ra, and Mut; and the relief above it (35) shows the king kneeling between the ram-headed Harmachis, receiving from the former a curved sword and a mace. The king holds a tame bird in his hand. The following sanctuary is that of Harmachis, and the reliefs are not unlike those already seen. The next recess contains the figures of Sekhmet, Ptah, and Harmachis; and the large relief above it (36) shows the king enthroned and carried by three hawk-headed beings called 'The Spirits of Pe' (a city of the Delta), and three jackal-headed beings called 'The Spirits of Nekhen,' i.e., Kom el Ahmar. These two cities were the archaic capitals of Lower and Upper Egypt. Before him go the standard of the shield and crossed arrows of Neith, the so-called scorpion sign, the emblem of Thebes, the disc of Hermopolis, and the jackals, Wepwat, of the south and north. Above this the king, holding the crook and flail, stands between Thoth and Nekheb on the one side and Horus and Uazet in the other. The goddesses Uazet and Nekheb are the patron deities of the two above-mentioned capitals. We next (39) see the barque of the king; for, like the gods, he possessed an image which was carried in this portable vessel in the temple processions. Another interesting scene here (40) shows him seated above the sign of union between Nekheb and Uazet, while Horus and Thoth lace together the stems of the papyrus and lotus plants, and Safkhet records the ceremonial union.

THE HALL OF SEKER

Between this last sanctuary and the passage on the east side, closed with an iron door, there is an open doorway leading into a three-columned hall, known to the Egyptians as the Hall of Seker. On the north wall, the reliefs show the king worshipping the hawk-headed Seker and the human-formed Tum. On the east wall are four recesses, of which the first contains the figures of Tum, Thoth, and Seker; the second of Osiris, Min-Ra (?), and a god whose name is now lost; the third of Seker, Ptah, and Seker again; and the fourth of Osiris, Tum, and Hor-ur of the south. Between these recesses the king is shown worshipping the gods. On the west wall, he offers four times to the hawk-headed Seker.

CHAMBER OF TUM

Two rooms led off the southern end of this hall, the first having a vaulted roof, and the second being now roofless. The first is the chamber of Tum, and in the reliefs, one sees the king adoring that god and the associated deities. On the east wall (41), at the top, the king kneels before a shrine containing the humanly-formed Ptah-Thenen, a disk-headed Amen-dwelling-in-Aten, a Djed-headed Osiris-Unnefer, a sphinx representing the king, and the lion-headed Sekhmet. Below this the king kneels before the lion-headed Tum, on whose head is his

LET'S LIBERATE THE TEMPLE

distinctive symbol of a hawk and lotus-flower, Ptah-Osiris, Shu, the hawk Horus perched upon the Uazet sign, Isis, Nephthys (?), Nekheb, and woman-headed hawk of Hathor. On the opposite wall (42), at the top, he worships before a shrine containing the mummified hawk of Seker, the lion-headed Tum, the ibis-headed Thoth, a naos in which is a lotus and a crescent-moon connected with the worship of Tum, a sphinx representing the king, and the lion-headed Tum holding a flail and sacred eye. Below this the king burns incense before a shrine containing a figure of Tum with a hawk and lotus upon his head, Nu, the primeval water, Khepera, the dawn, with a scarab on his head, Thoth, and damaged figures of Neith and Uazet.

Liberate the Temple. Medinet Habu, Mortuary Temple of Rameses III. Great Pylon of the Temple proper with Rameses slaying captives before Amon-Ra (left) and to the right, he slays captives before Ra-Horakhty, behind the tree.

FREDERICK MONDERSON

Liberate the Temple. Medinet Habu, Mortuary Temple of Rameses III. A small 18th Dynasty temple built by Hatshepsut and Thutmose, in the Great Temple's forecourt.

Liberate the Temple. Medinet Habu, Mortuary Temple of Rameses III. Columns under construction in the First Court.

LET'S LIBERATE THE TEMPLE

Liberate the Temple. Medinet Habu, Mortuary Temple of Rameses III. Defaced and destroyed Osiride Figures before square Pillars in the First Court.

CHAMBER OF OSIRIS

The second room, the Chamber of Osiris, has upon its walls some curious reliefs. On the east wall (43) we see the king kneeling before a naos containing the two hawks of Seker, and behind this is a representation of the sarcophagus of Osiris. The god, crowned with the crown of Upper Egypt, lies upon a bier, and Isis in the form of a hawk hovers over him, while the goddess in human form and Horus stand at either end of the body. Above this relief one sees Osiris holding a crook and flail, the jackal-headed Anubis, Nekheb wearing the crown of Upper Egypt, and three unnamed figures holding snakes and lizards, who are said to be giving life, might, and strength to the king. On the opposite wall (44) one sees a shrine containing two hawks, one representing Isis and the other Horus; and behind this is the sarcophagus of Osiris again. He lies on the lion-couch, so common in Egyptian tombs, while Isis and Horus bend over him.

FREDERICK MONDERSON

Behind this again is a shrine in which a now damaged figure of the hippopotamus goddess Taurt is shown. From these reliefs, it is clear that in this chamber were celebrated the mysteries connected with the resurrection of Osiris. Tradition stated that the god, after the murder and burial, came to life for a short time and had intercourse with his wife Isis, who afterwards gave birth to Horus.

THE OSIRIS HALLS

Behind the Sanctuary of Osiris, which, it will be remembered, is the third from the west end, there is a portion of the temple especially dedicated to Osiris. The visitor should enter it through the Osiris Sanctuary, and he will then find himself in a hall, the roof of which was supported by eight columns. On the north wall, the reliefs have been intentionally damaged, but are still good. The first relief at the top (45) shows the king offering before the shrine of Anubis, containing the jackal; and below this he worships at the shrine of Harendotus, in which is the figure of a hawk. The third relief (46) shows him opening the door of the shrine of Horus, which contains a hawk. The eighth relief (47) shown at the top the shrine of Heket, in which is the figure of frog; and below this the king opens the door of the shrine of Min-Harsiesis. The ninth relief (48) represents him worshipping at the shrine of the cow Shentait. On the south wall (49) is the great emblem of Abydos, the head of Osiris, having a large ornamental wig, placed upon a pole, while the king and Isis worship it. Next (50) is the ibis-standard of Thoth; then (51) the great Kherp or baton of Thoth, and the hawk-standard; next (52) the Djed-symbol of Osiris clothed, with a girdle and skirt; and (53) the king and Isis lift the same symbol. On the rest of the wall the reliefs show the king worshipping various gods. We see, then, that the reliefs in this hall were intended to give a kind of catalogue of the larger shrines and emblems employed in the Osiris worship. Three sanctuaries lead off the west end of the hall. The first is dedicated to Horus, and the fine colored reliefs show the king offering to that god, with whom are associated Osiris and Isis. The second chamber is dedicated to Osiris, and to the king who is here identified with that god. The brilliant

LET'S LIBERATE THE TEMPLE

reliefs show the king crowned and enthroned, wearing the insignia of Osiris, while Anubis, Isis, Thoth, and Harseosiris salute him; and on the end wall he is embraced by Osiris, with whom are Isis and Horus. The third sanctuary is dedicated to Isis, and the reliefs show the king worshipping her with Osiris and Horus. The four-columned hall with its three sanctuaries, which forms the east end of the Osiris Halls, is now so much ruined that it does not repay a visit.

THE LIST OF KINGS

One now returns to the Second Hypostyle Hall and enters the passage at the east side. On the south wall of this passage (54) is the famous list of kings. One sees Seti Ist holding a censer, and the young prince Rameses, afterwards King Rameses IInd, reading from a papyrus; and before them in two rows are the cartouches of a large number of the Pharaohs of Egypt, beginning with Mena and ending with himself. The third row of cartouches is a repetition of his own names. This list has been of great value to Egyptologists in fixing the position of certain of the less known Pharaohs; but it does not give the names of all the monarchs, and the spelling of some of the earlier names is defective.

A passage leading towards the south, and ending in a stairway, once led to the desert at the back of the temple; and it seems to have been used at the festivals in which the procession visited the tomb of Osiris. The reliefs date from the reign of Rameses IInd. On the west wall (55) that king and his son, Prince Amenherkhepshef, are seen catching a bull for sacrifice; and farther along (56) the king drags forward the elaborate barque of Seker. On the east wall (57) he and four genii pull at a rope which is attached to a net in which many wild ducks have been caught. These he and his son present to Amen-Ra and Mut. At the other end of the wall (58) he drives four sacrificial calves to Khonsu, and dances before a god whose figure is now destroyed.

UNFINISHED CHAMBERS

FREDERICK MONDERSON

Returning to the passage in which the list of kings is shown, one may pass through the iron door at its east end into several ruined and unfinished chambers. One first enters a hall of ten columns, in which the reliefs have never been completed. Those at the south-west corner, showing the slaughtering of cattle, are of good workmanship, and especially one figure (59) is noticeable for its spirited action. It represents a man pulling at a rope attached to the hind leg of a bull, and one can well see the tension of his muscles. The other chambers are hardly worth visiting. One hall contains reliefs representing the sacred barques, and a bench or shelf running around the walls seems to have been the resting place of the actual barques. Foreign inscriptions of the 6th Century B.C., and later Coptic inscriptions, are scrawled upon the walls.

Describing the nearby Temple of Rameses II, Margaret Brunson in *The Encyclopedia of Ancient Egypt*, New York Gramecy Books, (1991, 1999: 3) writes: "The temple of Rameses II, located to the northeast of the shrine of Seti I, is noted for its delicate reliefs, which provide a depiction of the Battle of Kadesh, carved into limestone. A red granite doorway leads to a pillared open court, and more reliefs depict a procession offering for the king. A portico on the west side of the temple opens onto small chapels honoring Seti I and various deities. Some of the deities have been provided with suites of rooms, and there is a humanoid Djed Pillar in one of the apartment chambers. Granite statues honor Rameses II, Seti I, the god Amon, and two other goddesses. The temple of Osiris in Abydos is located to the northeast of Rameses II's temple. Originally called Kom el-Sultan, the area has only a few remains of a limestone portico and ramparts. Cenotaphs dedicated to individuals were buried in the area."

LET'S LIBERATE THE TEMPLE

Liberate the Temple. Medinet Habu, Mortuary Temple of Rameses III. Colorful winged Vultures line the ceiling between the First and Second Courts.

Liberate the Temple. Medinet Habu, Mortuary Temple of Rameses III. Columns sandwiched by Pillars with broken Osiride Figures in the Second Court.

FREDERICK MONDERSON

Liberate the Temple. Medinet Habu, Mortuary Temple of Rameses III. More columns between Osiride Figures against square pillars in the First Court.

Even further, Brunson (1991, 1999: 3-4) states: "The Shunet el-Zbib, or Storehouse of Dates, the enclosure dating to the 2nd Dynasty (2770-2649), is in the northwestern desert. Two actual complexes, with massive inner walls and outer mud-brick walls, had main ramparts. The cenotaphs of the royal personages are located farther out in the desert, as a site known as Umm el-Ga'ab, the "Mother of Pots," because of the large numbers of vessels discovered on the surface – jars used for funerary offerings of the graves. To the south, cenotaphs of the Middle Kingdom and early New Kingdom were also discovered. A temple of Senwosret III (1878-1841? B.C.) stands at the edge of the desert. The king's cenotaph lays near the face of the nearby cliffs. A pyramid, possibly that of Ahmose I of the 18th Dynasty (1550-1525 B.C.), is located to the south of the temple. A mortuary complex of Queen Tetisheri, the grandmother of Ahmose, is also in the area. … Two stelae were discovered at Abydos. One, measuring 6 feet by 3 feet, was from the 13th Dynasty, placed there by Neferhotep

LET'S LIBERATE THE TEMPLE

I (c. 1741-1731 B.C.). The second records the plans of Tuthmose I of the 18th Dynasty (1504-1492 B.C.) to honor Osiris by endowing the god's temple with gifts."

VI.   Osiris - Universal God

"It is water which brings life to the soil, and Osiris is therefore clearly associated with the soil likewise."

Let us not forget, the quintessential role of water in this culture, and this is particularly so in regards Osiris generally represented as a mummy wearing the Osiris Crown, that is the white crown with two feathers; as well as scepter, and whip symbolizing his rank as king. Nonetheless, Osiris, besides being associated with water is also an agricultural god, given his waters "fertilize the land." In this respect, he is often pictured "green" for vegetation but Osiris is often called "the great Black" and is represented by that color.

In the fusion of Ra and Osiris worship

Theophile Obenga, expanding on deep thought, in referring to the Coffin Text, an offshoot of the Pyramid Texts, in *African Philosophy: The Pharaonic Period: 2780-330 B.C.* (2004) mentions four major acts of the great god Ra. He states: "Ra the creator, who emerged from Nwn in the primal period of creation." Nun, to recall, was a source of water, the first material from which everything came. Obenga states further regarding Ra:

"First, he created the air, giving all living beings breath throughout their time on earth. The gaseous envelope covering the earth, the atmosphere, is simply the air we breathe wherever we are in the world, the four winds, namely south, north, east and west. Ancient Egyptian tradition promised the blessed dead 'the gentle breath of the north wind.'"

FREDERICK MONDERSON

"Ra's second act was to create the waters: The Nile with its freight of loam, the lakes of the countryside, the sea, all the bodies of beneficial water. The spectacular rise of the Nile (the great flood) in the month of July was a cosmic event, essential for the life of the country, a blessing to the administrator as much as to the humble peasant."

"Ra's third accomplishment was the institution of equality and fraternity between humans (each man his brother). Evil (*isfit*) in the world is imputed to humans themselves, as free beings. There is a transcendent order, but humans, thus individualized, can obey or disobey it. Here the heart, ib, symbolizes the seat of liberty, the locus of the guiding principle of our behavior. To this faculty, the Greek Stoic philosophers gave the name hegemonicon. At one stroke, 'God' is rendered innocent of human evil. The heart, as the inner core of the human subject, expresses the ontological and the logical nature of being. This makes striving to do his or her work without necessarily taking orders from an external power. We are bonded to our ancestors in solidarity: we are part of our society; still, we are individually responsible for what we do. Here we see the ancient Egyptians, two thousand years before this era began, clearly asserting human equality and fraternity, moral freedom, human will, and the accountability for our actions as individuals."

"Ra's fourth accomplishment involved the use of liquid essences. Using water, sperm, sweat, saliva and tears, the demiurge created all the various forms of nature: humans, animals, everything that lives."

As such, then, we recognize, in a desert state such as Egypt, water and its uses are extremely important. Equally too, as an example, the country can get close to 3 inches of rain per year, more especially in the Mediterranean area to the north. In the United States, on the other hand, we get more than 76 inches of rain per year. Nevertheless, particularly in the religious mythology, we learn of:

1.   The "Pool of Life;"

2.   The "Pool of Earu;"

LET'S LIBERATE THE TEMPLE

3. The "Waters of Kher-Eha;"

4. The "Cool Pool" or "Stream of Nun" is where Piankhi the Ethiopian washed his face on way to Heliopolis where he was to be crowned and recognized as the Son of the Sun-god.

5. The "Water of Life and Good Fortune" is what washed the living Pharaoh;

6. Upon birth, the infant who will become Pharaoh was washed as the "Sun-God" was washed in his daily lustration in heaven and in his Sanctuary on earth;

7. As actual pharaoh, he was washed at the Ceremony of Coronation;

8. Pharaoh was washed or purified in the "House of the Morning" and when he entered the temple to perform the daily ritual. This was also called the Baptism. We generally see, on a panel outside on the temple wall, Horus and Thoth baptizing the king with streams of ankh.

9. The entire temple in its constituent parts was visited by the officiating priest and washed or purified for the daily service whether the pharaoh was present or not. Each room was visited and equally consecrated. It had to come alive before the ceremony could begin;

10. When the king visited the sanctuary or "Holy of Holies," the chamber is washed or purified by sprinkling holy water, this is called asperging. It can also be done by incense purification or fumigation. So, water, salt or natron, incense, even food and streams of ankh can "wash" or "purify."

11. Before the ritual is performed, the altar has to be washed or purified before materials used in the lustration of the god, viz., "Holy Water," perfume, ointments, oils, food, flowers, clothing, etc., were placed on it. Important, incense is never burnt on the altar, but either in the hands of the officiating individual or in an incenser in a corner.

FREDERICK MONDERSON

Liberate the Temple. Medinet Habu, Mortuary Temple of Rameses III. A large penis and a bull in the Second Court.

Liberate the Temple. Medinet Habu, Mortuary Temple of Rameses III. Rameses is assisted by helpers as he tills the soil in the Afterlife.

LET'S LIBERATE THE TEMPLE

Let us remember, the god himself is washed after he is invoked in his chamber as he is in heaven daily. Once everything is removed before his meal is placed on the altar, it is again washed. A scene at Abydos depicts Seti washing the god's altar with his bare hands. Remember, "Cleanliness is next to godliness."

12.   With the ceremony in the "Holy of Holies" finished, and this is done three times per day, the pharaoh uses the branch of a *hidn* tree to brush the sand floor and remove his footprints; all the while he retreats while still facing, never backing the god.

13.   Before he closes the "doors of heaven" and affixes the seal that locks it, he has to asperge or sprinkle water and incense the room to wash and purify the place to maintain the purity of the god's space until the next time he is invoked.

14.   The dead pharaoh was washed by Atum in Heliopolis as the *Book of Breathings* indicates as he hurried to the place where the gods are born.

15.   He was washed before, during and after mummification and again at the tomb before it is sealed.

16.   The dead pharaoh was washed upon his arrival in the heavenly abode, so that his presence would be as a pure one. Equally, along the way to the place of Judgment, the "Tree Goddess" pours four pitchers of water on him.

We know, certainly by the 5th Dynasty, the God's and the King's temple were housed in the same structure. This essentially continued through the Middle Kingdom. However, by the New Kingdom, the god's or worship temple became separate from the King's or mortuary temple. At Thebes, practically every New Kingdom monarch built a mortuary temple on the West Bank to be worshipped.

Seti was an exceptional pharaoh and a prolific builder who also repaired many structures that were damaged during the Amarna

FREDERICK MONDERSON

Revolution of the previous dynasty. He built his mortuary temple at Kurneh. However, some scholars believe the Hypostyle Hall at Karnak Temple was indeed a mortuary temple within a God or worship temple. Most important, "the temple of Osiris at Abydos was both a worship and a mortuary temple." This is because the Osireion in the rear is considered a mortuary cenotaph, where the Dead Seti is worshipped as a god.

As stated, therefore, the first temple came into existence from the waters of Nwn positioned on the sacred mound in the form of a structure within an outer enclosure wall, designed to separate the god and its power from everything outside. Similarly, each holy space had a pool or Sacred Lake for use in washing and other uses.

OSIRIS AND WATER, even further;

In the Pyramid Texts, we learn:

1. "Horus comes; he recognizes his father in thee; youthful in thy name of 'First water'"

2. King Rameses IV, says to the god at Abydos, "thou art indeed the Nile, great in the fields at the beginning of the seasons; gods and men live by the moisture that is in thee." Breasted (1933: 96)

So therefore, we see, Great fountains of water are identified with life giving qualities.

"Water is also a source of fertility."

"Water as a life-giving agency with which Osiris is identified."

LET'S LIBERATE THE TEMPLE

Petrie

1. Petrie discovered the tomb of Den-Setui - 5th king of the Ist dynasty. His tomb was lined with brick but floored with blocks of granite.

2. It was surrounded by 137 graves of family and nobles who served the king.

3. Petrie also discovered the tomb of King Khasekhemui, 9th king of the Second Dynasty, in whose tomb was found fragments of the royal Scepter made of sard and gold.

4. In the tomb of King Zer workmen found the arm of a mummy of Zer's queen with four bracelets of gold, turquoise, lapis lazuli, and amethyst.

5. The Frenchman Emile Amelineau (1897) and Flinders Petrie (1899) working for the **Egyptian Exploration Society** revealed a great deal of the history of Abydos.

In a stated example, Fred Gladstone Bratton in *A History of Egyptian Archaeology* (1968: 184) has indicated, the work of Flinders Petrie "contributed more to our knowledge of dynastic history than any other expedition in Egypt." He says further, "The significance of Petrie's excavation lies in the knowledge gained regarding the nature of the early Egyptian culture and the construction of archaic tombs." (184)

6. In 1912-1913, Eric Peet discovered an Ibis Cemetery at Abydos. "The expedition found hundreds of thousands of mummified jackals, cats, and other animals, all killed as sacrifice to Osiris, the god of Immortality."

Next, we ask the question, how did Osiris die?

There are different versions depending on the time and source. We are told,

1. He was tricked and sealed in a chest

2. He was assassinated

3. Drowned in his "new water" (The Inundation)

Liberate the Temple. Medinet Habu, Mortuary Temple of Rameses III. Rameses incenses Amon as Min while bureaucratic and sacerdotal personnel look on.

LET'S LIBERATE THE TEMPLE

Liberate the Temple. Medinet Habu, Mortuary Temple of Rameses III. Priests hoist several Barques aloft.

Liberate the Temple. Medinet Habu, Mortuary Temple of Rameses III. Rameses kneels with both hands empty and raised before squatting divinities.

FREDERICK MONDERSON

VIII. FURTHER RESEARCH

Calverly, A.M. and M.F. Broom. *The Temple of King Sethos at Abydos*. London and Chicago: 1933-1958.
Churchward, Albert. *Signs and Symbols of Primordial Man*. Buffalo, New York: Eworld, Inc., 1993.
David, A.R. *A Guide to Religious Ritual at Abydos*. Warminster, 1981.
Frankfort, Henri. *The Cenotaph of Seti I at Abydos*. London: 1933.
Harvey, S. "Monuments of Ahmose at Abydos." *Egyptian Archaeology* 4 (1994: 3-5).
Kemp, Barry J. "The Egyptian 1st Dynasty Royal Cemetery." *Antiquity* 41 (1967: 22-32).
Obenga, Theophile. *African Philosophy: The Pharaonic Period 2780-330 B.C.* Per Ankh: 2004.
O'Connor, David R. "The Cenotaph of the Middle Kingdom at Thebes." *Melanges Gamal Eddin Mokhtar* II (Cairo, 1985: 161-177).
Petrie, W.M.F. *The Royal Tombs of the Earliest Dynasties*. 2 vols. London: 1900-1901.

OBENGA

Obenga, Theophile. *African Philosophy: The Pharaonic Period 2780-330 B.C.* (Per Ankh, 2004).

The author says, "One Egyptologist sums up this reality concisely: "Egyptian society embraces the entire Universe: all elements and beings are registered participants, like parts of a single whole, collaborations in a single enterprise." What he means is that,

"In ancient Egypt, however, the human being was precisely god: human-god, a seamless whole, in effect. That a philosophy of wholeness should take form in the pharaonic 'polis' was altogether natural. For pharaonic society was a grand, organized, universal ensemble embracing the elements (sky, sun, moon, stars, fire, water, earth, vegetation); beings (gods, goddesses, spirits, kings and queens, viziers, the royal family); administrators of various central, provincial

LET'S LIBERATE THE TEMPLE

and local government departments (treasury, justice, army, temples); scribes and sundry craft-persons (carpenters, engravers, smelters, cobblers); together with peasants and herders - and the ensemble held for nearly twenty-five centuries of national history. In this system, nothing was completely independent, isolated from the overall pharaonic domain. The sacred and the profane were merely two aspects of a single socio-political reality incarnated by the pharaoh, the god-king."

TIME

Ancient Egyptians achieved a high degree of expertise in understanding time.

Their astronomical skills, their construction of the pyramids, their mummification of the dead, their ancient Osirian myth, their rituals for the periodic renewals of the pharaoh's vital energy - all this reflects a philosophy deeply concerned with the comprehension and use of time. In the unfolding of human destiny, this was an extraordinary endeavor, immensely complex, a development possible only in the fullness of time. So, time took on a cosmic aspect, and global time was conceived of as an eternity constantly flowing into the present, to become the past.

FREDERICK MONDERSON

Liberate the Temple. Dendera Temple of Goddess Hathor. The temple's Pronaos or First Hypostyle Hall with its screened walls supporting six Hathor head capitals.

Liberate the Temple. Dendera Temple of Goddess Hathor. Pharaoh in Double Crown offers an apron to enthroned Ra-Horakhty and Hathor in Double Crown.

LET'S LIBERATE THE TEMPLE

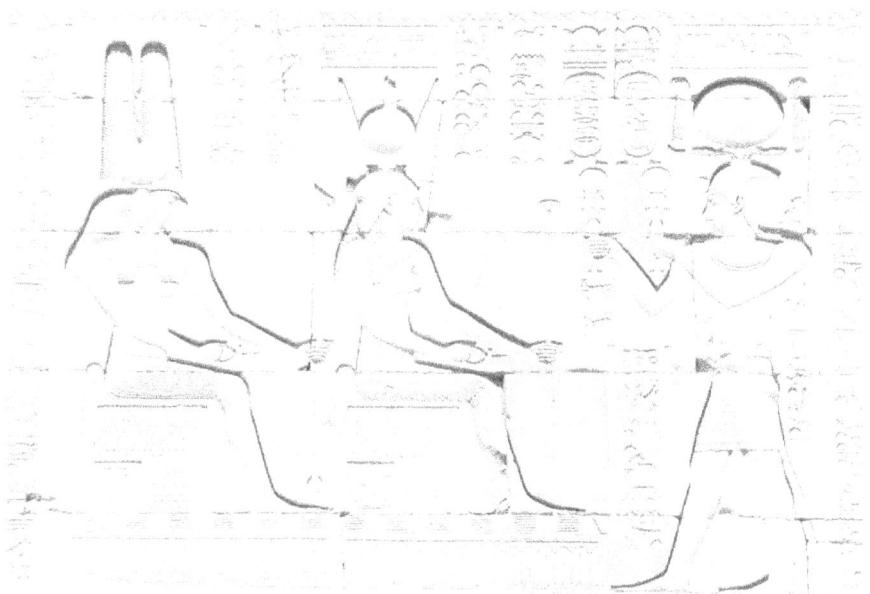

Liberate the Temple. Dendera Temple of Goddess Hathor. In fancy crown, Pharaoh offers two Sistrums to enthroned Isis (Auset) and Horus (Horus) wearing horns and disk.

Time, thus understood, was a dynamic process, periodically coming and going, always keeping humanity in touch with the totality of the cosmos. In pharaonic philosophy, this connection is essential. Time, a functional process beginning with the very origins of the world, reintegrates humanity into the totality of the universe. All the great rhythmic periodicities of life (years, season, months, the ritual schedules of work, worship and celebration) are so many affirmations of human destiny within the flow of time. Everything happens inside time; conversely, time imparts value and meaning to all that happens. In sum, time maintains all, time stabilizes all." (131-132)

"It is hard to reflect on time and its transitive nature, without an affirmation of the reflecting self, without thinking of one's own freedom. The linkage of humanity and the cosmos, the personal and the general, necessarily implies a transition to a higher mental level. That accomplishment can only be called thought, philosophy, a

FREDERICK MONDERSON

reflection of the world, the cosmic whole, this totality within which humans live and die." (133)

"The ancient Egyptians were convinced there was a higher order, living and eternal. They conceived of this deified cosmic order as a combination of justice and truth. They called it Ma'at. Given that premise, the process of living the inner life, deepening and protecting it, became synonymous with the exercise of intelligence. Whoever aspired to live forever the life of gods, in the company of the Blessed, had to make a conscious effort to live according to a set of 'rules' designed for the purpose of dominating death, transcending morality and affirming life." (219)

The straight path to eternal life was morality. Funeral rites, embalmment, sacrificial offerings to the deceased and to the skin cloaks during burial ceremonies, sarcophagi, statuettes, and inscriptions in the tombs - all this panoply imagined, invented and deployed in order to help the dead attain eternity, that is to say, to merge self and cosmic order, thanks to the achievement of bodily and spiritual purity. For only under conditions of absolute purity could the deceased take on the name of Osiris, ruler of the kingdom of the blessed.

"Egyptian temples were devoted to invocation of cosmic essence. In principle, each temple was built on the primal hill that rose from the watery abyss of Nwn., 'the ground of the first day." And practically every object in the Egyptian temple was imbued with cosmic significance: the temple foundations, the ritual statuary, the temple wells and pylons, the sacred pool, and the orientation of the temple itself. For instance, at Abu Simbel, the sun's rays penetrate all the way into the sanctuary on the day of the equinox. Just as remarkably, at Tanis in the Delta, the axis of the temple of Ant is in exact alignment with that of the temple of Amon at Karnak, in Upper Egypt.

LET'S LIBERATE THE TEMPLE

"The entire country, in effect, was criss-crossed with a veritable network of sacred lines. The processional axis of the burial temple of Queen Hatshepsut is at right angles to the Nile bank. Curiously enough, its projection across the river coincides directly with the main axis of the temple of Amon at Karnak. Historically, the worship of Amon, the Secret, Invisible One, like the architecture of the temple of Amon at Karnak, has lasted over 2000 years. Karnak, in Thebes, was a place of high privilege, filled with the presence of divinity." (547)

"The roots of the god Osiris date back to prehistoric times. The god had two basic aspects: fertility and burial rites, death and resurrection. 'I live; I die; I am the barley - I do not perish. For this reason, Osiris was the god of vegetation."

The ancient Egyptian "Holy Family" comprised Osiris, Isis and Horus.

Adolf Erman, *Manual of Egyptian Religion*. London: Archibald Constable and Co., Ltd., 1907 describes the following religious customs of the early period.

1.   Each temple must originally have been dedicated to one single deity who was considered to be the lord, but owing to the natural anxiety to secure the favor of other gods for the city others were added as secondary deities, and in the greater temples their numbers steadily increased in the course of centuries. Two of these, a goddess and a god, were generally regarded as the wife and child of the principal deity. Thus, Ptah of Memphis had Sekhmet for his consort, and Nefertum for his son, and Amon had Mut assigned to him as wife, and the moon god Khons as his child. The goddesses had at least one child: thus, Hathor of Denderah had the boy Ehi, and Buto a god Horus.

2.   The usual abode of the god was his chapel, in the last and most sacred apartment of the temple. This chapel was frequently made out of one single block of hard granite, which surrounded the sacred statue with an impenetrable wall; in front, a bronze framework was inserted and fitted with double doors. The place where this chapel stood, *the*

great place as it was called, was now the spot where the daily ceremonies were conducted.

3. Early in the morning the officiating priest stood in front of the holy of holies and commenced his performance, which in itself might have been completed in half-an-hour, but which must have lasted for hours, as every separate action had to be divided into a number of different actions, and each one of these had to be accompanied by a long speech. Would that there had been in these long speeches some trace of feeling for the sacredness of the place, the majesty of the god; but all personal feeling had long disappeared from the ritual, and it was celebrated in a way that could not well have been more absurd, as though the whole religion in every temple consisted only of the history of Horus and Set, and that of Osiris. When the priest loosened the sealed cord that closed the chapel, he had to say: The cord is broken, and the seal loosened – I come, and I bring to thee the eye of Horus, thine eye belongs to thee, Horus. Further, when he broke the clay of the seal, he said: the clay is loosed, the waters of heaven are opened, the veins of Osiris are stretched out – I do not come to drive away the god from his throne; I come to set the god on his throne. Thou remainest on thy great throne, god N., I have access (?) to the gods – an offering which the king gives – I am pure. He then draws the bolt; the finger of Set is withdrawn from the eye of Horus, that is excellent. The finger of Set is withdrawn from the eye of Horus, that is excellent. I loosen the leather behind the god. Oh god N., take thy two feathers and thy white crown out of the Horus eye, the right eye out of the right eye, the left eye out of the left eye. Thy beauty belongs to thee, oh god N.; thou naked one, clothe thyself... I am a priest, the king himself sends me, that I may behold the god. And now, as the door open, and the god is revealed, the priest says, the gates of heaven open, the gates of earth are undone. Homage (?) was paid to Keb when the gods said to him, 'Thou dwellest upon thy throne.' The gates of heaven are opened, and the nine gods appear radiant, the god N., thou naked one, clothe thyself."

LET'S LIBERATE THE TEMPLE

Liberate the Temple. Dendera Temple of Goddess Hathor. Hathor in horns and sun-disk squats in a Sun-Disk presiding over the land.

Liberate the Temple. Dendera Temple of Goddess Hathor. From a plant, a huge snake emerges and an individual with sistrum helps sandwich the "Great Bird" in the Crypt.

FREDERICK MONDERSON

Liberate the Temple. Dendera Temple of Goddess Hathor. The great snake emanating from the flower is hoisted by hands attached to Osiris' "Tet" or "Backbone" while a Baboon to the right holds two knives.

4. The ceremonies which the priest performed, were in the main the simplest possible. After he had offered incense and had filled the holy of holies with the perfume, he approached the chapel and opened it. He saluted the god with repeated protestations, and with chanting or repetition of hymns. He then took his vessels, which were close at hand in a box, and began the daily toilet of the god. Twice he sprinkled water over the statue from four jars, he clothed it with linen bandages which were white, green, red, and reddish in color, he anointed it with oil, painted it with green and black paint, and completed its toilet in other respects. Finally, he fed the god, by setting before him a variety of food and drink, bread, geese, haunch of beef, wine and water. Flowers also could no more be omitted from an Egyptian table of offerings than they could be from the dining-table of a noble.

LET'S LIBERATE THE TEMPLE

5.   For the official religion as it was accepted in the temples, there existed only the god and the king; he served them, he built their temples, and made offerings to them, and they rewarded *their beloved son* for his pious devotion with *life for millions of years*, with victory over his enemies and everlasting fame. The gods are no longer the gods of the Egyptian people, they are the gods of the Pharaoh *their son*. And this relation of the sovereign to the deities is carried yet farther. If the king built a temple he did it not so much from devotion to the god, as for his own future glorification. *He has made this as his monument*, thus begins every dedicatory inscription from the earliest times, and then follows the name of the temple which the king has built to the god *his father*.... It is a natural result of this idea that the temple scenes give the impression that the priests are not present, but that the king takes their place. On all the walls, the offerings and ceremonies are represented as they were performed before the god, but it is always the king who is officiating. Although we can understand that the king on some special occasion may have occasionally exercised priestly functions, yet that he should have taken part in the ceremonies of the countless temples of his dominions can only have been a theoretically possibility. The actual performers at the Egyptian ceremonies must have been the priests, even though they represented themselves in the rituals as merely the delegates of the king.

6.   Certain priestly orders are connected with certain professions. Thus, the high judicial functionaries of the Old Kingdom are at the same time priests of the goddess of truth, they physicians are priests of Sekhmet, the great artists are priests of Ptah.

7.   At the head of every temple was a high priest who acted as *overseer of all the sacred offices*, he is *initiated into divine books and divine thing* and *gives directions to the priests as regulating* the festivals. He has *a loud voice when he praises the god* and *a pure hand when he brings flowers and offers water and food upon the altar*. The administration of the temple properly is incumbent on him, and in war he has also to command the contingent provided by his temple. In the great sanctuaries, these high-priests frequently bore special antiquated titles. Thus, at Heliopolis the high-priest was called *He who is great in beholding*, perhaps because he could behold at

pleasure *the beauty of his lord*, i.e. the statue of the god; while at Eshmunen he was *great of the five*. At Memphis, where Ptah the god of artificers was worshipped, the title of the high-priest was the chief of the artificers, and in the Old Kingdom he held the position of superintendent of sculpture and all such artistic work; it appears that originally this combination of spiritual and worldly offices was shared by two persons, but towards the end of the Old Kingdom the king transferred every divine affair, and every duty that was in charge of the two high-priests, to Teti-Sabu, because his majesty trusted him especially.

8. These "priests" (literally divine servants) were not all of the same class. There was the *Kherheb*, whose duty appears to have been to read the ancient rituals at the ceremonies, and whose second title, *scribe of the divine books*, designates them clearly as learned students of the ancient sacred literature. What were the original functions of the so-called *we'b* priests is shown by the name, which is derived from the word for "pure;" we find them in sacrificial scenes, after examining the blood of the animal, declaring that it is *pure*. Other priestly titles which are frequently mentioned, such as that of the *divine fathers*, offers no explanation of their meaning.... for the greater number of these clerics the priesthood was only a subsidiary occupation; they formed the *hourly priesthood* of the temple, or as we may perhaps express it, alternating priests, who were divided into four sets, and alternately relieved each other in their duties.... Papyri ... in Berlin ... inform us that in addition to eight minor officials the permanent staff of the temple consisted only of the *prince and superintendent of the temple* (i.e. the high-priest) and the *chief Kherheb*, who were thus the administrators of the temple property and the directors of the ceremonies; nine other priests took regular turns there; a *superintendent of classes, a temple scribe,* and ordinary *Kherheb*, etc., and each time one of these classes entered on their duties, they took over the sanctuary and all its contents from the outgoing class, and relieved them of their charge.

LET'S LIBERATE THE TEMPLE

Liberate the Temple. Dendera Temple of Goddess Hathor. In the Crypt, with Seshat (left) and Isis enthroned (right) a large vessel emanates positive rays to Hathor Symbols of Sistrums above a huge necklace. Notice the boat that supports the two right sistrum columns.

Liberate the Temple. Dendera Temple of Goddess Hathor. Goddess Nuit, in her own Kiosk with Court, gives birth to the Sun in the morning and swallows it at evening time.

FREDERICK MONDERSON

Liberate the Temple. Dendera Temple of Goddess Hathor. How unfortunate. Hathor of all dignitaries in Egyptian history has suffered the most because "She looks so Nubian."

Liberate the Temple. Karnak Temple. In the rear, Nasser, utility man and friend.

LET'S LIBERATE THE TEMPLE

Liberate the Temple. Karnak Temple. Chief of Temple Security Handaka and Abdul, Brother Abdul's son, stand with ruins of the Hypostyle Hall and the Obelisks of Thutmose I (left) and his daughter Hatshepsut (right) in the rear.

FREDERICK MONDERSON

XXV. CONCLUSIONS

The intent of **Let's Liberate the Temple – A Dr. Ben-Jochannan Admonition** is that of one student-scholar's attempt to pay tribute to a great scholar, teacher, historian and humanitarian who was uncompromising in defense of the moral and intellectual capabilities of African people, irrespective where they belong on planet earth. In that earthly journey in which Dr. Yosef A. A. Ben-Jochannan challenged the oppression of African people fostered in sub-standard educational practices within and in non-colonial settings, distortion of the historical record and systematic omission of significant facts pertinent to the moral, psychological, social and spiritual even mental well-being of African people and their capabilities, many young minds were inspired and in process themselves became lights in the constellation of intellect Dr. Ben had created.

By the time of the turbulent world upheavals of Mid-20th Century, Dr. Ben-Jochannan had discovered Marcus Garvey and Duse Mohammed and they led him to further discover the wonders of the ancient Nile Valley culture that manifested so wonderfully-well through Ethiopia, Nubia, and finally Egypt, Kemet. So much so, by 1989, Dr. Ben had been conducting tours of Egypt for 50-years and exposing and enlightening those adventurous souls to the educational wonders of the temple.

LET'S LIBERATE THE TEMPLE

Liberate the Temple. Karnak Temple. Abdul and Dr. Fred Monderson with the ruins of the Hypostyle Hall and Thutmose I's Obelisk in rear.

Along the path of that wonderful journey of intellectual exploration, Dr. Ben further discovered and essentially preached African religion as a potent spiritual and social exhilir particularly as expressed in the temple in which cosmic consciousness sought to imbue human aspirations with a tenacity to be inventive and tremendously creative in manifold fields of intellectual pursuit and expression. And so, in the Egyptian temple Dr. Ben-Jochannan found, in addition to theology and spiritual sustenance, science, medicine, astronomy, and most particularly art and architecture. Like a prospector discovering a wonderful nugget or a classical diamond, Dr. Ben-Jochannan made that quintessential connection realizing divinity's intent to elevate human intellectual to function on a godly plane guided by the philosophic admonition of Ma'at that manifests in practices of justice, truth, righteousness and most important in moral and spiritual purity manifesting in thought and action, particularly when persons seek the solace of the temple.

FREDERICK MONDERSON

Yet, in that quest, Dr. Ben recognized the totality of the temple. He found the sum of its constituent parts and elements greater than the w hole. Therein he realized, the temple is essentially a divine construction designed to imbue cosmic consciousness in man to elevate his psychic being to higher realms of understanding, creativity and in process more humanistic.

In his traversing the Nile Valley from Abu Simbel, through Kom Ombo, Esneh, Edfu, Deir el Bahari, Karnak and Luxor, Ramesseum, and Medinet Habu, as well as Abydos and Dendera temples, the good doctor was painstaking in explaining the principal features of the temple, their meaning and in many respects was effective in enlightening his students. Consistent with this undertaking, he taught, wrote and self-published adhering to the philosophic admonition, "Publish or Perish." In those scholarly efforts he was strict, stern and laid down rules of conduct, temple behavior and dress while encouraging those who could visit the monuments to prepare well for the adventurous experience.

Seeking to determine which of the holy sites appealed more to him, those who were particularly familiar with his likes and dislikes seem to know he loved Abu Simbel, Deir el Bahari, Luxor but more especially Karnak Temple. As such, Karnak Temple could be considered his favorite and particularly its Hypostyle Hall. To fully appreciate the totality of that architectural wonder, he admonished, "Don't talk to me until you have visited Karnak's Hypostyle Hall 5 or 6 times."

Notwithstanding and in reflection, from the time Dr. Ben-Jochannan stepped through Karnak Temple's First Pylon and into the Great Court, the light of his majesty lit-up as he began pointing out the Theban Triad's Kiosk, the Temple of Rameses III, the North and South Colonnades with Sphinxes before them, altars in the Court, even the Taharka Column as surviving from his Kiosk. Next it was the Second Pylon, Hypostyle Hall, Thutmose I and Hatshepsut's obelisks, the Sacred Lake, the Sacred Scarab, and even the "Coca Cola temple." Dr. Ben, a "master of Karnak," enamored Brother Abdul who spent some 50 years in the temple and could offer greeting in a

LET'S LIBERATE THE TEMPLE

multitude of languages. More importantly, however, Brother Abdul "loved Nubian-Americans." He was saddened and expressed this over the devastation of Hurricane Katrina! Dr. Ben's associate, Professor George Simmonds, another "Master of Karnak" was an effective master teacher, a cultivator of intellect, patient, instructive and a great defender of the temple. He praised African people as originators and beneficiaries of the temple as a dynamo creating and generating knowledge that advanced the consciousness and intellectuality of humanity. As such, he demanded African people get credit for and share in the benefits the wonderful Nile Valley legacy bequeathed y "Mother Africa."

Liberate the Temple. Gathering of Friends at Luxor.
Ibrahim Soliman, Showki Abd Rady and the Driver.

Thus, this and more **Let's Liberate the Temple - A Dr. Ben-Jochannan Admonition** seeks to shine some light on in the process of mental and spiritual liberation as well as benefitting for the tremendous reservoir of knowledge the Black man created in Egypt. Continuing the education of all people in search of truth, exposing falsity, correcting distortions and including omissions, this work seeks to serve as a point of enlightening departure. Its aim is to

FREDERICK MONDERSON

help young scholars traveling the road towards intellectual autonomy seeking to develop problem solving skills and the benefits from being armed with a sound education.

Liberate the Temple. Medinet Habu Mortuary Temple of Rameses III. Egyptian Guide Showki Abd Rady points to seated statue of Goddess Sekhmet at the temple's entrance.

All the while, as both Dr. Ben and Professor Simmonds encouraged students to never forget as it relates to the Temple in Egypt, always remember as Dr. Leonard James has forever insisted, "The existential data contradicts the symbolic representation."

LET'S LIBERATE THE TEMPLE

THE TEMPLE OF KARNAK is oriented east to west and north to south

O, mighty Temple, Hatshepsut affirmed 'Karnak is the horizon on earth, the august ascent of the beginning, the sacred eye of the All-Lord, the place of his heart, which bears his beauty, and encompasses those who follow him.' Everlasting, you are a great dwelling of myriad years that is Shining like the horizon of heaven and established as an eternal work. Like the heavens, abiding upon their four pillars as a monument, great, excellent and useful for the Lord of Eternity, you are a favorite place of the Lord of the Gods, Amon and his consort, Amonauet. One whose hands are many, Suspender of the sky, you're the living lamp which rises out of the Ocean of Heaven, to support all things, for the Master of the Apts, the Beloved One!

Stela reveal New Empire furniture and utensils restored by Ahmose with gifts of gold rosettes, lapis lazuli, vases of silver, malachite, and vessels for the Ka. Jars with ointment, ebony, gold and silver houses, granaries, and gardens, all given when he established Amon, father of the gods, as Lord of Heaven. From the beginning, this House of Amon, Throne of Keb, with the serpent-diadem, is proclaimed the horizon on earth and horizon of heaven. It is the Throne of Horus before the Splendors of the Great House, whom the Great Ennead of gods has brought up to be Mistress of the Circuit of the Sun. This is the Splendid Place in which Amon loves to be, flourishing and established, with dark complexion, as ithyphallic Min, strong in his might.

At your City of the All-God, in the resplendent ascent from the Quay, two small Obelisks and Avenue of Ram-Headed Sphinxes stand before the Ethiopian Pylon, built during the XXVth dynasty, in Praise of the Beloved of the South and North. At the entrance into the Open Court, French Savants chronicled the dimensions of your revered Enclosure standing as a Seat of Truth, emblem of Ma'at. The Great Court centrally houses the surviving column of the colonnaded Kiosk of Taharka. The Shrine of Seti II abuts the Pylon's inner face at the west of the Northern Colonnade, while the Temple of Rameses III to

FREDERICK MONDERSON

the Southeast is east of the Southern Colonnade. Sheshonk's sculptures are nearby, in this place of the Lord of Truth, *Ipit Isut*, great in glory.

The statue of Rameses II, usurped by Pinudjen, and gateway to the Open-Air Museum, are also majestic features of your Court. Southwest and Southeast, mounds and unfinished columns, provide evidence of colonnade and pylon construction techniques evolved in your expansion. Within your holy seat, all foundation ceremonies began the day of the Feast of the New Moon. A later Sphinx and Altar in this Court celebrate first entrance into your sacred precinct, with its trapezoidal mud-brick enclosure wall, where Amon is Lord of Thebes. As Lord of all Gods, he commanded and all the gods came into being, and they fall down awe struck at his feet when they recognize His Majesty their Lord, Great One of Souls, Mighty One of Victory, his love brings the Nile.

Let's Liberate the Temple. Karnak Temple of God Amon. Hypostyle Hall. A center north-south aisle showing decorated columns.

LET'S LIBERATE THE TEMPLE

Further in older the temple, thus, as Amon looks out, not second but Fifth Pylon of Rameses II enclose the Hypostyle Hall to the West. It is a splendid and majestic philosophic expression of Kemetic/Egyptian architecture. Its manifestation further indicates structures of theological, philosophic, cosmological, epistemological, and scientific foundations of learning. How profound, Ben-Jochannan recommends six visits to comprehend this primeval forest of 12 Processional and 122 flanking columns, where Amon-Ra is King of the Gods. This Lord of Wisdom, Lord of Mercy, Lord of Magnanimity, is strong in apparel, of Beautiful face, coming from the Nubians. He is Ra, whose word is Truth, and whose rulings Thebes loves.

Sacred enclosure, Amenhotep III built your Processional Colonnade and Horemheb conceived the Great Hall. Begun by Rameses I, built by Seti I of fine sandstone and decorated by Rameses II, the walls portray Amen and other gods, worshiped in mysterious splendor. He sits on the Horus Throne of the All King, like Ra, forever established and Karnak is content. Seti's sculptures are to the north and Rameses' to the south, in this domain. Here Amon the Beautiful Bull, Creator of Everlastingness, Giver of Life is living in Truth, Forever in this beautiful divine resting-place. Mysterious Lion, a Bull for his City, a Lion for his People, the Bright God, excellent of counsel, he is the Good Protector in every truth.

Lord of Praises, the modern third, ancient fourth, Pylon of Amenhotep III, the "magnificent," enclose the central court. The fourth and fifth or second and third ancient pylons of Thutmose I enclose the first colonnade. Thutmose I, Horus Mighty Bull, Beloved of Truth, Shining-in-Beauty, in his petition for the God to recognize Hatshepsut's kingship as he had his, erected two pairs of Granite Obelisks for Amon Presider of Karnak, who is Lord of Eternity, Lord of Heaven, Ruler of the Gods, Ruler of Thebes. Amon, the Bull of godly countenance, darling in Karnak, Chief of the Great Ennead is the Judge of Horus and Seth in the Great Hall.

Splendid dwelling, your second colonnade abuts Thutmose III's sixth or first Pylon enclosing the Hall of Records listing his 17 campaigns.

FREDERICK MONDERSON

All stand on hollow ground, before the divinity with lofty plumes who looks out from his Sanctuary or Holy of Holies, and whose hidden shrine is the repose of the Lord of the Gods. There is divine presence in the great seat and Amon, resting upon his great throne, is enduring in his temple forever and ever. Chief of the Great Ennead of the Gods, sustainer of all things, maker of things below and above, he is Lord of Wisdom, Lord of Mercy, Treasurer of the Celestial Heights, Lord of Gods who lives on truth.

Beyond this "Throne of Thunder," the Middle Kingdom court esplanades the Akh Menu, Festival Hall of Thutmose III. To Paris Prisse de Avennes removed the Karnak Tablet from its revered Hall of Ancestors. Thutmose III built this temple at Karnak for his father Thutmose I, and as a monument to the kings of his fathers. In the rear a Temple of Rameses II faces the eastern gate. All this, in the name of the sole one with many hands, Maker of Beams, Maker of Light, whose adherents in oath swore, 'If Amon permits me to live.' Shield of the Bowmen and owner of all ships, Lord of the Highlands and Mountains, Chief Creator of Everything on Earth his disputations are greater than those of every God. Great of strength, there is none other that is like him.

Divine House, your eastern expansion at a limit, Thutmose III conceived the Seventh Pylon initiating the north/south axis that entrance the first or "Cachette court" with its rich hoard. To the east, Taharqa's Temple stands facing Hatshepsut's fallen obelisk. A summit in Cairo, another completely disappeared, her standing obelisk, the last of two pairs, with that of Thutmose I, are towering sites in the surrounding area. Senmut, Prophet and Steward of Amon, Queen's architect, erected his majesty's obelisks of red Aswan granite, with pyramidioms of electrum to radiantly illuminate the sands, like the Sun Disk of the Good God, Calf of the Heavenly Cow. The dweller in heaven, Amon whose name is hidden from the gods is a sweet breeze to him that calls upon him who preserves the weary.

August Abode, the Sacred Scarab of Amenhotep III rests near your Sacred Lake, where sacred barks floated at festive time, and priests washed as admonished 'let everyone who enters here be pure.' In the

LET'S LIBERATE THE TEMPLE

southwest corner of your enclosure, an east/west Ptolemaic Opet Temple perpendicularly abuts Rameses III's north/south Temple of Khonsu. On this axis, Hatshepsut built the Eight Pylon, enclosing the Second Court, while Horemheb built the Ninth and Tenth Pylons creating Third and Fourth Courts. In this last Court, the Heb-Sed Festival Temple of Amenhotep II celebrates the Beautiful Countenance of the God, the Only One who has no second, Father of the Father of the Gods. Your revered master is the dweller in the Horizon, Horus, Lord of him that is silent and gods obey His Majesty and extol the might of their creator.

Light of the World, beyond the Tenth Pylon, an Avenue of Sphinxes connected the Temple of Mut with its Sacred Lake and resplendent flower gardens. Temples of Khonsu Pa-Khered and Rameses III were in this enclosure. Nearby were Bark Stations of Thutmose III and Hatshepsut, and Sanctuary of Amen-Kamutef and Temple of Nectanebo II. North of your main axis is the Chapel of Osiris Hekadjet, Temple of Ptah, Temple of Thutmose, and beyond the Precinct of the War God Montu. A nearby Tomb of Osiris, together with exquisite gardens, all rest within your sacred abode of the Theban Triad Khonsu, Mut and Amon, most mighty of the Gods.

Mighty Karnak, Mountains yield stone to make your gateway great. People of Punt bring Perfume to make festive Amon's temple. Your Lord of All is a glaring lion with raging claws and a bull, firm of back and heavy of hoofs upon the neck of his foe. He is a bird of prey, flying high and seizing on him that assail him. The mountains are moved beneath him at the time of his terror.

Creator of Heaven, eldest of earth, Lord of what exists, Amon, the Double Crown is established on your head. Your Love passes throughout Egypt/Kemet when you send out light and rise with your two beautiful eyes. Your beauty seizes Upon Hearts. Your Loveliness makes arms weak.
Your beautiful operations make the arms Weak and hearts become weak at the sight of you, Great Hawk, making the body Festal. Sole One and Only with many hands, while men sleep good herdsman, you find fodder for your creatures. Jubilation and reverence to you for you created and care for mankind.

FREDERICK MONDERSON

Praise is given in the Great House, Ipit Isut palace where the fashioner of all gods and Ennead dwells, alongside the Lord of Earth, Sole King among the Gods. Karnak, you espoused thoughts and philosophical paradigms of Black African creativity in knowledge, enlightenment and inspiration. These principles issued forth from you are all part of Africa's gifts to the world in arts and architecture and metaphysics, theosophy, and religiosity. Beacon of Light, inspiration and hope; continue to radiate your blessings of health, prosperity, stability and purposeful vision to African families, men, women and children, who strive to make the world more loving and humane for humanity.

The TEMPLE OF LUXOR is oriented north to south

Amenhotep III, Mighty Bull, Shining in Truth, erected the Temple of Luxor for his father, Amen-Ra, Lord of Diadems. This Southern Isut, resting on three axes and made of fine white sandstone with walls of electrum and floor of Silver, is a favorite and joyous place for the Sovereign of Life, Health, Strength and Dominion. Amon, the Beautiful Bull of the Cycle of the Gods and Lord of the Upper and Lower World, the Ancient of Heaven, Chief Creator of the Whole Earth, and Lord of All Existence, left his Throne of Thunder, Karnak. Amid exuberant fanfare the Lord of Crown High Plumes, Lord of Adoration, journeyed to the Southern Isut for the Opet Festival of joy and festivity. Amon is the Sole and Only One, the Heliopolitan presiding in his Harim.

The Most Glorious One, Lord of Eternity, Mighty Lover of Power, whose alter ego is Ithyphallic Min, is satisfied with his son who is vigilant to seek that which is useful. Amenhotep, the Golden Horus, Great in Strength, Good God, Ruler of Thebes, is Lord of Strength and Mighty of Valor. This magnificent monarch praised the Maker of All Beings, Giver of Life and Doer of Justice. Amon, Bull, Beautiful Face, Creator of animals, worshiped here is Lord of Divine Grain.

LET'S LIBERATE THE TEMPLE

Even the Gods bow themselves before the majesty of Amon and extol their creator. They exult when they approach him who begat them. Master of the Land of the South, these gods Love his savor when he comes forth from Punt, being rich in sweet scents returning from the land of the Matoi.

Let's Liberate the Temple. Luxor Temple of Amenhotep III and Rameses II. The Great Processional Colonnade of Amenhotep with 14 massive columns; 12 at Karnak.

The Lord of Life, Prince of the Dew, Judge of the Combatants in the Great Hall, Beloved One of the Apts is pleased with his house of life. Indeed, a majestic view that reminds of a splendid age is Luxor Temple in the approach from Karnak to the north. In the Court of Nectanebo stand obelisks with hieroglyphic inscriptions and seated and standing statues of Rameses II. Some say vainglorious, others the "great" Rameses inscribed the Battle of Kadesh on the exterior of your First Pylon. In profound symbolist significance, the struggles between Good and Evil, Light and Darkness, instructs entrants into your Sanctuary, conquer the inner self before entering the holy place where the gods adore Amon's majesty, for he is living in truth every day.

FREDERICK MONDERSON

The Ramessean Front, oriented towards Karnak, rests on a subsidiary axis. It is different from the secondary Processional Colonnade, and principal axis of your original temple. Rameses' recognition is that Amon's Beauty Captivates the Heart. He is the Form One, Creator of everything that is, Only One, Creator of things that shall be. Men and women proceed from his two eyes. As Khephera in his boat who give the order, the gods came into being and these Gods say 'Welcome in Peace!' This great aged one, perception is his heart and command is his lips. His soul is Shu and his heart is Tefnut. His right eye is the day, his left eye the night and fate and the harvest god are with him for all people.

Entrancing the Pylon into your Great Court, visitors encounter a double inward colonnaded peristyle. To the right, Hatshepsut's shrine to the Theban Triad, Amon, Mut and Khonsu, was usurped by Thutmose III. To the left, rests the Mosque of Abu el-Haggag, Arab Saint of Luxor. Inward to the left, striding statues of Rameses stand between the columns. Inward to the right, statues of Rameses the 'Sun of the Rulers.' Nearby the southwest wall, anciently depicts the 'Plan of Luxor Temple' showing Rameses' sons and priests with fat cows in procession thereto. Here is worshiped Chief of the Apts, Lord of the Uret Crown, with Lofty Plumes, whose diadems of beautiful White Crown is high.

Beyond this Court, stands the Processional Colonnade of Amenhotep III, architectural splendor of Kemet. It is a fitting testament to the Lord of the Evening and Morning Barks, the Resplendent One in the House of Ben-Ben, who traverses the heavens in peace. Decorated by Tutankhamon in that mighty Amonian restoration, the Western Wall on your Processional Colonnade depicts the Opet Voyage to Luxor. The Eastern Wall equally recounts the return to Karnak, where drama, solemnity, fanfare, frolic and feast are vividly portrayed. The Sovereign on his Throne loved and revered, reigns high as in the heavens, broad as in the earth, deep as in the sea. 'Glory to Thee' says every wild creature; 'Praise to Thee' says every desert.

LET'S LIBERATE THE TEMPLE

Awe and reverence is offered for the Lord of Terror, Creator of Existences, who made mankind and created the beasts. It is he who makes pastures for the herds and fruit trees for men, who creates that whereby the fish live in the river and the birds under the heavens. As Lord of the Gods, the Nile comes at his will. He is the sweet, well loved, maker of the herbage that sustains all cattle, and gives warmth, life to all beautiful beasts. He is the creator of pasturage wherein herbs and flocks live and the staff of life for mankind. He makes live the fish in the river and the geese and feathered fowl of the sky, and when he comes mankind lives. He is the Lord of Grain who makes sustenance for the wild beast of the wilderness.

Your Court of Amenhotep highlights the original temple that challenges description, a testament to the magnificence of its builder and Greater Glory of the Lord of Sacrifices, the Bull of Offerings. Here, a Double row of eleven east and west columns stand perpendicular to a double row of eight split by a Central Aisle. In praise of the God with many names without number, atop a base, papyrus columns with triple bands and closed buds support abacus and architrave. Play of light and shade fascinates photographers who flock here, to imagine your aura amidst Amon's approval. He is the hawk-divine with outstretched wings, speedy one who carries away his assailant in the completion of an instant.

A majestic Hypostyle Hall, with four rows of 8 columns, is split by the Central Axis. Original and later Bark Sanctuaries for Khons and Bark Sanctuary for Mut surround a smaller Inner Hypostyle Hall, that occupying Roman legions modified as their chapel, recognizing that men issued from Amon's eyes and from his mouth gods came into being. These gods rejoice over the beauty of the Lord of Joy, Mighty in his Appearances.

In majesty, a Hall of 4 columns stand before, while 3 compartments with 3 columns each, front private apartments that enclose your Sanctuary for the Bark of Amon. To the rear rests the Sanctuary of Amenhotep III with two rows of 6 columns. A smaller room with 4 columns and 2 rooms with 2 columns each comprise the inner compartments giving service to Amon as Min in this Southern Harim. What a wonderful testament to the Lord of Lords who fashioned

FREDERICK MONDERSON

Himself, whose name is high and mighty and powerful. There is none that was made without him, the Great God, the Life of the Ennead.

Today as the modern town surrounds Luxor from the northwest, in the play of afternoon sunshade, a spectacular view is afforded from the northwest beyond the gates. O Great Grand Lodge, fount of knowledge and inspiration, radiate as of old when and where Africans imbibed, instructed and enlightened the world. Continue that ancient reverence, strengthen and protect your people that they may do good in the world to improve the lot of humanity.

ABYDOS TEMPLE OF SETI I

Abydos, home of Osiris, son of Nut and Seb, you remain one of the more memorable and religious sites of ancient Kemet. While favors of other gods rose and fell according to dynasties, Osiris worship endured and you Abydos boasted prominence in ten temples, for many millennia. Some say 15,000 B.C. or earlier, people of an African origin settled Abydos. Through Old, Middle and New Kingdoms, Ethiopian, Greek and Roman rule, your sacred city remained inspirational, awesome and divinely mysterious. Praises are sung in the southern heaven and adoration performed in the northern heaven, O One of Mysterious Forms in the Temples. Shu inspired fear of your august divinity Osiris Unnefer, and Tefnut created reverence for him.

Your godly master is father and mother of mankind, and Lord of Lords. Osiris' emblems included the mummy with curved beard, and he wore the white, *Atef* and *Ureret* Crowns, with scepter, whip, disk, horns, uraei, menat and sacred symbol. The **Djed Pillar** or backbone is the Power and Stability of the Lord of Heaven, of Holy Transformations, Lord of Life and Lord of the Two Horns, whose skin is of pure electrum. Worshiped in your sacred mansion, he is the Lordly Noble at the head of the nobles, with enduring office and established rule. He is the Goodly mighty one of the Nine Gods on whom men love to look. The north wind sprang from him, his seats

LET'S LIBERATE THE TEMPLE

were the stars of heaven that never set and the imperishable stars his ministers.

O, Osiris ithyphallic, coming forth from the body of Nut, you are the moon in heaven, Soul of Re. You rejuvenate yourself at your desire becoming young according to your wish and appear in order to dispel darkness. Anointed one, magic comes into existence to illuminate your majesty and bring your enemies to shambles. You are the Nile, great upon its banks at time of the beginning of the season, when man and gods live by the moisture that comes from you. Lord of Eternity, Seti built you a house like the heavens, an august adytum whose beauty illuminated the two lands. Lord of Praises, Lord of Maati, your seat is established into the land of holiness. You are remembered in heaven and earth and to you shouts of joy are raised at the Wag festival.

Among the Glorified, Osiris, Lord of Abydos, Prince of Eternity crowned King of Upper and Lower Egypt, you are from a distinguished lineage of rulers including predecessor Keb, then Seth, Thoth, and Maat. Holy God, you shone forth on the throne of your father as the sun when he rose on the horizon, when he sheds light on those in darkness. God of Vegetation you taught mankind the art and virtues of agriculture and established truth in Kemet when you overthrew your enemies and slew the powerful foes. Fear of you was widespread when, Lord of Rosta, Lord of Tazoser, King of the gods you enlarged the boundaries of your kingdom.

King of Kings, like the sun at dawn of day, you illumined and flooded the two lands, while your crown cleft the sky and consorted with the stars. All heaven was your domain and the doors of the sky opened before you of their own accord when you appeared, Lord commemorated in the town of Maati.

FREDERICK MONDERSON

Let's Liberate the Temple. Abydos Temple of Seti I.
An Inner Chamber of Osiris with smooth undecorated columns.

LET'S LIBERATE THE TEMPLE

The Legend of Osiris recounts your birth, life, marriage, kingship and murder of the Bull of Amentet. Tricked by your brother Seth, the great mighty one residing in Thinis was killed and his body dumped into the Nile River. Isis, your faithful wife, sister and adviser provided you safeguard and warded off enemies. She was subtle, with an excellent tongue, her word did not fail, and she was admirable in command. She sought you without wearying. The Glorious Master's dismembered parts were scattered throughout the land with the head at Abydos and heart at Philae. Full of mourning she traversed the land and took no rest until she found you. At the revivification of Osiris, Isis produced your son Horus.

First of the dwellers in the west, Beloved of his Father, Wennofre, blessed one promised hope and salvation to mankind. Unnefer, True of Voice, Great God of the dead, gods and men turn their faces towards him. Kings and men flocked to your court to establish endowments, erect stelae, and ascend the Staircase of the Great God. 'Welcome' was spoken by the Great Ones of Abydos who once ruled Kemet. The deceased were declared 'true of speech' and then received a place in the ship of the God. Even as Osiris Lord of the Tombs lives, they will also live, even as Osiris is not dead they also will not die, even as Osiris is not disposed, they also will not be destroyed. They will sojourn in the Field of Yaru to cultivate and raise grain twelve feet high.

Ceremonies to represent the Resurrection of Osiris were celebrated at Abydos, Philae and Dendera. In this Justification of Osiris, men journeyed to Abtu to learn to know the things of Osiris, Creator of Gods. Perhaps because the head was located there, the nature of Osiris remains more secret than all the gods. King of the dead, Chief of Abtu, who issued forth from Ra himself, is leader of every god with excellent laws. This palace at Abydos is a door of the dwellers in the netherworld, a Glorious Seat of Eternity, for the Ruler of the West, Lord of Souls.
The Great Ennead praised him and the Lesser Ennead loved him, while the firmament and its stars harken unto him and the Great Portals open to him.

FREDERICK MONDERSON

On entering this blessed enclosure of the mortuary temple of Seti I, completed by Rameses II, who put his name in many places, forty-two steps lead past the now destroyed First Pylon, causeway and First Court into the Second Court. Off to the left a hall with 10 columns stands central to magazines for storage. Two vestibules with single columns and an altar and single colonnade with 12 pillars depicting Rameses II lead into the Central Court of the Beautiful God, Lord of the World, incorruptible and immortal. Leader of every god, those in the underworld till the ground, those in the necropolis make an abeyance and the lands praise the approach of his majesty.

At this Throne of Osiris, House of Gold, Nomes of Kemet are represented on its doors. Twelve pillars front seven doors leading into the First Hypostyle Hall, all except the center closed by Rameses II. Pillared reliefs depict Rameses embraced by principal gods of Egypt. The King is beside a Sacred Tree while Ptah writes his name on its leaves and Thoth records his years. Hamarchis gives him the Crook and Osiris stands beside him. A double-row of 12 columns adorns this First Hypostyle Hall. Here the King is seen in several attitudes, burning incense, kneeling, giving gifts to the Gods, who offer power, life, stability, or purify him to illustrate his divine connection and origin. He breaks ground in the temple's foundation ceremony.

In the Second Hypostyle hall on two levels, three rows of 12 columns each split by inclined walkways lead to the Seven Sanctuaries of the temple's deities. Horus, Isis, Osiris, Amen-Ra, Horakhte, Ptah and deified Seti I are worshipped right to left. The right side is devoted to the Osiris Triad. The center and left to the three great state Gods of Thebes, Heliopolis, Memphis and the dead monarch. A beautiful expression for Osiris the great mighty one of heaven, king of them that are in the realm of the dead. Thousands praise him in Babylon, and men are in jubilation over him in Heliopolis.

The Osiris Sanctuary gives access to a western hall, or Inner Sanctuary of Osiris with 10 columns. Connected to the left, a Second Inner Sanctuary of Osiris, God of Truth and Life, Lord of Creation, has 4 columns. A Divine Palace in the place his heart loves, a glorious seat, excellent for giving jubilees to the king, is beautiful, pure, flourishing

LET'S LIBERATE THE TEMPLE

and excellent. North west of the Second Colonnade of the Second Hypostyle access gives the Hall of Ptah-Seker, with 3 columns and beyond Sanctuaries of Ptah-Sokar and Nefertum. Southwest of the Second Colonnade, is the Gallery of Kings with the Abydos Tablet, whose dead kings are called Osiris, servants of the Lord of Offerings, Governor of Amentet, the Glorious Master.

North of the Gallery of Kings, a Corridor leads to the Osireion beyond the temple, where the Book of Gates and Book of the Dead survive. Juxtaposed to the Gallery of Kings lies the Sanctuary of the Boats, with 4 columns. Further west along the Gallery, the Hall of Sacrifice with 8 columns, connects 4 rooms with 4, 2, 2 and 1 columns each. In this house of eternal worship, the most Chiefest of the Gods reside. He is firm of heart when he trods down the foemen because of reverence for him Atum fashioned in the hearts of men and gods and put the fear of him in all lands.

This august place, the City of Right and Truth, Endowed with Divine Rank and Dignity, is a splendid seat where resides the Ruler of Eternity, whose Soul is Existing for Vigilance as Lord of Everlastingness. Author of Invocations in the Region of the Tree Ner, Master of Invocations in Ant, whose name is Stable in Men's Mouth, he has promised everlasting life and illumination to all humanity, what a wonderful gift of Africans to the world!

RAMESSEUM – Temple of Rameses II

O mighty and picturesque architectural masterpiece, wonderful creation of lordly User-Maat-Ra While the ancient Greeks misnomered the Memnonium or Ozymandias, Diodorus Siculus described your beauty and Champollion christened the Ramesseum.
In ruin your beauty is awesome, in use spectacularly divine as befitting the august Amon-Ra to whom it was dedicated. Evidence indicates the priestly class was educated within your precinct where important mathematical rolls were discovered.

Your First Pylon entrance and inner face are now destroyed.

FREDERICK MONDERSON

Let's Liberate the Temple. Ramesseum Temple of Rameses II. Native Egyptian Guide Showki Abd Rady stands beside the broken statue of the king before the Osiride figures backed by square pillars.

FIRST COURT

The First Court with two current entrances is at the East Side of the south side of the temple, with another at the West Side of the same area.

The monarch has splendidly recounted, on your walls, events of the Battle of Kadesh fought around 1388 B.C.

The king's bravery, the Hittite despair and the satisfactory conclusion is retold throughout the land, viz., Luxor, Karnak, Abu Simbel, Beit Wali and so on.

Far end on the North Pylon, eighteen towns are shown captured by the king in the eighth year of his reign.

Among the fourteen now remaining, Jerusalem, Damascus, Askelon, Beth-Anath, and Meron are numbered.

LET'S LIBERATE THE TEMPLE

In the Pylon's center, the Egyptian camp is pictured with a wall of shields, wicker doorway and groups of sentries.
Features as chariots, baggage-wagons, soldiers talking and fencing, and the sudden attack of the Hittites are shown.
Next Rameses is shown to the right taking council from his generals. On the South Pylon, the king escapes in his chariot, drives the enemy before him, the charioteers behind while he grasps his enemies by the hair and slays them.

THE SECOND COURT

Two seated colossal stood on the right and left of the Second Court. From a single piece of granite quarried at Aswan, they each stood mightily.
Weigall gives measurements of: "57 or 58 feet in height; the length of the ear is 3 ½ feet; the breadth of the face from ear to ear is 6 ¾ feet; the breadth of the foot across the toes is 4 ½ feet; and the area of the nail upon the middle finger is about 35 square inches."

On the partial remaining front wall, a row of Osirian figures stood against square pillars of which only four now remain.
Bases of double rows of columns are all that remain at the north and south side of the court.
The court's west side was formed by a gallery or terrace. The roof was supported by a row of Osiride statues and a row of columns, of which only few remain.
West face of the front wall, from the Battle of Kadesh, Rameses races his chariot through those of his enemies.

He chases the enemy into the Orontes River, along with the King of Aleppo, who seems to be drowning.
The City of Kadesh remains in Hittite hands on the Orontes River.
Above, on the wall, the Procession of the Festival of Min is shown.
At the west-end, three flights of stairs lead to a raised terrace with Osiride pillars, and behind them the king enjoys the company of the gods.

FREDERICK MONDERSON

East face of the wall, on the right, Rameses kneels before seated deities Amen-Ra, Mut and Khonsu.
Thoth writes his name in the tree of life granting immortality.
On the left, the Theban war god Monthu and Thum lead him to Amen-Ra, while below his many sons are represented.

GREAT HYPOSTYLE HALL

Forty-eight columns supported the roof of this Great Hypostyle Hall. The graceful Processional Columns have calyx capitals and are well preserved. The Clerestory created, allowed light to enter the Hall.
Inside the entrance hall, the siege and capture of a Syrian town, Dapur is illustrated.
On the rear wall, Rameses II receives scepters of rulership from Amen-Ra, accompanied by Mut.
A Procession similar as at Luxor Temple, shows the king's sons in attendance.
Right of the doorway, Rameses II receives the ankh symbol of life from a seated Amen-Ra. Behind the god stands Khonsu. Behind the king stands Sekhmet. Below another procession of princes is shown.

FIRST SMALL HYPOSTYLE HALL

Eight papyrus bud columns supported the roof of this First Small Hypostyle Hall. The ceiling displays remarkable astronomical features. Inscriptions indicate sacred books of Thoth, the god of writing, and wisdom, were kept in this hall.
Right and left of the entrance, a procession carries sacred Barques of the Theban trinity, Amen-Ra, Mut and Khonsu.
At the far end of this hall, to the right, the king sits among the foliage of the Heliopolitan tree of life.
A seated Atum, with Safkhet, the goddess of history, and Thoth, the Ibis, writes the king's name in the tree of life, thereby guaranteeing him immortality.

LET'S LIBERATE THE TEMPLE
SECOND SMALL HYPOSTYLE HALL

Right of the entrance of this Second Small Hypostyle Hall, the king makes offerings to Ptah and Sekhmet. Badly ruined, yet four of this room's columns remain. Other rooms and chambers remain, all in a dilapidated state.

MEDINET HABU Temple of Rameses III.

ENTRANCE PYLON

The Pavilion of Rameses III is patterned after Asiatic models with two crenellated towers above the gateway and contains several apartments. A small court at the entrance has guardhouses on each side. To the left of the Pylon, the King smites Egypt's enemies before Amon Ra and to the right he repeats the same before Ra-Horakhty.

FIRST COURT

Galleries left and right of the entrance of the First Court are supported on one side by columns with calyx capitals and the other with square pillars with Osiride figures.
The Court is preserved but the Osiride figures were damaged during Christian times.
On entering, face of the left or South Pylon, a battle illustrates Libyan defeat in the eleventh year of the king's reign.
He charges the Libyan enemy wearing beard, long hair and heavy side-locks. He slays and scatters them for "sixty miles of butchery."
The king, his infantry, and Sardinian mercenaries in horned helmets with Philistines in feathered headdresses are victorious.

FREDERICK MONDERSON

From the royal entrance on the south, not the main entrance to the east, affords one a panoramic view of the Court. Hence, the palace or south side with columns views the Osiride figures across the Court.

On this wall, moving west, the king returns from the war in his chariot with his pet lion at his side. Fan bearers, soldiers, nobles, priests are present.

Beyond a doorway he slays Asiatics, slays foreigners, and soldiers engage in sports of single sticks, wrestling, fencing with forehead, chins and knuckles protected by pads.

Farther on, the king and his nobles inspect horses of his chariots held by grooms while one blows on his trumpet.

Left side of the west wall, Rameses presents Amen-Ra and Mut with three rows of captives.

The top row of prisoners is Sagalassians of Pisidia; the middle row Danaans; and below Philistines.

Right side of the west wall, an inscription recounts the king's war in Syria during his eighth year of rule.

Greek and Asiatic nations threatening Egypt from the coast of Palestine and Rameses and his army vanquishes this enemy.

Across the Court, behind the eight Osiride figures on the north wall, the king presents two rows of prisoners to the Theban trinity, Amen-Ra, Mut and Khonsu.

Arthur Weigall in **A Guide to the Antiquities of Upper Egypt** (1910) mentions an inscription recording the King's speech to the gods, with reference to captives in which he states: "I carried off their people, all their possessions, all the splendid stones of their country, they are all placed before thee, O Lord of Gods.... I have carried them away: the males to fill thy storehouse, the women to be the servants of thy temple."

Further along on the wall, with his pet lion at his side and fan bearers behind, the king drives Libyan, Syrian and Philistine captives.

Next Rameses steps down from his chariot, stands on corpses of an enemy, then attacks an Amorite city by shooting arrows at the defenders. Sardinian mercenaries carrying round shields and wearing

LET'S LIBERATE THE TEMPLE

horned helmets lead the attack. They place scaling ladders on the walls and gain a foothold.

Let's Liberate the Temple. Medinet Habu Temple of Rameses III. Image of the Horus Hawk sporting a disk of the Sun.

SECOND COURT

The Second Court has a gallery on its four sides whose roofs are supported by five columns on the north, five on the south, eight square pillars with Osiride figures on the east and eight similar figures on the west.

The west side gallery has eight columns behind pillars.

Early Christians converted the Court into a church, destroyed the Osirian pillars and plastered the ancient reliefs.

On the left, the king presents prisoners of Asia to Amen-Ra and Mut.

Riding his chariot, Rameses drives prisoners before him while his Egyptian and Philistine bodyguards and fan-bearers walk alongside.

Next, he slays enemies with shooting arrows.

FREDERICK MONDERSON

High above, the king walks towards the temple along with four standards of four primitive tribes of Egypt.
The adjoining wall depicts the king in his chariot, grooms hold the horses, and he turns to inspect cut hands and other prisoners.
Right side of the entrance, the Theban Triad, Amen-Ra, Mut and Khonsu greet three headed figures representing, according to Weigall: "The spirits of Hierakonpolis (the first capital of Upper Egypt), the goddess Nekheb, Lady of that city, the king, the goddess Uazet, Lady of Buto, (the first capital of Lower Egypt), and three jackal headed figures representing the spirits of that city."

On the adjoining wall, Rameses is purified by Thoth and Horus, before he officiates at a religious ceremony. He walks behind a sacred barque carried by priests to meet the barque of Amen-Ra also carried by priests. High above, the Festival of Min is represented.

Below on the wall the king makes offerings to the barque of Amen-Ra now resting in its shrine.
Above the Festival of Min, the king is carried, in his portable throne, by soldiers wearing feathers, while courtiers walk behind their Lord.
The gallery of the west end shows the king with gods and below his sons and daughters.

THE GREAT HYPOSTYLE HALL

The Great Hypostyle hall is in a ruined state. A Christian village was built here.
Portions of the twenty-four columns above ground were destroyed and only their bases remain. Scenes show the king in presence of the gods.

On the left side, with bow in hand he leads a number of captives and presents Asiatic vases to the Theban Triad, Amen-Ra, Mut and Khonsu.
Both sides of the hall contain rooms dedicated to various gods.
In Chapel a Rameses, deified, is worshipped by sons and daughters who bring offerings to him and his queen.

LET'S LIBERATE THE TEMPLE

Chapel B is dedicated to Ptah of Memphis; Chapel C is dedicated to Osiris; and Chapel D again to Ptah and nearby his headless statue of alabaster.
Chapel E is dedicated to Amen-Ra and on the right wall fat bulls are brought in and slaughtered for the festival.

In the Small Hypostyle Hall, two rows of four each horizontal column support the roof.
A doorway on the left, leads to a series of small chambers where mysteries of the king's life in the underworld were centered.
The first is a two-columned chamber leading to a room with a stone bench for offerings.
Next are two chambers. On the right an arched chapel is dedicated to Osiris, God of the Dead. Scenes on the right wall of the left chamber, the king is in the underworld ploughing and reaping the fields.
Canals and pools of Paradise are pictured while the gods of the underworld sit beside the water.
Opposite, on a wall, the king addresses Osiris while his four genii rise from a lotus-flower.

The final room depicts sacred emblems and sacred Cattle.

THE TEMPLE OF DENDERA

The Temple of Dendera, Home of the Goddess Hathor enjoyed a long and illustrious history. Throughout dynastic rule, Hathor was revered and temples erected in her honor from earliest times to the Greco-Roman conquest, boasting sixty-one priestesses and eighteen priests. In the present temple of the Mistress of Dendera, Queen of the Gods, traditions are continued allowing glimpses of worship and reverence for this ancient goddess Hathor, the Mother of Light and Mistress of Heaven. Identified with Isis as the Mother Goddess, Hathor was a cow from Central Africa.

Goddess of universal nature, Hathor, the first act of Creation, is the female counterpart of Ra. Dendera, the Sacred Abode of Hathor, Goddess of Joy and Love, is also the House of Horus. Beautiful of

FREDERICK MONDERSON

Feasts, the Daughter of Ptah, she wears the vulture headdress with uraeus and disk, and symbols such as the sistrum and Menat, an emblem of joy and pleasure. Hathor, the Lady of the Malachite Country is the Patron Saint of the Mines of Sinai and Patron Goddess of singers, dancers and merry makers. This Black-skinned Daughter of Nut is also the great goddess of pleasure, Lady of Rejoicing and Mistress of Song. Daughter of Ra and equally Wife of Ra, the Goddess of the Star Sothis, Hathor is the Second Sun in Heaven.

Lady of Heaven, great Mother of the World, Hathor is the Mother of her father, and Daughter of her son. The Eye of Ra, Dweller in the Disk, the Great Goddess of Pleasure is Mother of Every God and every Goddess. Wife, mother, daughter, she is true, good and represents the best in woman. More beautiful in her person than another woman, Glorious in heaven, mighty upon Earth, the Divine Lady is Mistress of the Valley. The great one, the Moon within the Night sky and whose eyes are the Sun and Moon, she represents the Powers of Nature. The Mistress of Hotep, Lady of Amentet, Lady of the Underworld, is giver of resurrection and immortality.

Seven Hathors were worshiped at Dendera, where bare yet erect ruins of the Entrance Pylon give access to the Great Court littered by later temples and modern conveniences. Here the public gathered for the Intoxication Festival of the Golden One, the Daughter of Ra who had no equal.

The entrance Pronaos or Great Hypostyle of the Place of Drunkenness, the Place with Pleasant Life, comprises a colonnade of 4 rows of 6 horizontal Columns. The first row of massive engaged-columns and three rows of smaller ones are split by a Central Aisle, with east and west doors that exit the sides. The ceiling is decorated with figures of the astronomical drama in the House of the Chronographer and Chronologist of Thoth. This Female Counterpart of Thoth is also Patroness, Chieftainess and Sovereign of Thebes.

The inner Hypostyle Hall or Hall of Appearances for religious ceremonies has three rows of two columns, each enclosed by six compartments, also with 2 side doors. The Hall of Offerings, where

LET'S LIBERATE THE TEMPLE

the goddess enjoyed her Repast, has an opening to the west. To the east, a compartment and juxtaposed opening gives access to lengthy stairs to the roof, also a point of exit for processions.

The Hall of the Cycle of the Gods, or Central Hall, the largest self-contained or enclosed area in the temple, gives access to the Sanctuary, the great place. Here were shrines and barks of the gods.

From the Central Hall a number of rooms surround the Great Place while the actual Sanctuary, the Great House containing Hathor's principal statue, rests directly behind the Great Place. In a semi-circle to the east of the Hall of Appearances is located a place for preparing ointments and incense. Then, come a chamber for flowers and a room for remains of the Goddess' meal. West of the Hall of Appearances, first is located the treasury, and then a chamber for the supply of water with an exit, probably to a well.

From the east, a room connects the Hall of Offerings, and nearby another room for garments and ointments of the Goddess' toilet. Next are 11 rooms arranged in a semi-circle. First, the place where the goddess's mother gave birth and depictions on the wall shows the king bringing milk and linen to Hathor. Next chapels of Osiris Sokaris and of Horus, uniter of the Two Lands; three rooms connected to the actual, centrally located Sanctuary, then a chamber for Hathor's cult musical instrument, the Sistra.

In addition, there's the room where the statue of the God was purified with water. Then comes the Second Holy of Holies, and the Fire House for bringing incense and for burnt offerings. Further the Abode of Ra and musical room for the great neck-chains, which rattled, with movements of the dancers. Then come three rooms for feasts on the day of the Child in the Nest, Hathor's birthday, and the New Year.

West of the Hall of the Cycle of the Gods, a doorway gives access to the Court of the Goddess Nut. Beyond, the Chapel of the Goddess Nut depicts the Lady of Heaven giving birth to the Sun that traverses her body, the Sky, to be swallowed up at evening-time.

FREDERICK MONDERSON

On the east, the stairway to the roof leads to the Chapel of Hathor where the Goddess bathed in the sun, her father, and nearby a Chapel of Osiris, where his mysteries were performed. The morning and evening ritual of the God and Goddess repeat in perpetuity.

EDFU TEMPLE OF HORUS

Wonderful temple of the triad Hor-Behedet, Hathor and Hor-Ema-Tawi.
The ancient legend of the winged disk named this the "Place of Piercing."
Home of Horus, the one General of Winged Disk with uraeus on each side
Who crushed the rebellion against Ra-Horakhte when he embarked from Nubia.
Since ancient times great builders from Imhotep, and Hatshepsut, Seti I, Rameses III, Rameses IV, whose cartouches have been found nearby, and Nectanebo I, have glorified this sacred place of religious importance and jovial festivity.

For the "Feast of Victory and Good Union" or "Feast of Beautiful Meetings" Hathor's exquisite Barge left Dendera to celebrate with Horus and were met with tambourine music, chanting priests and bouquets of flowers.

FIRST PYLON AND ENCLOSURE WALL

Monumental pylon and enclosure wall with prodigious hieroglyphic inscriptions best preserved in Egypt, depicts the holy place, history and aspects of ancient mythology.
Ninety-seven years to complete and one hundred and eighty years in construction your plan allows a deeper understanding of the essential features of an Egyptian temple.

LET'S LIBERATE THE TEMPLE

The winged disk and two uraeus above the cornice; holes for flag poles, double nature of your pylon's depictions and two falcons as temple symbols; greet the visitor to this Majestic example of late Egyptian temple architecture. The falcon represents Ra and guarantees cosmic harmony.

THE GREAT COURT

Besides the principal exit and entrance, your court holds four with two other exits elsewhere in the enclosure wall.
Your eastern and western (vertical) and Southern (horizontal) colonnades boast twelve and ten columns respectively.
These 32 columns employ a wide variety of capitals, each different and adjoins a roofed ambulatory on three sides of the court, all with prodigious illustrations.
The eastern colonnade shows the king coming "Forth from the palace, crowned, incensing, standards, purification, wand of office, festive boats, All before the gods."
On the west, the king leaves the palace, priest, standards, purification, with festival boats, all in presence of glorious ones of the "City of Pe" and "Glorious Ones of the city of Hierakonpolis."
In this "Court of the Appearance of the Protecting Hawk," Priests made "offerings three times per day."
North end of the Court, before the Pronaos, stands two remaining hawks, symbolic of your resident deity.

PRONAOS

The Pronaos entrance to the temple proper, boasts six columns with varied palm and floral capitals, with six screened columned walls with uraeus on their cornice façade.
Within this "Chief of the First Hall," Khent, stands two additional rows of six each horizontal column, all divided by the central axis running from "Orion in the South to the Great Bear in the North."
Left and right of the center aisle stand two small chapels.
Your left or west chapel is the Chamber of Consecration with golden vases from which the pharaoh was consecrated before performing

rituals of the actual festival. A scene portrays the pharaoh being purified by Horus and Thoth.

The right or east chapel housed the Temple Library or "Chamber of the Papyrus Rolls of Horus and Horakhte" arranged by the Chief Ritual priest of the Twelve hours of the day.
Here and on the doorway of the great Hypostyle Hall scenes represent the four senses, hearing, sight, taste and reason as a small figure worshipping a scribe's palette.
Simpkins mentions relief that depict the "King, in company with Horus and Seshat, pegs out the ground, for the future building, cuts the first sod, purifies the ground so that the building on it may be holy, raises the first block of stone, incenses the whole temple. Presents the completed building to Horus and finally offers Horus the Emblem of its decoration."
Other ceremonies are also represented and the pharaoh is shown dancing before the god of your reverence.

THE SMALL HYPOSTYLE HALL

The Small Hypostyle hall is of smaller size but of greater beauty than the Great Hall and houses two rows of three each vertical columns each side of the center aisle with beautiful floral capitals.
The noon sun lights this hall through perpendicular shafts in the roof. In this "Festal Hall" were celebrated important festivals.
Scenes depict Ptolemy Philopator offering an image of Ma'at to the Solar Boat captained by two Horus Figures.
The King again leaves the palace, led to Horus by Hathor, pegs out the temple limits, breaks ground, offers weights of gold to Horus and presents your august plan to the god.
Again, a priest in sacerdotal leopard skin walks beside the Barques of Horus and Hathor as the king burns incense.

LET'S LIBERATE THE TEMPLE

On the west was the "Chamber of the Nile" where pure well water was kept.
Next, the "Laboratory" where ointment and perfumes for anointing the god were kept.
Opposite on the east was the treasury housing valuables and religious items.

HALL OF THE ALTAR OF OFFERINGS

In this hall stood your Altar of Offerings, where the daily ritual was performed.
This "Pure Place" illustrate the Solar Bark's voyage through the twelve hours of the day.
At Sacred times as "Festival of the New Year" the God Horus was taken to the "Court of the New Year" on the roof.
Bas-reliefs on the lengthy staircase to the roof, up one side, down the other, shows the "procession carrying the god's statues to be recharged with divine solar energy."

HALL OF THE REPOSE OF THE GODS

Lying before the Sanctuary scenes show the king and his wife Arsinoe offering Horus and Hathor a scribe's palette.
He binds captives before Horus and the infant Horus is shown rising out of the marshes at his birth.
A doorway to the west leads to the Chapel of Min.
All the walls show him worshipping this god of fertility, generation and growth.
An upright Penis from his navel, balancing a flagellum, the god was worshipped at his principal shrine at Coptos and at many temples throughout the land for he reigned over the fields and over the families as patron who renews life.
East of the hall of the repose of the Gods, stands a little chapel with two columns, reminiscent of Dendera's chapel.

FREDERICK MONDERSON

The depiction reminds, the goddess Nut rules the heavens.
Scenes show the King and Queen enthroned, the Seven Hathors or fairy godmothers beating tambourines and Min worshipped in relation to childbirth.

THE SANCTUARY

Only the king or his high priest could enter the Sanctuary, yet moderns transgress this taboo.
The Neolithic shrine placed here by Nectanebo I was transferred from the older temple.
An altar also rested here.
Relief shows the king as high priest, opening the lock and door of the shrine and incensing the deities.
Every morning the high priest woke the god, dressed and served him food and sang hymns in his honor. At night they prepared him for bed.
From the Sanctuary's door, looking south down the middle aisle or central aisle, one gets a panoramic view of the size and depth of the temple.
Six doorways with double doors span the distance from entrance to Sanctuary and only the king or senior priests could enter the inner vestibules.

CHAMBERS BEHIND THE SANCTUARY

In ten chambers behind and encircling the Sanctuary, entered from its left and right, interesting connections with the temple and its ritual are revealed.
First is the "Chamber of Spread-wings" for the gods who protect Osiris and seeks vengeance on his enemies.
In the "Chamber of the Throne of the Sun" several deities accompany the hawk headed Sun god.
The "Chamber of Khonsu" that member of the Theban triad, is shown similar to Horus, while other gods accompany him.
The "Chamber of Hathor" places the goddess with other deities.

LET'S LIBERATE THE TEMPLE

The "Chamber of the Victor," right behind the Sanctuary, has an altar in the center and an inscription calls it the "Great Throne of the Dispenser of the Sun's Rays."
The "Chamber of the West" is dedicated to Osiris and his attendant demi-gods are shown.
Then there is the "Chamber of Osiris."
There is also a "Chamber of the Tomb" of Osiris.
The "Chamber of the Throne of the Gods" and "Chamber of the Linen" round out these rooms behind the Sanctuary.

THE OUTER CORRIDOR

The Outer Corridor, best entered from the northeast corner of the Forecourt, termed the "Passage of Victory" richly illustrates the conflict of Horus and the enemies of Ra.
Profusely illustrated the Eastern Passage begins with the king smiting kneeling captives, and in presence of Horus, Hathor and young Horus, "Uniter of the Two Lands."
The king with Khnum, Horus and Thoth, is shown with a net in the marshes catching birds, animals and men.
The king leaves his palace with 5 standards of the Jackal of the South, the Jackal of the North, the Ibis of Hermopolis, the Hawk of Edfu and the Scepter of Thebes.
He is purified by Horus and Thoth, crowned by Nekheb and Ouadjit, led by Horus uniter of the two lands to Horus of Edfu, and stands before Horus of Edfu. He is again crowned by Nekheb and Ouadjit.
East end of north corridor, Horus in a shrine is carried by three hawk-headed and three jackal-headed figures.
The King leads, holding a sistrum and a pot of incense and directs the shrine to the lion-headed goddess Sekhmet.
Opposite the king leaves the palace with standards. He also leads the shrine of Horus to goddess Mut.
Moving south the west corridor of "Passage of Victory" shows the king using ropes to pull a sledge with the sacred boat of Horus.
A boat in sail with Horus and Isis is next.
The king on land, and Horus in a boat in sail spears

FREDERICK MONDERSON

HATSHEPSUT'S TEMPLE AT DEIR EL BAHARI

Deir-el-Bahari, you are Hatshepsut's monument for her father, the good God, Amon Lord of Heaven. Queen Makere, the ever living, a brilliant emanation of Amon-Ra ruled the Black and Red Land. One who had no enemy in any land, she boasted 'my fame is among the sand-dwellers, my boundary extends from Punt to Asia and the Asiatics are in my grasp.' She ruled like the Son of Isis and strong like the Son of Nut, so her temple shall be unto eternity like an imperishable star. He, father Ra himself is united with his body and he is the great one who is in Heliopolis, the begetter of the Primordial Gods. One falls down dead on the spot for terror if his mysterious unknowable name is pronounced. No god can address him by it, his with the soul, whose name is hidden, for that he is a mystery.

Amon, Lord of the Two Lands established her name on the Ished Tree in life, stability, and satisfaction. Makere, living forever, female Horus, shining in Thebes, is Beloved of Amon, Lord of Diadems. Boasting, 'my father Amon favors me and my nostrils are filled with satisfying life,' she is truthful in sight of her father. Fresh in years, beautiful to look upon, with fidelity of heart, Hatshepsut is Amon's Daughter of Truth who glorifies him. Divine of Diadems who abounds in deeds and Favorite of the Two Goddesses, she boasted, the Royal Lord 'Ra, the electrum of Kings, loves me.' Beloved, she built him a temple called Tcheser Tcheseru, 'Most Splendid,' because the gods fawn at his feet when they know his majesty their lord. All gods make the boast in him, in order to magnify themselves with his beauty, for his is so divine.

An inscription depicts Senmut, the Steward of Amon, architect and confidant of your Queen, giving praise to Hathor for the sake of life, prosperity and health of Makere. Monuments abound justifying Hatshepsut's right to rule. Praising Amon, maker of all beings, Lord of the Terrestrial Thrones, Senmut erected two obelisks at Karnak,

LET'S LIBERATE THE TEMPLE

where their rays flood the two lands and the Sun rises between them as he dawns in the Horizon of Heaven. This master of Mankind, King, Lord of All Gods, created the fruit trees, made the green herbs and sustains the cattle as he traverses in the firmament in Peace, King of Upper and Lower Egypt.

Let's Liberate the Temple. Hatshepsut's Temple at Deir el Bahari. The Sanctuary in the Upper Court on the Upper Terrace.

An Avenue of Sphinxes then Causeway led from the Nile into your august temple oriented southeast by northwest. Imitating Mentuhotep's earlier structure, Deir el-Bahari is built in three terraces when one-story structures were the norm. Trees and lions greet the visitor at the precinct entrance pylon, where flagstaffs flew the colors. Pillars alternate with columns in the First Court and the central ramp's South Colonnade. In this Lower Terrace, the Mythological and Obelisk Colonnades recount significant milestones in the queen's reign, in praise of the god of the beginning, firm of horns and fair of face, who is crowned in the House of Fire.

FREDERICK MONDERSON

Majestic and alternating eleven columns and pillars in each arrangement are symbolic of Hathor, Goddess of the West. While the North Colonnade speaks of things Mythological, the South portrays the inspiration and acquisition of Obelisks at Aswan, set up for the Supreme Majesty of the Land, Lord of Adoration, Amon of Karnak. The Lord of Life is fearful, terrible, great of will and mighty in appearance. He abounds in victuals, creates substance and abides in all things for he is unique in his nature, this goodly Bull of the Nine Gods.

The second ascent of the central Ramp splits the Second Court in rise to the Second Terrace.
The Pillared Birth and Coronation Colonnades to the North and Punt Colonnade to the south remind of the august deeds in Hatshepsut's reign. Against the north cliffs, the true Northern Colonnade with 15 columns fronts chapels of worship. Subjects of these scenes, bespeak immortal remembrance and infamy for ruler and architect, some say lovers, whose innovation, is a wonderful and splendid architectural and artistic creative work. Senmut praised his majesty Hatshepsut and glorified her master, Amon-Ra, who created the gods and lifted up the sky. He is the Lord of Rays who created light.

The ascent to the Upper Terrace reveal twenty-two pillars before columns in similar arrangement where the Third and Upper Court are surrounded by two rows of 42-each columns, all before the Sanctuary. North and south Chapels to the Sun and Hatshepsut provide meaning to the structure. Northeast and southwest of the Second Court, Chapels to Anubis and Hathor respectively employ twelve and thirty-six columns, Hathor with eight pillars, and each chapel with outer and inner Sanctuary.
In your blessed abode, the Lord of the Ninth Day of the Month Festival in whose honor men keep the Sixth and Seventh Day, the Sole One who made all that is, the One and Only who made all that exists, is perpetually worshiped.

Though his name is hidden from his children, his beauty captivates the heart and love of him makes languid the arms. Love of him makes

LET'S LIBERATE THE TEMPLE

feeble the arms and his adherents' hearts forget when they look upon him.

August abode, Senmut fashioned your portals to praise his beautiful Queen Hatshepsut. Her father Amon is God extraordinary. His beneficence creates the light, his eye overthrows the enemy, of a kind heart Amon, hears the praise of the prisoner. He rescues the fearful from the oppressor and judges between the miserable and strong. These things and more your precinct represents as it withstood the ravages of time. Yet, it still, retains the power, aura, awe and majesty of its ancient mystique.

Moderns revealed 40 royal mummies in the Deir el-Bahari "cache" and another 153 mummies, in this northern Coptic Convent or Sanatorium of healing. Senmut secreted his tomb in the Second Court and deposited figures of his-self throughout. He decorated, covered, and painted the walls, to foil his adversaries' anticipated destructive acts. Later, when the upper stucco gave way they revealed his artistry, a labor of love.

THE TEMPLE OF KOM OMBO

Beyond the now destroyed Pylon, five columns each in the East and West Colonnade,
perpendicular to six columns split by Double Aisles and Central Altar, form the Forecourt of the twin deities Haroeris right and Sobek, left.

The Grand Hypostyle Hall, comprise three rows, the first engaged and 2 stand free of five columns, numbering 15.
Double Aisles envelope the Central three, separating the halls of the respective gods.

The Second Hypostyle Hall with two rows of five columns similarly disposed, entrance the First, Second and Third Vestibules.

FREDERICK MONDERSON

The Double nature of the temple dictated Double Sanctuary with Double Priesthood for worshiping the twin deities. Northeast and west, inner Corridors bound walls enclosing the small Hypostyle Hall to the front of the Sanctuary.
Northeast and west Outer Corridors envelop the Twin Temples.

Beyond the West Wall, a Nilometer and Well, both served many purposes in the Temple.

Liberate the Temple. Karnak Temple of God Amon. Temple of Amenhotep II. This temple on the North/South axis between the Ninth and Tenth Pylons boasts square pillars.

LET'S LIBERATE THE TEMPLE

Let's Liberate the Temple. Karnak Temple of God Amon. The Hypostyle Hall. Decorated shaft, open umbel capitals, a hidden die and the architrave overhead, spanning the void.

www.ingramcontent.com/pod-product-compliance
Lightning Source LLC
Chambersburg PA
CBHW071641160426
43195CB00012B/1322